MW01156346

THE
STANDARD DOYLE
COMPANY

"The interplay of ideas and the oblique uses of knowledge are often of extraordinary interest."

SHERLOCK HOLMES in
The Valley of Fear

THE STANDARD DOYLE COMPANY

CHRISTOPHER MORLEY
ON
SHERLOCK HOLMES

EDITED, AND WITH AN INTRODUCTION,

BY STEVEN ROTHMAN

FORDHAM UNIVERSITY PRESS

NEW YORK

Morley, Christopher, 1890–1957.
  The standard Doyle company : Christopher Morley on Sherlock
Holmes / edited, and with an introduction, by Steven Rothman. —
New York : Fordham University Press, c.1990.
  xii, 429 p. : ill. ; 21 cm.
  ISBN 0-8232-1292-0
  1. Doyle, Arthur Conan, 1859–1930. 2. Holmes, Sherlock
(fictitious character). 3. Baker Street Irregulars (Organization :
U.S.).   I. Rothman, Steven. I. Title.
PR4624.M65   1990   823.8—dc20   90-82073

Jacket drawing by Jeff Decker

CONTENTS

SHERLOCK HOLMES AND DR. WATSON: A TEXTBOOK OF FRIENDSHIP

POEMS

PREFACE

This volume is a by-product of my love for the literature of both Arthur Conan Doyle and Christopher Morley, whose writings I have studied for much of the last quarter-century. My goal was to gather Morley's Sherlockian writings under one cover for both the scholar of Sherlockiana or Morleyana and the general reader with some interest in Holmes or Morley. Representing almost thirty years of productivity and a number of genres, these writings are impressive when read together (though the haste of composition and the very frailty of hebdomadal journalism cannot be escaped).

Much of this material first appeared in *The Saturday Review of Literature* in Morley's columns titled "The Bowling Green" and "Trade Winds." I spent many hours going through the *Review* issue by issue, from its inception in 1924 through 1940, when Morley stopped editing "Trade Winds." ("Bowling Green" ceased in 1938.) I was aided in this search by the *Index, 1924–1944* to the *Saturday Review* published in 1971 by R. R. Bowker (but I found that many references to Sherlock Holmes were not indexed). I also owe a debt of gratitude to Ron De Waal's two-volume Sherlockian bibliography. I have tried to be complete, but a few things may have missed my search (particularly contributions to the *Book-of-the-Month Club Newsletter*, which I was unable to see).

The reader seeking further information on Morley might be rewarded by reading the following (full citations can be found in the list of works cited at the end of this volume): for his life, Helen McK. Oakley, and Mark I. Wallach and Jon Bracker; for his books, Alfred P. Lee, Guy R. Lyle and H. Tatnall Brown, Jr., and Anna Lou Samuelson Ashby. Major collections are available for study at Haverford College, the Harry Ransom Humanities Research Center of the University of Texas at Austin, and the Bryant Library, Roslyn, New York.

Morley also figures in several of the autobiographies of his contemporaries, including Felix Riesenberg, Vincent Starrett, Frances Steloff, and his brothers Felix and Frank.

I would like to thank the following people without whom I could not have proceeded: the late Seymour Adelman and the late

Charles Bell, for their early encouragement and faith in my abilities; the late Carl Anderson, for his memories; Peter Blau, for his many resources; Blythe Morley Brennan; the late Helen Hare Cain; Louise Morley Cochrane; George Fletcher, for his patience; David Holmes; Jon Lellenberg; John Ruyle; Philip Shreffler, for allowing some of these thoughts to have had earlier public appearances in *The Baker Street Journal*; the staffs at Haverford College Library, the University of Pennsylvania Library, and the Rosenbach Museum and Library; and my many friends in the Sherlockian world, for their patience on the subject and their encouragement. And I would like readers to join me in thanking my wife, Janice Fisher, without whom this would be an unwieldly and illegible pile of foolscap, but under whose lovingly (if severely) wielded blue pencil a book was born.

The texts have been slightly standardized typographically, although Morley's often idiosyncratic punctuation has been retained. Material is arranged chronologically within each section. Every selection concludes with a citation of its source; the two following, being so frequent, are briefly cited thus:

BSJ   *The Baker Street Journal* (Original Series or New Series)
SRL   *The Saturday Review of Literature*

A complete listing of the sources will be found in the Works Cited section at the end.

CHRISTOPHER MORLEY, CA. 1948,
by Lotte Jacobi

INTRODUCTION

E VERY MOVEMENT NEEDS ITS POINT MAN—the fellow who actually goes out on the road, climbs a stump, and starts to preach the received truth to the as-yet-unbelieving masses. Though others may be more inspired or delve deeper into the mystery, one lone fearless voice gives the movement form out of the void. This truth is obvious from the Bible onward.

Christopher Morley was just such a voice for the Sherlockian movement. There were prophets who had preached before him—scholars who dared to say in print that Conan Doyle had indeed given us a remarkable character—but they were few and their words not far-reaching. It was Kit who, bubbling over with love for Holmes and for literary games, infected the world.

He was uniquely suited for this task. Born May 5, 1890, to English-born parents, he was among the first generation to grow up on the Holmes stories. By the time the stories stopped in 1927, Kit was himself well established as that now extinct phenomenon, the Man of Letters. Well read in all of Western literature, he made his living reading, writing, commenting, publicizing, lecturing—the whole exhausting panoply of putting oneself and one's ideas before the public. He was not just a best-selling author, literary columnist, and reviewer, but also a poet (of light verse and more serious stanzas), a playwright, and a quiz-show panelist. From 1920 till his death Kit seemed omnipresent to those who loved and knew books and writing.

Still, he was somewhat out of step with the literary scene, a fact that has perhaps contributed to his current obscurity. Though he worked in Manhattan, he lived on Long Island. Though he was in France at the same time as Scott and Zelda and Hem, he was there with his family and didn't

1

live on the Left Bank. Though he worked for a weekly magazine, it was *The Saturday Review of Literature* and not *The New Yorker*. Though he drank many rounds with his friends, it wasn't often at the Algonquin's Round Table.

Over this long career he wrote much about the Great Detective in all the manners and styles for which he was so well known. These writings greatly influenced both his contemporaries and the following generation of Sherlockians, but were published in a great variety of locations, some quite obscure. I have endeavored to assemble them all under one cover for the first time, to aid both the most fanatical Morleyan or Sherlockian scholar and the casual reader.

A BRIEF BIOGRAPHICAL SKETCH

Kit spent his first ten years among the gardens and meadows at Haverford College in Pennsylvania, where his father was a professor of mathematics. In a retrospective essay he recalled:

> I think I had the happiest childhood that ever was. Sometimes people tell me what marvellous times *they* had as boys and girls, but I am never convinced that they had half as merry a career as I.
>
> In the first place I had the good sense to choose a professor as my father. Professors have vacations from June to September, and this particular professor had a passion for going to a new place every summer. That means glorious excitement for the children. In the second place, while I elected to be an American, I chose parents who were English, and who had the jolly habit of spending a summer in England every few years. And thirdly, in addition to my father and mother, uniquely delightful people as they seemed to me, my covenant with life included also two excellent younger brothers. To a boyhood so enriched and

2

fortified I must admit no impediments—save only that I never had a sister.

This happy life included the books that were to remain his lifelong companions. In his 1931 novel *John Mistletoe*, a slightly fictionalized autobiography, he wrote:

> In the old wing of the Haverford Library there was a little gallery, reached by an iron ladder. It was rarely visited, used for the storage of an antique collection of classical and theological texts annotated in German, and some thousands of legal volumes in scaled and exhalatory calf. Behind the bookcases, on the outer side of the building, high up by the tops of the tall windows, ran a dusty little passage, somewhat tremulous underfoot and carpeted with rough cocoanut matting. In the days when the undergraduate literary societies turned over their private collections to the college library, certain volumes of juvenile fiction, esteemed too frivolous for general circulation, were sequestered in a remote corner of that gallery. . . . [W]hen Mistletoe was perhaps eight years old [the librarian], with an air of much mystery, piloted him up the iron ladder, introduced him to the enchanted concealed pathway round the gallery, and then under pledge of secrecy, where the bottom shelf looked out on the old greenhouse arch, disclosed the cache of tattered volumes. . . . That, I think, was Mistletoe's fullest introduction to the joys of secret reading.

When the century turned, Kit's father accepted the Professorship in Mathematics at Johns Hopkins University, and the family moved from the verdant glories of the Main Line to the harsher urban tracts of Baltimore. In a talk given at Haverford in 1958, Frank Morley, the youngest of the three brothers, recalled his brother at thirteen:

> My conviction is that it was the move from Haverford to Baltimore in 1900 which turned Kit into a bookman. I don't think it was with him entirely an original sin. I think it was

3

something which greatly developed in the circumstances. Only a Haverfordian courtesy would have described Christopher at the age of ten as a chubby lad. He was a fat boy, fatted with strawberries and chicken salad outside Founders Hall. . . . When school hours were over I don't visualize Christopher using the Baltimore streets as playground so much as a means of transit to and from the Enoch Pratt Free Library.

Kit, in his famous essay "In Memoriam Sherlock Holmes," recalled his reading:

I then put in two or three years in reading everything else of Dr. Doyle's. One walked downtown to the old Enoch Pratt Free Library on Mulberry Street in Baltimore and got out a book—*The Firm of Girdlestone*, or *The Captain of the Pole Star*, or *Beyond the City*, or *A Duet*, or *Round the Red Lamp*, or *The Stark Munro Letters*, or *The Doings of Raffles Haw*. For I specialized chiefly in the lesser known tales, and deplore Sir Arthur's tendency (in his autobiography) to make light of some of these yarns. As for *The White Company* and *The Refugees* and *Micah Clarke* and *Uncle Bernac*, these were household words. When one found at the library a Conan Doyle he had not read, he began it at once on the walk home. It was quite a long trudge from Mulberry Street to the 2000 block on Park Avenue, and the tragedy often was that, loitering like a snail, almost like the locomotion of a slowed moving picture, the book was actually finished by the time one got home. There was all the journey to do over again the next day.

In the Christopher Morley Alcove in the Haverford College Library is a much-read copy of Conan Doyle's 1900 work *The Green Flag*, inscribed to Kit on the flyleaf from "Uncle" John Harkness, mathematics professor at Bryn Mawr College. The book is stamped "C.D.M.P.L. [*C*hristopher *D*arlington *M*orley *P*ublic *L*ibrary] No. 1." Thus Conan Doyle can be shown to have entered Kit's life as early as his tenth birthday, and Sherlock Holmes soon followed.

By 1900 less than half of the Sherlockian canon had been published. (Imagine the joy of reading *when it was published* about *The Hound of the Baskervilles*, which appeared in August 1901.) Kit devoured each case. As his two younger brothers learned to read he would lead them up to the attic and sit them down with a bound volume of *The Strand Magazine* to receive the truth.

Recalling these tutorials, Kit's youngest brother Frank wrote (in *Christopher Morley or The Treasure of the Abandoned Mine*):

> The books he borrowed were what you might expect: Mayne Reid, Jules Verne, Rider Haggard, Conan Doyle, Stevenson, Kipling and all. A point to be made is that though the books he chose were so to speak "easy" books, he did really read them and think about them: each was more than a passing daydream. . . . My father got examination papers for his students; very well, so soon as Felix and I could be hurried on for Kit's tuition, there we were, poor things, studying *The Hound of the Baskervilles* or *Twenty Thousand Leagues Under the Sea* in order to withstand Kit's examination. . . . It was Kit who brought back the examination material, and flung it at you. I am not saying the stuff was difficult to read, but you had seriously to read it. In companionship with Kit in boyhood you had to have specific responses to specific questions. . . . There I was at the age of four . . . beckoned . . . to the Sherlock Holmes stuff in the attic. The first of the Sherlock Holmes stories that I remember reading at the age of four was *The Adventure of the Abbey Grange*. What lasting harm this may have done to my character I don't know; I have never put my children at such an age to such lurid reading; but my point is that Kit felt an urgency that this escapism should be shared. His urgency affected both Felix and me.

Thus, by the age of twelve, Kit was already feeling his vocation, had already begun to make his first tentative climb upon that soapbox.

By 1906, back at Haverford College as an undergraduate, Kit began his practice of forming fellowship and informal organizations. There were the Maltworms, an exclusive club of two, and the three brothers McGill, sons of a mythical importer of woolen goods. Page Allison, who would be his lifelong friend, was Mifflin McGill, and Kit was Andrew McGill, who would later be a character in Kit's first novel, *Parnassus on Wheels*.

Kit was an excellent student and wrote his honors thesis on Robert Louis Stevenson, an author for whom he and Doyle shared the greatest esteem and affection. One of four members of his class to be elected to Phi Beta Kappa, Kit was also awarded a Rhodes Scholarship to New College, Oxford.

He sailed to Oxford in the autumn of 1910 and found it, like Haverford, a paradise for him. In the title poem of *Parsons' Pleasure* are these lines:

> Two breeding places I have known
> Where germinal my heart was sown;
> Two places from which I inherit
> The present business of my spirit:
> Haverford, Oxford, quietly
> May make a poet out of me.

In 1911, Ronald Knox, a young don at Oxford's Trinity College, presented a paper entitled "Studies in the Literature of Sherlock Holmes." The paper was a *succès fou* and Knox read it all over Oxford. As Kit recalled in his introduction to his own Sherlockian textbook,

Studies in the Literature of Sherlock Holmes . . . was in the tradition of a much older classic of reverse English—what is now called double-talk—Archbishop Whately's *Historic*

6

Doubt Relative to Napoleon Buonaparte. The device of pretending to analyze matters of amusement with full severity is the best way to reproach those who approach the highest subjects with too literal a mind. This new frolic in criticism was welcome at once; those who were students at Oxford in that ancient day remember how Mr. Knox was invited round from college to college to reread his agreeable lampoon; it was first printed in a journal of undergraduate highbrows (*The Blue Book*) then appropriately edited by W. H. L. Watson.

Kit's own first published work, a traditional thin volume of verse entitled *The Eighth Sin*, was published by Blackwell in November 1912. The curious title comes from a letter of Keats: "There is no greater Sin after the seven deadly than to flatter oneself into an idea of being a great poet."

Coming down from Oxford in 1913 with an Honours degree in Modern History, and now affianced to Helen Fairchild, an American he had met in London, Kit set about looking for a job. A short time before, he had written in his journal this self-appraisal:

Mine is (as I have remarked before in my journal) what Tennyson calls "a second-rate sensitive mind" and of such there are many on the market. I seem to be clever in a superficial way, adaptable to my surroundings, and tho' not personally prepossessing yet not ill-mannered . . . and yet, curiously enough, with plenty of self-depreciation, I think I have *genuine ability* if I can find the appropriate channel for it. What is it to be? Writing is all very well as an *hors d'oeuvre* but not as the pièce de résistance. One must have some more reliable mode of bread winning. Teaching? I might do well at it but I doubt if I have the ability for valuable research work, which is the only sure way of promotion in that profession. The diplomatic service? This appeals to me—but seems to need both private means and influence, neither of which I have.

7

Having at length decided on publishing, he made repeated assaults on the firm of Doubleday, Page & Co. Later, Kit recalled an interview in which he pulled out of his pockets lists of books that he felt the firm should publish. Mr. Doubleday then asked him, "What kind of job would you like best around this place?" Without hesitation Kit replied, "Yours!" He worked for Doubleday for the next four years, editing, writing copy, selling books, and developing the esteem that never left him for "the Boys," the travelers in books whose job it is to convince the stores to stock them.

During his sojourn at Doubleday Kit achieved several milestones. In June 1914 he married Helen Fairchild, and that same year he wrote his first novel, *Parnassus on Wheels*. He then returned briefly to the city of his youth and worked for *Ladies' Home Journal*, and then the Philadelphia *Evening Public Ledger*, before going back to New York in 1920 to write the column for the *Evening Post* that he christened "The Bowling Green."

The Three Hours for Lunch Club was another of Kit's semi-mythical societies. Its rationale was to be truant from one's workplace with agreeable friends doing agreeable things: lunching, drinking, sightseeing, book shopping. The THLC met whenever Kit was so moved, whenever a friend from out of town came by or two or more friends met with him. They would have jaunts to Brooklyn, to Hoboken, to Philadelphia. The title first appeared in "The Bowling Green" when he threatened to write a book called *How to Spend Three Hours at Lunch Time*.

Though no such book was written, many adventures of the THLC were recorded. Often a book was picked out of the bargain bin to serve as a minute book and souvenir of the meeting. Many such volumes exist, signed by those assembled and often slightly spotted with (prohibited) red wine.

Over the years the Club became a part of the heart of

Kit's readership and a part of his way of entertaining friends. The spontaneous grand event made from a tour of the mundane was just the sort of thing he constructed in his columns and so delighted doing in real life.

Kit's time at the *Evening Post* drew to a close when his old boss from Philadelphia, Cyrus H. K. Curtis, bought the failing paper. One of his first acts was to fire the staff of the Saturday paper's Literary Review supplement—which included Kit. The move precipitated the formation of *The Saturday Review of Literature* in 1926. In his final "Bowling Green" column for the *Evening Post*, Kit, never at a loss for an apposite quotation, cited *The Taming of the Shrew* (IV.1, 37). The opening lines of Grumio's speech read, "A cold wind, Curtis, in every office but thine; and therefore fire. . . ." It was, alas, killed in the later editions.

The chronicles of the THLC moved to the *Saturday Review* with Kit. Indeed, writing for an audience interested in books, Kit was able to expand his coverage of his little outings. Over the next dozen years "The Bowling Green" traveled the vast landscape of Kit's interests. Several of his novels were serialized in the column, and many of his best essays first appeared there.

When Kit left the *Evening Post* he also left daily journalism. He had written by this time over twenty books: volumes of poetry, collections of essays, novels, short stories, and plays. To heighten his break with the past, he gathered up his wife and children (Christopher Jr., Louise, Helen, and Blythe) and awayed to France. A place near the sea, at Mont-St.-Michel, proved perfect for both family and author. Two volumes came from this foreign interlude: *The Romany Stain*, a collection of essays mostly about France, and *Thunder on the Left*, the tragedy/fantasy about growing up that showed, to any still doubting, that Kit's was a talent of considerable stature and worthy of mature consideration.

Of Kit's essays little needs to be said, as many of the different types are represented here (albeit on one subject).

But his novels were another matter. He captured the reading public with his first novel, *Parnassus on Wheels*, a gentle romance about a bookseller and his horsedrawn bookshop and the middle-aged woman who escapes her drudge's life of caring for her famous writer–brother to caravan across New England. *The Haunted Bookshop* is, in a way, a sequel, but Roger Mifflin and Helen have settled into "Parnassus at Home" on Gissing Street in Brooklyn. This book is really an adventure story, a Buchan-and-water tale of an assassination attempt upon President Wilson. Next was *In the Sweet Dry and Dry* (1919), written with Bart Haley, a completely ephemeral story of Prohibition. Then came *Kathleen* (1929), a novel of Oxford undergraduates discovering a letter from Kathleen and all setting out to discover her and fall in love. *Where the Blue Begins* (1922) is the anthropomorphic tale of Mr. Gissing, a dog, and his search for God. (Kit once said, "This is a 'dog story' in the same sense that *The Hound of Heaven* is one.") *Pandora Lifts the Lid* (1924, with Don Marquis), *The Arrow* (1927), *Pleased to Meet You* (1927), *I Know a Secret* (1927), and *Rudolph and Amina* (1930) round off the 'twenties in a vigorous growth of titles. All in all, Kit's list of "A" titles—that is, bibliographically speaking, major works—numbers over 170 items, an impressive achievement.

The books continued to pour out of Kit's pen (for, until *Kitty Foyle*, he wrote most of his books in longhand). There are slight fantasies and burlesques, volumes of poetry, the fictionalized autobiography *John Mistletoe*, books of travel, and more volumes of essays. Among the novels that stand out are *Human Being*, the story of Richard Roe, an Everyman, and *The Trojan Horse*, an all-too-prophetic look ahead to the coming of the Second World War by a look back to Chaucer's *Troilus and Cressida*. There were countless introductions to books by others, and dozens, if not hundreds, of essays, poems, and stories that never have been collected.

Another adventure on a distant shore came when Kit and the Three Hours for Lunch Club leased the Old Rialto Theatre, 118 Hudson Street, Hoboken, New Jersey, in the summer of 1928. From there they issued pamphlets and advertisements luring jaded New Yorkers to "seidel over to Hoboken." The Old Rialto began its season on September 3 with "The Barker," followed by one-week runs of other stock melodramas. A dramatization of Kit's "Pleased to Meet You," with music by Jerome Kern, opened on November 29. Their biggest hit, "After Dark; or Neither Maid, Wife nor Widow," a rewritten production of Dion Boucicault's melodrama of the underworld, opened December 10, 1928, and ran for 437 performances. In 1929, after the crash, the crowds, in Kit's words, "postponed coming." He was left with large debts due in part to overexpansion and in part to his overtrusting his partners. In a letter years later, he wrote, "Think of the matter as a Romantic Memory. That's the way I myself remember Hoboken which cost me, in the net, about 30,000 dollars."

The 1939 novel *Kitty Foyle*, which was Kit's only best seller, was a turning point in his career. The book was a tour de force first-person narrative about the life and loves of a "white-collar girl" from a working-class neighborhood, her affair with a Main Line blueblood, and her struggle to make her own way in the world. Before, Kit had been popular with the critics and the reading public. Afterward, he seemed to have lost some of the critics' love, and he never gave the public another *Kitty* (despite his publisher's urgings).

Thorofare (1942) was another semi-autobiographical novel, based on Kit's Anglo-American background and his Baltimore youth. Like its hero Geoff, Kit was part of a quartet of like-minded boys who called themselves the Sign of the Four. The advanced student of Holmes and Morley could profit from rummaging out the allusions to Baker Street.

11

The 'forties did not prove to be his most prolific decade, although he wrote many poems that appeared in a great variety of newspapers and magazines. Kit also became more and more of a public figure. He promoted his books on a number of national tours. He was frequently heard on the radio, where his ability to talk amusingly and spontaneously was valued. He became a panelist on "Information Please" both in the United States and on the BBC version. He was also among the original five members of the Editorial Board of the Book-of-the-Month Club, a post he held from 1926 until 1954. Though none of his own books was selected by the BOMC, he was quite influential in choosing what the country read for twenty-five years. All these appearances took away time from his writing, and the books appeared less often. He worked on several novels that were never published, including *Thorofare II*, which continued Geoff's story in (I am told) the same semi-autobiographical mode, and *Miss Libby*, a fantasy novella about the adventures of the Statue of Liberty after she swims ashore to Manhattan. He finished the decade with his last, perhaps best, and certainly darkest novel, *The Man Who Made Friends With Himself*, in which Richard Tolman, literary agent, is haunted—perhaps—by his Doppelgänger.

By the late 'forties his name had begun to fade from the scene. In England he was regarded as a Man of Letters, but at home he was already something of the past. He had hoped that Doubleday would issue a two-volume set of his collected essays and poems for his sixtieth birthday in 1950, but nothing ever happened. In 1951 he had the first of the strokes that bit by bit diminished him. Little writing except letters and poems occurred. His final collection of poetry, *Gentlemen's Relish*, was published by W. W. Norton in 1955. He died on March 28, 1957.

KIT AND THE B.S.I.

The boy who devoured Conan Doyle's books in Baltimore became the man who, author and columnist, still livened at

the thought of Baker Street. When Kit was in his early
forties, a time when men often begin remembering fondly
the carefree joys of their childhood, Sir Arthur died. This
gave rise to both an article on Doyle and a re-evaluation of
the importance of the character of Sherlock Holmes. Bit by
bit, Holmes crept more and more into Kit's columns.

The Baker Street Irregulars existed as an idea in print
before they had a formally informal gathering. In the May
1, 1926 "Bowling Green," Kit told of a meeting with an
English printer:

> We found ourselves, I don't know just how, embarked on a
> mutual questionnaire of famous incidents in the life of
> Sherlock Holmes. "What was the name of the doctor in
> 'The Speckled Band'?" he would ask, and I would counter
> with "Which mystery was it that was solved by the ash of a
> Trichinopoly cigar?"

In the August 2, 1930 issue appeared "In Memoriam:
Sherlock Holmes," commissioned by Doubleday as the
introduction to *The Complete Sherlock Holmes*. Kit received
the largest sum ever paid up to then by a publisher for an
introduction (nearly enough to send him to Baker Street).
It was money well spent; the collection has never been out
of print. "In Memoriam" is the single most reprinted
Sherlockian essay, and the finest. Only Kit would begin an
introduction to another's book by quibbling with the author
over the character, and only Kit would end by blessing the
patients of Dr. Doyle who so little exercised his medical
skills. Almost everyone among the converted cites this as
milestone, if not epiphany, on the path to Baker Street.

On January 7, 1933, Kit wrote:

> I have not looked up the date, but if, as an astrologer has
> suggested, Sherlock Holmes was most likely born in Janu-
> ary, some observance is due. Therefore, if the matter has

never been settled, I nominate January 6th (the date of this issue of the *Saturday Review*) as his birthday, and reproduce herewith a new portrait, specially done for the occasion by our staff artist W.S.H. [William S. Hall]. (The year of Holmes's birth is thought to be 1853.)

January 6, seemingly selected so casually, was also the birthday of Kit's younger brother Felix ("The Second Stain").

His readers responded immediately. Letters on Holmes appeared not only in his "Bowling Green" and "Trade Winds" columns but also as correspondence to the editor. Such illustrious Sherlockians as Edgar W. Smith (later to be first editor of *The Baker Street Journal*) and James Keddie (founder of the Speckled Band of Boston) first appeared in "The Bowling Green." Until the founding of *The Baker Street Journal* in 1946, "The Bowling Green" was the only place for American Sherlockians to share their researches in print. It must be our Ur-text when researching Sherlockian scholarship.

In the first issue of the *Saturday Review* in 1934 (January 6!), a letter by one Charing Cross of Staten Island appeared under the heading, "Sherlock Holmes and Cocktails."

Sir:— Last year—on what evidence I cannot guess—you announced that January 6 was the date of Sherlock Holmes's birthday, and 1853 the probable year. That seemed to be about right: I remember that the beautiful Irene Adler, "*the* woman," the only one toward whom Sherlock might conceivably have felt an impulse of sentiment, was born ("in New Jersey") in 1858. (Where in New Jersey, I wonder?)

Anyhow, every year about Christmas time I get out my Conan Doyles and read Sherlock again. And your comment lately about cocktails having gone back to 25 cents reminded me that Holmes considered even that price a trifle high. In *The Adventure of the Noble Bachelor*, you remember, he examines a hotel bill in which a cocktail costs a shilling

14

and a glass of sherry 8d. He deduces that the bill was from "one of the most expensive hotels."

Will not the Hotel Duane on Madison Avenue, which you say is frequented by Sherlock Holmes's publishers, invent a Sherlock Holmes cocktail in honor of the birthday? I will offer the 2-volume edition of the Complete Stories as a prize for the most appropriate formula.—Of course there should really be two; the *Sherlock* and the *Mycroft*. What a subtle and softly influential philtre the *Mycroft* would have to be!

Another thought: what evidence can you give of Sherlock's religious feelings, if any?

Kit had, of course, pulled the old journalist's trick of writing himself a letter on a subject of interest. The next week's "Trade Winds" column ran the following:

The "Baker Street Irregulars," a club of Holmes-and-Watson devotees, held its first meeting on January 6, the date now accepted as Sherlock Holmes's birthday. Mr. Malcolm Johnson, editor of the Crime Club books, proposes that the Baker Street Irregulars publish once a year a rare private item of Holmesiana.

Frank Morley ("The Three Garridebs"), the youngest of the three Morley brothers, is a vital link in the Irregular chain. In the May 19 edition of the *Saturday Review* there appeared a letter from "Tobias Gregson, late of Scotland Yard," in which Gregson reveals a crossword puzzle apparently constructed by Mycroft Holmes and discovered at the Diogenes Club. Kit offered membership in the BSI to anyone who submitted a perfect solution within the fortnight. Six did. Tobias Gregson was Frank Morley, who had created the crossword puzzle as an anodyne to boredom during an Atlantic crossing. That there is only one ambiguous question among the 47 set is tribute to the thoroughness with which Kit schooled his brothers in the lore of

15

Sherlock Holmes. In the brotherhood and scholarship of the Morleys were rooted all the aspects of modern Sherlockiana: the clubbishness, the scholarship, the quiz, the desire to disseminate the truth and indoctrinate others.

Although the earliest meetings of the BSI are somewhat shrouded in mystery, we know that the first formal dinner was held at Christ Cella's restaurant on June 5, 1934. The eight men present delighted in each other's company, and the meeting was a resounding success. The next recorded meeting, on December 7, 1934, has always been known as the Woollcott dinner. Alexander Woollcott, *New Yorker* columnist and radio personality, came as a guest of Vincent Starrett and did his best to alienate the Irregulars while trying to claim credit for all that happened. Woollcott wrote up his impressions of the dinner in the *New Yorker* of December 29, 1934, in an essay entitled "The Baker Street Irregulars." Kit, who had little love for this fellow former Philadelphian, resented ever after Woollcott's intrusion and the unwanted publicity for what had been meant as a gathering of "kinsprits."

But Woollcott's uninvited presence at the first dinner underscores the fact that the BSI was escaping Kit's control from its conception—a most unruly child. In a 1949 essay, "On Belonging to Clubs," Kit wrote:

> And still, poor soul, I had this morbid hanker for inventing clubs. Surely the most innocent impulse of my life was my boyish passion for the corn of Conan Doyle. I invented something called the Baker Street Irregulars; a simple group of a dozen devotees who met, Dutch, to discuss what amused them. It was taken up by that resonant soundingboard Woollcott, and then by *Life* magazine. The quiet speakeasy where we met was trampled into covercharge by runners and readers and their dames. Our scrapbook of minutes was stolen by some biblioklept; our simple punchinello (Christ Cella) died of ambitious hypertension. Truly, men in Clubs have an urge toward Deficit, Damnation and

Death. Now the scholarly group of Baker Street find themselves swaddled, or saddled, with a publishing business, an
annual meeting, and a province of pulp. They have about
30 scionist branches whose letters have to be answered. But
not by me.

We must lay the blame for the quiz aspect of the meetings firmly at the doorstep of 2026 Park Avenue, Baltimore,
where the young Kit first used it both to instruct and to
subjugate his younger brothers. But Kit could take quizzes
as well as give them. The Minutes of the meeting of the
Baker Street Irregulars for Friday, January 5, 1945, report
(on page 3) that, "Under the sponsorship of Mr. Wm. S.
Hall, a 'last-line' contest was next prepounded, the object
being to identify, with the respective tales from which they
were taken, the twelve closing paragraphs or passages
quoted. First prize in this contest, a holograph letter from
Dr. Watson's literary agent, was won by Mr. Morley, with
all but one quotation correctly identified."

In August 1938 Kit received a self-effacing letter from
Edgar W. Smith, a vice president of General Motors, sending him some essays on Sherlock Holmes: "The Long Road
from Maiwand," "Up from the Needle," and "The Curious
Incident of the *Tour de Force*." He closed by writing, "Starrett also told me something of the Baker Street Irregulars.
Is this band still operating, and is membership in it beyond
the realm of my aspirations?"

This letter received the highest accolade from Kit: an
immediate response. On August 12, 1938, his reply announced that he had sent "The Curious Incident" for
immediate publication in "The Bowling Green." About
the Irregulars he wrote, "The BSI lead a vague and sporadic
existence. They haven't met now for a couple of years, but
some time next winter there will be a dinner and surely
you must be handsomely inducted."

The friendship grew quickly. By January 7, 1939, Smith

17

was writing to Kit as "Dear Porky." By 1940 he was helping to arrange the BSI dinner. And by the autumn of that year he was referring to himself as acting secretary of the Baker Street Irregulars.

When *The Baker Street Journal* began in 1946, it brought Kit's new column, "Clinical Notes by a Resident Patient." These same years also saw Kit prepare an edition of the Canon for high-school students: *Sherlock Holmes and Dr. Watson: A Textbook of Friendship*.

As the Irregulars became more institutionalized, Kit began to retreat. By 1948 Smith was proposing the incorporation of the Baker Street Irregulars to protect the publishing of the *Journal*. Over his protests at the idea of being involved in a corporation (especially after his disastrous involvement in Hoboken theater), Kit was made president of the BSI Inc. and duly signed stock certificates for those who bought shares. Unfortunately his suggested name for the new corporation, The Standard Doyle Company, was disregarded.

It was also at this time that both Smith and Kit began to feel that their annual dinner had far too many participants, and they began trying to chop the list back to about thirty right-thinking men. Just before the 1947 dinner, Kit wrote to Smith:

> My theme song would be that Moriarty's spider web have tried their best to break up the B.S.I. by overcrowding and disorder. I would continue by saying (if I remember it) that when the impossible have been eliminated (as we have tried to do) those who remain are the Truth.

Later that year he continued:

> My considered opinion remains that the demise of the Murray Hill gives perfect alibi for omitting any public meeting this year; I think Jan 9 would be a perfect date for

a meeting of only the Solid Core, in secret. . . . Unless everyone is notified, no one should be notified. One must be cruel to be kind. In the old days of simplicity, no one wailed when we went some four years without a Stated occasion.

Even more strongly in a letter to a Sherlockian (who shall remain anonymous), Kit explains reprovingly why the man could not be invited to that year's dinner:

Your kind note grieves and embarrasses me! The more so because what you affectionately suggest is, on any genuine Sherlockian principles, impossible. Can you imagine Sherlock himself, or Dr. Watson, or even the Great Paraclete Mycroft, attending such a disorder as those meetings were of latter years? No!

The dissolution of the old Murray Hill made it possible, without offense or prejudice, to dissolve the roaring riot of those occasions, which had become, as any sensitive man would observe, a burden rather than a privilege and which were, especially for those who had to try to orchestrate them, an ordeal by shouting. Imagine yourself in the case of the Gasogene & Tantalus, who used to get back to their lairs in just such condition as Dr. Huxtable on the bearskin hearthrug. Think of the thready pulse, the three-day chin! Not even a return ticket to Mackleton (in the watch-pocket) could assuage such exhaustions.

To show you I am sincere, I told our Grand Manciple Edgar Smith last year that I myself would never again attend a meeting such as have been hurly-burlied in recent years. . . . The little group that first met back in 1934 had no intention of starting a mass movement. Those whose kind and consanguineous feelings are similar can best serve themselves, and best serve Sherlock, by meeting on their own. . . . I implore you to Have Fun, as S.H. and JHW and Mycroft would have suggested, in a little meeting of your own. Not depend on a huge rioting assembly of accidentalists to amuse you.

The BSI meetings had been becoming an increasing burden to Kit. In an unsent letter dated January 4, 1947, he wrote,

> As I found myself saying last night, at the annual dinner of the Baker Street Irregulars (surely one of the most grotesque and yet strangely and touchingly revealing of human associations; the N.A.M. or the C.E.A. (do you know what that is? College English Association) or the C.I.O. or the frigging A.P. are kindergartens compared to it, in psyche) found myself saying to old Edgar Smith, one of the v.p.'s of General Motors, how ghastly it is that the bores and dimwits identify themselves to you; nay, force it upon you; in the first ten minutes. If for the love of Jay Finley Christ, they wd only keep shut you'd maybe not guess it for yrs.; but they have (by infernal compulsion, poor bastards) to let you know in the first ten minutes that they are bloody nuisance fools. By the time Elmer Davis and I left the co[c]ktail room for the salle à manger we knew that poor [*del.*] was a human liquorice; but he spent the next two hrs enforcing our suspicion upon us. Can you imagine: in a mtg of ostensibly grown-up people he began yowling for autographs.
>
> When I think, soberly and sourly (the way I think) what man had done to better men, I am really griped.

In another letter written the same day:

> More gruesome (it was a very good meeting on the whole, and several convives, particularly Peter Greig, kept shouting it was the Best of All) the pay-off came when old Dr. Maitland, the Medical Examiner of the City of New York, mischievously decided to show up the sentimental lads who pretend they are interested in Crime. He dragged in a projection machine, about 11.30 pm, and began to show slides on a screen. . . . They were still at it when I left; handing over to the conscientious Edgar. But it will take me a time, and a determination, to forget those pictures.

20

I prefer to remember the drunken member from Baltimore who kept insisting, without awareness, that Sherlock Holmes had perfected the haemogoblin test—to which I felt it my duty to warn the excitable colleagues that the haemogoblins wd get them if they didn't watch out. Bob Leavitt, and Rex Stout, and specially Prof Starr of Temple Univ., Phila., were admirable. Starr's psychiatric study of Mary Morstan and her mental illness (so tenderly concealed by Watson) was delightful and in the best vein. Rex Stout made a brisk onslaught on Edmund Wilson Jr. (who was Edmund Wilson, the unfortunate Sr.?) which was somewhat obscene but well received. By not serving any highballs until after the soup we kept some of the wild men under wraps.

At the end of that year, in a memo to Edgar Smith about the "Blue Carbuncle," Morley reminisced about a Christmas past:

I should like to say something, when appropriate, about old Christ Cella, in whose speakeasy on 45 Street the earliest mtgs of the BSI were held. He died some time while I was abroad, maybe in October. He is part of the Blue Carbuncle saga because it was he who provided the Goose which was cooked for our 1st Xmas dinner, 1935 or whenever it was, and how baffled he was when (after hunting all over town) I found in a Woolworth's on Nassau Street (down town) the exact sort of blue-glass star-jewel, an awful thing with pseudo-iridiumpointillists which he was to cook, inside the goose. That certainly shook him. He pleaded and promised himself to do it, and he got it inside the entrails of the Goose somehow, so that when it was carved (by me) it appeared as phænomenon. But I never could explain to old Christ why it had to be done. . . . I feel to remind you-all sometimes, that those who have known the BSI since they became so throngy and thrombotic, must sometimes remember the humble origins of the fathers of the Church.

Though increasingly disenchanted with the size and tumult of the Irregulars' dinners, Kit remained intrigued by the possibilities of canonical research. On December 15, 1949, for example, he wrote to a friend, Helen Hare (later Cain):

> I want to sell the BSI boys the idea of adopting *colors* for the club: to be shewn in either a rosette for the lapel, or even in a necktie. The colors, of course, to be
>
> *Purple, Blue and Mouse*
>
> these being the three shades through which Sherlock's dressing gown passed in its fadings. A fine rich purple; a pleasing "electric blue" (like the dress Violet Hunter had to wear in Copper Beeches!); and then a furry, soft, comfortable mouselike gray. . . . I thought maybe, if not imposing yr gallant patience, you wd stitch together a small rosette in these colors for me to wear at the Dinner—or even a necktie! The colors must be in that order of juxtaposition: purple, blue, gray. Don't you think it wd be handsome?

The resulting tie was a great success at the 1950 dinner, although Kit found

> the *blue* . . . a little too dark to be strictly in the canon! You see, my theory is that the *blue* was sun-faded from the original purple, just as the *mouse* was faded from the blue; . . . the three allusions in the stories to the dressing gown's color were all to the same gown, in successive stages of heliotropic chemistry.

In 1986 the BSI adopted an official tie patterned after the original.

Kit also, despite his disgruntlement, remained active in planning the BSI dinners. On November 16, 1949, he wrote to Edgar Smith's secretary, the long-suffering Ruth Freiberg:

> Don't let anyone, not even Dr. Huxtable, get you into an

angst or swivet about the mtg of the B.S.I. The club is now mature & deeply investitured enough to carry on by natural own steam—provided of course EWS is there to preside. . . . All that is necessary to do—and I take full personal responsibility (after all I invented the society!)—is to send, to the same mailing list used in '49, a notice like this:

Owing to Buttons' absence, visiting Peshawur, Pondicherry Lodge, the Agra Treasure and the various curses of our Indian possessions, the annual meeting could not be planned and codified with the usual protocol and assiduous notification.

It will be held at the Racquet & Tennis Club at 6.30 p.m. on January 7, 1950. Members who notify and pay the score (cheques to Edgar W. Smith) will receive interesting souvenirs, and will be called upon, as time allows, to deliver any conanical meditations on their minds. This will be an *ad hoc* and impromptu gathering. In so far as possible, the established rituals will be followed, but only as mood and impulse suggest. Please come prepared to contribute or controvert. Mrs Hudson's menu will be duly prepared. The charge, to cover everything, will be $12. Curfew at midnight. Commuters advised to take the third cab.

But as Kit's health worsened in the 'fifties he was able to attend few meetings. He continued his "Clinical Notes" column and his correspondence with Sherlockians. Indeed, a few of his best canonical writings were done in this period. But the increasing institutionalization (necessary though it was, as he grudgingly admitted) had little appeal to the evangelist in Kit. He loved the tent meeting approach of building his congregation through personal appeal, but when that church became built upon too solid rock it had less need for him and he for it.

Kit was a model Irregular, witty and wise. He was that perfect idolator of Doyle, the reader who was "a boy that is half a man, and a man who is still half a boy." The vitality in what is today the Baker Street Irregulars is the vitality that was Christopher Morley.

Kit's life of enthusiasm and enthusiasm for life were personified in his literature; his ebullient mind was a constant source of ideas and interpretations. He saw so much of interest in the world and he wanted to share it with his friends and his readers—and he saw little difference between the two. His boundless productivity and the charm of his web of words continue to impress the sensitive reader.

That Kit saw greatness in Conan Doyle does not surprise. That he convinced the world to look beyond the "detective fiction" label is his real achievement. As he put it several times (e.g., "Clinical Notes," July 1946, for one variation on the theme):

> Some hard-minded readers may be inclined to think it silly that a group of grown-up men should dally so intently over a literature of entertainment for which even its own author had only moderate regard. Let me conclude then by reiterating what I have said before, that there is no printed body of modern social history—and I include all the Keyserlings and Spenglers and Paretos and other brows like Dover Cliff—that whether of purpose or unintentionally contains so rich and varied pandect of the efficient impulses of its time.

HELEN AND CHRISTOPHER MORLEY BESIDE THE *MEDIA*,
ON WHICH THEY HAD JUST CROSSED FROM NEW YORK TO
SOUTHAMPTON IN JUNE 1951; KIT IS WEARING
THE B.S.I. TIE
Photo courtesy Louise Morley Cochrane

HHC (Bz.)

tremendous thanks

on Jan 6 19*50*

~~CORN EXCHANGE BANK TRUST COMPANY~~

for wonderful necktie

		DOLLARS	CENTS
SILVER	*I have just seen*		
BILLS	*here at the Bank*		
CHECKS	*on way to BOM*		
LIST EACH CHECK SEPARATELY	*Club mtg — had no*		
	time yet to go up		
	to office — will write		
	after the mellay — but		
	hugely grateful —CMFS		

ON HIS WAY TO A BOOK-OF-THE-MONTH CLUB MEETING
AND THEN THE ANNUAL DINNER OF THE BAKER STREET
IRREGULARS ON JANUARY 6, 1950, MORLEY HASTILY
THANKS HELEN HARE CAIN, IN PITTSFIELD, FOR MAKING
THE B.S.I. TIE

CHRISTOPHER MORLEY, ROBERT KEITH LEAVITT, HELEN
HARE, AND LOUIS GREENFIELD, IN MORLEY'S STUDIO AT
46 WEST 47TH STREET IN JUNE 1946
Doubleday publicity photo by Louise Thomas for *Bartlett's
Familiar Quotations*

NIGEL BRUCE AND CHRISTOPHER MORLEY IN THE MID-
'FORTIES AT THE MORLEY HOME, "GREEN ESCAPE"
From the Bryant Library local history collection, Roslyn,
New York

FREDERIC DANNAY, ELMER DAVIS, WILLIAM S. HALL,
CHRISTOPHER MORLEY, AND REX STOUT AT THE B.S.I.
DINNER ON JANUARY 3, 1947
New York Herald Tribune

CHRISTOPHER MORLEY, CLAYTON RAWSON, EDGAR W.
SMITH, AND FREDERIC DANNAY AT THE B.S.I. DINNER
ON JANUARY 6, 1950. THE PUNNING "VALENTWINE!"
REFLECTS KIT'S USE OF THIS MAGAZINE PHOTO TO SEND
GREETINGS ON THE FOLLOWING FEBRUARY 14TH
Publishers Weekly

ESSAYS

Morley made his name as an essayist. His newspaper columns and later his *Saturday Review of Literature* columns made him a national figure on the literary scene.

The following essays originally appeared in "The Bowling Green": "In Memoriam Sherlock Holmes," "Was Sherlock Holmes an American?," and "Doctor Watson's Secret." "Notes on Baker Street," "A Southdown Christmas," and "An American Gentleman" also appeared in the *Saturday Review*.

"In Memoriam" appeared in three slightly different forms: the first in the *Saturday Review*, August 2, 1930; the second in the Doubleday Memorial Edition of the Holmes stories; and the third—the version printed here—in Kit's volume of essays *Internal Revenue*. This version expands upon the various Mrs. Watsons and quotes from S. C. Roberts. As Kit chose to include it in his volume, I read it as the definitive "In Memoriam."

These essays are the core of Kit's serious contribution to Sherlockian scholarship and are still cited frequently by contemporary commentators. They show the willingness to examine and illumine anything catching his eye, the attention to even trivial detail, that is his (and Holmes's) hallmark.

IN MEMORIAM
SHERLOCK HOLMES

IT WAS UNFAIR of Conan Doyle to say (as he did in his delightful autobiography, *Memories and Adventures*) that Dr. Watson had never shown a gleam of humor nor made a single joke. Let me refute that at once. In the first chapter of *The Valley of Fear* the good doctor, after some rather sharp taunting by his friend, caught Holmes fairly off guard. They were speaking of Professor Moriarty.

"The famous scientific criminal," says Watson, "as famous among crooks as——"

"My blushes, Watson!" Holmes murmurs in a deprecating voice.

"I was about to say, as he is unknown to the public."

Even Holmes admitted that this was "a distinct touch."

But another evidence of Dr. Watson's mischief was his frequent sly allusion to the unrecorded adventures. All Holmes-and-Watson lovers must have brooded sadly on the titles of those untold tales. "The shocking affair of the Dutch steamship *Friesland*, which so nearly cost us both our lives," the case of Wilson the notorious canary-trainer, the repulsive story of the red leech, the story of the Giant Rat of Sumatra "for which the world is yet not prepared," the singular affair of the aluminum crutch, the Curious Experience of the Paterson Family in the Island of Uffa—these are some of the yarns we have had to do without; having only the melancholy assurance that the documents were safely on file in that famous dispatch box in the vaults of Cox's Bank at Charing Cross. Perhaps most of all I deplore that we never were told "the story of the politician, the lighthouse, and the trained cormorant." In this allusion we surely find Watson in a deliberately pawky vein.—We hoped against hope for some of these stories; we can never have them now.

27

But there is one omission in the long Holmes–Watson history that some generous survivor could supply. It must not be forgotten that it was a certain "young Stamford," also a medico, who first introduced Watson to Sherlock Holmes; and the chance that brought this about was that Stamford and Watson met at the Criterion bar in London. Young Stamford was so specifically outlined in those first pages of the *Study in Scarlet* that I had always thought he might reappear some day in one of the adventures. I don't believe he ever did. But at least his immortal service in bringing the pair together should be remembered. A small tablet in that famous bar-room would be a graceful memento; I think it should be erected by the London publisher who bought the complete copyright of *A Study in Scarlet* for £25. And in any healths drunk in the matter by visiting pilgrims I suggest also a grateful side-look to the gallant Murray, the orderly who saved Dr. Watson's life in Afghanistan.

The whole Sherlock Holmes saga is a triumphant illustration of art's supremacy over life. Perhaps no fiction character ever created has become so charmingly real to his readers. It is not that we take our blessed Sherlock too seriously; if we really want the painful oddities of criminology let us go to Bataille or Roughead. But Holmes is pure anesthesia. We read the stories again and again; perhaps most of all for the little introductory interiors which give a glimpse of 221B Baker Street. The fact that Holmes had earlier lodgings in Montague Street (alongside the British Museum) is forgotten. That was before Watson, and we must have Watson too. Rashly, in the later years, Holmes twice undertook to write stories for himself. They have not quite the same magic. No, we are epicures. We must begin in Baker Street; and best of all, if possible, let it be a stormy winter morning when Holmes routs Watson out of bed in haste. The doctor wakes to see that tall ascetic figure by the bedside with a candle. "Come, Watson, come! The game is afoot!" If that is not possible, then I prefer to find Holmes stretched on the sofa in a fit of the dumps; perhaps he is scraping on the violin, or bemoaning the dearth of imaginative crime and reaching for the cocaine (a habit he evidently outgrew, for we hear little of it in the later adventures). We have a glimpse of the sitting-room, that room we know so well. There are the great volumes of scrapbook records; the bullet marks on the walls; the mysterious "gasogene" which appears occasionally in English fiction and which I can only suppose to be some sort of syphon-bottle. (There is also a sort of decanter-holder called a "tantalus" now and then set out on the sideboard; another mystery for American readers, and now more than ever true to its name.) The Persian slipper for tobacco and the coal-scuttle for cigars don't appeal to me so much. They are more conscious eccentricities. In comes Mrs. Hudson with a message, or a "commissionaire" with a letter, and we are off. Gregson and Lestrade will get the credit, but we have the fun. Already we are in a hansom rattling through the streets to Waterloo or Charing Cross or Paddington. (Holmes rarely takes train at Euston or King's Cross or Liverpool Street.)

It is a kind of piety for even the least and humblest of Holmes-lovers to pay what tribute he may to this great encyclopædia of romance that has given the world so much innocent pleasure. Already the grandchildren of Holmes's earliest followers are beginning upon him with equal delight. I was too young to know the wave of dismay that went round the English-reading world when Sherlock and Professor Moriarty supposedly perished together in the Reichenbach Fall, but I can well remember the sombre effect on my ten-year-old spirits when I first read the closing paragraphs of the *Memoirs*. The intolerable pathos of the cigarette-case on the rocky ledge; the firm clear handwriting of that last stoic message! I then put in two or three years in reading everything else of Dr. Doyle's. One walked downtown to the old Enoch Pratt Free Library on Mulberry Street in Baltimore and got out a book—*The Firm of Girdlestone*, or *The Captain of the Pole Star*, or *Beyond the City*, or *A Duet*, or *Round the Red Lamp*, or *The Stark Munro Letters* or *The Doings of Raffles Haw*. For I specialized chiefly in the lesser known tales, and deplore Sir Arthur's tendency (in his autobiography) to make light of some of these yarns. As for *The White Company* and *The Refugees* and *Micah Clarke* and *Uncle Bernac*, these were household words. When one found at the library a Conan Doyle he had not read, he began it at once on the walk home. It was quite a long trudge from Mulberry Street to the 2000 block on Park Avenue, and the tragedy often was that, loitering like a snail, almost like the locomotion of a slowed moving picture, the book was actually finished by the time one got home. There was all the journey to do over again the next day.

But all that time I knew, deep in some instinct, that Holmes was not really dead. In the first place I had noted that the date of his Reichenbach crisis lacked only one day of being my own birthday; and I felt positive that the eve of my festival would not have been marred by the death of my hero. So you may imagine the thrilling excitement—in 1903, wasn't it?—when *The Return* began printing in *Colliers'*. Then we saw how Dr. Doyle had got himself out of his predicament. He had revived Holmes, but (to be fair all round) he had killed off Mrs. Watson. We had been tolerant of Mrs. Watson because she was née Mary Morstan in *The Sign of the Four*, but obviously she was a little in the way. Her patience was certainly exemplary in allowing the doctor to rush off on various expeditions; but it could not last. One of the unsolved questions, by the way, is the second Mrs. Watson. Evidently the good doctor, who was always persevering, had tried again; for Holmes in January 1903 (see *The Adventure of the Blanched Soldier*) refers to an existing Mrs. Watson. But who or why this second lady we have no data. S. C. Roberts, in his delightful pamphlet *Doctor Watson*, offers the ingenious suggestion that the Deutero–Mrs. Watson was the cool and aristocratic (but also imprudent) Miss Violet de Merville of the story *The Illustrious Client*. Mr. Roberts says:

> Watson's second marriage took place at the end of 1902 or at the beginning of 1903, a few months after the affair of the Illustrious Client. Now this adventure must have made a more than ordinary impression upon Watson's mind. Instinctively chivalrous, he was a man to whom a woman in trouble made a specially vivid appeal. Violet de Merville, moreover, was "beautiful, accomplished, a wonder-woman in every way." After the terrible exposure of the true character of her fiancé, what more natural than that Watson should, after a fitting interval, make inquiries as to her recovery of health and spirits? It may be objected that Miss de Merville moved in exalted circles, and that a retired practitioner would not have the *droit d'entrée* to her society. But here a significant fact must be considered. Miss de Merville's father was a soldier, and a soldier who had won distinction in Afghanistan—"de Merville of Khyber fame." With such a father-in-law Watson would at once be on common ground.

Mr. Roberts goes on to the specially ingenious suggestion that the story (*The Mazarin Stone*) which follows the first allusion to Watson's second marriage may be from the hand of Mrs. Watson II. It is not told by Dr. Watson himself, and it may well be that in the preoccupation of resuming medical practice, the good doctor turned over to this accomplished lady the task of editing one of the memoirs. The objections to Mr. Roberts's theory are grave, however. In the first place we nowhere learn, in the story of the *Illustrious Client*, that Dr. Watson actually met Miss de Merville; Holmes speaks of it as a possibility ("Perhaps you may meet her before we are through"), but Watson himself makes no comment. It was about the 14th of September, 1902, when the horrid episode of Baron Gruner and the vitriol took place. After so serious a shock it would have taken Miss de Merville some time to recover. We know that she was fond of Mediterranean cruising; I think it most probable that she would have gone for a winter voyage to recuperate; and it is improbable that she could have already become Mrs. Watson by January 1903.

The other possible candidate for Dr. Watson's hand would be Kitty Winter; she was imprisoned for vitriol-throwing but given "the lowest possible sentence." On the whole I fear that Mr. Roberts's theory, though very tempting, is difficult to accept.

One of the blissful ways of passing an evening, when you encounter another dyed-in-the-blood addict, is to embark upon the happy discussion of minor details of Holmesiana. "Whose gold watch was it that had been so mishandled?" one may ask; and the other counters with "What was the book that Joseph Stangerson carried in his pocket?" Endless delicious minutiæ to consider! There was Dr. Verner, "a distant relative of Sherlock Holmes," who bought out Watson's practice. Undoubtedly this was an Anglicization of the name of Holmes's grandmother Vernet. She was French, a sister of the French military artist of that name. (A real and very distinguished family of painters, incidentally; undoubtedly suggested to Doyle by his own artistic family inheritance. I wonder if the Vernet family in France realize that the world-famous detective has thus been grafted onto their genealogy?) Or there are the glimpses of Moriarty to be talked over: his youthful treatise on the binomial theorem "which had a European vogue." Or Mycroft Holmes, seven years older than Sherlock; we would gladly have heard more of him and of the Diogenes Club. How was it that Dr. Watson happened to cherish a portrait of Henry Ward Beecher, but had never had it framed? Or we might air a minor grievance that the devoted Mrs. Hudson had never been implicated in a mystery of her own. There was a mystery about a landlady, but a certain Mrs. Warren was brought in for the purpose. And why did Gregson and Lestrade gradually fade out of the picture? Why does Billy the page-boy remain only a phantom? Holmes speaks once of having been at college: what college was it? And Dr. Watson's wound from the "Jezail bullet": was it in his shoulder or in his leg? apparently Sir Arthur was not quite sure.

In the matter of editions there is also room for much gossip. As with all esteemed authors, there is too much talk of first editions and fine copies and not nearly enough about the chance examples and shabby second-hand culls that we more frequently encounter. Does no one else take pleasure in phony copies, piracies, wretched reprints jobbed off for mail-order sets and department store trading? What an oddly miscellaneous spectacle is the collection of any average Doyle enthusiast. My own fortuitous gathering of Doyles ranges (by gift or purchase) from the bound volumes of *The Strand Magazine* for 1891–93 in which Holmes's adventures and memoirs first appeared, down to S. C. Roberts's admirable pamphlet. I have some genuine firsts among them, but not less prized are the queer and abominable copies picked up from time to time at hazard. My American edition of the *Stark Munro Letters* (Appleton '95) has the rubber stamp of the Y.M.C.A. Library, Montreal. *Beyond the City*, vilely impressed on brittle yellowing paper, was sponsored by F. Tennyson Neely, 1894. *A Study in Scarlet* is one of a set imprinted W. R. Caldwell and Co. *The Firm of Girdlestone* carries the name of Siegel Cooper & Co., New York and Chicago. Most mysterious of the lot is *A Case of Identity and Other Stories*, from The Optimus Printing Company, 45–51 Rose Street, New York, down by the Brooklyn Bridge. Next after Oscar Wilde, poor old Conan Doyle must have been utilized by more will-o'-the-wisp publishers than any other modern writer.

Such are the minutiæ that Holmesians and Doyleites explore with innocent satisfaction. Even in the less successful stories we remain untroubled by any naïveté of plot; it is the character of the immortal pair that we relish. It is not mere chance that they are well loved. Doyle himself must have been a singularly lovable man. There is an anecdote in his *Memories and Adventures* that reveals very clearly the fine instinct of delicacy in his massive personality. He was visiting George Meredith in the latter's old age, and they were walking up a steep path to the little summerhouse Meredith used for writing. In Doyle's own words:

> The nervous complaint from which he suffered caused him to fall down occasionally. As we walked up the narrow path I heard him fall behind me, but judged from the sound that it was a mere slither and could not have hurt him. Therefore I walked on as if I had heard nothing. He was a fiercely proud old man, and my instincts told me that his humiliation in being helped up would be far greater than any relief I could give him.

I can think of no truer revelation of a gentleman than that.

The character of Holmes, Doyle has told us, was at any rate partly suggested by his student memories of Dr. Joseph Bell of the Edinburgh Infirmary, whose diagnostic intuitions used to startle his patients and pupils. But there was abundant evidence that the invention of the scientific detective conformed to a fundamental logic in Doyle's own temper. The famous case of Oscar Slater was one example; another was his ingenuity in transmitting news of the war in cipher to British prisoners in Germany. This he did by sending books in which he had put needle-pricks under various printed letters so as to spell out the desired messages; but beginning with the third chapter, believing that the German censor would examine the earlier chapters more carefully. Of his humor there is a pleasant income tax story. In his first year of independent medical practice his earnings were £154, and when the income tax paper arrived he filled it up to show that he was not liable. The authorities returned the form with the words *Most Unsatisfactory* scrawled across it. He returned it again with the subscription *I entirely agree.* As many readers must have guessed, *Round the Red Lamp* and *The Stark Munro Letters* were very literally drawn from his own experiences in medicine.

"Art in the blood is liable to take the strangest forms," Sherlock Holmes once remarked. Undoubtedly Doyle was thinking also of his own inheritance (both artistic and Irish) and certainly he himself, though he looked so solidly Watsonian, gave his friends many surprises in the mutations of his vigorous career. One of the quaintest of these must have been his collaboration with Barrie in an operetta. Of the final spiritualist phase only those who have made careful study of those problems can profitably speak. But there was no stage of the life, from the poor student doing without lunch to buy books to the famous author enduring painful hostility for his psychic faith, which did not reflect the courage, the chivalry, the sagacity we would have expected from the creator of Holmes. Certainly it was characteristic of that student of mysteries to attack the greatest one we know.

Those of us who in earliest boyhood gave our hearts to Conan Doyle, and have had from him so many hours of good refreshment, find our affection unshakable. What other man led a fuller and heartier and more masculine life? Doctor, whaler, athlete, writer, speculator, dramatist, historian, war correspondent, spiritualist, he was always also the infracaninophile—the helper of the under dog. Generous personality, his virtues had always something of the fresh vigor of the amateur, keen, open-minded, flexible, imaginative. If, as Doyle utterly believed, the spirits of the dead persist and can communicate, there is none that could have more wholesome news to impart to us than that brave and energetic lover of life.

A blessing, then, on those ophthalmic citizens who did not go to that office at 2 Devonshire Place, near Harley Street, where in 1891 Dr. A. Conan Doyle set up consulting rooms as an eye specialist. It was there, waiting for the patients who never came, that he began to see the possibilities in Sherlock Holmes. No wonder that Dr. Watson too sometimes rather neglected his practice.

> *Internal Revenue*; the version used to introduce Doubleday's *The Complete Sherlock Holmes* also appeared in *Prefaces without Books*

WAS
SHERLOCK HOLMES
AN AMERICAN?

> "I think the fellow is really an
> American, but he has worn his accent
> smooth with years of London."
>
> —*The Three Garridebs*

A CAPRICIOUS SECRECY was always characteristic of Holmes. He concealed from Watson his American connection. And though Watson must finally have divined it, he also was uncandid with us. The Doctor was a sturdy British patriot: the fact of Holmes's French grandmother was disconcerting, and to add to this his friend's American association and sympathy would have been painful. But the theory is too tempting to be lightly dismissed. Not less than fifteen of the published cases (including three of the four chosen for full-length treatment) involve American characters or scenes. Watson earnestly strove to minimize the appeal of United States landscapes of which Holmes must have told him. The great plains of the West were "an arid and repulsive desert."[1] Vermissa Valley (in Pennsylvania, I suppose?) was "a gloomy land of black crag and tangled forest . . . not a cheering prospect."[2] Watson's quotation from the child Lucy,[1]—"Say, did God make this country?"—was a humorous riposte to Holmes, spoofing the familiar phrase Watson had heard too often in their fireside talks. There is even a possible suggestion of Yankee timbre in the Doctor's occasional descriptions of the "well-remembered voice." The argument of rival patriotisms was a favorite topic between them. Watson never quite forgave

[1] *A Study in Scarlet.*
[2] *The Valley of Fear.*

Holmes's ironical jape when after some specially naïve Victorian imperialism by the Doctor (perhaps at the time of the '87 Jubilee) Sherlock decorated the wall with the royal V. R. in bullet-pocks. (Or did the Doctor misread as V. R. what was jocularly meant to be V. H.—because Watson too insistently suggested a sentimental interest in Miss Violet Hunter of the *Copper Beeches*? An H. in bullet-pocks, if the marksman's aim was shaken by a heavy dray in the street, or by the neighboring Underground Railway, might well look like an R.)

Why, again, does Watson write "It was upon the 4th of March, as I have good reason to remember," that the adventure of the *Study in Scarlet* began? And why was Holmes still at the breakfast table? It was the 4th of March, 1881, and Holmes was absorbed in reading the news dispatches about the inauguration, to take place that day, of President Garfield.

Was Holmes actually of American birth? It would explain much. The jealousy of Scotland Yard, the refusal of knighthood, the expert use of Western argot, the offhand behavior to aristocratic clients, the easy camaraderie with working people of all sorts, the always traveling First Class in trains. How significant is Holmes's "Hum!" when he notes that Irene was born in New Jersey.[3] And Watson's careful insertion of "U.S.A." after every American address, which always irritates us, was probably a twit, to tease his principal. True, as Inspector MacDonald once said,[4] "You don't need to import an American from outside in order to account for American doings." But let us light the cherry-wood pipe and examine the data more systematically.

Holmes's grandmother was "the sister of Vernet, the French artist."[5] This of course was Horace Vernet (1789–

---

[3] *A Scandal in Bohemia.*
[4] *The Valley of Fear.*
[5] *The Greek Interpreter.*

1863), the third of the famous line of painters in that family. Horace Vernet's father (who had been decorated by Napoleon for his *Battle of Marengo* and *Morning of Austerlitz*) came from Bordeaux and Horace's grandfather, the marine painter, from Avignon. Here we have an association with the South of France which Holmes acknowledges by his interest in Montpellier[6] where he probably had French kindred. Like Sir Kenelm Digby, who delivered there the famous discourse on the Powder of Sympathy,[7] Holmes knew Montpellier as an important center of scientific studies. (See *The Empty House*.) It is deplorable that our Holmes researchers have done so little to trace his French relationship. It is significant that though he declined a knighthood in Britain he was willing to accept the Legion of Honor in France.[8]

Much might be said of Sherlock's presumable artistic and political inheritance from the Vernets. His great-uncle's studio in Paris was "a rendezvous of Liberals."[9] Surely the untidiness which bothered Watson at 221B is akin to the description of Horace Vernet "painting tranquilly, whilst boxing, fencing, drum and horn playing were going on, in the midst of a medley of visitors, horses, dogs and models."[10] Holmes's grandmother, one of this radical and bohemian and wide-travelling family, brought up among the harrowing scenes of the French Revolution and the Napoleonic wars, may quite possibly have emigrated to America.[11] It is not inconceivable then that at least one of

[6]*The Empty House*. Cf. also *The Disappearance of Lady Frances Carfax*.

[7]Ann Macdonell: *The Closet of Sir Kenelm Digby* (1910), p. xxxi.

[8]*The Golden Pince-Nez*.

[9]*Encyclopaedia Britannica*, article "Vernet."

[10]Ibid. Perhaps Sherlock as a child got his first interest in boxing and fencing from great-uncle Horace.

[11]Turning to the telephone book, as Dr Watson did for Garrideb, I find that several of the Vernet (Verner) family came to the U. S. There are 2 Vernets in Brooklyn, 3 Verners in Manhattan, 1 Verner in Floral Park, L. I.

Holmes's parents was an American. My own conjecture is that there was some distant connection with the famous Holmes household of Cambridge (Mass.). Every reader has noticed Holmes's passionate interest in breakfasts: does this not suggest the Autocrat of the Breakfast Table?

I will not cloud the issue with futile speculation, though certainly it is of more importance than many of the controversies (such as, was Holmes's dressing gown blue, purple, or mouse-colored?[12]). But before proceeding to recount some specific passages which prove our hero's exceptional interest in America let me add one more suggestion. The hopeless muddle of any chronology based on the *Gloria Scott* and *Musgrave Ritual* is familiar to all students; Miss Dorothy Sayers has done her brilliant best to harmonize the anomalies. But all have wondered just what Holmes was doing between the time he left the university and his taking rooms in Montague Street. My own thought is that the opening of the Johns Hopkins University in Baltimore in 1876, and the extraordinary and informal opportunities offered there for graduate study, tempted him across the water. He was certainly familiar with papers in the chemical journals written by Ira Remsen, the brilliant young professor who took charge of the new laboratories in Baltimore. Probably in Baltimore he acquired his taste for oysters[13] and on a hot summer day noted the depth to which the parsley had sunk into the butter.[14] In that devoted group of young scholars and scientists, and in the musical circles of that hospitable city, he must have been supremely happy. His American-born mother (or father) had often told him of the

---

[12]Elementary. This particular gown was blue when new (*The Twisted Lip*). It had gone purple by the time of the *Blue Carbuncle*. During the long absence, 1891–94, when Mrs Hudson faithfully aired and sunned it in the back yard, it faded to mouse (*The Empty House*).

[13]*The Sign of the Four*.

[14]*The Adventure of the Six Napoleons*. Holmes's interest in the butter-dish is also shown in *The Musgrave Ritual*.

untrammeled possibilities of American life. The great Centennial Exposition in Philadelphia (1876) was surely worth a visit; there he observed the mark of the Pennsylvania Small Arms Company.[15] During his year or so in the States he travelled widely. He met Wilson Hargreave (who later became important in the New York Police Department[16]) perhaps in connection with the case of *Vanderbilt and the Yeggman*, a record of which he kept in his scrapbook.[17] He went to Chicago, where he made his first acquaintance with organized gangsterism.[18] I suggest that he perhaps visited his kinsmen the Sherlocks in Iowa—e.g., in Des Moines, where a young member of that family, Mr C. C. Sherlock, has since written so ably on rural topics.[19] He must have gone to Topeka;[20] and of course he made pilgrimage to Cambridge, Mass., to pay respect to the great doctor, poet and essayist. From Oliver Wendell Holmes, Jr., then a rising lawyer in Boston, he heard first-hand stories of the Civil War, which fired his interest in "that gallant struggle." Indeed he spoke to Watson so often about the Civil War that Watson repeated in the story of *The Resident Patient* the episode of the Henry Ward Beecher portrait which he had already told in *The Cardboard Box*.[21] It is interesting to note,

[15]*The Valley of Fear.*

[16]*The Dancing Men.*

[17]*The Sussex Vampire.*

[18]"My knowledge of the crooks of Chicago," v. *The Dancing Men*. Cf. also allusions in *The Valley of Fear* and *The Three Garridebs.*

[19]C. C. Sherlock: *Care and Management of Rabbits* (1920); *The Modern Hen* (1922); *Bulb Gardening* (1922), etc.; v. *Who's Who in America*. Iowa is a great apiarian State; undoubtedly from the Sherlock side came the interest in roses, bee-keeping, etc.

[20]Otherwise how could he know that there was no such person as Dr Lysander Starr? (*The Three Garridebs.*)

[21]There was no duplication in the stories as first printed: *The Cardboard Box* in *The Strand Magazine* of January 1893, *The Resident Patient* in August of the same year. In the latter story as it absurdly appears in the collected editions the description of the "blazing hot day in August" is repeated for

in passing, that when Holmes spoke in that episode of having written two monographs on Ears in the *Anthropological Journal*, the alert editor of the *Strand* at once took the hint. A few months later, in October and November 1893, the *Strand* printed "A Chapter on Ears," with photos of the ears of famous people—including an ear of Dr Oliver Wendell Holmes. Surely, from so retiring a philosopher, then 84 years old, this intimate permission could not have been had without the privileged intervention of Sherlock.

Speaking of *The Strand Magazine*, it is odd that our researchers do not more often turn back to those original issues which solve many problems. The much belabored matter of Holmes's university, for instance. There was never any question about it, for in Sidney Paget's illustrations Holmes is clearly shown sitting in Trevor's garden wearing a straw hat with a *Light Blue* ribbon.[22] (He was, of course, a boxing Blue.) Why has such inadequate honor been paid to those admirable drawings by Paget?—Oxford was unthinkable to Holmes; with what pleasure he noted that Colonel Moran[23] and John Clay[24] were both "Eton and Oxford."

In *The Bruce-Partington Plans* one of our most suggestive

"a close rainy day in October." The explanation is that Dr Watson withheld *The Cardboard Box* from book publication for 24 years; perhaps because it revealed some anti-American bias in his never having had the portrait of Beecher framed. But the Beecher incident showed Holmes's keen observation, and in compiling the *Memoirs* Watson carelessly spliced or trepanned it into *The Resident Patient*. Then, when he republished *The Cardboard Box* in *His Last Bow* (1917), he forgot this.

[22]*Strand Magazine*, Vol. V, p. 398. While speaking of the *Gloria Scott*, has it been pointed out that Holmes never admitted to Watson why he chose Mrs Hudson's lodgings? She was the widow of the ruffian Hudson who blackmailed old Mr Trevor—and so more than ever "a long-suffering woman." And of course the rapid disappearance of Watson's bull-pup was because Holmes had been bitten by one in college days.

[23]*The Empty House.*

[24]*The Red-Headed League.*

SHERLOCK HOLMES WEARING CAMBRIDGE RIBBON
Drawing by Sidney Paget in *The Strand Magazine*

passages occurs. "You have never had so great a chance of serving your country," cries Mycroft. But is Holmes moved by this appeal? "Well, well!" he said, "shrugging his shoulders." All emotions, we know, were abhorrent to that cold, precise mind,[25] and certainly militant patriotism among them; at any rate until many years later when bees, flowers, Sussex, and long association with the more sentimental Watson had softened him to the strange outburst about "God's own wind" on the terrible night of August 2nd, 1914.[26]—Plainly he resented Mycroft's assumption that

[25]*A Scandal in Bohemia.*
[26]*His Last Bow.*

England was his only country. Mycroft, seven years older, had earlier outgrown the Franco-American tradition of the family. If Mycroft had ever been in the States he had striven to forget it; indeed no one can think of Mycroft without being reminded (in more respects than one) of the great expatriate Henry James.[27]

That Holmes had a very special affection and interest in regard to the United States is beyond question. He had much reason to be grateful to American criminals, who often relieved him from the ennui of London's dearth of outrage. The very first case recorded by Watson was the murder of Enoch J. Drebber, the ex-Mormon from Cleveland. Irene Adler, *the* woman, was a native of New Jersey. In *The Red-Headed League* the ingenious John Clay represented the League as having been founded by the eccentric millionaire Ezekiah Hopkins of Lebanon, Pa., "U.S.A." In *The Five Orange Pips*, Elias Openshaw emigrated to Florida, rose to be a Colonel in the C.S.A. and made a fortune. Although Watson tries to prejudice the reader by painful allusions to the habits of these people, there is plentiful evidence that Holmes considered America the land of opportunity. (Watson preferred Australia.) Both Aloysius Doran[28] and John Douglas[29] had struck it rich in California. Senator Neil Gibson,[30] "iron of nerve and leathery of conscience," had also made his pile in gold mines. Hilton Cubitt, the Norfolk squire, had married a lovely American woman;[31] and Holmes was glad to be able to save Miss Hatty Doran from Lord St Simon who was not worthy of her.[32] He yawns sardonically at the *Morning Post*'s social

[27]It is possible that Mycroft's experience had been in Canada, not the U. S.—Sherlock says Mycroft was known at the Foreign Office as an expert on Canada (*The Bruce-Partington Plans*).

[28]*The Noble Bachelor.*

[29]*The Valley of Fear.*

[30]*Thor Bridge.*

[31]*The Dancing Men.*

[32]*The Noble Bachelor.*

item which implies that Miss Doran will gain by becoming
the wife of a peer. That case is a high point in Holmes's
transatlantic sympathy. He praises American slang, quotes
Thoreau, shows his knowledge of the price of cocktails,
and utters the famous sentiment:—

> "It is always a joy to meet an American, for I am one of
> those who believe that the folly of a monarch and the
> blundering of a minister in far-gone years will not prevent
> our children from being some day citizens of the same
> world-wide country under a flag which shall be a quartering
> of the Union Jack with the Stars and Stripes."

Which reminds one obviously of the fact that when Holmes
disguised himself as Mr Altamont of Chicago, the Irish-
American agitator, to deceive Von Bork, he greatly resem-
bled the familiar cartoons of Uncle Sam.[33] He visited Chicago again in 1912–13 to prepare himself for this role; I
wish Mr Vincent Starrett would look up the details.

Holmes's fondness for America did not prevent him from
seeing the comic side of a nation that lends itself to broad
satiric treatment. In *The Man with the Watches*, one of the two
stories outside the canon,[34] Holmes remarks of the victim
"He was probably an American, and also probably a man of
weak intellect." (This rhetorical device for humorous purposes was a family trait: we find it in Mycroft's description
of the senior clerk at the Woolwich Arsenal—"He is a man
of forty, married, with five children. He is a silent, morose
man."[35]) After his long use of American cant for Von Bork's

[33]*His Last Bow.*

[34]The other is *The Lost Special*; both are to be found in *The Conan Doyle
Stories* (London: John Murray, 1929). Holmes appears in both these stories
by obvious allusion, but Watson suppressed them, probably because
Holmes's deductions were wrong. [See "Two Suppressed Holmes Episodes," below, pp. 177–178.—S.R.]

[35]*The Bruce-Partington Plans.*

benefit Sherlock says "My well of English seems to be permanently defiled."[36] But these japes are plainly on the principle "On se moque de ce qu'on aime." He kept informed of American manners and events: when he met Mr Leverton of Pinkerton's he said "Pleased to meet you" and alluded to "the Long Island cave mystery."[37] He knew "the American business principle" of paying well for brains.[38] He did not hesitate to outwit a rascal by inventing an imaginary mayor of Topeka—recalling for the purpose the name of the counterfeiter of Reading years before.[39] (Those who escaped him were not forgotten.) But nothing shows more convincingly his passionate interest in all cases concerning Americans than his letter about the matter of *The Man with the Watches*, alluded to above. Even in Tibet, where he was then travelling as "a Norwegian named Sigerson,"[40] he had kept up with the news. This was in the spring of '92; how Watson, after reading the letter in the newspaper, can have supposed his friend was really dead passes belief. There are frequent humorous allusions to American accent,[41] the shape of American shoes,[42] American spelling.[43] I suspect that Holmes's travels in these States never took him to the South or Southwest;[44] for he shows a curious ignorance of Southern susceptibilities in the matter of race,[45] and in spite of his American

[36]*His Last Bow.*

[37]*The Red Circle.* The mystery, on true Sherlockian principles, is that there are no caves on Long Island.

[38]*The Valley of Fear.*

[39]*The Three Garridebs, The Engineer's Thumb.*

[40]*The Empty House.*

[41]*The Hound of the Baskervilles.*

[42]*The Dancing Men, The Valley of Fear.*

[43]*The Three Garridebs.*

[44]The "remarkable case" of the venomous gila lizard (v. *The Sussex Vampire*) need not suggest Arizona. It probably came from Number 3, Pinchin Lane (*The Sign of the Four*).

[45]*The Yellow Face.*

Encyclopaedia[46] he did not know which was the Lone Star State. Let it be noted that the part of London where he first took rooms (Montague Street, alongside the British Museum) is the region frequented more than any other by American students and tourists.

That Holmes was reared in the States, or had some schooling here before going up to Cambridge, seems then at least arguable. His complete silence (or Watson's) on the subject of his parents suggests that they were deceased or not in England. A foreign schooling, added to his own individual temperament, would easily explain his solitary habits at college.[47] If he had gone to almost any English school the rugger jargon of Cyril Overton would have been comprehensible to him[48] or he might have picked it up from Watson, who played for Blackheath.[49] Watson, moreover, if he knew more about Holmes's family, may have been moved by jealousy to keep silent. Already he had suffered by the contrast between the corpulent Mycroft and his own older brother, the crapulent H. W.[50] Or his neglect to inform us may just have been the absent-mindedness and inaccuracy which we have learned to expect from good old Watson—and which were even acquired by his wife, who went so far as to forget her husband's first name and call him "James" in front of a visitor.[51] The Doctor has hopelessly confused us on even more important matters—that

---

[46] *The Five Orange Pips.*
[47] *The Gloria Scott.*
[48] *The Missing Three-Quarter.*
[49] *The Sussex Vampire.*
[50] *The Sign of the Four.*
[51] *The Man with the Twisted Lip.* This was probably the cause of the first rupture between Dr and Mrs Watson. Has it been pointed out, by the way, that there is premonitory allusion to a second Mrs Watson in *The Disappearance of Lady Frances Carfax*, where Watson evades Holmes's question as to who was his companion in the hansom? Also the Doctor had been bucking himself up with a Turkish bath.

both Moriarty brothers were called James, for instance. Considering the evidence without prejudice, the idea that Holmes was at any rate partly American is enticing.

As Jefferson Hope said,[52] "I guessed what puzzled the New Yorkers would puzzle the Londoners." So I leave it as a puzzle, not as a proven case, for more accomplished students to re-examine. But the master's own dictum[53] is apposite:—"When once your point of view is changed, the very thing which was so damning becomes a clue to the truth."

"Bowling Green," SRL, July 21 & 28, 1934; also in
Streamlines and *221B*

[52]*A Study in Scarlet.*
[53]*Thor Bridge.*

48

DOCTOR WATSON'S SECRET

I SPOKE SOME TIME AGO of the secret in Sherlock Holmes's life, his American connection. Perhaps it is permissible now to remark upon an even more carefully hidden arcanum, Dr Watson's clandestine marriage.

The infuriating inconsistencies of Watsonian chronology have cost scholars many a megrim. The more carefully we examine them the more deeply confused they seem. Some authorities (e.g., Miss Dorothy Sayers) have attempted to account for slips on the theory that Watson misread his own handwriting in his notes. Others (e.g., Mr. S. C. Roberts) have fallen back upon the regrettable hypothesis that occasionally the Doctor was not "in his normal, business-like condition." Still others (e.g., Mr R. E. Balfour) reject from the canon stories that appear incompatible. It is true that *The Sign of the Four* begins with neither Holmes nor Watson in completely rational state. Watson had had Beaune for lunch, which affected him so that he thought it was his leg that pained him (instead of his shoulder). Holmes had taken a 7% solution of cocaine. Holmes's addiction to the drug was (at that period) habitual; but why had Watson taken the Beaune on that particular day? We shall see. It was to screw up his courage for an imminent ordeal.

Let me digress a moment, at the risk of repeating matter familiar to all genuine Holmesians, to note a few of the outstanding anomalies which must be reconciled. The case of *The Noble Bachelor* is dated (by the hotel bill, the high autumnal winds, and the age of Lord St Simon) as October 1887. This, Watson says, was "a few weeks before my own marriage." And the somewhat elastic time-allusions in *The Stockbroker's Clerk* also imply that the wedding took place late in the year. On the other hand both *The Crooked Man*

49

and *The Naval Treaty* distinctly suggest that the marriage was in the spring or early summer.

How may these contradictions be reconciled? Surely not by the assumption that good old methodical Watson ("the one fixed point in a changing age") was simply careless or muddled. Watson wove a tangled web in his chronology because he was deliberately trying to deceive. Why not adopt the reiterated thesis of the master himself: when you have excluded the impossible, whatever remains, *however improbable*, must be the truth. The truth must be that Watson had contracted a secret marriage with Mary Morstan, some time before the adventure of *The Sign of the Four*. His allusions are perfectly comprehensible if we realize that he is sometimes referring to the actual date of that union; and sometimes to the purely fictitious occasion (late in the autumn) which he and his wife agreed to represent to their friends as the time of the nuptial.

The extraordinary year 1887 is crucial in any study of Holmes–Watson history. All scholars have noted the exceptional number of important cases assigned to this year. Particularly, beginning early in February, there was the business of the Netherland-Sumatra Company which took Holmes abroad. Watson, now in full health and vigor, did not spend his entire life sitting in Baker Street, or even at his club playing billiards with Thurston. How and when he first met Mary Morstan we do not know; probably in connection with the earlier case when Holmes was "of some slight service" to her employer, Mrs Cecil Forrester. (I like to think, incidentally, that Mrs Forrester's "tranquil English home," with the stained glass in the front door, the barometer and the bright stair-rods, was in Knatchbull Road, Camberwell, for which Boucicault named the villain in *After Dark*.) At any rate, both Watson and Miss Morstan were lonely and financially insecure. Their romance was immediate, but both were afraid to admit it to their associates. Miss Morstan would lose her position; Watson would incur the annoyance of the misogynist Sherlock.

I will be as brief as possible, for once this hypothesis is grasped, all experienced Watsonians will observe the wealth of corroborating circumstances. Let us re-examine the chronology of the year 1887.

First of all, we cannot accept Mr Roberts's conclusion that *The Sign of the Four* belongs to 1886. The facts are positive: Mary Morstan had received six pearls, one every year, beginning in May '82. She calls that "about six years ago"; in reality it was only just over five years, but she thought of it as six because she had that number of pearls. Also she says her father disappeared in "December 1878— nearly ten years ago." From the beginning of the year '87 her grieving heart would naturally think of the bereavement as in its tenth year. Even in her sorrow her precise mind could not reckon it so until the calendar year '87. I accept July 1887 as the date of the *Sign of the Four* adventure— preferring to follow the postmark on Sholto's letter rather than Watson's subsequent reference to a "September evening." As for the yellow fog (rare in July, surely?) seen by Holmes, it was at least 7% cocaine. But mark well: we now have for the first time an explanation of Watson's mysterious telegram that morning. He and Mary Morstan Watson, weary of meeting by stealth, had at last decided to break their news to Holmes. The mystery of the pearls, which they had often discussed, was an additional motive. Watson had gone to the Wigmore Street Post Office (as a matter of fact isn't it just around the corner in Wimpole Street?) not primarily to *send* a wire but to receive one. Addressed *Poste Restante* was a message from Mary. She had received the puzzling letter from Thaddeus Sholto and appealed to her husband for advice. He wired back telling her to come to Baker Street. And the Beaune for lunch was his attempt to fortify himself for the revelation to come. Observe, throughout the narrative, how slyly old Watson concealed from Sherlock the fact that he and Mary were already intimate.

Recapitulate, then, the events of 1887. Early in the year, probably February or March, while Holmes was absent in the Netherland-Sumatra business, Watson and Mary Morstan were secretly married. They met as and when they could, but told no one. Their anxious and surreptitious bliss was interrupted by the news (April 14) that Holmes was ill in Lyons. Watson hurried to France, he and Sherlock returned together, and spent April 25–27 at Reigate (*The Reigate Puzzle*—originally published as *The Reigate Squire*). Perhaps this was followed by the matter of the Grice Patersons in the island of Uffa—where *is* Uffa, by the way? But if it is (as it sounds) in the Hebrides, Shetlands or Orkneys, the Grice Patersons would have sense enough not to go there until midsummer.

Holmes was in aggressive spirits after the Reigate visit; Watson was gloomy. His secret preyed on his mind; he wrote many letters to Mary. (He had in his desk "a sheet of stamps and a thick bundle of postcards.") At the time of the Jubilee (June 21) it was the shooting of the V. R. into the wall that finally convinced Watson he must make a break. "With me there is a limit," he said in *The Musgrave Ritual*. He made up his mind to take charge of his own check-book, find a home, and resume practice. *The Sign of Four*, coming just when it did (July 8), was a happy coincidence. His anxieties about Miss Morstan becoming heiress of the Agra treasure were just as sincere as if he had really been only a suitor. Since their marriage had been concealed, everyone would be sure to think him a fortune-hunter.

After the excitement was over, the pair went through the appearance of a formal engagement for the benefit of Holmes and Mrs Forrester (not to say Mrs Hudson). May it not have been Watson's now frequent visits to Knatchbull Road that brought the Camberwell Poisoning to Holmes's attention? No doubt soon after *The Sign of the Four* Mary had her summer vacation, and she and the Doctor used this for a furtive honeymoon—perhaps in "the glades of the New Forest"; Southsea would have been a little too public. So when the elated husband, narrating *The Five Orange Pips*, speaks of his wife he forgets that she was not at that time known as such. It was not until November that he found a home of his own, left Baker Street and set up housekeeping in Paddington. The *Noble Bachelor* affair in October preceded by a few weeks what they agreed to call their "marriage." They simply told their friends, about Guy Fawkes Day, that they were going to slip off quietly to a registry office. Probably the medical practice was bought as of January 1, 1888.

Sitting on a pile of cushions with plenty of shag tobacco, and following the master's cardinal principle, the preceding seems to me the only possible solution. This chronology harmonizes many apparently conflicting statements. It makes intelligible the allusions at the beginning of *A Scandal in Bohemia* (March 20–22, 1888). It gives sense to Watson's eagerness that Sherlock should become interested in Violet Hunter; how delightful, the Doctor thought naïvely, if he and Holmes should both marry governesses—and alumnæ of the same agency, for undoubtedly Mary, too, had been a client of Westaway's. When the case of *The Stockbroker's Clerk* came along in June '88, Watson jumped at the chance to go to Birmingham with Holmes. He thought he might be able to persuade Sherlock to run out to Walsall (only 8 miles away) to see Miss Hunter at the school where she was headmistress.

I must not weary you in the matter of Dr Watson's private affairs; but there is just one more point which is essential to mention. We were arguing that the correct date of *The Sign of the Four* is July (1887) rather than September. The most apparently damning evidence against July has been ingeniously pointed out by Mr H. W. Bell in that indispensable little volume *Baker Street Studies* (London: Constable & Co.). Holmes insisted on Athelney Jones staying for dinner—for which he had ordered "oysters and a brace of grouse." Neither of these are in season in July. But is not this precisely what Holmes meant by his following remark to Watson: "You have never yet recognized my merits as a housekeeper." Surely he was calling attention to his cunning in being able to procure these luxuries when they were impossible for most people.

If my suggestion is acceptable that Dr Watson and Miss Morstan had been secretly married in the spring but agreed to pretend that it didn't happen until autumn, other chronological reconciliations are possible. We now see that *The Naval Treaty* (in "the July which immediately succeeded my marriage"—viz., the next July after their collusive wedding-date in November) must have been in July '88. The treaty had been drawn up in May of that year, obviously in view of the illness of Frederick III of Germany and the probable succession of the young Kaiser—whose temperament was only too likely to necessitate readjustments of the European balance of power. There were two other cases in that month, you remember: *The Second Stain* and *The Tired Captain*. Watson's ingrained mixture of duplicity and na-ïveté in regard to the date of the Morstan marriage is delightfully shown when years later he sets down the story of *The Second Stain*. It happened, he says, "in a year, and even in a decade, that shall be nameless"—quite oblivious that in his earlier reference he had mistakenly dated and identified the episode.

From here on the succession of events is fairly plain. *A Case of Identity* is evidently late spring of '88. *The Crooked Man* is the summer of '88. Myself I should prefer to place *The Engineer's Thumb* in '88 ("not long after my marriage," he says), but Watson positively assigns it to summer '89.

54

The Valley of Fear must have been in January '89;[1] followed in June by *The Man with the Twisted Lip* and that autumn by the great *Hound of the Baskervilles*. Watson's long absence from home and practice while visiting Baskerville Hall may well have been another trial of Mrs Watson's disposition; but we find her in June 1890 generously urging the Doctor to accompany Holmes to Boscombe Valley. Immediately after returning from Boscombe Valley Holmes became interested in *The Lost Special* (one of the cases outside the legitimate canon, never recorded by Watson). 1890 closes with *The Red-Headed League* and *The Blue Carbuncle*; it is pleasant to think of Holmes and Watson sitting down cheerfully to the post-Christmas goose: their last intimacy before the tragic events of April and May 1891.

It is also possible to believe that Watson's innocent and timid subterfuge of the secret marriage quite escaped Holmes's attention. Sherlock had grown into the habit of regarding Watson as a lay figure who would never do the unexpected; the great detective was intensely absorbed in his own ideas and except on those mischievous occasions when he turned the full focus of his observation upon his companion he was not likely to speculate much on Watson's private thoughts. And a man of Watson's upright, simple and candid nature, once driven in upon himself, can develop surprising foxiness. It pleases me to think that the self-sacrificing Doctor was dashing enough to seize the romance that came his way. His pangs, his honorable yearnings, his necessities for concealment, gave him (every student has noticed) a special tenderness for women in distress. In brooding the problem of his later marriage one could be tempted to wish that the superb Grace Dunbar of

[1] See, however, Mr A. G. Macdonell's disturbing suggestion that it was ten years later. In *Baker Street Studies*, edited by H. W. Bell (London, 1934).

Thor Bridge might have been the second Mrs Watson. (She also had been a governess.) But knowing Senator Neil Gibson, it is unlikely.

Having caused endless embarrassment by his transparent attempts to disguise the facts of his first marriage, no wonder Watson said nothing whatever about the second. And apropos the second matrimony (which all scholars agree to place about the end of 1902) it is interesting to note that Watson chose to establish his renewed ménage in Queen Anne Street. It crosses Harley Street, is only a stroll from 221B, and still very near the Wigmore Street Post Office. The other most famous resident of that immediate neighborhood is *The Young Man with the Cream Tarts*.

"Bowling Green," SRL, December 15, 1934; also in *Streamlines* and (as by "Jane Nightwork") in *221B*

WATSON À LA MODE

WATSON WAS COUTURIER AT HEART. I don't need to remind you that he was first attracted to Mary Morstan because she was "dainty, well gloved, and dressed in the most perfect taste." What he admired about her neat tailleur of grayish beige was that it was "untrimmed and unbraided." He so approved the small turban "relieved by a suspicion of white feather in the side" that he watched it from the window as Miss Morstan went down Baker Street. It was not until a later occasion, when Mary sat under the lamplight in the basket chair, dressed in what the Rev. Herrick would have called her "tiffany," that Watson learned she did the dressmaking in Mrs. Forrester's household. Shyly he praised the "white diaphanous material, with a little touch of scarlet at the neck and waist." She replied "I made it myself," and what more surely enlists a prudent man's enthusiasm?

Watson's detailed description of Miss Mary Sutherland, in the *Case of Identity*, was of course because he was so horrified by her *mauvaise tenue*. The hat was "preposterous," slate-colored straw with a huge red feather; the black jacket was beaded and fringed and had purple plush at the neck and sleeves; the fur boa and muff[1] were undoubtedly scraggly. The gray gloves were worn through. The dress (above the unmated shoes) was a "brown darker than coffee." Darker than Mrs. Hudson's coffee does that mean, implying that it was not brewed strong enough for Watson's taste? Anyhow poor Miss Sutherland's costume horrified Watson's taste in millinery and mode. It was a taste keenly trained at that time, for he had not long been married.

As far back as *Silver Blaze* (1881) Watson became aware

---

[1] Is not H. W. Bell in error (*Sherlock Holmes and Dr. Watson*, p. 63) in calling them *feather* boa and *feather* muff?

of the financial possibilities of the dressmaking business. He made no special comment at the time on Mme. Lesurier's bill, which included an item of 22 guineas for a single costume, the "dove-colored silk with ostrich feather trimming" for Straker's fancy lady, but we may be sure he made a mental note. In the early cases we hear little of falbalas and fanfreluches; even poor Helen Stoner's frill of black lace was not mentioned as glamour, but because it hid the five livid bruises on her wrist. But see, after the meeting with Mary Morstan, how much more technical, realistic (even carnal) the Doctor's female observations become. Just for the fun of parallel columns, let us compare a few of Watson's comments with Holmes's more delicate and spiritual remarks about the same clients:

HOLMES	WATSON
(*Irene Adler*)	
The daintiest thing under a bonnet. A lovely woman, with a face that a man might die for.	Her superb figure outlined against the lights.
(*Mrs. Neville St. Clair*)	
This dear little woman.	A little blonde woman . . . clad in light mousseline de soie, with a touch of fluffy pink chiffon at her neck and wrists . . . her figure outlined against the flood of light.
(*Violet Smith*)	
There is a spirituality about the face.	Young and beautiful, tall, graceful, and queenly.
(*Anna Coram*)	
Attired like a lady.	At the best she could have never been handsome.

58

(Lady Hilda Trelawney Hope)

The fair sex is your department.	The most lovely woman in London . . . subtle delicate charm, beautiful coloring of that exquisite head . . . white gloves . . . framed for an instant in the open door . . . dwindling frou-frou of skirts.

Characteristic of Holmes's comments is his description of Violet de Merville: "a snow image on a mountain; beautiful with ethereal other-world beauty." Typical of Watson is his note on Grace Dunbar: "a brunette, tall, with a noble figure." He liked them framed in doorways, and preferably lit from behind. Certainly Watson would not so often have said "I have seldom seen," or "One of the most lovely I have ever seen," unless it was feminine contour that preoccupied him. At the Abbey Grange, Lady Brackenstall elicited his double instinct for both form and garb:—

> I have seldom seen so graceful a figure, so womanly a presence, and so beautiful a face—blonde, golden-haired, blue eyed . . . a loose dressing gown of blue and silver . . . a black sequin-covered dinner dress.

These boudoir details filled Watson's mind so that he apparently gave no medical attention to the hideous plum-colored swelling over one blue eye.

Watson's cotquean regard for galloons and trimmings was more discreet in his own home. Of his wife's friend Mrs. Isa Whitney he only remarks that she was "clad in some dark-coloured stuff." How much livelier when off on the road with Holmes! See Miss Turner of Boscombe Valley: "One of the most lovely young women that I have ever seen in my life . . . violet eyes shining, pink flush, her natural reserve lost." There were moments perhaps when Watson thought that loss of natural female reserve an excellent thing. And was not his special sympathy for bright freckle-faced Violet Hunter because of the unpleasant electric-blue dress (again "a sort of beige") she had to wear?

Watson's silences are sometimes as revealing as anything he says. He was too shrewd to argue against Holmes's frequent foolish complaints that women's motives are inscrutable. The behavior of the woman at Margate who had no powder on her nose (v. *The Adventure of the Second Stain*) would have been no surprise to Watson. If the Doctor had written the story of *The Lion's Mane* we would surely have seen beautiful Maud Bellamy in clearer circumstance. She had "the soft freshness of the Downlands in her delicate coloring," writes Holmes (in the new vein of sentiment that bees and Sussex inspired), but if only Watson had been there we might at least have seen "a touch of white at the neck and wrists."

Am I too fanciful to think that good old John Hamish Watson was the first Victorian to do justice to the earliest white-collar girls? Do you remember Laura Lyons of Coombe Tracy whose fingers "played nervously over the stops of her Remington typewriter"?[2] Her cheeks were "flushed with the exquisite bloom of the brunette, the dainty pink which lurks at the heart of the sulphur rose." Watson never made more candid confession than then: "I was simply conscious that I was in the presence of a very handsome woman." It was a consciousness warmly and widely diffused, and always double, for the creature herself and for her covering. He spoke with equal enthusiasm, at the same time, of Beryl Stapleton "with her perfect figure and elegant dress."

There are other passages, but I have said enough to remind students of Watson's specific interest in miladiana,

[2] *The Hound of the Baskervilles.*

"over many nations and three separate continents," a theme which few but Mr. Elmer Davis[3] have ever examined candidly, and which is so murky that it has even led to the gruesome suggestion of Mr. Rex Stout in his atrocious venture "Watson Was a Woman."[4] It has glowwormed others into the uxorious theory that Watson was thrice married. My own notion is offered only as a speculum into the unknowable.

Mary Morstan, a clever dressmaker, found time on her hands after she and Watson moved into the house in Paddington. The medical practice was not lucrative (we know that their slavey Mary Jane was of a very humble order), there were no children, and John Hamish ("James") kept up his frequent sorties with Holmes. Watson, with his special interest in dressmaking, encouraged Mary in her ambition to start a little business of her own. The Agra pearls were sufficient capital. Mrs. Cecil Forrester and friends were sure customers, and the business spread. What else was the needlework which Mrs. Watson laid down that evening when her husband, giving his first yawn, heard Kate Whitney at the bell? Begun at home, by '89 or '90 the business needed seamstress help and an atelier. Watson would not wish his friends to know that his wife had gone into trade, so for her business style she adopted some name of fantasy which has not yet been identified. A business directory of London in the early '90's would undoubtedly shew some Mme. Agra, or Mme. Boulangère, or Mme. Medico, or Morstan Styles, *confections de dames*, doing business a little west of the haute couture. The bills were not as steep perhaps as those of Lesurier on Bond Street, but it was a sound middle-class connection. And Watson, though he had countenanced this, was horribly ashamed.[5]

[3]"The Emotional Geology of Baker Street," in *221B*.
[4]In *Profile by Gaslight* (New York: Simon & Schuster, 1944).
[5]*London of Today*, by C. E. Pascoe, a lively annual handbook, lists in the 1891 edition, among fashionable modistes, *Mme. Oliver Holmes*. [Editor's note: This note does not appear in the BSJ.—S.R.]

What else would account for the Doctor's contradictory and baffling references? Mary was properly fond of him, but she had her own life to live, without benefit of Sherlock. The "sad bereavement" to which Watson referred when Holmes came back in '94 was not bereavement by death, but the fact that Mary and he had separated. Divorce, even if desired, was socially impossible in the holy deadlock of those days. Watson, I have pointed out before ("Dr. Watson's Secret"), had a sly ("pawky") camouflage of his own. As time and success went on, Mary wearied of giving her whole time to dressmaking; and Watson, at the age of 50, even grew a little fatigued with Holmes. Watson's so-called second marriage was when he and Mary decided to resume mutual bed and board. So Watson's second wife was actually his first wife; and there never was a third.

Holmes was too genuine a philosopher to have called Watson's first marriage "selfish." He knew it was part of the destiny of average mankind. He did think it selfish when, after ten years of separation, Watson and his wife decided to make a second try. So when John and Mary set up housekeeping afresh in Queen Anne Street about the autumn of 1902, Holmes began looking for property on the Sussex Downs. Mary farmed out the dressmaking business and said she had always wanted to write. Her first (and last) attempt was *The Adventure of the Mazarin Stone*.

Mary Morstan's influence on women's wear was not lost. Morstan Styles (or whatever the trade name was) became a limited company and she and John still drew dividends. In 1914 the Doctor, long relieved of money anxieties, was "still the same blithe boy."[6] The business spread to the U.S. after the First War. How else do you account for *Morstyle Frocks, Inc.*, in the Manhattan telephone book; or *Morston Textiles* (Morstan & Watson), ibid.?

> BSJ (OS), 1 No. 1 (January 1946) as by "Jane Nightwork"; also in *The Ironing Board* and *Sherlock Holmes by Gas-Lamp*

[6]*His Last Bow.*

AN AMERICAN
GENTLEMAN

IT WAS REALLY ODD that last night for no discoverable
reason (except what Keats might have called the ignoble
dearth of good narcotics) I picked up Stevenson's *The
Dynamiter*. That delicious little prologue in the Cigar Divan, never improved in brio by anyone, is what the bishop
was called, social soporific. It sends one off with a smile.
But it also sent me off with the familiar thought, why is it
never sufficiently suggested that Sherlock Holmes was born
out of the ribs of Robert Louis and Fanny Stevenson? Poe
and Gaboriau and Dr. Joseph Bell are all very well, but the
spark that lit young tinderhearted (*sic*) Conan Doyle was
surely the Prince–tobacconist of Bohemia. Even the divan
in Rupert Street ("mouse-colored plush") may have fa-
thered the much more famous mouse-colored dressing
gown. That was the wicked stinging and punctuating effect
of Stevenson's words. They were hypodermic, needled into
one's self. It's amusing to note a recent revival of curiosity
in R.L.S. among the stricken middle generation. It is
naturally disturbing to the deliterated to find words used
with such wasteful delicacy. But the best of him will be
forever breathing and forever young, to improve poor
Keats's tubercular line. It is a pity that poets have to be
outlived to be improved.

I must keep to my theme. Sometime toward the end of
'85 or early '86 young Dr. Conan Doyle read *The Dynamiter*.
His natural interest in Stevenson (a few years' senior graduate of the same university) was professionally enlarged by
the well-known rumor that R.L.S. was a very ill man; an
invalid, possibly moribund, at Bournemouth. The famous
dedication (in *Underwoods*) to no less than eleven doctors
had not then been written (1887, I think?) but there is

always a crapevine among medical men, and if Dr. Doyle
hadn't been so overdrawn in Southsea he might well have
wished to move a few miles westward to Bournemouth to
serve as interne to the immortal Dr. Scott—whose sinister
initials were T. B. (Thomas Bodley Scott; see that noble
dedication). I think it probable that Dr. Doyle would rather
have been Stevenson's medical adviser than anything else
he could think of. Young H. G. Wells, then a draper's
assistant in Southsea (his employer was a patient of
Doyle's), was as ruddy and shrill as only H. G. would have
been at nineteen.

The MS of *The Firm of Girdlestone* was already shabby
with to-and-fro. The "rustle of the greengrocer's lungs," as
Doyle called it, and "the throb of the charwoman's heart"
were worth only about eighteen pence a visit. His self-
imposed family obligations were large; the hard-earned
£250 a year was (as his Inland Revenue critic wrote on the
form) "most unsatisfactory." I imagine him, say some
rainywindow evening about Christmas 1885, after a visit to
the Southsea Circulatory Library (of which he was the most
faithful customer) sitting down to swoon himself with his
idol's new book, *More New Arabian Nights: The Dynamiter*. I
won't bruise you with all the obvious parallels, but only
seven pages in, what did he read:

> "Do you then propose, dear boy, that we should turn
> detectives?" inquired Challoner.
> "Do I propose it? No, sir," cried Somerset. "It is reason,
> destiny, the plain face of the world, that commands and
> imposes it. Here all our merits tell; our manners, habit of
> the world, powers of conversation, vast stories of uncon-
> nected knowledge, all that we are and have builds up the
> character of the complete detective. It is, in short, the only
> profession for a gentleman."

I could quote more, and zealously apropos; but it will do
no one harm to re-examine *The Dynamiter* for himself; the

Irgun Zwai Leumi of 1885. The point, sharpened by a hundred razor passages in those preposterous stories (completely witty and completely blah), is that A.C.D. went to bed that night in Bush Villa with a new idea in his simple and workable occiput.

It was not only a detective that he had in occiput, but even, God forgive him, a Mormon interlude. He had no idea, nor does it matter, that he was unconsciously mismating Edgar Poe's detective with Fanny Stevenson's appalling Mormon feuilleton. But if you want to suffer, which is part of a literary critic's duty, reread *A Study in Scarlet* (written 1886) and then that grevious chapter in *The Dynamiter*, "The Story of the Destroying Angel." He did it again, thirty-five years later, in *The Valley of Fear*. He never shook off the unconscious influence of that emphatic woman; nor did anyone else.

The intimations of literary heredity, the cross-fertilities of suggestion, are more subtle than any bookish Burbank has ever put in *précis*. No one has ever had the courage, let us say, to suggest the bloodstream osmosis between Hemingway and Kipling (of which, prudentially, Hemingway is least aware). But the exciting thing, in the woe and wizardry of art (I beg you remember this), is that one man's poison can be another man's meat. The most forgettable thing one artist ever did (Stevenson's futile, delightful *Dynamiter*, for instance) can be the accidental takeoff and jet-bomb for another man's felicity. Neither of them will know it. Only the true lover of human frequencies and modulations will ever guess; and will keep it to himself.

I said it was odd; this was what I meant. I fell on sleep thinking about Doyle's subconscious impulse from Stevenson. I thought about it again, as one does, this morning, brooding in the only privacy that still exists, the bathtub. (Much more private than Mr. Hoover's two aspiring secrecies: prayer and fishing.) It was in my mind, and futile at that, to remark Doyle's unconscious increment from R.L.S.

That leads one to think (few people do?) of their own impulsives from behind the swing. I thought of Don Marquis, and Simeon Strunsky, and William Hazlitt, from whom I myself have been ungrateful and unconscious to plunder. It is the people from whom you steal who are the zodiac over your Grand Central. People who are just catching trains don't have time to look at the ceiling.

I said it was odd: about midmorning I went down to the depot, got my copy of *The New York Times*, and saw that our dear old Lloyd Osbourne died yesterday. *Loia*, as the Samoans called him, unspoiled old innocent, was perhaps the greatest American Boy (barefoot, with cheek) since Whittier and Mark Twain. Who remembers the immortal dedication:

> To LLOYD OSBOURNE
> An American Gentleman
> In accordance with whose classic taste the
> following narrative has been designed. . . .

Just about fifty years ago I had an earache; in the therapy of that era, I was put to bed with a baked onion poulticed on me, and given a paper-bound piracy to read. How well I remember it, as soon as I got interested in the Admiral Benbow I forgot my ear, and haven't thought of it since. But I never forgot (I always read all the front-matter of books; sometimes it's the best of them) L. O., the American Gentleman. Nor do I forget that he was collaborator in what shrewd judges (for instance Rudyard Kipling) have said is a Test Book. *The Wrong Box* (1889) is the kind of book you don't mention except to Initiates (as Kipling said). I have always felt a little bashful about it because my father read it on his honeymoon. It was then, and remains for those who know a smile from a smirk, "judicious levity." Twenty-five years ago I used to see Lloyd Osbourne around the mid-forties, perhaps at the Coffee House Club.

I never told him, and I'm sorry, that when driving the highways of North America I often thought of him. They have a way of painting, before arterial crossings, the sedative abbreviation SLO. Always, putting on the brakes, I used to think of him. His full name was Samuel Lloyd Osbourne—the last of a relentful generation. He entertained angels awares.

Never make up your mind (if that's what it is) about literature until you have no personal interest in it. All I'm trying to say is that just as Lloyd Osbourne's rainy day in Scotland in 1881 helped to create *Treasure Island*, so did his stepfather's illness in Bournemouth in 1884–85 help to beget Sherlock Holmes.

Piety is the love of things that have been loved before, by better men than yourself. There is no piety if you don't say it.

SRL, September 20, 1947; also in *The Ironing Board*

67

NOTES ON BAKER STREET

LIKE ALL OTHER learned and scientific societies, the Baker Street Irregulars exchange notes of research about this time of year. They are too wise to hold stated meetings, which would belie their name and take the fun out of their indoctrinated amateurishness; and the accumulated records of their memoirs and adventures have been lying in a publisher's drawer now for several years pending certain final perfections of accuracy. If you must know, one of the niceties that has delayed them is to obtain an accurate reckoning of how much Sherlock Holmes spent on hansom cab fares in his journeys as described by the Doctor. A gentleman in London was commissioned to itinerate all these journeys as exactly as possible (by taxi), keep account of the cost, and make a prorated diminution according to price scales in the '80's and '90's. Then, however, the difficulty began. Was this envoy to have his actual expenses paid by the Club (which has no treasury)? or should he be reimbursed only what the travels cost Holmes?

The overhead charges of literary work (are you listening, Income Tax?) have never been properly appreciated by outsiders.

However, the album in question will eventually appear. Its title will be *221B*, it will have 221 pages and an additional B page, and will (I hope) be set in Baskerville type.

As evidence of the affectionate fidelity of the clan, mark a letter from Mr. P. M. Stone of Waltham, Mass., who reports that he has loaned to the Waltham Public Library his own collection of Sherlockiana, on show there until January 28. There are about 75 items, he says, including the excessively rare original *Study in Scarlet* (*Beeton's Annual*, '87), and monographs, drawings, autograph letters, book-plates, posters, theatre programs, whatnots of all kinds relating to the Master. "It will be interesting to see," says Mr. Stone, "how many enthusiasts, in an industrial city of our type, turn out to reacquaint themselves with an idol of their youthful days."

It has always surprised me that so few of the Baker Street investigators go back to one of the prime sources, viz., *The Strand Magazine* of '91 to '93. A careful study of the *Strand* text is prerequisite for any solid Sherlockian scholarship. Consider the problem faced by Mr. Greenhough Smith, editor of the *Strand*, when his most successful feature, the first 12 of the *Adventures*, came to an end in June '92. Anyone familiar with the anxieties of magazines must be amused and instructed by Mr. Smith's valiant efforts to fill the gap while Dr. Watson was taking a six-months' recuperation. July '92 a short editorial note remarked "It will be observed that this month there is no detective story relating the adventures of the celebrated Mr. Sherlock Holmes. We are glad to be able to announce that there is to be only a temporary interval. . . . Powerful detective stories by other eminent writers will be published."

Shrewdly enough the *Strand* followed this up, the next month, with an illustrated interview (one of a famous series, done by Harry How) showing—yes, we must name him, I suppose—Conan Doyle in his home at South Norwood, and giving the first intimation that Dr. Joseph Bell in Edinburgh, one of Doyle's old teachers, was the suggestion-germ of Holmes's character. But the powerful detective stories by other hands were not so easy to find. Dick Donovan's series of *Romances from a Detective's Case Book* were a terrible let-down, though Mr. Donovan was given a strong build-up as the author of *Tracked to Doom*, *Caught at Last*, *Who Poisoned Hetty Duncan?* etc. Dick Donovan was in a tough spot, and felt it, as you can see by the way he tried to imitate the characteristic opening strokes of the Watson method. Observe Mr. Donovan in the September '92 issue:—

> It was a bitter night in December, now years ago, that a young and handsome man called upon me in great distress, to seek my advice and assistance. It was the third day after Christmas, and having dined, and dined well, I had ensconced myself in my favourite easy chair, before a cheerful fire, and was engaged in the perusal of Charles Dickens's "Cricket on the Hearth," when my visitor was unceremoniously ushered into the room. He held his dripping hat in his hand, and the heavy top-coat he wore was white with snow, etc., etc.

The intention was excellent, but Oh what a difference. The series called *Shafts from an Eastern Quiver* tried hard to give some continuity of thrill; and Grant Allen wrote *The Great Ruby Robbery* (illustrated by Sidney Paget, who did Holmes and Watson for the *Strand*; in spite of villainous engraving it was a notable job) and even Greenhough Smith himself lent a hand with a pedestrian mystery of his own. Some Baker Street student should monograph Greenhough Smith, editor of the magazine for so many years. I have always respected him for having had the gumption to rehash some of Bataille's great French criminal trials, though his treatment was heavily uninspired. Anyhow as Watson's first regular editor he deserves our homage. May it not have been Watson's own suggestion (see *The Five Orange Pips*) that impelled Smith to get a sea story by Clark Russell to help fill in? It's in the August number of that year, *A Nightmare of the Doldrums*, with the editorial blurb: "A Terrible Story of the Sea, only to be read by people of strong nerves."

Mr. Greenhough Smith must have been a happy man, one day in that autumn of '92, when the MS of *Silver Blaze* was actually in his hands and he could put a teaser in the November issue:—

70

Next month will appear the first of the new series of "The Adventures of Sherlock Holmes." Admirers of that eminent detective are also informed that "The Sign of Four," the story of the wonderful adventure by which he gained his reputation, can now be obtained at this office. Price 3s 6d.

That was a little disingenuous, but one remembers that Watson had sold the *Study in Scarlet* outright (for £25) to another house, and there was no way Newnes, the *Strand* publisher, might reprint it. He probably would have if he could: in the *Strand* for December '91, for instance, he printed "A Vision of Saint Nicholas, by C. C. Moore" with no intimation that it had ever appeared anywhere before.

But Mr. Greenhough Smith's wits were keenly at work during those difficult months while his readers were hallooing for more Sherlock. Have a look at the September, November and December 1892 issues. There were three extraordinary cartoon features, called *Club Types*: a series of deliciously mischievous little figures representing the characteristic foibles of famous London social groups, each club in its own humor. They were done by a young man who must have been still an undergraduate at Oxford? They were signed first H. M. Beerbohm, and then H. Maxwell Beerbohm. These, which so few collectors have ever spotted, were the *Strand* reader's compensation for doing without Sherlock.

SRL, January 28, 1939

REPORT FROM
BAKER STREET

AS TRAVELING INSPECTOR for the Baker Street Irregulars, lately returned from some weeks in London, may I make my brief biennial report? The anomalous situation whereby the Moriarty brothers were able to keep all Sherlock Holmes stories out of print for some years, is now relieved. Books, though in short supply, are now available again in Britain, and possibly also in U. S. A. But this is a story for which the world is not prepared.

Baker Street still shews influences of Holmes and Watson. The modern building which has subsumed the historic Number 221 is aptly opposite the Lost Property Office of London Transport. It harbors ancillary offices for methyl, carbon dioxide and carbonic acid gas, which would have interested Holmes the chemist. There is also an Inspector of Taxes, perhaps planted there by Professor Moriarty; and on the 7th floor, under the convenient address of 221B (by permission of H. M. Postmaster General), the *London Mystery Magazine*—known to the wiseacres as the Shand Magazine. Holmes and Watson have of course been nationalized by the Labor Government and have become ecumenical excise. The building itself, headquarters of a great real estate and building enterprise, carves on its façade a lighthouse and the motto "security." These were suggested by the most famous of Holmes's untold stories, that of the Lighthouse, the Politician and the Trained Cormorant. As Mr. Churchill has been getting ready to say, politicians and trained cormorants are identically the same, "redundant."

The prevailing magnetism of Dr. Watson, who encouraged his wife into the millinery business, is shewn by the large number of modistes and dress shops on Baker Street. As Holmes said, the fair sex was Watson's department.

I offered a version of this report to *The Times* of London, but the Editor, in a most courteous letter, said that readers of *The Times* might be confused; they are literal-minded, he said, and might think I was writing about Real People. As I was.

It is generally accepted by scholars (and the Vice-Chancellor of Cambridge, Holmes's own university, will confirm me; I mean Mr. S. C. Roberts, biographer of the two greatest fantasts in our language, Boswell and Watson) that the house that best approximates identity with Mrs. Hudson's lodgings is the blitzed frontage still numbered 111. I enclose a snapshot* taken this summer by J. C. Iraldi, a vagrant idealist. The hope of a tablet on that or any other agreed-upon site has long been mooted by enthusiasts. The Criterion Bar in Piccadilly Circus is grimly in process of transformation into a Puritan Maid soda fountain and therefore less apropos. But when the ruins of 111 Baker Street are cleared and the game is afoot for a new building, the Baker Street Irregulars (30 branches in U.S.A.) will be eager to design and subscribe a bas-relief plaque (subject to the approval of the Borough of Mary-le-bone) as a focus of pilgrimage for all American zealots.

Next after London Bridge the place in England most happily imagined by Americans is the one that never existed. No matter how literal the readers of *The Times* of London, let us create for it a local habitation.

The New York Times Book Review, November 27, 1949

*Editor's note: Not reproduced here.—S.R.

THE BAKER STREET
IRREGULARS
OF NEW YORK

O N A FOGGY AND DRIZZLING EVENING in January, 1950, at a club in New York City, 50 men drank a standing toast. It was in regret and homage to their own boyhoods; it was occasioned by the soon approaching demise of *The Strand Magazine*. Some 30 of the convives were members of the Baker Street Irregulars, a club whose membership is limited to 60—the number of the Sherlock Holmes stories. The others were delegates from "scionist" societies, viz., satellite chapters from other faubourgs of cities, of which there are about 30.

Surely it is a unique tribute to an author whose name, officially, is never mentioned. The traditional *mystique* is that Holmes and Watson are so much more real than their creator that except by privilege from the Chair (known as The Gasogene) the Agent is never mentioned by name.

Whatever decision the British electorate may reach at the forthcoming polls, nothing can ever change the world-wide magic and renown of Holmes and Watson. They are fixed in parallax; dioscuri of modern fiction; stylised as the lion and the unicorn. I know even less about economics than Lord Beveridge, but I suspect that Holmes and Watson are the largest and most luscious of Britain's Invisible Exports.

And (since you insist) the Baker Street Irregulars, of New York, now enjoying their sixteenth year of lively homage, actually began with four schoolboys in Baltimore about the year 1902. They called themselves then, and still do, The Sign of the Four. One is the senior professor of Greek at Harvard; one is a physicist of the Naval Research Laboratory in Washington, and knows more than anyone needs to about undersea explosions; one is a renowned physician in Baltimore; and the last is your reporter.

The fundamental doctrine of the B.S.I., when they set aside for an evening the irrelevant trivialities of their own lives, is that the Holmes–Watson saga (officially denominated by Mr. Elmer Davis "THE SACRED WRITINGS") is more actual, and more timely, than anything that happens to ourselves or happened to its mortal mouthpiece. The greatest art is the annihilation of art.

I once went to Somerset House, or whatever it's called, to "search" the will of Sir Arthur Conan Doyle. I couldn't help wondering whether in his final testimony he had made any mention of his humble passports to immortality. I paid my shilling (just as Holmes used to at "Doctors' Commons") and read the document, in his own clear masculine hand—so like the map of the Priory School neighbourhood. Not a word about the incubus Holmes . . . and yet Holmes, even in profile and robe and headgear, is pretty nearly the Dante of our modern inferno.

With profound insight the B.S.I. have adopted as their colours the three shades of Holmes's dressing gown. It faded as all mortal energies do: from royal purple to blemished blue; from heliotroped blue to mouse. Mouse, by the way, was the colour of the settees in Simpson's famous Chess Divan, as reported in R.L.S.'s *New Arabian Nights*, from which A.C.D. unconsciously borrowed so much.

So the B.S.I. published for three years a quarterly journal (whose motto was: "When was so much written by so many for so few?"), but if you can get from your bookseller (Argus Bookshop, Mohegan Lake, N.Y.) those three volumes you will have the best winter evening reading of a lifetime. Myself, I would rather have them than a first Bristol Cream of Wordsworth and Coleridge's *Lyrical Ballads*.

Wordsworth and S.T.C. were also greatly anxious about affairs in 1798. But now we need to know, as Holmes asked Watson, "What do you know of the black Formosa corruption?" How I would have loved to ask Madame Generalis-

75

sima Chiang that question, just before she took off by plane lately—she is obviously the Irene Adler of South-East Asia.

Or when Holmes spent the great hiatus (1891–94) in Tibet, wasn't he making arrangements 60 years ahead for what's getting ready now? Or the reptilian Moriarty, oscillating his cobra brow over the dynamics of an asteroid, was doubtless precursing uranium and hydrogen bombs, all fission spent. What could the great untold story of the Politician, the Lighthouse, and the Trained Cormorant have suggested but the career of Sir Stafford Cripps?

These are the hints the B.S.I. follow through. Why did passengers on the G.W.R. *have* to take lunch at Swindon? Exactly how (and with what type scalpel) do you nick the tendons of a horse? What was the precise layout of the rooms in Baker Street? Was Sherlock illiterate, I mean could he read? Why did Watson always have to read aloud to him all letters and telegrams? Why did Holmes never eat fish but always game, beef, and boiled eggs; Why did he never drink tea? Why was he such a poor marksman? These are the paraleipses or paralipomena to which we devote the most innocent diversion of our lives.

Myself I do not wholly agree with the tradition that A.C.D. should never be formally mentioned. I loved him long before his heirs and assigns and agents were born, and I find in his writings the most delicious asymptotes to the Holmes–Watson codex. As I have often said, how ridiculous he was only Knighted—he should have been Sainted.

My Christmas carol of last year was this:

> What opiate can best abate
>   Anxiety and toil?
> Not aspirins, nor treble gins,
>   Nor love, nor mineral oil—
> My only drug is a good long slug
>   Of Tincture of Conan Doyle.

The Sunday Times, London, January 29, 1950; composite text from *The Sherlock Holmes Letters* and *The Sherlock Holmes Scrapbook*

A SOUTHDOWN
CHRISTMAS

PERHAPS IT IS only at Christmas time that I become consciously aware of one of my routines. Every year at this season I find myself (in spite of more supposedly important duties) rereading some special old favorites. Perhaps the three most habitual, in this ecstasy of evasion, are George Gissing, O. Henry, Leonard Merrick. It is at other seasons that I find myself (maybe that phrase is significant?) busy on W. W. Jacobs, Cutcliffe Hyne, A. Edward Newton, Bill Footner. Instantly after Christmas, as usual, Sherlock Holmes (*The Blue Carbuncle*) is my 7 per cent cocaine. The medical men tell me that it was really morphine, not cocaine; but I hold that off until St. Agnes Eve (January 20) when I reread Keats. And remember (one of the great moments) that midshipman at Annapolis who construed Keats's Morphean amulet as a morphine omelet.

A few weeks ago, in the great sunshine anticyclone of October, we were round-and-about Eastbourne (Sussex), which I hankered because apparently few Americans had heard of it. The hotel (in the intervals of reckoning surcharges) insisted that eighty U. S. citizens had been dumped there by the Cunard Line for last summer's Coronation. We were evidently caught in the overdraught of those luxurious transients, but we had a wonderful time. The South of England annual croaky (croquet) tournament was being held; day after day we sat on the sidelines of their billiard-table verdure, rolled and planished, and even saw old Sherlock himself, in deerstalker cap, stroking huge diagonals and clicking his intended ballistic. It is the only game for intentional old men; but also I liked, one day of gusty wind, the lady who bound her rearward skirts with Scottish tapes for fear she would be airborne.

77

Those were perfect days. You'd have to go back to Asbury Park, say in the Eighties, to find anything like it over here.

But my prime purpose, obviously, was to seek and identify the cottage to which, some fifty years before, Sherlock Holmes had retired to keep bees. I was too simple to realize that Holmes's report, describing it as at the very rim of the Channel cliffs, was evidently intended to mislead the gunmen of Moriarty and Moran. So when I thought I had found the probable spot, and asked the gardener at work, "Does anyone here keep bees?" I got the apocalyptic reply: "You can't keep bees here: too windy."

So, not to bore you with delicious detail, I once more drew a compass arc at five miles from Eastbourne pierhead; attached nylon threads to homing bees working westward from the gorgeous dahlia beds of Eastbourne's municipal gardens, and with huge effort and struggle (helped by Southdown Bus #12) I calculated the vector. So, over Beachy Head and the geological gullies of Birling Gap and Cuckmere Haven, I followed my beenomial theorem. The graph led us to Sherlock's favorite own pub, The Tiger, in East Dean; thence up the rugged hill to the gloriously ancient church of Friston, with its dew-pond and circuit of tank traps. The cottage (we photographed it) isn't far away; but I hope I'm as discreet as Mrs. Hudson. It has a pinewood windbreak to shelter the bees. I think of it as I thought fifty years ago of the Virgilian motto at McCoy Hall in Baltimore: *Sic Vos Non Vobis*. No one maybe since Dr. Gildersleeve has thought of that so sentimentally as I.

You'd be surprised to learn how much leeway, or drift, a nectar-heavy bee can sag in climbing those Downs—he better pause (and usually does) at the golf club, half way the rump of Beachy Head, where George Gissing was snowed under in a winter walk, February 1888. Eastbourne, gay and trimly dight beneath the great amphitheatre of hills, must be a God-rest-you-merry place of pause for

Christmas when the line of the Downs, "so noble and so bare," is white with snow. I hope the great buses halt at the brow to hear chimes rising. Here in Salamis we can also (when the plumbing doesn't murmur too loud) hear church bells in the valley below; they lose all sectarian timbre and catch pure Wordsworthian music of dissent.

But I've delayed too long to mention my best of routineering. As we take our vacation always in late autumn (leaving after the September 15 income taxes, returning in time to pay December local dittoes) I have always, these weeks before Christmas, a crate of second-class mail to brood. But specially (and it grieves me to think how few enjoy them as I do) the autumn crop of lists from second-hand booksellers. The grievance of my time of life is the sudden awareness of doom that strikes say about 2 A.M., then the plumber's damnable diapason rustles loudest in chateau Shabby, then the breath comes briefest and trial spears of pain shoot sharpest in the innocent lobes of the brainy sponge. Mind and heart, or is it that mysterious sweetbread called pancreas, are hostile to sleep. (No wonder Shakespeare praised sleep so highly. I hope he had plenty, but I doubt it.) Then even my tested darlings (Gissing, Merrick, O. Henry) make me only more and more nervous. But always, while cocoa is heating, ready are the strong heaps of book catalogues. I have boxes and boxes of them; haven't even gone through 1951 and 1952 yet. But here (and Goodspeed's of Boston will know I'm quoting their *Flying Quill*) I find old Toplady, the coxcomb who wrote "Rock of Ages." In 1777 he wrote from Knightsbridge to a young lady in Soho "in reply to her naïve theological wonderings":

> I am most deeply & clearly convinced that the saints in glory know each other . . . it seems impossible that the unfallen Angels, who have lived together in Heaven, shd not be perfectly acquainted.

My "Saints in Glory," who have seen me through so many hours either boredom or bankrupt, I like to believe with The Rev Gus, assemble toward Christmas; they chaw me special bacon (leaner than you ever get from Long Island supermarkets). Can't you imagine even Rudyard Kipling and Hilaire Belloc, who both loved Sussex so much they wouldn't speak to each other, coming round into the same corner of the sheepfold. Or I can hear Gissing and O. Henry ribbing each other; and arguing whether one was luckier than the other. O. Henry's stuff, so stupidly attempted to be preserved *en masse*; and Gissing's short stories (so much better than his dour novels) quite lost and forgotten. I couldn't help telling George (when I saw him halfway uphill in the snowdrift) how I had compiled a volume of chosen short stories (from the three or four posthume collections of same) and begged a preface from one of the most sensitive New York booksellers. But all that Lawrence Gomme really remembered was how he and other children happened to live next door in Surrey, and had pelted G.G. with conkers and pebbles as the poor bloke paced the garden path, brooding his sentimental Ryecroft.

Kipling, of course, was chafing Will Porter (O. Henry to him) for assuming (since Porter knew only river steamers) that the *Kaiser Wilhelm* (NDL) had paddle-wheels ("Past One at Rooney's"). Also, said Rud, the horrible stumer that O. Henry made in assuming that all triangles were either right or equilateral. Hell, cried Rudyard, you never heard of scalene? No, admitted O.H., always in his soft Ca'lina dialect, Miss Lina didn't tell me. But how the hell did *you* write anything so terrible as *Brugglesmith*? Then I think Uncle Rud fell upon poor Merrick for not knowing what was a taffrail, and O. Henry was sore at Merrick for ribbing Duluth (*One Man's View*, 1897). Gissing also said Merrick had been unfair to Eastbourne, both in its own name and as "Sweetbay" in so many theatre stories. But Merrick, always agile, said that (1) *The New Yorker* had imitated him in that, and (2) as for his best known book, most people thought it had been written by Conrad.

Likewise, Merrick added, that Christmas lunch in the first chapter of *The Actor Manager* is gloomy enough for even you, George. Saints in Glory can get savage when they discuss each other's Christmas stories. Remembering the outcry when I had proclaimed Watson's *Blue Carbuncle* better than Dickens's *Carol* (never really whooped up except by saccharinists like FDR) I snowslid down the eastward scarp of Beachy Head. That southernmost breakage of Britain's geology makes me nervous. Wives, daughters, and even strangers love to go much too near the terrifying cliff, which is plainly fissionable. As they say in Britain, it's too close to the knuckle. Maybe that is where the hambone of literature is sweetest?

I remember the young woman who bought a fashionable headgear which was labeled Luxurious Leopard. But when she asked the honorable salesmiss, "Is this really leopard?" the sprite replied, "That's the trade name. Ackshully, it's stenciled rabbit."

I rather enjoy Stenciled Rabbit in my late-at-night Christmas Reading. Beautiful, when you read them again, the curious rhythm of surrealism that enchants you. For instance, how few of O. Henry's New York stories suggest it; they are likely to be impacted with twinges of time and topic, with the coarse slang of Park Row. This was the poor fellow's attempt to give Bob Davis and Gilman Hall and Bill Johnstone the sort of thing they thought their readers wanted. How cruel it was to reprint him *in toto*, in two gravid volumes. One quarter of the weight would have been quantum suff. They did the same with Rudyard; they always will; as they did with Chaucer, and Dante, and Shakespeare; even, when his time came, with Willie Maugham. So, and no wonder, publishers thought of the South Downs as sheep ranges. O. Henry might have had

81

something to say about that. The southdown sheep, with
their black stockings, have been replaced by crocodiles of
little girls, longlegged in black wrinkles, from Bathhouse
to Broodhouse.

These (I realize now, when the first snow is impending
over the immortal Downs) were autumn thoughts, begotten
and beguiled in the dangerous kindness of shriveling sunshine. We learn beauty most sharply in our own acids of
decay, when the sky (with the keen detachment of a
grandparent) watches the children's frolic before bedtime.
I'm not quite sure now, were we talking of bees, or sheep,
or stenciled rabbits? I know that in late sunlight, in the
dearth of philosophical pessimists, I think of George Gissing. He is at this moment (here is the News Angle) being
remembered in his birthplace (Wakefield, Yorkshire) by a
public-library exhibit. He shines for me with a grim metallic luster. His personal infelicities have been hidden with
more than British tightness of lip. How astonished the boys
of Yale would be to learn that they are inheritors (from
George Matthew Adams) of the most complete and dour
collection. Or did Mr. Adams give these books and MSS to
Dartmouth? I grieve to say, I just don't remember. Equally
I disremember some of Leonard Merrick's glories of un-
timeliness. He had a marvelous success in the Tauchnitz
editions, about fifteen volumes I should guess. Continental
readers were specially pleased by his oddly prim old-bach-
elor–spinster sense of scandal; it is only equaled by *Life*
magazine's gusto for pelvic cheesecake. And he never
guessed (I know, because I asked him) how much harmless
joy he gave American readers in the innocent girl's despair
when hexed by the Parisian madame of the cabaret. "After
a moment the girl passed out." (*When Love Flies Out o' the
Window*, Chapter 6.)

I was relieved when a distinguished neurologist, while
we were riding tipcat in sturdy little *Media*'s smokeroom

(we were hove-to in a November gale SW of Eire), told me that he suffers from the same habit that afflicts me. When reading, and particularly when rereading, his chosen Stenciled Rabbit, he finds that his eyes soon close in tender hypnosis. But his mind goes on reading, inventing luscious supplement where attention ceased. "Aye indeed," I cried (seeing him below me as *Media* threw her heels aloft), "until the peripheral nerves of the brain"—these, I had read, were one of his specialties—"reactivate, and you say to yourself, 'It can't be as good as that!' " We agreed with mutual assent, and sealed it with another Old Fashioned.

Sometimes the best of these Sleepy Saints in Glory is Merrick. He has, for me, just the tenderest delicacy of social cynicism, the "gun-flint" savor of the dry sauterne. O. Henry and Gissing swing almost too fiercely (like *Media*?) from sardonic to saccharine? Gissing doesn't even bother (as in his *Human Odds and Ends*) to finish his short stories; they are often half-told episodes, the dark meat left on the plate to be served by some carver of leftovers. Kipling was too shrewd to leave anything in the fridge for futurity. There is still the soot-stain on one of the rank of Tudor chimneys, at Bateman's, where Frank Doubleday, arriving unexpected one summer day, saw a plume of smoke, rushed upstairs, and found the little shagbrowed man heaving armfuls of MS into the hearth. "Nobody's going to make a monkey of me after I'm dead." But Kipling knew much more about bees than Sherlock Holmes. Actually, still at Bateman's the honey of his bees is on sale in jars in the front hall. Burwash, in the valley of The Weald, is good shelter for nectar on wings: from the glorious flower gardens of Eastbourne (you should study those dahlia beds up by the Wish Tower) the bees coast NE past Hurstmonceux and Brightling Needle, easy finding to Puck and Pook's Hill. As dusk comes on Kipling's study is the most haunted place I know. The study, still with pen-and-pencil tray and folio paper and pipecleaners on the work-table, with the silver

inkstand and sagging bookshelves, is bewildered with stories untold. The National Trust caretakers are naïve and
easily shaken off. I went upstairs again, in quiet secrecy,
and thought I recognized Kaa and Baloo and Bagheera in
the shadows. And as for bees, "The Mother-Hive" is one
of the greatest of political parables. Written (when? some
thirty or forty years ago) it antedates and prophesies everything of the recent Harry Sinister White affairs. The infil-
tration of Communists into our great executive ganglia isn't
just a joke; the wax moth in Kipling's fable (based I'm sure
on actual beehive contaminations) would give such lineback
coaching as the FBI never dreamed.

So the mind comes, or came, back to the bees. Mr. James
Montgomery, BSI, in his this year's *Christmas Annual* (Phil-
adelphia, 1953) suggests the Downland English Honey,
from Polegate, Sussex (within the five-mile reach from
Eastbourne) as probable nectar from Sherlock's own bees.
That is possible, of course; we used to see it in windows on
Eastbourne's handsome shopping street Terminus Road.
That was where the mother of Leonard Merrick's young
actor was startled to see her son carrying his baggage on
Sunday. The Downland Honey was always available at our
own hotel (with surcharge). But (this has puzzled you
already) the bees I talk about were both real and imaginary.
We know little about Holmes's imaginary insects, except
that he segregated the Queen (as he also segregated Miss
Adler); and like any beekeeper (or publisher) in winter he
set out sugar-water to tempt them home. Let's not be too
scientific: all I know about bees is that they're by instinct
busy; they do their private airy dance for directional radar;
then travel straight. And somehow the stories we most
enjoy, in our sleight of sleep, are when however impeded
they find their dormitory on Wuthering heights.

And the wind that gripes and flings them sideways, the
wind that wuthers and buffets? Is it all the brigaded stupors

that confound every homebound bee? Is it the fatal wax-work of everyday chance, the plumber, the carpenter, the editor in his office, the rats in the cellar, the oil burner in swoon? Can a bee heave-to in gale like the *Media*? The shadows of December afternoon are long and athwart. Perhaps that is why, in my ritual rereadings, I relish most the honey-bearers stricken in cross-currents. So often I recall O. Henry's reply to the editor when reproached for not meeting a promised deadline. The indignant editor said, in effect, "Some day I'm coming to give you a good strong kick with heavy shoes. I never go back on *my* promises." To which O.H. replied, "It's easy to keep promises that can be pulled off with your feet."

So I get an almost crazed enjoyment from watching some of my old beloveds, the windstricken bees, slanting heavily toward their skeps. Take Joseph Conrad, for instance (but I don't read him again until January), maybe I miss most of all his one incredibly gruesome comic yarn—"The Black Mate" (maybe it was in *Tales of Hearsay*?). But I lent it, years ago, to an old pal; and, of course, never saw it again. Except in a few academic essays, critics and readers have never grown up to Conrad. How simple were his actual storms and typhoons compared to the psychic storms he faced in his stories. The dreadful Donkin of *The Nigger* is the waxmoth cell of modern Communism. Both Conrad and Kipling rewrote, in the latest years, their earliest themes, with dangerously canny restatement.

As for the bees, whether the phantom creatures of the phantom Holmes or the actual honeymakers of Bateman's, all I know of them is that they are busy, and subject to wind-pressure. I also went, as straight as roads pursue, to see old Hilaire Belloc's home near Horsham, which he had so often and so magniloquently surrealized. His candle still burned a ruby spark in the sacristy upstairs, and in lyke-wake mood we followed him to the freshly sodded grave at West Grinstead. Those of his own persuasion will be pleased to remember his Sussex Christmas described in *Conversation with an Angel* (1929). It was truly thrilling to see H.B.'s windmill alongside his miscellany cottage, and recognize it as a symbol of himself. So also (and how different) was Kipling's carefully guarded Bateman's, trimly alleyed with trees, and the muddy Saxon brook.

But publishers were setting out their saucers of sugar-water for the Christmas season. Having had my own privately valued experience as a forgotten man, curiously I studied the weather graphs every day alongside the Band Stand. I even queried the text of our old beloved "Foggy Foggy Dew" as sung by the soloist of the Irish Guards. It wasn't what I had learned from Alf Harcourt and Carl Sandburg? No, it was a sophistication per Benjamin Britten, and I complained to the Erse baritone. But I took one of Mr. Holmes's favorite excursions to the sloping field below Battle Abbey, where poor Harold and his Saxons were lured downhill by shouts of false surrender. The only patriotic notice I saw was the simple Saxon warning, BEWARE OF THE BULL. As Holmes used to say, How wise if all invaders since 1066 had heeded it. Then followed his strident laugh. . . .

We withdrew (in good order) across the Pevensey Levels, where the old castle ruin casts some of history's longest shadows. There is truly honey in the sunset breeze from Beachy Head. The second-hand bookstore on Seaside Road was still open, and the shrewdest huntsman among us found what the occasion desired, a well-read copy of *Puck of Pook's Hill*. Maybe that will be my next rereading.

SRL, December 26, 1953

INTRODUCTIONS

Kit was always popular as a master of ceremonies for a newly launched book. Here are several examples of him in varying moods of prefatory enlightenment. His payment by Doubleday for the introduction to *The Complete Sherlock Holmes* was the largest ever, at that time, for an introduction—nearly enough to get him to Baker Street.

Kit wrote prefaces, introductions, or forewords for over fifty books. Many of these were posthumously collected as *Prefaces without Books*. In the introduction to that volume, Jerome Weidman recalls being taken by Max Schuster, of Simon and Schuster, to call on Kit at his hideaway loft on West 47th Street. When Kit, responding to the bell, came down from his aerie on the freight elevator, he expressed his disgust with Schuster for dragging him from his work (but was charming to Weidman, whom he had never met). When asked by Kit what he was working on at present, Weidman responded that he was writing an introduction to a volume of his short stories. "Good," said Kit, slamming the door in their faces; "Introductions can be fun."

FOREWORD

MR. EDGAR SMITH AND DR. JULIAN WOLFF have given every Baker Street student an opportunity to light the cherry-wood pipe. Perhaps henceforward the Gazetteer will be as necessary as the Gasogene. From Abbas Parva to Zion many topics for meditation are offered. How come a Bull Ring in Birmingham? Is Charlington Heath actually in Sussex or Surrey? I rather wish our editor had listed Long Island* (where the Cave Mystery happened). But, as he well knows, to have caulked every seam would have left his sea-lawyer friends no pleasures of quibble.

And Holmes, himself no mean cartographer (you remember the *Priory School* terrain), would have enjoyed the maps. Here for the first time we get a tempting glimpse of Uffa, *insula incognita*. I am not *quite* sure of the rig of some of Dr. Wolff's vessels: but to pester the matter would put one in a class with the notorious canary trainer. It pleases me to point out to Mr. Starrett that New York gets five entries (and Brooklyn one) as against Chicago's four. I wish Dr. Watson's allusions to New York were not so vague. If we could include *The Lost Special* and *The Man with the Watches* in the canon (as I maintain we should: you'll find them in the John Murray volume of other-than-Holmes stories) we'd have two new savory entries for Manhattan: a hotel called The Johnston House, and "Bassano's Library, Broadway." Bassano's is obviously Brentano's—but where is the Johnston House?

Fulworth, of *The Lion's Mane*, is I suppose really the *Lul*worth remembered for John Keats. So, in the oddly blended mood known to the zealot, one passes into the fog (like the cutter *Alicia*) and disappears. In a world of repulsive stories and Red Leeches here is pure innocence.

May 17, 1940.

Baker Street and Beyond

*He now has.—*Ed.* [Edgar W. Smith].

89

A LETTER FROM
ROSLYN HEIGHTS,
NEW YORK

My dear Edgar:

I hadn't heard from old Stanley Hopkins for a long time, but I took the liberty of telling him your plan. Now to my great delight comes a long letter addressed to you in my care, which I have carefully copied. (You mustn't mind my keeping the original for my collection: it is written with a J-pen on wrapping paper from the Army & Navy Stores.)

There are one or two flashes that really give us a new slant on Mycroft: I'm specially tickled by the old fellow remembering Mycroft's punning misquote from Horace. There is as much sense in Horace as in Hafiz, as I think George Sand wrote to Gustave Flaubert. Anyhow, Hopkins is always pithy.

The game is afoot! Yrs.

CHRISTOPHER

Green Escape
Roslyn Heights,
New York.
April 15, 1942.

Letters from Baker Street

A LETTER FROM
YOXLEY, KENT

It was good of you, my dear Mr. Edgar Smith, to apprise me that your Irregulars have agreed to subsume *The Lost Special* and *The Man with the Watches* into the full canon. Mr. Mycroft Holmes once remarked when we were discussing this very point "They are definitely canon-fodder." There was a touch of *motif* in Mr. Mycroft's feeling, for I can admit you to an interesting secret. The "elaborate and plausible hypothesis" in the *Gazette* was of course the work of Mycroft Holmes, who may have had his own reasons for wishing to puzzle both the Yard and the remaining members of the Moriarty circle. You correctly remark that Mr. Sherlock Holmes was then in Tibet—"doing a polyphonic motet in Lhassa," Mycroft said once. Mycroft was not without fraternal malice. "Professor Moriarty was not the only man who had a brother," he used to say, and always added a Latin tag I did not understand: "Non omnis Moriarty." Anyhow you will observe how warily Dr. Watson refrains from stating the authorship of the *Gazette* letter; he only says it was *"over the signature"* of a well-known investigator. Internal evidence in the letter itself (even including the sneer at American mentality, which was far from S.H.'s attitude) shows it as the kind of fine-spun speculation characteristic of Mr. Mycroft Holmes, sitting with a Bradshaw in the Diogenes Club; too indolent even to make the single inquiry at Euston which would have quashed his theory. Remember too that the *Gazette* is not a regular newspaper at all but an official record of government appointments, etc., and only a government officer (which Mr. Mycroft was) could have access to its columns.

With all his errors, our old friend Watson was a writer of strong artistic conscience. He did not include these sketches in the canon because they were only his rough log, his aide-mémoire for future use. *What no one has hitherto suspected*, they were the memoranda he intended to use in telling two of the famous Unpublished Stories. What is here called *The Lost Special* is the material he proposed to amplify as *The Papers of Ex-President Murillo*; and the tragic story of the young (and I am afraid epicene) fellow with the time-pieces was to have introduced the atrocious affair of the card scandal at the Nonpareil Club. The little round mirror, by the bye, is still in the criminal museum at Scotland Yard. I remember Watson also saying he might tell the story under the title of *The St. Pancras Case*, transferring the incidents from the London & Northwestern line to the Midland; as his friend Thurston had let him in for some L. & N. W. shares.

But as you know Dr. Watson never found time to work up these notes into his careful narrative form. There were reasons for this. The episodes happened in 1890 and 1892 when he was busy with his medical practice; also at that time (as Mr. S. C. Roberts has gently pointed out) the first Mrs. Watson was in a sad state. When the delayed explanations came out, some years later, much had happened to alter the public mind. In 1897 the horrifying scandal of the Oscar Wilde trial was still only too pungent in people's nostrils, and a man of Dr. Watson's delicacy was unwilling to go into clinical detail in the matter of young Edward X, whom even his own brother called a Mary Jane.

There were a number of curious points in these two affairs which your Irregulars might wish to study further. Mr. Holmes's suggestion of a possible criminal society of colliers (doing mass-murder) caused much public agitation; when the matter of an 8-hour law for miners came up in Parliament not long later (in March '92) it was voted down in Commons. As you may have suspected, the mysterious Horace Moore (who applied for the second Special) was one of the Moriarties; in fact the Professor's brother. He was an amateur of railways, appreciating their opportunities for mischief, and later got a post as a station master in the West of England (Boscombe Valley, I think) which caused much grief to innocent travellers. Dr. Watson's notes were always precise, and any large-scale map of Lancashire will show you all those stations on the L. and W. C. Railway, though he gives the name of Barton Moss to the famous peat-bogs of Chat Moss. How many of your Americans know what was a "parliamentary train," even if they are familiar with the phrase in the Mikado's Song in Gilbert and Sullivan? (I often wondered why Dr. Watson never mentioned Mr. Holmes's great fondness for those operettas; he made a point of attending their openings when possible. He took me with him to hear *The Pirates of Penzance* once when Watson had migraine, and often twitted me by playing "A Policeman's Lot," etc., on his fiddle. Mr. Mycroft Holmes rarely went to the theatre, even the stalls were too narrow for his figure; but he cleverly deduced from the fact that the young American had not used his readmission ticket to the Lyceum, that he was a person of feeble intellect; since Sir Henry Irving and Ellen Terry were playing Shakespeare there at that time.)

A parliamentary train, of course, was a train with third-class carriages, as made mandatory by Act of Parliament in the early days of railway traffic.

Sparrow MacCoy, so your Mr. Wilson Hargreave once told me, was one of the same gang as Birdy Edwards. I always thought Hargreave or some of your Pinkerton men should have been a little quicker to look up the records at the Johnston House in New York. They might have laid hands on McPherson.

So what you really have here is two of the Adventures in case-book form, before the Doctor had given them his special alterative treatment. I felt a strong interest in both those cases because I was a youngster on the Force and Inspector Vane was grooming me for detective work. They proved that neither of the Holmeses was always right. But I mustn't bore you with an old fellow's gossip; 76 now, and living down here in Kent not far from a place you've heard of. But I'm still not entirely a crock, and do my share as a Senior Warden—we've had plenty of plastering in this region. It's pleasant to recall days when there was nothing worse than Giant Rats in Sumatra, or blow-pipes in the Andamans, and a harpoon seemed a terrible weapon.

My best to you all,

Sincerely yours,

STANLEY HOPKINS, O.B.E.

Chief Inspector C.I.D. (Retired)

The Bilboes, Yoxley, Kent,
Easter Sunday, 1942.

Letters from Baker Street

MEMORANDUM

ORTY YEARS AGO Sherlock Holmes came back to life. In memory of that return, and in gratitude for more than forty years of as good pleasure as the world of print affords, this little compilation has been edited with the kind approval of the publishers concerned (Doubleday, Doran and Company, Inc., and Harper and Brothers), and Messrs A. P. Watt of London, representatives of Sir Arthur Conan Doyle's estate. I am under special obligation to Mr. Denis Conan Doyle for his interest and assistance, and to Mr. Bernard De Voto for expert comment on the Western interlude in *A Study in Scarlet*.

The book was prepared with special reference to the needs of younger readers. Two experienced teachers, Miss Hortense L. Harris of Gloucester, Massachusetts, and Miss J. Grace Walker of Cicero, Illinois, have been kind enough to read the copy throughout and have made valuable suggestions as to how much comment high school students can endure. But I believe some older readers also may find information and amusement in the notes. I have a livelier hope of this since I have seen undoubted evidences of pleasure in a highly critical assistant not previously interested in Holmes and Watson. I refer to my former secretary, who cheerfully served as task force and test tube. I dedicate this first annotated textbook of Sherlock Holmes to Ensign Elizabeth Barrett Winspear, U.S.N.R.

New York City
November, 1943

Sherlock Holmes and Dr. Watson

INTRODUCTION

THERE WERE NO RATION BOOKS in those days, and it is good to know that Sherlock Holmes and Dr. Watson always had a substantial breakfast. When the reader first sits down with them for the morning meal in the old sitting room on Baker Street, it is one of the most perfect moments that fiction can contrive. Neither of the two is in the easiest of tempers when we join them unseen. Sherlock, like Oliver Wendell Holmes, was an Autocrat at the Breakfast Table, and even Mrs. Hudson, most patient of landladies, was a little annoyed to be hustled for Dr. Watson's coffee and boiled eggs at an unexpectedly early hour. She may have wondered whether she had made a mistake in accepting these unconventional lodgers. Yet at that moment all unawares she was putting on immortality, and we as readers are entering our privilege in one of the most complete illusions ever created by art. The illusion is so persuasive that all readers everywhere have instinctively agreed to think of Holmes and Watson as actual people. The habit is now well established. *The Sign of the Four* was scarcely published in *Lippincott's Magazine* of February 1890 when a Philadelphia tobacconist (I expect it may have been John Middleton) wrote to Conan Doyle asking where he could obtain Holmes's essay "Upon the Distinction between the Ashes of the Various Tobaccos." Even in recent years the editor of an important Swiss newspaper, the *Journal de Genève*, was still receiving requests for the issue of May 6, 1891, which was supposed to contain an account of Holmes's death in the Reichenbach Fall. One of the most interesting reports of fiction's power on an unspoiled mind is in a letter from Robert Louis Stevenson in Samoa in 1893. Stevenson, nicknamed Tusitala, "The Teller of Tales," by the Samoan natives, used to exercise his imagination by improvising fables for them—perhaps to encourage them to tell him their own legends in return. One day he told his native overseer the story of "The Engineer's Thumb" (one of Holmes's adventures not included in this selection). Stevenson confesses that it was not easy to make the story intelligible: the tale involved railway trains, a hydraulic press, counterfeit money, all of which were quite outside the Samoan overseer's comprehension. Even the idea of crime was difficult for the listener to grasp. But Stevenson tells in his letter to Conan Doyle how this narration enhanced his prestige among his simple employees. They thought of him with added reverence as the master who had a friend to whom this extraordinary adventure had literally happened.

I mention Stevenson not merely at random: his *New Arabian Nights* and *The Dynamiter* had a strong influence on the imagination of young Dr. Doyle. There are many curious blood transfusions in literature. The least successful episode in *The Dynamiter* was the Mormon fantasy written by Stevenson's wife: it need not be examined too harshly, since Fanny Stevenson invented it chiefly to amuse her husband while he was ill in bed. But Dr. Doyle was evidently impressed. When he interpolated a Mormon theme into *A Study in Scarlet* he probably thought he was taking a cue from his much admired fellow alumnus of Edinburgh. Actually he was imitating Mrs. Stevenson. Doyle's version of the Latter Day Saints is now a tedious interruption and in this edition I print it only in synopsis. But it is well to remember that in the late Eighties no young writer could possibly take up the pen without having Stevenson in mind. Few writers in any age can set their notions down on paper without either imitating or reacting from what is then fashionable in print.

There was another and more important influence preceding Holmes and Watson. I think Doyle was always a little shy of admitting to us how much he owed to Poe. It is amusing to find Sherlock Holmes so condescending about Poe's detective Dupin. If anything is plain in literary history it is that our well-beloved sitting room at 221B Baker Street is derived from the "book-closet" at 33 Rue Dunot, Faubourg St. Germain, where Dupin and his unnamed friend used to sit smoking in perfumed candlelight. One might even imagine that the rugged A. C. Doyle took the habit of signing himself A. Conan Doyle because it was almost an echo and anagram of C. Auguste Dupin. To open the story with a little essay on analysis, to close with a pat quotation from the classics, to introduce a baffled policeman, to tell the story by the confession of the simple marveling stooge—this was Poe's own strategy. One concludes that Gregson of Scotland Yard must have been kin to the Parisian Prefect of Police, "Monsieur G——." From Dupin, Holmes learned the value of inserting an advertisement in the newspapers (See "The Murders in the Rue Morgue"), and the trick adopted in "A Scandal in Bohemia" is exactly that of "The Purloined Letter." Doyle learned from Poe the value of eccentricities to fix a character in the reader's mind. Dupin and his friend used to sit all day in the dark; they even smoked in the dark, which seems to prove that Poe himself was no smoker. For Holmes more ingenious habits were invented, but the purpose was the same.

I have sympathy with Mr. John B. Opdycke who in editing *The Adventures of Sherlock Holmes* for Harper's Modern Classics (1930) said he could not bear to harass the student with any explanatory notes. To do so may look like pedantry in its most heavy-footed tread. Yet a few explanations are really needed for the reader of another land and another generation. The innocent misunderstandings of English and Americans in their casual allusions have often been a hobby with me. I remember how bewildered American readers were when Mr. A. P. Herbert in his gorgeous murder tale, *The House by the River*, spoke of a character so obscure that "his death would only be reported on the front page of the newspapers." This would be meaningless if one were not familiar with the make-up of the London *Times* and other important British journals where the front page is not news but only obits and small advertising. Similarly I have seen an English visitor puzzled by a note on American railroad timetables that Daylight Saving is in effect between certain dates, but Standard Time is observed "during the balance of the year." My Englishman could only interpret "the balance of the year" as the equinoxes. These are trivial instances of the large comedy of two languages which overlap but have broad fringes of difference. Sherlock Holmes himself was keenly aware of diversities in English and American usage; more than once (for instance in "The Three Garridebs") the solution depended on them. Indeed Holmes's use of American slang was so accurate that it has been suggested he was of United States birth or lineage.

The most valid reason for adding notes to the text is that the saga of Holmes and Watson is a gateway into a vanished world. In his deliberately historical novels—*Micah Clarke*, *The White Company*, *Sir Nigel*, etc.—Doyle fortified himself with painstaking research and crowded his narrative with documented fact. As often happens, the more he piled in conscientious detail the more he lost the magic of illusion; but in the stories about Holmes and Watson, where his only purpose was to entertain, he became historian in spite of himself. His casual allusions to costume, transportation, morals, science, politics, meat and drink, social habits of all kinds, are a revealing panorama of the late Victorian age. The value is not only in clothes and furniture and machines. It is manifest in the simple but complete revelation of a national temperament. Perhaps Doyle himself, in Irish blood, Scottish education, English living, was intuitively gifted to divide and reveal two aspects or humors of the island race: the quick-witted Holmes, the plodding Watson. The one supreme and secret weapon which made it impossible for the Nazis to win the war was that queerly enduring thing, the character of Britain. It has never been more naïvely and completely suggested than at 221B. The way to prove this to one's self, absurd as it may seem, is to ask of any dilemma in British national existence, What would Holmes and Watson do about this? You will find the British Parliament or cabinet or army or navy or visiting mission doing exactly that. I am sometimes tempted in referring to Doyle to use the word *naïf* too often. If so I mean it in the best sense, implying the intelligence that instinctively relies on its natural and unargued impulses. It does not imply that Doyle was only a Watson. When in his own career, problems of the Baker Street sort were submitted to him, more often than not he solved them just as Holmes would have done.

One of the pleasantest traits in his large and manly character was a complete absence of jealousy. No writer of modern time was more promptly and deliberately imitated, which he sensibly regarded as true compliment; he was not even annoyed when his own brother-in-law (E. W. Hornung) made a great success of the stories of Raffles, the chivalrous crook, and his companion Bunny, obvious burlesques of Holmes and Watson.

II

I remember my friend Mr. Edgar Smith of the General Motors Company telling me that on a business trip to Washington he had an appointment with the Secretary of State. In the anteroom he met Mr. Elmer Davis, head of the Office of War Information. While waiting to see the nation's chief diplomatic officer these two found themselves discussing appropriate episodes in the career of Sherlock Holmes, who also was often consulted in problems of high politics. Mr. Davis remarked that though there have been more important authors than Conan Doyle, in his own experience no other writer has provided so large a fund of both pleasure and useful information. I have elsewhere admitted that for a student of my taste more of reliable social history and speculation can be had in Doyle than in a whole shelf of Keyserlings and Spenglers. The enthusiast likes to dream of the great omnibus volume in which the whole Sherlockian codex would be annotated from end to end for a new generation. Lest one suppose that explanations are unnecessary, take at random a few examples of casual passages. How many young readers know what is a wax vesta? A gasogene, or a tantalus? A commonplace book? a Crockford? a Bradshaw? A wideawake, or a billycock? A London growler? a penang lawyer? When Holmes says he is going to Doctors' Commons, or has had a letter from a tide-waiter, what does he mean? What was the *Pink 'Un* that the poultry dealer had in his pocket? It would require a bibliographical expert to explain allusions to the "yellow-backed novels." (Is there a suggestion of comparative tastes when on the journey to Boscombe Valley Watson relaxed with a yellow-back whereas Holmes carried a pocket Petrarch and wanted to talk about Meredith?) And what sort of image rises in the young reader's mind when he hears of the friend who was invited every year by Squire Beddoes "to come and shoot over his preserves"? The natural visualization would be some mischief on pantry shelves. For the student of the law the stories are rich in comedy. One may wonder about the technical bigamy committed by Mrs. F. H. Moulton ("The Story of the Noble Bachelor") or the Musgrave family keeping as private property the historic Stuart crown, which should surely be locked in the Tower of London ("The Musgrave Ritual"). There can be no doubt that the proceedings in "Silver Blaze" would have meant scandal and imprisonment for all concerned, including Sherlock himself. In their errors as much as in their felicities the stories are perfect romance. There is something almost godlike in the simplicity that would use duplicate openings for two different stories ("The Cardboard Box" and "The Resident Patient") and never through some forty years bother to alter them. In the American editions they are there still. As I write this, I learn that a distinguished publishing office (The Limited Editions Club) is preparing a complete text of all the Sherlock Holmes stories, in which for the first time the English and American editions will be collated and a permanently accurate version rendered.

III

Doyle once wrote a verse to the effect that his favorite reader was "the man who's half a boy or the boy who's half a man." It is a sound instinct that has led boys of several generations to love him, for certainly he led the kind of life boys covet. One of the most difficult decisions he had to make must have been when the captain of a Shetland whaler offered to make him harpooner if he would stay for a second trip instead of returning to medical school. This Arctic interlude of seven months (at the age of 20) was one of several interruptions in his medical course when he was trying to help pay his tuition at Edinburgh University. The adventures of students working to supplement meager funds are a familiar topic and one that Americans and Scots have specially in common. In this connection one thinks of Doyle's fellow student (J. M. Barrie, a year younger) who in that memorable address on Courage, at St. Andrews University, paid his deepest tribute not to the college itself or its distinguished graduates, but to "the poor homes of Scotland" that sacrificed so much to send their boys in search of learning. What an odd pair Doyle and Barrie must have been: the small, dark, gnome-like J. M. B. with hands and feet like a child's, and the huge blond athlete Doyle, well over six feet, 46-inch chest, "16 stone" (viz., 224 pounds) of solid bulk. I wish someone might have taken a snapshot of them sitting together on the beach at Aldeburgh in Suffolk, arguing what would be the most tactful way to kill Sherlock Holmes.

Few writers have made more efficient use in fiction of their own experiences. When Sherlock Holmes once remarked "Art in the blood is liable to take the strangest forms" of course it was Doyle's own family of which he was thinking. A. C. D. was the son of the youngest of four artistic brothers, themselves sons of a talented Irish cartoonist. One of Conan Doyle's uncles was the famous Dicky Doyle (1824–1883), whose work still appears every week on the cover of the English humorous paper *Punch*. This uncle illustrated Dickens's *Christmas Stories* and Thackeray's *The Newcomes*; one of his drawings that was pleasantly known was the label for the once famous *Apollinaris* bottled water. The little sketch plans included in some of the Sherlock Holmes stories, particularly "The Priory School," "The Naval Treaty," "The Golden Pince-Nez," show that Conan Doyle also had a crisp touch as draftsman. I think one may guess that when Dr. Watson alluded to the misfortunes of his older brother he was mindful of Doyle's brilliant and unsuccessful father; and surely the number of stories based on the romantic hazards of governesses were suggested by the fact that three of Doyle's five sisters had to earn their living in that employment.

The reader who looks up Doyle's delightful autobiography, *Memories and Adventures*, will find the whole story of an exciting career told with the utmost charm and good humor. Mr. Hesketh Pearson, who had access to family papers in preparing his biography of Doyle, reports the amusing fact that even in his own diaries Doyle often went wrong on dates. This is comforting to those who have noticed Dr. Watson's uncertainty in chronology.

The love of physical combat evident in many of the tales

was a part of young Arthur Doyle's own character. As a small boy in Edinburgh he lived in a kind of dead-end street where there was great rivalry between those who, like himself, lived in small "flats" (apartments) and the more well-to-do boys from the "villas" (viz., detached houses) on the other side of the street. Young Doyle was chosen as pugilistic champion of the boys from the flats. His schooling would seem severe to boys today: at the age of ten he was sent away to a famous Jesuit boarding school (Stonyhurst) which allowed only one vacation a year. There followed a year at a Jesuit school in Austria after which he returned to study medicine at Edinburgh. His allowance was small and his usual lunch was a mutton pie which cost twopence (4¢)—not a lavish meal for a young giant. But not far from the stall that sold mutton pies was a secondhand bookstore and outside the door stood a barrel of books with the sign "Your Choice for 2d." (Viz., twopence. The abbreviation *d* for penny comes from the Roman coin *denarius*.) From his teens young Doyle was a passionate accumulator of books and often went without the mutton pie to add a volume to his private shelf. George Gissing's test of an author used to be "Has he starved?" and Doyle could qualify. Several of his writings recall those hard-pressed student days in the old gray capital of the north, but important for our present theme is the professor of surgery whose classes he attended. When Stevenson first read the Sherlock Holmes stories he wrote to Doyle: "Surely this is my old friend Joe Bell?" It was indeed. Dr. Joseph Bell, who chose young Doyle as his classroom assistant, came back to Doyle's mind when he depicted the character of Holmes. Bell had an extraordinary gift for diagnosis more than merely medical. When the patient was brought in for examination in front of the class he could specify character and trade with remarkable accuracy. Also he had the tall thin figure, the high beaky nose and strident voice which we now recognize as the detective's. Dr. Bell was enormously pleased when he found himself simulated in fiction; he offered many suggestions for plots which Doyle regretfully admits were not practical.

By the time Doyle was twenty years old his father was in a sanitarium and the young student found himself the head of a large embarrassed family. A book written some years later, *The Stark Munro Letters*, gives a substantially truthful record of the student's vacation struggles to earn money by serving as a medical assistant in various parts of England. His experiences were probably not very different from those of any other young doctor, but he found time to write remarkable letters describing them to a friend. This friend insisted that Doyle should put some of this gift into fiction, and while he was still a student he was able to sell his first story for three guineas, about fifteen dollars. This was "The Mystery of Sasassa Valley," published in the famous old Scottish magazine *Chambers's Journal*. From the very beginning of his literary career we see Doyle under American influence, for his first attempts were reminiscent of Bret Harte, who was at that time United States Consul in Glasgow.

IV

If one tried to invent the perfect training for a writer of adventure one could hardly imagine experience more stimulating than Doyle's. The profound effect made on him by the vast crystalline spaces of the Arctic is suggested by his story "The Captain of the Pole Star." The whaling voyage was soon followed by a quite opposite experience when he went as ship's surgeon in a trading steamer down the West Coast of Africa. The heavy, fever-tainted air of the equatorial coast was very different from the Greenland ice floes; the young doctor fell ill and for some days was unable to attend the passengers for whom he was responsible. He describes this voyage with his usual humor in *Memories and*

Adventures, and says he found—just as Dr. Watson did at the beginning of *A Study in Scarlet*—that the weakness following a disease is useful for making good resolutions. He decided that the career of ship's surgeon, however alluring for the thrill of strange scenes, had no professional future. He gave up drinking cocktails, with which the colonists of West Africa tried to forget their troubles, and determined to settle down to the laborious humdrum of a provincial practice. He also declined the offers of a recruiting sergeant who had spotted the powerful young man on a vacation visit to London. It was a close decision for he was without job or funds at that moment and to "take the Queen's shilling" for service in Afghanistan must have been an adventurous impulse. Certainly the idea stayed in his mind, for Dr. Watson served in that same campaign and received the much-disputed wound; but Dr. Doyle settled in Southsea, a suburb of the great naval base of Portsmouth. The humors and hardships of a young doctor's life in a strange community are described in *The Stark Munro Letters* (1894), a book still interesting to medical students. The rigors of professional etiquette were strict in those days; the doctor must always wear his silk hat and frock coat in public, and not to have a neatly uniformed maid to open the front door was a confession of failure. But Doyle could afford no servant and pretended, every time he answered the bell, that it was just an accident. Then he had the happy thought of inviting his small brother Innes Doyle to come and live with him and masquerade as a page. The proper uniform (a dark tunic with rows of brass buttons) was not available, but that also was always explained as the chance of the moment. Perhaps this gave A. C. D. his interest in boys-in-buttons—bellhops, we would call them now—for Mrs. Hudson, the landlady on Baker Street, engaged one as soon as Holmes and Watson showed signs of prosperity. Nor is it forgotten that in the play *Sherlock Holmes* this same role of the page boy was played in England by an actor who afterward became as famous as Holmes himself—Mr. Charles Chaplin.

Speaking of famous names, Doyle used to remember that one of his patients in the years at Southsea was the proprietor of a "draper's shop" (where cloth, linens and dress goods are sold) and on his professional visits Dr. Doyle must often have seen a young clerk then working as the draper's assistant. His name was H. G. Wells, then collecting impressions which he used afterward in the well-known novel, *The History of Mr. Polly.*

Sometimes after waiting indoors all day for the patients who did not come, the burly young doctor used to go out late at night, vigorously polish his brass plate, and then set off for a short furious walk for exercise, across Southsea Common and along the waterfront. He saw transports putting off past the Isle of Wight, heard the whistles of liners going down to sea, and must have had envious twinges. But he had already started practice in debt, and also he was obstinately faithful in trying to help his father's family. Once in childhood he said to his mother, "When you are old you shall have a velvet dress and gold glasses, and sit in comfort by the fire," and he was proud that the time came when that was true.

How often it happens that what looks like ruin proves salvation. Doyle always had energy enough for three ordinary men and in the discouragements of a small medical practice he found time to go on writing stories. This was more necessary than ever after his marriage (to the sister of a patient). He broke into the famous *Cornhill* and *Blackwood's* magazines, and struggled manfully with a novel called *The Firm of Girdlestone*, which still remains almost a classic of melodramatic naïveté. But it can be kindly considered by lovers of Baker Street, for among the characters is a certain Mrs. Hudson, distressed widow of a sailor done to death by a rascally shipowner. One would like to believe her the same Mrs. Hudson whom Doyle afterward set up in decent prosperity at 221B. And then in 1886 came *A Study in Scarlet*. It went the rounds of the publishers for many months, but the only offer made for it was so unpromising that the disheartened author almost threw the manuscript into the bottom of a drawer. A publisher offered £25 ($125) for all rights, with the further stipulation that it would be more than a year before the story could be put in print. It appeared as part of a Christmas annual in 1887, and Doyle never received a single penny more than that first payment. Probably not even in the case of *Paradise Lost* or *The Vicar of Wakefield* or any other of our classics has the disproportion between payment and earnings been more extreme.

Even with *A Study in Scarlet* and *The Sign of the Four* behind him, and also the vigorous historical novel *Micah Clarke* which was accepted by Andrew Lang for one of the most ancient and eminent English publishers, Dr. Doyle still thought of his writing as only an occasional assistance to the household budget. He decided to become an eye-specialist, invested his savings in study under experts in Vienna, and returned to set up an office as close as he could afford to Harley Street, which is the Royal Road of London specialists in medicine. Every day he walked to his office from his lodgings in Montague Street—where incidentally Sherlock Holmes lived before meeting Watson; a byway of modest rents alongside the British Museum. Though he sat patiently from ten to four in his consulting room, no one came to consult. To pay the bills he reverted to the idea of Sherlock Holmes, and if any eye-sufferer had arrived with his vision not too impaired, he might well have seen pages of the doctor's small neat script protruding from under the blotter. Then came a serious attack of influenza. In the clarity of mind accompanying the lassitude of convalescence Dr. Doyle made another decision. He abandoned his practice, rented a small house in the southern suburb of Norwood, and set about earning his living entirely by writing. The first series of the *Adventures* began to run in

The Strand Magazine in July 1891. Famous as they now are, the rate of pay was not lavish. Mr. Hesketh Pearson tells us that the average fee for the first six tales was £30 ($150) but was raised to £45 in the second six. After the twelve *Adventures* Doyle wanted to do something else, but the success of the stories in the *Strand* had been so remarkable that the editor, Mr. Greenhough Smith, insisted on another series as soon as possible. It is entertaining to study in the files of the *Strand* for 1892 the various efforts made by the editor to placate his readers with other features while they waited for the promised continuation of Holmes and Watson. Most of the substitute attempts were barefaced and painful imitations, but among his experiments Mr. Greenhough Smith did achieve one discovery hardly less important than the Holmes and Watson series. It was a portfolio of cartoons by a young man then fresh from Oxford who signed himself H. Maxwell Beerbohm. You know him now, I hope, as Max Beerbohm; in his own vein the most perfect writer of our lifetime.

Six months release was all Dr. Doyle was able to obtain. There were other reasons too why he had to continue a steady output. His wife was taken ill with what was called in those days "galloping consumption." For her health costly journeys to Switzerland and Egypt were advised. Sherlock Holmes made this possible so it was perhaps ungrateful that Dr. Doyle chose a Swiss waterfall as the scene of Holmes's death. Probably no catastrophe in fiction ever aroused so much dismay among devoted readers; of the thousands of protests the author received, his favorite was always a telegram from a lady who said simply, YOU BRUTE. But poor Doyle was trying hard to think of other things. During his stay in Switzerland he happened to read the *Memoirs of Marbot*, one of Napoleon's most temperamental generals. This was the inspiration of the gorgeous tales of Brigadier Gerard which began in *The Strand Magazine* in 1894 and which among connoisseurs are hardly less esteemed than the more famous adventures of the detective.

V

No quality was more evident in Conan Doyle than his always inquiring and inventive mind. He wrote once, "I have an occasional power of premonition which exercises itself beyond my own control, and which when it really comes is never mistaken." He was alluding chiefly to the studies in spiritualism which occupied the later years of his life; particularly to his somber belief, expressed in 1924, that humanity was fast approaching some gigantic crisis. But the wide exploring range of his temper was illustrated in countless other interests as well. The modern passion for skiing can be credited partly to him since he was the first to introduce this Scandinavian sport into Switzerland. Or we find him beside a marshy little pond in Surrey experimenting with a rifle to test the possibilities of high-angle fire—and almost wounding an innocent artist who was quietly sketching on the other side of the pond. The suggestions he made to the War Office were pigeonholed but he always believed that they were an early approach to the trench howitzer. This episode was a result of his experience in South Africa when he went with a volunteer medical unit in the Boer War. He saw there the full effect of the enteric fever which had stricken Dr. Watson: from one small field hospital sixty men a day were buried. Years later he said it still turned him sick to think of that smell reaching miles out into the veldt, the odor of pollution and disinfectants. The jocular address that he wrote at that time on letters home was "Café Entérique, Boulevard des Microbes, Bloemfontein." One believes that it was in the long voyage back from Capetown that his friend B. Fletcher Robinson, a war correspondent, told him the "West Country Legend" that became *The Hound of the Baskervilles*.[1] Not less important was his realization that a modern government needs to make use of intelligent publicity. Having seen the Boer War at firsthand he was appalled by the defamation of the British troops spread all over the world from German sources. In a month of furious application he wrote a small book *The War in South Africa* (1902) which was distributed in twenty languages and published in Germany itself by the famous Tauchnitz. Almost single-handed Doyle was able to give the world a quite different picture of the troubles with the Boers; it was this achievement that brought him his knighthood.

In whatever phase we notice, he was doggedly and courageously pursuing his earnest projects. How delightfully diverse they were. He was a pioneer in raising the social esteem of modern prize fighting—so much so that he was invited by American sportsmen to referee the championship Jeffries–Johnson fight in 1910. Only distance and other engagements prevented him from accepting this high compliment. Long before the American merchandisers he foresaw the financial possibilities of greeting cards, and served many years as a director of the renowned printers of Christmas and picture cards, Raphael Tuck and Company. He was chairman of the board of a brass band instrument factory. Many other investments, equally romantic, were less rewarding, such as gold mines in Africa and Australia, coal mines in Kent, and a Spanish Armada galleon sunk off the coast of Ireland. He was an unsuccessful candidate for a seat in Parliament; he agitated endlessly for a tunnel under the English Channel. He stood up for the officers of the *Titanic* when she was sunk by the iceberg; he gave

---

[1]Mr. Vincent Starrett tells me that Fletcher Robinson's death, years later, also was a topic of supernatural rumor: it was attributed to the baleful influence of an Egyptian mummy whose displeasure he was supposed to have incurred.

largely of time and money to remedy miscarriages of justice in some famous criminal cases; and equally characteristic, he assisted the chambermaids at a hotel in Brighton to organize successfully for higher wages. I think with special pleasure of his sending one of his books to prisoners of war in Germany with an accompanying letter explaining that the first couple of chapters might be slow but the story would improve about Chapter 3. The intelligent prisoners were shrewd enough to divine that this meant something. Beginning with Chapter 3 they held the pages to the light and saw that Doyle had laboriously pricked out certain letters with a needle. Reading these in succession they spelled out messages of what was happening at home.

There can scarcely be many examples in literature where the writer of well-loved books was so exactly what the reader would hope him to be. The faithful obstinacy of Watson, the priceless intuition of Holmes are both apparent throughout. Even when Holmes retired from detective practice it was to the intellectual interest of beekeeping. Evidently that occupation is by no means remote from human problems. We learn from a recent biography of the Wright Brothers that when every newspaper and scientist regarded them as forlorn fanatics their only encouragement came from the editor of a magazine famous in its field, *Gleanings in Bee Culture*. Not the least of the values of the Holmes and Watson epic is that it opens into civilized concerns from a hundred alluring directions. Of the many continuations of Sherlock Holmes the only one worth record approaches him among the beehives. See, for your own delight, that engaging and terrifying book by Mr. H. F. Heard, *A Taste for Honey* (1941).

Doyle's political ideas were simple and firmly held. He was always a campaigner for Anglo-American friendship. No one was ever more earnestly convinced that the collaboration of all the English-speaking peoples is of critical importance to the world. To this hope he dedicated his novel *The White Company* in 1891. In the *Stark Munro Letters*, published in 1894, Dr. Munro is supposed to be writing to his American friend, Bertie Swanborough, of Lowell, Massachusetts:—

> Will civilisation be swamped by barbarism? It happened once before. . . . But what could break down the great country in which you dwell? No, our civilisation will endure and grow more complex. Man will live in the air and below the water. Preventive medicine will develop until old age shall become the sole cause of death. Education and a more socialistic scheme of society will do away with crime. The English-speaking races will unite, with their centre in the United States. Gradually the European States will follow their example. War will become rare but more terrible. The forms of religion will be abandoned, but the essence will be maintained; so that one universal creed will embrace the whole civilised earth, which will preach trust in that central power, which will be unknown then as now. That's my horoscope, and after that the solar system may be ripe for picking. But Bertie Swanborough and Stark Munro will be blowing about on the west wind. . . .
>
> Man himself will change, of course. The teeth are going rapidly. . . . And the hair also. And the sight. Instinctively, when we think of the more advanced type of young man, we picture him as bald and with eye-glasses. . . . On the other hand, there is some evidence in favour of the development of a sixth sense, that of perception.

VI

So when we climb the seventeen steps to the sitting room on Baker Street we are in a scene prepared and enriched for us by the pleasure of millions. The convention of accepting Holmes and Watson as real passed beyond argument long ago. They have the reality that accrues only to the great symbols and cartoons. There are no haggling comparisons in that realm of "life beyond life"; the detective and the doctor move with all the other great pairs of masculine good humor: with Don Quixote and Sancho, with Crusoe and Friday, with Jim Hawkins and John Silver, with Huck and Tom. Their adventures are a textbook of friendship.

Even the graduate school of Sherlockian criticism is of decent maturity. It was in 1911 that the Reverend (now Monsignor) R. A. Knox wrote for a club at Trinity College, Oxford, his humorous paper (with shrewd overtones of theological satire) "Studies in the Literature of Sherlock Holmes." This new frolic in criticism was welcome at once; those who were students at Oxford in that ancient day remember how Mr. Knox was invited round from college to college to reread his agreeable lampoon; it was first printed in a journal of undergraduate highbrows (*The Blue Book*) then appropriately edited by W. H. L. Watson. Cambridge University followed some years later (1931) with Mr. S. C. Roberts's delightful little biography of Dr. Watson. The literature of this field is now considerable; the pleasantest introduction to it is Mr. Vincent Starrett's *The Private Life of Sherlock Holmes* (1933). These references need not disturb the beginning reader, who concerns himself with little more than attentive enjoyment, but they are needed to frame the picture.

The student of composition will be aware of the skilled simplicity with which the stories are told—particularly the shorter tales in which the author had adapted and stylized his formula. To the unspoiled participant, as to the Samoan overseer, they simply seem to happen. No school of journalism earnestly instructing reporters to begin with a provocative "lead" has devised more sure technique of seasoning the reader's curiosity. Even after the plots are familiar there is still permanent satisfaction in the vivid little interior or stage-set that always begins the adventure. Each reader will discover his own favorites among these masterly

114

prologues. Is it a night of driving rain when Holmes and Watson sit on either side of the coal fire, and the long rasp of carriage wheels grinds against the "kerb" below? It may be Watson the heavy sleeper roused before daylight in his bedchamber upstairs, Holmes in the famous dressing gown leaning over him with a candle and the deathless words "Come, Watson, come! The game is afoot!" Or perhaps a railway carriage (always first-class, reserved) "flying westward at fifty miles an hour." Holmes wears his ear-flapped traveling cap and is filling the compartment with discarded newspapers. His motto at the beginning of each exploit might well be that of Will Rogers, "I only know what I read in the papers." Sturdy Watson waits patiently for his friend to whet the keen blade of his observation on that solid grindstone mind. You will be surprised to find that we know more details of Watson's behavior and appearance than we do of his great master. His service revolver bulges in his pocket, his large boots show the slashes of a careless maidservant who scraped off the mud; his left cheek also may be scraped, for after leaving Baker Street for domesticity, Watson's shaving mirror never had a good light. The worthy doctor carries his handkerchief in his coat sleeve, a habit dating from army days, since the uniform tunic had no pocket for the purpose. We see him filling his pipe with the Arcadia mixture and suspect he favored that blend by inheritance from his creator's friend, J. M. Barrie. When Holmes has finished the news, and condescends to tell Watson what it's all about, the detective usually predicts that by the time they reach the spot marked "X" the local police will have trampled out all traces "like a herd of buffalo." This, his frequent phrase, is surely a suggestion of his visits to the United States. Is it trivial or absurd to apply to these imaginary characters the same close attention which is the principle of the stories themselves? Holmes's axiom, so often repeated to the patient Watson, is not a bad motto: "When you have eliminated the impossible, whatever remains, *however improbable*, must be the truth." We must remember, of course, not to be too hasty in defining the impossible.

There is a special and superior pleasure in reading anything so much more carefully than its author ever did. Perhaps to do so is a sound beginning in scholarship. To eliminate the impossible from Dr. Watson's narratives is to many readers as profitable enjoyment as crossword puzzles. There are inconsistencies, slips of the press, and textual variants almost as cherished as disputed passages in Chaucer or Shakespeare. The very frailties of Watson as reporter may be made an introduction to the vintage delights of textual criticism. Veterans of Sherlockian research like to regard the revised London editions published by John Murray as "the Canon." It is true that someone apparently made a conscientious attempt in that reprinting to strain out the errors; but also succeeded in introducing new confusions (for instance in the cipher of "The Dancing Men," which is imperfect in the John Murray text). The stories given here have been collated with both texts but I confess a lingering affection for the American versions with all their luscious errata which should keep a reader alert. What a thrill of excitement (or annoyance) the customer experiences when he discovers the famous duplicate passages in "The Resident Patient" and "The Cardboard Box"; or finds Mrs. Watson (in "The Five Orange Pips") visiting her mother, when we know that lady died years before. Or the famous American misprint, never corrected, that the horse Silver Blaze was descended from "Somomy." It should be *Isonomy*, a famous thoroughbred of those days.

What other body of modern literature is esteemed as much for its errors as its felicities? The saga of Holmes and Watson endures as a unique portrait of a friendship and of a civilization. It is not strange that in our recent years of turmoil and dismay there has been so keen a nostalgia for the shape of things gone by. The Victorian age had many cruel faults yet in some phases it reached the highest accomplishment and assurance human beings have known. When Watson is talking we know where we are. Right is right and wrong is wrong; an aristocrat always looks like an aristocrat; he has a high beaky nose, wide-open haughty gaze, and sags a little at the knees. Mrs. Hudson's joint of cold beef is on the sideboard (no one dreamed of an icebox in those days), and Holmes is smoking the cherrywood pipe which he reserves for disputatious mood. Let us enter the argument. So, in Vincent Starrett's phrase, we revisit a world "where it is always 1895." What would we not give for a similar accidental charade of the age of Shakespeare or Milton or Ben Franklin?

Sherlock Holmes and Dr. Watson

A CHRISTMAS STORY
WITHOUT SLUSH

SURELY ONE OF THE MOST UNUSUAL THINGS in the world: a Christmas Story without slush. It makes me sad to think that the one perfect reader for it, the man who more than any other would have delighted in its economy and skill, never saw it. I mean, of course, Charles Dickens. How much Dickens might have learned from it, if he had been capable of learning! I am quite serious when I say that, as a story, *The Blue Carbuncle* is a far better work of art than the immortal *Christmas Carol*. The latter, canonized by over a hundred years of sentiment, is more legendary than legible. It contains deathless scenes of sheer genius, but all clanked and labored together by a heavy drag of mechanical framework. And, as a collector, I would rather have Sidney Paget's original drawings for this story, in the old *Strand Magazine* for January 1892, than Leech's color plates for the *Carol*.

How long does it take for any piece of writing to become a classic? There are still fine old people, in their 70's and 80's, who must remember reading *The Blue Carbuncle* in that old magazine with its pale blue cover picturing Southampton Street, Strand; or in the Harper edition of the *Adventures of Sherlock Holmes*, autumn 1892. Harper tried as nearly as possible to imitate, in cloth binding, the blue tint of the magazine. Readers thought of it, naturally, as just another adventure of Sherlock Holmes. It never fell into the Trade's most profitable groove as a "Christmas story." It was a just-after-Christmas story, and it was good entertainment. They didn't (and mostly readers shouldn't) realize it was superb art. It hasn't a word too many or too few, and it doesn't rely (like O. Henry's famous *Gift of the Magi*) on sleight of hand. It nowhere breaks its chosen mood.

It's interesting, by the way, to reflect that both Dickens and Doyle were about the same age (say 31 or 32) when *Carol* and *Carbuncle* were written. It's a critical age, when hope and disgust and domestic overheads are all in unstable balance. The frustrated young doctor who wrote *The Blue Carbuncle* probably had no idea it was a masterpiece in its kind. But a great many devotees quite independently have learned to reread it during the Christmas octave. I used to wish that Franklin Roosevelt would sometimes vary his (widely publicized) habit of reading the *Carol* aloud to his family on Christmas Eve. After all, he was also a Baker Street Irregular, and (if I know anything about families) the younger generation would have enjoyed the change. But if you pause to think, there were strong psychological reasons for F.D.R.'s fixation on Dickens. Tiny Tim also had a leg brace; and I feel sure that F.D.R. got an annual guffaw out of Dickens's malicious allusion to the U.S.A. Even in his little homily of love, Dickens, like Jack Priestley, couldn't resist a barb for the gigantic daughter of the West. Scrooge, you will remember, found some of his fiscal paper as worthless as "a mere United States security."

But let us stick to our goose. Here is a post-Christmas story for frostbitten people. It happened on Friday, December 27, 1889. Dr. Watson, not very long married, had quite properly spent Christmas and Boxing Day with his wife and patients. Then Mrs. Watson went to visit her aunt, of whom we know too little.[1] The Doctor, though too mannerly to boast of it, had an evening or so off leash. There is no other genteel way to account for his double visits to Baker Street on December 27. He called on Holmes to wish him, in his restrained way, "the compliments of the season." That is the first frosty phrase to remember. Not a Merry Old

---

[1] I believe she was actually Mrs. Cecil Forrester, of Camberwell, where Mrs. Watson had been employed as governess. The family grew so fond of Mary Morstan, later Mrs. Watson, that she called Mrs. Forrester "Aunt."

Christmas, not Jocund Yule; just the bashful British meiosis, Compliments of the Season. Wary old Watson, one of Britain's great understatesmen. No emotional Heilige Nacht, no Tannenbaum, no vast substantial Fezziwigs, no lachrymous Yuletide yowling. Compliments of the Season, Old Boy; and how are you, Holmes?

We know how he was. Particularly if we have relished Sidney Paget's drawings (*Strand*, January 1892) we have memorized those tantalizing glimpses into the immortal sitting-room: the horsehair sofa, the dressing gown, the pipe-rack. What pipes! How Dunhill would be shocked: a few dirty clays and straight-stem bulldogs, and the cherry-wood for disputation. Never a droopy bowl as the movies and California vintners insist, their horrible curly calabashes and processed chin-briars. After Holmes had his tooth knocked out in Charing Cross Station (see *The Adventure of the Empty House*) he had to wear falsettoes. He couldn't denture a gooseneck pipe.

But more minutiae. The basket chair. Few Americans know what is a basket chair ("Minty's Varsity Chair") invented (at Oxford?) to help students fall asleep beside the fireplace. Look closer still into Paget's drawings: see Watson's velvet-collared topcoat, and Ascot tie. See Holmes's caped ulster; very dear to me, because my dear Old Man (my father), when he emigrated to U.S.A. in 1887, had just such a garment. It was pale sandy-color with reticulations of green. He wore it until about 1900, when we moved to Baltimore; then my Mother cut it down to be a dressing gown for me. I wore it to and from the bathroom until about 1910. Then my younger brothers took over. It was very likely re-dyed, like Holmes's own, which experts remember started purple, then mouse, and then grey. The gradual solstitial fading of Holmes's dressing gown is one of the statutory documentations of life as it happens. It is one of the accidentals that prove that Doyle was a great uncon-scious artist, as all artists are.

120

This wonderful wintry story of the Blue Carbuncle offers all sorts of opportunities to scholars. It has everything that a Xmas fable wants: frost-crystals on the windows, brisk outdoor walking, and Holmes's slippers warming by the fire. It has in it one of the most famous passages in fiction, the deductions made from the old battered and greasy derby hat. That is plainly an attempt to imitate the equally famous series of inferences made from H. Watson's gold watch in *The Sign of the Four*; and even excelled some years later by the glorious deductions made from *Whitaker's Almanac* (the predecessor of Golenpaul–Kieran's) in *The Valley of Fear*. That is what fiction exists for, to make delightful the impossible and unbelieved.

Are we scholars? Are we talking about the Impossible? How could our hero Sherlock get advertisements into all the afternoon papers by mid-morning? How come the plumber was working on Sunday at the Cosmopolitan Hotel? (If Friday was the 27th, the 22nd was Sunday.) How come that Sherlock's fire "crackled"? It was certainly a soft-coal fire, which never crackles? Why does Sherlock say that the solution was "its own reward"? We know perfectly well that he must have taken a percentage of the Countess of Morcar's offer (£1000) because he had these items at least to pay: the cost of advertisements in seven or more evening papers; the sovereign bet at Covent Garden; the cost of the four-wheeler, and the fresh goose, and the broken window. I am perfectly sure that on the morning of Saturday, December 28th, Holmes (still feeling the holiday spirit) went round to the shop on Tottenham Court Road, paid for the broken window, and charged it to account. The Xmas goose, judging by Breckinridge's mark-up, cost Holmes (per Mrs. Hudson) probably 16/6, and I dare say he wrote off the woodcock too as "Entertaining client." Much has been said about Holmes's housekeeping, but no one has remarked his passion for meat, and bird-game. We have records of his meals of grouse, pheasant, partridge, woodcock, and pâté de foie gras; cold beef, and eggs, and oysters. But he never ate fish; he can't have been English? There was some talk about trout in the Shoscombe case, but only as pretext.

Scholars, I said? What was poor Henry Baker doing in the British Museum? You may or may not notice that when he comes to Baker Street (I wish we knew which newspaper it was where he saw the advt.? Myself I think it was *The Star*) he quotes Horace (*Satires*, I. iv, 62). Actually he misquotes, *disjecta membra*. So I think he was doing research, reading and devilling and misquoting, for Dr. Thorneycroft Huxtable's *Sidelights on Horace*, which had a European vogue. Dr. Huxtable was too busy, as schoolmaster (see *The Adventure of the Priory School*), to do his collations for himself. I know the place, here called The Alpha, where Henry Baker joined the goose-club. It is at the corner of Museum and Great Russell Streets. It used to have, in the old days (about 1924), the most beautiful crosscut rose-and-white jambon of ham waiting for slice behind the bar. And crisp crusty secants of fresh bread.

Ham makes me think of *The Pink 'Un*, that Breckinridge had in his coat pocket. How many of our young readers will know, and how do people know if you don't tell them, *The Pink 'Un* is a sporting paper, printed on pink sheets, something like our American *Police Gazette*?

There are many kinds of readers; the best and brightest of them probably wish to be amused, not to deduce nor infer. For either kind this chillblain comedy is perfect. It is as traditional as Homer, as corny-modern as Billy Rose, the suitor of O. Henry. You can read into it subtleties the author had no notion of, for instance that the crook Ryder and his girl-friend Kitty Cusack got the simple plumber to the hotel on Sunday (December 22) because that would be the day when the Countess of Morcar was out at a party. Or you can worry about what is a *commissionaire*, one of the corps of uniformed veterans (G.I.'s) founded in 1859, who run errands and take messages and do doorman work at hotels and theatres. So read the story first (aloud, if you have any friends patient enough) and don't worry about details.

Years ago I amused myself one Xmas by making a model stage-set for a toy theatre, to represent this story on Baker Street. I fixed cellophane windows crystallized with frost; the coal fire, the scuttle, the fiddle, and Holmes's slippers. There was the fresh goose (16 shillings and 6d) on the sideboard, and of course the decanter of brandy, Watson's universal specific. The detective, in purple gown, lounged among his crumpled papers, and studied the old billycock with forceps and lens. Watson was just coming in at the door, carrying (what Sidney Paget forgot) his medical bag. My truly great invention was the Sherlock Holmes Cherubs that hovered in air looking in the window. They were the face of the Great Sleuth, in accipitrine and oblique perspective, but supported by feathery wings. It seemed to me a wonderful Idea, uniting both motives: the dominant skull of Sherlock (whose hair was receding fast on top, according to Sidney Paget) and the sacred wings of the Season. Some of them had little deerstalker hats for the wintry weather. I wish I could find my drawing for that scene. I couldn't ever do it again; no artist can do anything twice. But I hope to persuade some young sculptor to design a Sherlock Holmes Cherub as a Xmas Card for the Baker Street Irregulars.

This most kindly and unintentional of Christmas Stories belongs in what that good man Oscar Firkins (of the University of Minnesota) once called "the warm little hollow between Christmas and New Year." That should be, if human beings were as sensitive as one would like to suppose, a moment of peace.

The Blue Carbuncle; also in *The Ironing Board*

INTRODUCTION

THERE IS AN AUTUMNAL SADNESS in the Case-Book. These great monolithic figures fade gradually away across the Sussex downs. We see Sherlock (now realizing what he lost in losing Watson) trying to keep the doctor by making him partner in the "agency" or "firm." We see an equally pertinacious character, the unidentified second Mrs. Watson, infuriated by Holmes's published remark that Watson had "deserted him for a wife," keeping the doctor's ear to the stethoscope in Queen Anne Street. How much, if you know the neighbourhood, the Queen Anne Street address suggests: both of Watson's nostalgia for Baker Street and the Wigmore post-office, and of his enforced revival of professional ambition. The most gruesome testimony to the tensions of that time is Mrs. Watson's attempt to write one of his adventures for him. The dreadful *Mazarin Stone* (obviously written by one who had never visited 221B personally) is proof how far she would go to keep Watson's mind on his practice. Privately, I think she may also have written *The Three Gables*.

But there is plenty of Canon-fodder in the Case-Book for the interlinear student. Twice running they dine at Simpson's in the Strand; Holmes was trying to show Watson that "this agency" could afford costly victual. And why was it that Watson saw the news-vendor's bulletin between the Grand Hotel and Charing Cross? He had just left the Turkish Bath in Northumberland Avenue. He took Turkish baths before every marriage.

Holmes was more shaken by Watson's second nuptial than his cold precise mind cared to admit. He was 49, the ascetic bachelor's most sensitive era. His fury at the maddening Violet de Merville, with her deep-freeze passion, leads on to the superb governess Grace Dunbar, and the peasant-clear allure of Maude Bellamy. "No young man would cross her path unscathed." To any psychologist, how much that implies unsaid! Holmes's mind went back to Violet Trevor, who died of diphtheria in Birmingham, perhaps his girlish ideal in college days; and to Irene Adler of *A Scandal in Bohemia*. But now, instead of an imagined sister (*Copper Beeches*), he thought of Violet de Merville as if she were an imagined daughter. People who have imagined a daughter have at least imagined intercourse; and, like every intellectual Sherlock, have shuddered at such indignity.

It is only by willingly descending into the depths of carnal absurdity that one may later acquire spiritual aggradation. Sherlock almost learned this in that astonishing episode of *The Illustrious Client*—but not quite. How much more Watson would have gained in a Mediterranean Cruise! They are still amusingly offered in the Agony Column of the London *Times*.

The Case-Book is our last loving glimpse of 221B Baker Street. We see how carefully Holmes has tutored Watson in deviation tactics, so that he himself instinctively alters all facts. Take the Blanched Soldier: he misstates the Priory School case (his £12,000 fee!) and even drives to Euston to take train to Bedford. I've mislaid my most precious 1894 Bradshaw, but I'm pretty sure you'd have to go to St. Pancras to embark (Midland Ry.) for Bedford. There are plenty of *dubiosa* in the text to class the Case-Book with what are called in Shakespeare study the Bad Quartos. For instance, the interpolation of South American wives whenever an excess of jealousy, or fidelity, would seem un-British; or of an Austrian nobleman when fiendish Lust is required. There is a higher morbid percentage of moral caducity in this than in all the other gospels. It shows the cross-currents of both Holmes and Watson in their febrile fifties. Unhappily they strove, as men will in that time of life, to remingle their young forces. But it was never sure, were they trouting for touts, or touting for trouts? (*Shoscombe Old Place*).

So it is not surprising that scholars have been reluctant to comment frankly on the Case-Book; even now, twenty-five years after its first publication, one speaks warily. As Holmes said to the Shoscombe trainer, our thoroughfare is Baker Street, not Harley Street; yet a just assessment of the Case-Book tangle would require a skilled psychiatrist. For here we see, under the terms of the Baker Street Axiom (when you have eliminated the impossible, etc.), the Immortal Friends in the tide-rips of conflicting purposes. Holmes is softening, becoming more emotional, convincing himself that he needs "the soothing life of Nature," even dims his clear hard eyes when Watson is wounded.

And Watson, newly remarried in 1903, resents being called back to Baker Street for what sounds at first a trivial problem (*The Creeping Man*). Watson, for the first time in his career, and under pressure that he carefully conceals, was definitely busy. His often-mentioned attractiveness to women was beginning to pay off. It did not, like Baron Gruner's, have a European vogue; but it kept the doorbell busy on Queen Anne Street. Nothing is more sinister in the Case-Book than Watson's despairing silence about his own affairs.

Holmes, now for the first time accessible by telephone, shows a strange world-weariness. Mrs. Hudson's new cook, who hardboils the eggs, was no help. "I was alone," he says, with sad brevity. He retired (say January 1904) to Sussex and cocaine? It was only his fiftieth birthday, but he had lived hard. Among the papers he took in were, of course, *The Manchester Guardian* and *The Baltimore Sun*. (I have suggested before that he was one of the earliest students at the Johns Hopkins, in 1876.) No one read with more interest the reports of Dr. Osler's famous farewell address at the Johns Hopkins (February 22, 1905), quoting Trollope on the chloroforming of men at the age of sixty. It is more than coincidence that the last testimony we have (*His Last Bow*) showed him at that age. And there was always the blue phial of prussic sent him by Eugenia Ronder. How one wishes that Harold Stackhurst might have had more evenings free, to drop in!

Here we see, in confused and partly apocryphal form, a human creature becoming immortal, putting off corruption, putting on (in the minds and hearts of devotees) incorruptibility; and, as is grievously human, most violently fallible in the agonies of approaching change. The enormous spread of the Sherlockian *mystique* in recent years is grim enough evidence of our universal *angst*. It is only too plain, in these final evangelisms, that Holmes had strangely persuaded himself of his long-wished little farm in Sussex. The Times Book Club was around the corner in Wigmore Street; and, like everyone else, he had read Kipling and even Belloc (at Horsham!) on Sussex. You don't know Holmes, and his country-squire lineage, if you don't realize his primary sentimentalism. But, like anyone else who retires from business to beatitude, vacation soon becomes vacuity, and boredom grows morbid. Watson's occasional comments, though carefully vague, might suggest in Holmes a cerebral neoplasm. It may be that Watson's death in 1942 (by coronary explosion, when he thought that his native Australia was about to be invaded by the Japanese) was the last impediment to what Sherlock had long had in mind . . .

You can't have gods without *Goetterdaemmerung*. Remains their poor symbolic reliques. I don't go along Baker Street without saying to myself, *This was the kerb that ground a thousand wheels*. And remember that it was in Baltimore that

Holmes learned his first great bee-keeping line from Vergil, the motto of the Johns Hopkins University—

> *Sic vos non vobis*
> *Mellificatis apes.*

The Case-Book of Sherlock Holmes; also in *Introducing Mr. Sherlock Holmes*

INTRODUCTION

THOSE FORTUNATE RAMBLERS in old bookshops who have chanced on a copy of Dr. Huxtable's *Sidelights on Horace* will remember the famous passage (in his enlarged 2nd edition) where the good dominie pays his gratitude to Mr. Sherlock Holmes. He analyzes one of the most famous of the odes to suggest that Horace and Holmes were destined kinsprits; he even finds in the number of the immortal *Integer vitae* (Book One, 22) an inverted clue; he finds the initial letters of the first two words a suggestion of John Watson; Mauris points to Moriarty; *venenatis sagittis* is the cocaine needle; and then possessed by a frenzy (like all who have been beset by codes and ciphers) he finds

> FuSce, pHarEtRa,
> . . . vel quae LOCa, etc.,

and steadies himself with the reflection that the Latin had no K.

I don't think the old classic intended to be taken too seriously; he goes so far as to suggest that the *silva Sabina* was St. John's Wood, and Lalage was Irene Adler—of whom, he justly says, Sherlock's last glimpse showed her *dulce ridentem*.

As the editors of this *3rd Case-Book* may have grunted, again quoting Horace, *Heu, heu, quantus adest sudor.* Or even as I shall now digest it:—

> Non omnis moriar, as Horace said;
> And Holmes: I shall not be completely dead,
> My work will be prolonged, non vi sed arte—
> My career was more than Moriarty.

Individually I quite agree with Mr. Honce when he suggests that too much intentional whimwham can become, to us grizzled old Baker Street hands, rather jejune. But then here we have the proper answer, in young Cherry, or even in recently so young Jerry. This is a game which leads into all sorts of education; I can even imagine Cherry, for instance, getting interested in Horace because she hears he was like S. H. in temperament. The best learning or culture any of us ever got was when our schooling became a game, or a self-produced play in a toy or impromptu theatre.

I would wager that Morris Rosenblum (see within) is most successful as a Latin teacher when he tangles Horace up with Sherlock, or with Eugene Field. I could tell you some sorry episodes of juvenile mischiefs committed right here in Long Island, by high school kids who never learned, nor were inspired to invent, games of their own. Some of the outland phantasy may sometimes seem like corn and soupstock to the ageing cynic—but every police-dog was a puppy once. Alas, I am no classic: I envy and revere people like M. Rosenblum and Elmer Davis: I got no further in Vergil than *stant litore puppes* (end of Book VI, isn't it?)— the pups are on the beach. The barbarity of our modern education seems to be, we don't give them beaches to land on that lead anywhere for an open run.

I much enjoyed my skim-through of the *3rd Case-Book*. I got it suddenly, just preparing for a holiday (I've been dreaming of going to Sherlock's Eastbourne region, on the Sussex coast, even ferreting out the Long Man of Wilmington, who had nothing to do with Dupont). A news story recently, about safes and files left open in the Pentagon, showed me that Percy Phelps at the F.O., and Bruce-Partington Plans at Greenwich Arsenal, are still timely. And the stunning piece by Mr. Grazebrook (with its data about Violet de Merville and her Mediterranean cruise) pleased me amain. And others too; never mind what the *aes triplex*, the high brass, may say. This is a game, and any game is worth playing if it keeps us briefly away from the abyss. Indianapolis, as I remember it, is the only paulopost-

Victorian ambience still urgent. If anyone chafes you, remember that the paper matchbook is slow to strike in humid weather; so good luck, indeed, from

CHRIS

The Illustrious Client's Third Case-Book

SHERLOCK HOLMES AND DR. WATSON

Sherlock Holmes and Dr. Watson appears, at first glance, to be an anomaly among these other writings. It is a textbook: *A Textbook of Friendship* is its subtitle. This 1944 volume includes *A Study in Scarlet*, *The Sign of the Four*, "The Final Problem," "The Adventure of the Empty House," and "The Adventure of the Bruce–Partington Plans," all set out as text for the high-school student, plus introductions, topics for discussion, bibliography, and a guide to all the adventures.

This was not Kit's first venture at designing a textbook. He had edited two volumes, *Modern Essays* and *Modern Essays: Second Series*, in the 'twenties, which had been designed to be marketed to the high-school reader. He had also occasionally turned professor, teaching in 1930–1931 at his alma mater, Haverford College, courses in Shakespeare, Chaucer, and Advanced Composition. Kit could always be described like Chaucer's Clerk: "gladly wolde he lerne, and gladly teche."

The introduction sets forth at length Kit's love for Sherlock Holmes and his admiration for Conan Doyle as an author while it puts the stories in a context for the reader of the 'forties. Unfortunately, this labor of love was cold-shouldered by the educative community and sold poorly.

The book's "Memorandum" and "Introduction" are included above, pp. 95–117, in the "Introductions" section of this volume. There is also, in the "Fictions" section, pp. 419–421, below, a brief pastiche, "The Adventure of the F.W.L.," which appeared on the dust jacket.

TOPICS FOR DISCUSSION:

A Study in Scarlet

1. PAGE 23.   Dr. Doyle's title for his first Sherlock Holmes story was consciously highbrow. In the art jargon of that day paintings were frequently called "A Study in Such and Such a Color." For instance Whistler's "Nocturne in Green and Gold," or the Portrait of his Mother, often alluded to as "A Study in Black and Grey." Whistler was at the height of his renown when *A Study in Scarlet* was written.

2. PAGE 25.   *irretrievably ruined*—What evidence can you suggest, from Dr. Watson's later adventures, that his health had not been damaged as severely as he thought?

3. PAGE 36.   Do you think Holmes's theory about overcrowding the mind is sensible?

4. PAGE 37.   After getting to know Dr. Watson, in this and the following stories, it might be amusing to draw up a schedule "John H. Watson—his limits," as he did for Holmes.

5. PAGE 39.   *nondescript*—Does Dr. Watson really mean "nondescript," having just successfully described them? Would *various* or *miscellaneous* be a better adjective?

6. PAGE 52.   *simious*—Can you suggest a more usual form of the adjective?

7. PAGE 53.   *Albert chain*—Can you suggest why the watch-chain, stretching across the waistcoat, was so called in that era?

8. PAGE 72.   *more stately tread of the landlady*—Our first opportunity to visualize the famous Mrs. Hudson. What do you deduce?

9. PAGE 77.   In "The Disappearance of Lady Frances Carfax" Holmes was able to pass as a French workman in the cabarets of Montpellier, a city where he was always very much at home. Would Dr. Watson have had more difficulty in masquerading as a Frenchman?

10. PAGE 82.   *free and familiar*—The result of reading Mr. Stangerson's copy of *The Decameron*?

TOPICS FOR DISCUSSION:

The Sign of the Four

1. PAGE 121. *velvet-lined armchair*—If Mrs. Hudson drew up an inventory of the room's contents, to be sure nothing got lost during Holmes's long absence in the years 1891–94, what would the list mention?

   Doyle once prepared a "property plot" for the stage version of the story "The Speckled Band" (published by Samuel French). This gives his own idea of the furnishings of the Baker Street sitting room. His list includes "easy chair in red tapestry with high loose cushion under which is large scrapbook," but forgets the important work-table for chemical experiments.

2. PAGE 124. *my wounded leg*—Advanced students may be reminded of another famous disablement in literature, that of Uncle Toby in *Tristram Shandy*.

3. PAGE 135. *fervently*—What do you deduce?

4. PAGE 140. *It was a September evening*—A paragraph of unusually vivid description. Can you point to other passages in this story of similarly lively effect?

5. PAGE 175. A barometer was usual in the hall of every middle-class English home. Does this suggest anything about the British climate? Do not forget that in our own day the umbrella became the universally recognized emblem of a British prime minister, Mr. Neville Chamberlain.

   We have said that the Sherlock Holmes stories have acquired unexpected values as a social history of their period. Can you think of any modern American writers of whom that is true? Perhaps O. Henry?

6. PAGE 207.   You might compile a list of the wardrobe required by Holmes in his various impersonations.

7. PAGE 208.   *The whole thing is irregular*—Students of law will find many interesting topics in Holmes's career, particularly his habit of compounding or conniving at a felony. In plain terms, he frequently refrained from prosecuting or informing when he felt his own judgment was better than the law.

8. PAGE 250.   *unstrapped my wooden leg*—Do you remember an incident in *Treasure Island* that might have suggested this?

TOPICS FOR DISCUSSION:

"The Final Problem"

1.   Why does the "death" of Sherlock Holmes seem so dramatically fitting? What means does the author employ to build up suspense before the final tragedy?

2. PAGE 258. What would have been "matters of supreme importance" to the French government in 1890–91? Look up in any history of France. Might one of them have been the German plans for building a powerful navy? Perhaps Holmes suggested to the French cabinet their new policy of a closer understanding with Russia. How did the French develop this policy in the summer of 1891?

    Probably when Holmes wrote from Narbonne and Nîmes (both in the South of France) he was taking a few days off to study the Roman ruins. Narbonne is famous for its honey; it may have been there he first got interested in beekeeping.

3. PAGE 260. *binomial theorem*—As a suggestion for research: Explore (in other stories not included in this volume) the evidences that there were also two Mrs. Watsons.

4. PAGE 265. Imagining yourself a stage director, consider the "singular interview" between Holmes and Moriarty as if it were a scene in a play. What instructions would you give the two actors for their behavior? What is it that makes Moriarty seem specially dangerous?

5. PAGE 271. *Newhaven*—Look up the route in an atlas. If you had an hour to spend in Canterbury between trains, what would you most wish to see?

6. PAGE 273. the Strasbourg *salle-à-manger*—the dining room of their hotel. Under less anxious circumstances Holmes, who enjoyed good food, would have taken time to enjoy Strasbourg's world-famous goose-liver pie (*Pâté de foie gras*), but it cannot be digested in haste. Their spending only half an hour for dinner is a tribute to what?

7. PAGE 275. As a matter of historical fact, the village of Meiringen was almost entirely destroyed by fire in 1891; perhaps this was an act of revenge or malice by the Moriarty gang. (See Baedeker's *Switzerland*, 1899 edition.) It is distressing to learn from Baedeker that the Reichenbach Fall is now reached by a "wire-rope railway"; there is a refreshment pavilion near the fatal path, and "on summer evenings the fall is illuminated by electricity."

TOPICS FOR DISCUSSION:

"The Adventure of the Empty House"

1. PAGE 289.   How does the author effectively suggest the deep affection that Watson felt for Sherlock Holmes?

2. PAGE 295.   *my own sad bereavement*—That is, the death of Mrs. Watson. Do you think Mrs. Watson may have disapproved of Holmes? A similar situation in actual life was the attitude of Mrs. Boswell toward Dr. Johnson.

    Holmes himself first suggested the parallel when he said "I am lost without my Boswell." Mr. S. C. Roberts has followed up the clue in his admirable little biography *Doctor Watson* (Criterion Miscellany No. 28, London, 1931).

3. PAGE 298.   *my infinite variety*—Would you deduce that Holmes was not entirely ignorant of English literature? What famous passage is he quoting? Where else in this story does he quote the same author?

4. PAGE 304.   *Von Herder*—Advanced students will remark the curious parallel of the air gun and wax bust in one of the least successful stories, "The Mazarin Stone" (in the *Case-Book*). That story is one of the two not told either by Watson or by Holmes. It has been conjectured that it was set down by the second Mrs. Watson. *His Last Bow* is also from some unidentified hand, perhaps that of Mycroft Holmes.

5. PAGE 307.   *Eton and Oxford*—The most dangerous man in London had of course been Professor Moriarty; the "worst man in London" you will find in the "Adventure of Charles Augustus Milverton."

141

Whom did Holmes consider the smartest man in London?

6. PAGE 308. Discuss Holmes's theory of character development. (He suggests somewhat the same idea in *The Hound of the Baskervilles*.)

TOPICS FOR DISCUSSION:

"The Bruce–Partington Plans"

1.   Among detectives created by modern writers is there any one whose reluctance to leave his own premises reminds you of Mycroft Holmes? See the stories by Rex Stout.

2.   Sherlock Holmes said it was fortunate for the community that he was not himself a criminal. If he had been, what sort of crimes would he have been likely to commit?

3.   PAGE 315.   If the political allusions in this story should lead into discussion of Anglo-American history, profitable reference can be made to Walter Lippmann's *United States Foreign Policy* (1943). Lord Salisbury's famous memorandum dealt with the Monroe Doctrine. He said "No statesman, however eminent, and no nation, however powerful, are competent to insert into the code of international law a novel principle never recognized before." Mr. Lippmann points out how ignorant, even to this day, most Americans are of the history and implications of the Monroe Doctrine.

Doyle's prescience in political affairs has been acutely analyzed by Dr. Felix Morley in an essay, "The Significance of the Second Stain," included in *Profile by Gaslight*.

Germany's special interest in her North Sea coast, as a base for possible invasion of England, is the theme of *The Riddle of the Sands*, by Erskine Childers, one of the best stories of international plotting ever written. This novel, first published in 1903, was reissued in 1915, in 1927, and in 1940. Readers who look it up will be astonished by its foresight.

4. PAGE 316.   Does Mycroft Holmes's unique position in the government remind one of an important official without portfolio in recent United States history? Suggest a parallel with Mr. Harry Hopkins.

5. PAGE 323.   We do not know what was playing at the suburban Woolwich Theatre the night of Monday, November 18, 1895. The sensation of that year in the metropolitan theater was *The Importance of Being Earnest*, by Oscar Wilde, but it had been quietly closed on May 8, 1895.

6. PAGE 336.   Both Oberstein and La Rothière are also mentioned in "The Adventure of the Second Stain."

7. PAGE 338.   A large-scale map of London shows that the original of Caulfield Gardens was probably Courtfield Road or Courtfield Gardens. Their relation to the railway is much as described.

A GUIDE TO
THE COMPLETE
SHERLOCK HOLMES

(The dates are those of first
publication *in books*.)

A STUDY IN SCARLET (1887)

A very unpleasant American was found dead in an empty house in a small street in London. There were no signs of a wound, yet the word RACHE was scrawled in blood on the wall. . . . Dr. Watson's first introduction to the sordid and gruesome details of violent crime.

THE SIGN OF THE FOUR (1890)

Sherlock Holmes is roused from boredom and cocaine by Miss Morstan's appeal. Shall she keep the blind date with an Unknown Friend? The thrilling story that follows extends from the great mutiny in India years before to a man hunt down the river Thames, and still leaves time for Dr. Watson's quiet love story.

THE ADVENTURES OF SHERLOCK HOLMES (1892)

(1) "A Scandal in Bohemia"

The first of the long series of shorter tales, and one of the most charming. Holmes relieves the King of Bohemia from an embarrassment, but finds the American prima donna Irene Adler more attractive than the royal client he is serving. Holmes outwits her at first, but she retaliates brilliantly. He refuses to shake hands with the King of Bohemia and keeps Irene's photograph as a souvenir. Perhaps the only evidence of romantic sentiment in the great detective's career.

(2) "The Red-Headed League"

A red-headed pawnbroker spends eight weeks copying the *Encyclopaedia Britannica* with a quill pen, but in the meantime what was his assistant doing in the cellar? This was "a three-pipe problem," but the knees of a pair of trousers gave Holmes the clue.

(3) "A Case of Identity"

Mary Sutherland, the typist, was thrilled when romance came into her life. Her suitor also was skillful with a typewriter, but when he left her waiting at the church she consulted Holmes. Holmes felt the case could best be settled with a horsewhip.

(4) "The Boscombe Valley Mystery"

"Air and scenery perfect" was the allure that Holmes used to tempt Watson to accompany him to the countryside in the West of England where murder had been committed. The crime had its origin in far-off Australia, and Watson (who had been in that country) might have been quicker in recognizing some of the clues.

(5) "The Five Orange Pips"

A Confederate veteran, for dire reasons, "exchanged the charming climate of Florida for the lonely life of an English provincial town." Holmes was consulted too late to avert the tragedy, but this is one of the most successful of all the stories in conveying the sense of impending horror. The effect is enhanced by the September gale that was raging when young John Openshaw came to Baker Street to tell of the sinister message: "Put the papers on the sundial."

(6) "The Man with the Twisted Lip"

Dr. Watson gallantly left his evening armchair to rescue one of his patients from an opium den in the slums of East London. There he unexpectedly met Sherlock Holmes who was investigating the mysterious disappearance of Mr. Neville St. Clair. This gentleman had apparently been drowned in four and a half feet of water, his pockets weighted with 691 copper coins.

(7) "The Adventure of the Blue Carbuncle"

Christmas, "the season of forgiveness," leads Holmes to let a badly frightened thief escape without punishment. Some of his shrewdest deductions lead up to the crisis, particularly the inference from a man's hat that his wife no longer loves him.

(8) "The Adventure of the Speckled Band"

One of the most famous cases, in which the brutal Dr. Roylott terrorizes his twin stepdaughters and twists Holmes's poker into a curve with his bare hands. Why did the smoke of Dr. Roylott's strong cigar bother his stepdaughter in another room, and why was the bed clamped to the floor?

(9) "The Adventure of the Engineer's Thumb"

One of the railway men at Paddington Station brought this case to Dr. Watson, and the good doctor after treating the wounded engineer referred the mystery to Holmes. (This was the story that so excited Stevenson's overseer in Samoa.) By the time they reached the scene of the outrage there was nothing Holmes could do, but Watson always felt a special pride in having started the investigation.

(10) "The Adventure of the Noble Bachelor"

This story is particularly famous for Holmes's pro-American sentiments. He serves a supper of congratulation for an attractive American couple, and thinks the lady has done well to escape becoming the bride of the aristocratic Lord St. Simon. We realize from one of Holmes's deductions how prices have changed since 1887: the hotel bill lists the cost of a bedroom as 8 shillings ($2) and a glass of sherry 8d (16¢)—Holmes knows therefore that it is one of the most expensive hotels in London.

(11) "The Adventure of the Beryl Coronet"

Dr. Watson thought it was a madman coming along Baker Street that winter morning: it was the portly banker Alexander Holder, whose despair was shown by his strange behavior. Holmes saved him from a scandal that would have involved an exalted name, but the story itself is less attractive than its brilliant opening.

(12) "The Adventure of the Copper Beeches"

The Copper Beeches was the name of the house in Hampshire where Mr. Rucastle paid high wages for a governess who would do unusual things—cut her hair short, wear an electric blue dress, and listen to comic stories. Behind these trivial demands was something much more sinister.

THE MEMOIRS OF SHERLOCK HOLMES (1894)

(1) "Silver Blaze"

This fine story, which shows Holmes at the top of his form, involves various problems of ethics. The crime was caused by a woman's excessive taste for expensive clothes, yet the actual murderer was not human, and all concerned (including Holmes) might have been prosecuted as accomplices in crooked gambling.

(2) "The Yellow Face"

Holmes asked to be reminded of this case if he ever showed himself overconfident. Except for the opening deductions based on the visitor's pipe it is one of the least satisfying of the tales.

(3) "The Stockbroker's Clerk"

When you discover that young Mr. Pycroft's well-paid job in the Franco-Midland Hardware Company involves no work except checking off the names of hardware-dealers in a directory of Paris, you may be reminded of the task set for the pawnbroker in "The Red-Headed League." And the reason for it is equally sinister.

(4) "The *Gloria Scott*"
Squire Trevor, father of Holmes's college friend Victor Trevor, fainted when young Holmes (then a college student) remarked on the initials tattooed on his arm. The mystery of Mr. Trevor's past is well told, but equally interesting is the glimpse of Holmes's youth.

(5) "The Musgrave Ritual"
Watson's insistence that Holmes clean up his papers brought out this strange story. Like the preceding case, it began with a friendship of Holmes's college days. The Ritual concerns one of the most precious relics of English history, and one doubts whether even "some legal bother," as Holmes says, would keep it in the private possession of the Musgraves.—Another problem is whether Watson realized that the Ritual would only be correct at a season of the year when the sun's declination was the same as at the date of the original formula.

(6) "The Reigate Puzzle"
(Known in the English editions as "The Reigate Squires.")
Holmes was recuperating from a breakdown, and he and Watson were staying with an old friend of Watson's army days. But the scrap of a note found in a dead man's hand rouses Holmes more than any tonic. We know from *The Sign of the Four* his interest in handwriting, and he sees at once that the scrap of paper is extraordinary. . . .

(7) "The Crooked Man"
This is one of the few times when Holmes left Baker Street to stay overnight in Watson's home—perhaps the

unfamiliar surroundings dulled his faculties, for the case of Colonel Barclay's death is one of the least absorbing. The best element of suspense is, what sort of animal can run up a curtain?

(8) "The Resident Patient"

A case that greatly interested Watson, since the client was a young doctor struggling to establish a reputation as a nerve specialist. Dr. Trevelyan had acquired what many young doctors dreamed of, a wealthy patient entirely under his care. But then a Russian nobleman came to consult him, and passed into a trance while the doctor was questioning him. . . .

(9) "The Greek Interpreter"

Here we meet Sherlock's older brother, Mycroft Holmes, visit the unusual Diogenes Club, and hear the mystery of Mr. Melas the interpreter, who lived in the same house with Mycroft. Mr. Melas was in great danger, and would have been killed by the ancient device of charcoal fumes, except for Watson's medical skill.

(10) "The Naval Treaty"

This problem—which Watson laid before Holmes at the appeal of Watson's former schoolmate "Tadpole" Phelps—involved a document of great import, a secret treaty between England and Italy. Mr. Phelps was entrusted with the responsibility of copying the papers, but he made the mistake of leaving them on his desk while he went for a cup of coffee. The story ends with one of the best of the Baker Street breakfasts, including ham and eggs, curried chicken, and both tea and coffee.—The easy way in which state documents are left about is always an amusing feature of the stories.

(11) "The Final Problem"

Readers were appalled by Holmes's disappearance, but at any rate Watson told the story in the right tone of voice. None of the episodes surpasses this in effective suspense and intimate suggestions of character.

THE HOUND OF THE BASKERVILLES (1902)

Probably the masterpiece. There are moments of anxiety and shock which no story in this vein has improved. From the moment when Holmes, looking at Mrs. Hudson's well-polished silver coffeepot, sees the image of Watson studying the "Penang lawyer" (a walking stick) the reader is carried in an absorption we would not spoil by giving any hints. Holmes rarely laughed and when he did so it boded ill for evildoers. Toward the end of this superb tale we hear his strident and dangerous mirth.

THE RETURN OF SHERLOCK HOLMES (1905)

(1) "The Adventure of the Empty House"

This story first appeared in *The Strand Magazine* in London, and in *Collier's Weekly* in New York, in October 1903. The American publication included the drawings by the most devoted of all Holmes's illustrators, Mr. Frederic Dorr Steele. Those who were schoolboys in 1903 can well remember how we waited for the issues of *Collier's*, and families squabbled and cried "Dibbies on it first!"

(2) "The Adventure of the Norwood Builder"

Holmes was able to refute all Lestrade's theories and rescue "the unhappy John Hector McFarlane" from suspicion of having murdered the builder. Holmes spent an hour crawling about the lawn in an August sun, discovering only some trouser buttons; but the thumbprint on the wall was the clue that made his eyes shine.

(3) "The Adventure of the Dancing Men"

One of the most famous of the stories, introducing the bizarre cipher of the little acrobatic figures. Holmes's expert study of all forms of secret writing (he was the author of a monograph *An Analysis of 160 Ciphers*) enabled him to read the threatening messages. His "knowledge of the crooks of Chicago" convinced him they meant what they said.

(4) "The Adventure of the Solitary Cyclist"

The beautiful Violet Smith, a music teacher, was not as solitary as she wished to be. As she rode on her bicycle through the picturesque countryside of Surrey she was mysteriously pursued by another rider. Holmes thought it might be only "some trifling intrigue" and sent Watson to investigate. Later Sherlock went himself, and got into a fist fight.

(5) "The Adventure of the Priory School"

Dr. Watson always thought the startling arrival of Dr. Thorneycroft Huxtable, M.A., Ph.D., one of Baker Street's most dramatic moments. What had happened to cause such despair and fatigue in this burly schoolmaster, principal of the famous Priory School and author of *Huxtable's Sidelights on Horace*? Holmes was able to give interesting sidelights on cloven feet. Experts have observed some differences between the English and American printings of Watson's sketch map of the Derbyshire moor.

(6) "The Adventure of Black Peter"

The adventure began with Holmes practising driving a harpoon into the body of a pig hung up at Allardyce's butcher shop, where Mrs. Hudson bought her meats. This had a bearing on the murder of the whaling skipper Peter Carey. The case introduces for the first time a young detective-inspector from Scotland Yard, Stanley Hopkins (born 1865), whom Holmes considered very promising.

(7) "The Adventure of Charles Augustus Milverton"

Charles Augustus Milverton was "the worst man in London," a trader in scandal and blackmail. Holmes considered him a poisonous reptile and threw down Milverton's calling card with disgust. In this brilliantly told story Holmes and Watson do a little housebreaking on their own account, and Watson is almost grabbed by the police. His wounded heel is better than in the old days, for he achieves a two-mile run across Hampstead Heath.

(8) "The Adventure of the Six Napoleons"

Even Lestrade pays handsome tribute to Holmes's masterly work in this case, and the cold reasoning temperament of the detective is moved for a moment to a human relish for applause. One reason for his success was knowing how to make use of the newspapers. And we learn that Mrs. Hudson reserved a "lumber-room" at the top of the house for Holmes's files of old papers.

(9) "The Adventure of the Three Students"

At St. Luke's College the examination paper in Greek for a valuable scholarship consisted of sight translation from Thucydides. But Mr. Soames, the lecturer in Greek, went out to tea and left the paper on his desk. Which of the three students had cheated by looking at the Greek text?

(10) "The Adventure of the Golden Pince-Nez"

It was a drenching November night when Stanley Hopkins came to consult Holmes, bringing a pair of nose glasses that had been found by the body of the victim. Holmes comforted Hopkins with a cigar and a hot toddy, but the mystery was really solved by smoking cigarettes. The case, dealing with political exiles, seems quite contemporary in tone.

(11) "The Adventure of the Missing Three-Quarter"

The telegram perplexed Holmes; it said: TERRIBLE MIS-FORTUNE, RIGHT WING THREE-QUARTER MISSING. It was queer that Watson, an old player of English Rugby football, didn't explain that this meant that one of the Cambridge team had disappeared on the eve of the Oxford–Cambridge game. Holmes and Watson go together to Cambridge to study the problem, and Holmes gets out his hypodermic syringe, but not to use on himself. However, Oxford won the game.

(12) "The Adventure of the Abbey Grange"

"Come, Watson, come! The game is afoot!" is the lively opening of this adventure, while the doctor is still abed on a cold winter morning. Again young Stanley Hopkins appeals to Holmes for assistance, and they find a tragedy in high life at the picturesque old Abbey Grange. One of the richest men in Kent has been brained with his own poker. Holmes's knowledge of port wine and sailors' knots leads to the solution.

(13) "The Adventure of the Second Stain"

"The fair sex is your department," Holmes said to Watson. What was the secret concealed by Lady Hilda Hope, "the most lovely woman in London"? Lestrade is baffled—so much so, indeed, that he now looks like a bulldog, whereas in the early days he was always compared to a ferret. This story of international intrigue and diplomatic secrets has complete charm in spite of its naïveté. In the introduction Watson tells us that Holmes has retired from London and "betaken himself to study and bee-farming on the Sussex Downs."

THE VALLEY OF FEAR (1914)

A fine and most ingenious opening starts this long story at excellent pace, but then Watson reverts to the ancient device of *A Study in Scarlet*. The long interpolation of the background story is a disappointment, and the epilogue is perfunctory and out of key. Scholars have attributed the mystical ending to the unidentified Other Hand that was active in some of the later narratives.

HIS LAST BOW (1917)

(1) "The Adventure of Wisteria Lodge"

Grotesque was a word that always put Holmes on the alert. When Mr. J. Scott Eccles telegraphed that he had had a grotesque experience Holmes was eager to hear the details. When Mr. Eccles went for an overnight visit with Señor Garcia, why did he find the house deserted in the morning?

(2) "The Adventure of the Cardboard Box"

This story, first written for the *Strand* in 1893, was withheld from book publication until 1917; the author believed it made unchivalrous reflections on female character! The very respectable Miss Cushing receives an unpleasant package in the mail: a tobacco box filled with coarse salt in which are two "very singular enclosures." When you observe Holmes suddenly staring at Miss Cushing's profile you are getting "warm."

(3) "The Adventure of the Red Circle"

"Unmitigated bleat" was Holmes's cruel description of the sentimental messages in the newspaper *Personals*, known in the London press as the Agony Column. But in his daily scrapbook of these advertisements he found a clue to the mystery of Mrs. Warren's lodger, who had not been seen for ten days and communicated with the landlady only on scraps of paper.

(4) "The Adventure of the Bruce-Partington Plans"

As in several other stories, we here find vital government secrets not very carefully guarded. But we accept the simplicity of the plot without demur for the sake of meeting again the lethargic Mycroft Holmes—who astonishes his brother by coming round to Baker Street in person.

(5) "The Adventure of the Dying Detective"
Holmes's pretense that he was dying of a fatal and rare disease, the "black Formosa corruption," was a notable piece of acting and made lifelike (or deathlike) with theatrical effects. It deceived both Mrs. Hudson and the anxious Watson; why the performance was necessary is for the reader to learn. After three days' fasting Holmes was eager for a liberal meal at Simpson's famous chophouse.

(6) "The Disappearance of Lady Frances Carfax"
When Holmes telegraphed Watson asking for a description of the Rev. Dr. Shlessinger's left ear, Watson thought it only an ill-timed jest. But as usual Holmes had his reasons. A gruesome and excellent story, and with an unexpected suggestion of romance: when Holmes deduces that Watson had had a companion in the cab, is it not the first suggestion that the doctor is courting a second Mrs. Watson?

(7) "The Adventure of the Devil's Foot"
In some moods Holmes believed this story of the Cornish Horror the strangest case he ever handled. It happened when he and Watson were vacationing in the unusual landscape of Cornwall. In their investigation both were nearly overcome by the strange effects of the West African drug, *radix pedis diaboli* or devil's foot root.

(8) "His Last Bow"
This story produces a curious effect because it is not told as usual by the faithful Watson, but by some unidentified narrator who has evidently had access to official records—perhaps Mycroft Holmes. The date is just before the out-

break of war in August 1914, and we learn how Sherlock prepared himself by two years of impersonation (as "Mr. Altamont, of Chicago," who looked like a caricature of Uncle Sam) to come to his country's aid in the hour of crisis.

THE CASE-BOOK OF SHERLOCK HOLMES (1927)

(1) "The Adventure of the Illustrious Client"

The last collection of tales, the *Case-Book*, put the zeal of Watson lovers under some strain: few of the dozen stories seem to show the old magic. This is one of the best: Holmes undertakes to rescue the beautiful Miss de Merville from her infatuation for the Austrian Baron Gruner, "perhaps the most dangerous man in Europe." He has "waxed tips of hair under his nose," like some other dangerous Teutons. Holmes's special agent in the underworld, Porky Shinwell, is called upon for help, and Dr. Watson masquerades as a collector of Chinese porcelain, but the dénouement comes by still another hand.

(2) "The Adventure of the Blanched Soldier"

Sherlock himself writes this story, partly to show Watson how he thinks it ought to be done; and also because "the good Watson had at that time deserted me for a wife, the only selfish action which I can recall in our association." It is presumed, however, that this was Watson's second selfishness. Holmes's own account of the pale-faced soldier is a grievous anticlimax; nothing else could have shown us how much he owed to Watson's charm as a writer.

(3) "The Adventure of the Mazarin Stone"

This narrative, reported by some unknown hand, is so singular a mixture of several plots and persons already familiar, that many experts have wished to exclude it from the Canon altogether. Even the arrangement of the Baker Street rooms is different from what we expect. The effect is of a story written on hearsay by some sensational journalist who had no personal knowledge of the facts.

(4) "The Adventure of the Three Gables"

In spite of intimidation Holmes goes to see why someone is so anxious to purchase Mrs. Maberley's country house with all its contents. The clue is page 245 of the manuscript of a novel, on which an embittered young author had unconsciously mixed his pronouns.

(5) "The Adventure of the Sussex Vampire"

The beautiful Peruvian wife of an English athlete (who had played football against Watson) was suspected of being a vampire. She had sucked the blood of her own child. And why was the pet spaniel paralyzed? The best thing in this queer tale is Holmes's method of indexing his scrapbooks.

(6) "The Adventure of the Three Garridebs"

A huge fortune was supposedly offered to the American Mr. Garrideb if he could find two others of the same unusual name to share it. This might not have been so difficult in the U. S.—there are three listings of a very similar name in the 1943 Manhattan telephone directory—but the real purpose (as in "The Red-Headed League" and "The Stockbroker's Clerk") was to gull a simpleton. Holmes shows unusual emotion when Watson is wounded.

(7) "The Problem of Thor Bridge"

Though late in the long series, this case ranks with the best. The introduction, though brief, is packed with valuable allusions, tells us of Dr. Watson's dispatch box in Cox's bank vault (crammed with the records of the untold stories), and mentions the solitary plane tree in the back yard on Baker Street. In America we would call it a sycamore or buttonwood. Holmes showed himself a match for the world-famous American senator, J. Neil Gibson, who looked like a debased Abraham Lincoln; and Watson again met and admired a magnificent governess.

(8) "The Adventure of the Creeping Man"
Holmes was ahead of his time in foreseeing the uses of dogs in detective work, and this case was another instance of "the peculiar behavior of the dog in the night-time." Why did Professor Presbury's faithful wolfhound attempt to attack his master? The solution lay in some dangerous experiments in modern medicine which made Holmes dubious about the future. He was already (this was 1903) thinking of "that little farm of my dreams."

(9) "The Adventure of the Lion's Mane"
A young science teacher went swimming and died in agony on the beach, apparently flogged to death. Holmes himself tells the story, and much better this time. The peaceful seclusion of his bee-farm in Sussex, where he lived alone with a housekeeper (presumably Mrs. Hudson), had improved his writing. His villa was probably at Birling Gap, west of the great promontory of Beachy Head, and near the famous chalk cliffs known as the Seven Sisters. In the garret of his house Holmes kept all the books he had gathered in a lifetime, and one of these (a volume of natural history) showed him what had happened.

(10) "The Adventure of the Veiled Lodger" .
There is also a lion's mane in this story, but quite different from the preceding one. A landlady comes to consult Holmes about her lodger, Mrs. Ronder, who has only allowed her face to be seen once in seven years. When the milkman saw her at the window he was so startled he dropped his milk. Holmes fortified himself for the meeting by one of his favorite meals (cold partridge and white wine) but even so he was shocked by the tragedy of Ronder's Circus.

(11) "The Adventure of Shoscombe Old Place"

As in "Silver Blaze," a horse and a dog are the explanation of the mystery; and here also there are legal anomalies that may puzzle students of law. Dr. Watson was always interested in horse-racing: in order to find out what was happening at the training quarters of the horse *Shoscombe Prince* (entered for the Derby) he and Holmes pretend to be fishermen and catch some trout for their supper.

(12) "The Adventure of the Retired Colourman"

When Holmes ate two boiled eggs for breakfast it meant he was on someone's trail. Not satisfied with Dr. Watson's preliminary investigation Holmes went himself to see why Mr. Amberley had been painting his strong room at a time when he would more properly have been secluded in grief and dismay. But Mr. Amberley was a chess player, "the mark of a scheming mind." The history of Sherlock Holmes ends, as it began, with the official police getting the credit.

NOTE FOR ADVANCED STUDENTS

A COMPLETE BIBLIOGRAPHY of Sherlockiana would almost require a book in itself. Vincent Starrett's *The Private Life of Sherlock Holmes* contains a valuable reference list. For the convenience of readers who may wish to pursue the subject I mention here only a few of the more important titles.

A. Conan Doyle: *Memories and Adventures*. Boston, 1924.

R. A. Knox: *Essays in Satire*. London, 1928.

Frederic Dorr Steele: *Sherlock Holmes: Farewell Appearances of William Gillette*. New York, 1929.

——: "Sherlock Holmes in Pictures." *The New Yorker*, May 22, 1937.

S. C. Roberts: *Doctor Watson*. London, 1931.

H. W. Bell: *Sherlock Holmes and Dr. Watson: The Chronology of Their Adventures*. London, 1932.

T. S. Blakeney: *Sherlock Holmes: Fact or Fiction?* London, 1932.

Vincent Starrett: *The Private Life of Sherlock Holmes*. New York, 1933 (reviewed by Elmer Davis in *The Saturday Review of Literature*, December 2, 1933).

H. W. Bell, editor: *Baker Street Studies*. London, 1934.

Walter Klinefelter: *Ex Libris A. Conan Doyle*. Chicago, 1938.

Edgar W. Smith: *Appointment in Baker Street*. New York, 1938.

——: *Baker Street and Beyond: A Sherlockian Gazetteer*. New York, 1940.

——: *Letters from Baker Street*. New York, 1942.

Vincent Starrett, editor: *221B: Studies in Sherlock Holmes*. New York, 1940.

Hesketh Pearson: *Conan Doyle: His Life and Art.* London, 1943.

Edgar W. Smith, editor: *Profile by Gaslight.* (Another collection of studies by members of the Baker Street Irregulars.) New York, 1944.

"THE BOWLING GREEN"

Kit began his column "The Bowling Green" in February 1920, when he moved from the Philadelphia *Evening Public Ledger* to the *New York Evening Post*. It appeared six days a week on the editorial page through the end of 1923, when he resigned from the *Evening Post*. "The Bowling Green" reappeared in *The Saturday Review of Literature* when the magazine began in August 1924.

The "Green" was an anthology column, common enough in its day. Like others of its ilk—Franklin Adams's "Conning Tower" in the *New York World*, Don Marquis's "Sun Dial" in the *New York Sun*—"The Bowling Green" was an eclectic collection of poems, essays, short stories, and novels (in serialization) by its "conductor" (as Kit often referred to himself). The "colyums" (to use another Morleyism) also depended on correspondence from readers and short pieces from contributors. Many eminent Sherlockians such as Vincent Starrett, Edgar W. Smith, Belden Wigglesworth, James Keddie, Sr., and W. S. Hall appeared in the "Green."

Kit also used the column to chronicle the adventures of his Three Hours for Lunch Club, which would retire to the docks, or Hoboken, or far-flung Philadelphia, for conversation and cocktails. Their meetings were often memorialized by Kit grabbing a handy book and having all present inscribe the volume (usually now wine- and ink-spotted).

The column ran regularly through the April 2, 1938 issue. (Kit continued as contributing editor to the *Review* through March 29, 1941.) The pieces included in this section give a good flavor of Kit as essayist and paragraphist. Several of the longer essays that appear in a separate section of this book originally were published in "The Bowling Green."

A MAN MAY HAVE this uncanny gift [the ability to write of life as a foreigner] and yet have no narrative art. He may not be as easy to read as our adorable old Conan Doyle, for example, who must never be forgotten as a king among story tellers. Who has begun a tale more delightfully than the opening of almost any Sherlock Holmes episode taken at random? For instance "The Adventure of the Beryl Coronet"—

> "Holmes," said I, as I stood one morning in our bow-window looking down the street, "here is a madman coming along. It seems rather sad that his relatives should allow him to come out alone."

Can that be surpassed for embarking the reader's attention?

(November 14, 1925, p. 294)

The other day I had the good fortune to meet a famous English printer who is visiting in this country; and instead of talking about Plantin and Caslon and Bruce Rogers we found ourselves, I don't know just how, embarked on a mutual questionnaire of famous incidents in the life of Sherlock Holmes. "What was the name of the doctor in 'The Speckled Band'?" he would ask; and I would counter with "Which mystery was it that was solved by the ash of a Trichinopoly cigar?" "Who was the fellow who had the orange pips set on him?" he cried; and I, "What was the adventure they cleaned up early enough in the evening to go and hear a concert at Queen's Hall?" Our hosts were startled to find us so passionately happy in this pastime, which might well have gone on for hours. We concluded that since Sir Arthur is writing some new Holmeses, the real thing to do would be a book all about Mycroft Holmes, the mysterious older brother, in which Sherlock would appear only as an amateurish and promising youngster.

(May 1, 1926, p. 755)

I promised to write a note about William Gillette's "The Astounding Crime on Torrington Road," and I haven't done so. I said I would do it aboard *Caronia*, but I know I shan't. So let me say here, with affectionate respect, that Mr. Gillette has been worthy of his high detecting associations. It is a notably ingenious tale, the best possible anodyne.

(August 20, 1927, p. 55)

There is no need for me to lament the passing of Sherlock Holmes, the ignoble dearth of good shockers.

(February 4, 1928, p. 571)

I am inclined to agree with Vincent Starrett who says (in his introduction to *Fourteen Great Detective Stories*, in the Modern Library) that he believes Mr. Austin Freeman's Dr. Thorndyke "the best detective since Sherlock Holmes."

(April 7, 1928, p. 741)

We were speaking of carelessness often committed by even the most famous writers of detective stories. One thing that has often interested me is how an obvious error will persist through innumerable editions, no one ever taking the trouble to correct it. I believe that the discrepancy in dates in Conan Doyle's story "The Red-Headed League" has continued through all editions (in this country at least) since the story was published in 1891. Vincent Starrett reprints it unchanged in his recent collection *Fourteen Great Detective Stories*.

(April 21, 1928, p. 785)

The pleasantest reading encountered lately was S. C. Roberts: *Doctor Watson*, one of Faber and Faber's Criterion Miscellany pamphlets (one shilling in London). Mr. Roberts, distinguished Johnsonian, offers a biographical reconstruction of Sherlock Holmes's friend and attempts to resolve the famous problem of Dr. Watson's marriages. A delightful bit of serio-spoof, a Must item for all Holmesians. The first Mrs. Watson (née Mary Morstan, you remember) died during the period between 1891 and 1894 while Holmes was supposed to be dead in Reichenbach gorge. But Holmes himself, in the story of the *Blanched Soldier*, speaks of another Mrs. Watson existing in 1903.

Mr. Roberts has carefully studied all the clues and offers the ingenious suggestion that the Deutero–Mrs. Watson was the cool and aristocratic (but also imprudent) Miss Violet de Merville of the story *The Illustrious Client*. Mr. Roberts says:—

> Watson's second marriage took place at the end of 1902 or at the beginning of 1903, a few months after the affair of the Illustrious Client. Now this adventure must have made a more than ordinary impression upon Watson's mind. Instinctively chivalrous, he was a man to whom a woman in trouble made a specially vivid appeal. Violet de Merville, moreover, was "beautiful, accomplished, a wonder-woman in every way." After the terrible exposure of the true character of her fiancé, what more natural than that Watson should, after a fitting interval, make inquiries as to her recovery of health and spirits? It may be objected that Miss de Merville moved in exalted circles, and that a retired practitioner would not have the *droit d'entrée* to her society. But here a significant fact must be considered. Miss de Merville's father was a soldier, and a soldier who had won distinction in Afghanistan—"de Merville of Khyber fame." With such a father-in-law Watson would at once be on common ground.

Mr. Roberts goes on to the specially ingenious suggestion that the story (*The Mazarin Stone*) which follows the first allusion to Watson's second marriage may be from the hand of Mrs. Watson II. It is not told by Dr. Watson himself, and it may well be that in the preoccupation of resuming medical practice, the good doctor turned over to this accomplished lady the task of editing one of the memoirs. The objections to Mr. Roberts's theory are grave, however. In the first place we nowhere learn, in the story of the *Illustrious Client,* that Dr. Watson actually met Miss de Merville; Holmes speaks of it as a possibility ("Perhaps you may meet her before we are through"), but Watson himself makes no comment. It was about the 14th of September 1902 when the horrid episode of Baron Gruner and the vitriol took place. After so serious a shock it would have taken Miss de Merville some time to recover. We know that she was fond of Mediterranean cruising; I think it most probable that she would have gone for a winter voyage to recuperate; and it is improbable that she could have already become Mrs. Watson by January 1903.

The other possible candidate for Dr. Watson's hand would be Kitty Winter; she was imprisoned for vitriol-throwing but given "the lowest possible sentence." On the whole I fear that Mr. Roberts's theory, though very tempting, is difficult to accept.

But his essay, together with that of Father Ronald Knox in *Studies in Satire,* is a necessary addition to the Holmes–Watson codex.

(March 7, 1931, p. 645)

In having a ransack among some books before locking them up for the winter, I wondered why we hear so much about first editions and fine copies and not nearly enough about the chance examples and shabby second-hand culls that we more frequently encounter. Does no one else take pleasure in phony copies, piracies, wretched reprints jobbed off for mail-order sets and department store trading? Consider Conan Doyle for instance: what an oddly miscellaneous spectacle is the collection of any average Doyle enthusiast. My own fortuitous gathering of Doyles ranges (by gift or purchase) from the bound volumes of *The Strand Magazine* for 1891–93 in which Holmes's adventures and memoirs first appeared, down to S. C. Roberts's admirable pamphlet *Doctor Watson* (which no one has yet printed in this country) attempting to clear up the mystery of Watson's second marriage. I have some genuine firsts among them, but not less prized are the queer and abominable copies picked up from time to time at hazard. My American edition of *The Stark Munro Letters* (Appleton '95) has the rubber stamp of the Y.M.C.A. Library, Montreal. *Beyond the City*, vilely impressed on brittle yellowing paper, was sponsored by F. Tennyson Neely, 1894. *A Study in Scarlet* is one of a set imprinted W. R. Caldwell and Co. *The Firm of Girdlestone* carries the name of Siegel Cooper & Co., New York and Chicago. Most mysterious of the lot is *A Case of Identity and Other Stories*, from The Optimus Printing Company, 45–51 Rose Street, New York. I wonder where Rose Street is? Next after Oscar Wilde, poor old Conan Doyle must have been utilized by more will-o'-the-wisp publishers than any other modern writer. These casual oddities of imprint always give me much innocent pleasure.

(October 17, 1931, p. 203)

Some time ago we lent W. S. H. [William S. Hall] a copy of that delightful book, *A Duet*, by A. Conan Doyle. W. S. H. read it on shipboard and though he does not moisten easily he reported that his eyes were damp when he finished. It is the day by day story of a young married couple; it immediately became W. S. H.'s favorite Doyle, and in his customary diligence he rooted about until he found some autograph letters from Doyle concerning the book's original publication. And the pleasantest discovery he made was that good sentimental Dr. Doyle left his regular publisher and gave the MS to Grant Richards—then a beginner in the field—because "this book *ought* to be published by a young married couple."

169

W. S. H. discovered the following letter written (1898) by Doyle:—

UNDERSHAW,
HINDHEAD,
HASLEMERE.

My dear Grant Richards

The only valid reason I can ever give a publisher for quitting him is that I can get better terms. So if I come to you with "A Duet" my terms must be high. But they would be put in a convenient form . . . as thus.

1. No advance.
2. Half yearly accounts.
3. Two shillings per copy on 6/ book.
4. You guarantee to fairly spend £100 in advertising.
5. The form to be such as I approve.

How does this strike you? If too high or too anything then let me know at once.

I propose to sacrifice the serial rights of this book and bring it out at once in book form. This will in itself be an interesting experiment & should, I believe, help the sale of the book materially. To bring it out at a low price would be a second experiment and I think it would be well to try one experiment at a time. Therefore let it be 6/.

The book will be from 60 to 70000 words. Over 50000 are done—so it should be ready for appearance early in March. I shall have what I have done typed without delay.

This is only the English rights of course.

I am on very friendly terms with Smith and must return to him, so don't be hurt when I do so with my next book. The fact is that this book *ought* to be published by a young married couple and so I give you the refusal of it.

I shall be in town on Wednesday morning if you wanted to see me on any point—but I shall be rather rushed.

With kind regards

Yours very truly,
A. CONAN DOYLE

(December 24, 1932, p. 342)

170

I have not looked up the data, but if, as an astrologer has suggested, Sherlock Holmes was most likely born in January, some observance is due. Therefore, if the matter has never been settled, I nominate January 6th (the date of this issue of the *Saturday Review*) as his birthday, and reproduce herewith a new portrait, specially done for the occasion by our staff artist W. S. H. (The year of Holmes's birth is thought to be 1853.)

SHERLOCK HOLMES.

(January 7, 1933, p. 367)

On a recent romantic visit to Mexico City, W. S. H. found at the American bookshop there a Tauchnitz edition of a Conan Doyle story new to him and to us—*The Poison Belt*, one of the adventures of the bristly scientist Professor Challenger. W. S. H. points to a passage in that story as the high apex of British temperament. Professor Challenger is speaking to his faithful and well-trained man-servant:—

171

"I'm expecting the end of the world to-day, Austin."
"Yes, sir. What time, sir."
"I can't say, Austin. Before evening."
"Very good, sir."

Another of Conan Doyle's pleasant minutiæ in the Professor Challenger stories is emphasizing the prickly temper of the scientist by calling his home "The Briars," Rotherfield.

(February 25, 1933, p. 450)

F. M. M. [Felix M. Morley, C. M.'s younger brother], who has been reading Vincent Starrett's *Private Life of Sherlock Holmes* with much pleasure, adds another proof of Mr. Starrett's contention that Holmes has passed over from fiction to actuality. In the story *The Final Problem* Watson wrote that an account of Holmes's death was printed in the *Journal de Genève* of May 4, 1891 (or some such date)—and M. Chapuiset, the present editor of that excellent paper, says that every year he receives letters asking for copies of that issue.

(November 25, 1933, p. 290)

The Bowstring Murders by Carr Dickson (and published by Morrow) begins very well, just what doddering Digby needed; he has a bulimy for Gothic castles and shrieks at night; but he wondered on page 3 about the chaps taking a train from *Charing Cross* to Suffolk. It's very important that mystery-story-writers don't get their London railway stations mixed up. Sherlock Holmes never did. Our impression is that all trains to East Anglia leave from *Liverpool Street*. Can one go to Suffolk from *Charing Cross*?

(December 23, 1933, p. 371)

SHERLOCK HOLMES AND COCKTAILS

Sir:— Last year—on what evidence I cannot guess—you announced that January 6 was the date of Sherlock Holmes's birthday, and 1853 the probable year. That seemed to be about right: I remember that the beautiful Irene Adler, "*the* woman," the only one toward whom Sherlock might conceivably have felt an impulse of sentiment, was born ("in New Jersey") in 1858. (Where in New Jersey, I wonder?)

Anyhow, every year about Christmas time I get out my Conan Doyles and read Sherlock again. And your comment lately about cocktails having gone back to 25 cents reminded me that Holmes considered even that price a trifle high. In *The Adventure of the Noble Bachelor*, you remember, he examines a hotel bill in which a cocktail costs a shilling and a glass of sherry 8d. He deduces that the bill was from "one of the most expensive hotels."

Will not the Hotel Duane on Madison Avenue, which you say is frequented by Sherlock Holmes's publishers, invent a Sherlock Holmes cocktail in honor of the birthday? I will offer the 2-volume edition of the Complete Stories as a prize for the most appropriate formula.—Of course there should really be two; the *Sherlock* and the *Mycroft*. What a subtle and softly influential philtre the *Mycroft* would have to be!

Another thought: what evidence can you give of Sherlock's religious feelings, if any?

CHARING CROSS

St. George, Staten Island

I like Mr. Cross's suggestion about the cocktail, and will be pleased to forward for his judgment any suggested formulæ. In regard to Irene Adler ("a face that a man might die for" was Holmes's astonishing description) I have always maintained that she was born in Hoboken.

Of Holmes's religious feelings: I've always supposed that the beginning of his atheistic tendency was the fact that if he hadn't been on his way to the college chapel he wouldn't have been bitten by Trevor's bull terrier. (See the story of the *Gloria Scott*.) It must have been a bad bite; he was laid up for ten days. But he was a student of the Bible (see *The Crooked Man*).

(January 6, 1934, p. 395)

THE BAKER STREET IRREGULARS

Sir:— Since you have resumed the annual *escarmouche* about Sherlock Holmes, may I point out that Mr. Vincent Starrett, in his recent agreeable memoir, is surely in error in saying, "It was in 1902 that Conan Doyle received his knighthood from a grateful Queen." The Queen died in January, 1901.

Whatever beverage your Holmes-and-Watson club chooses for its ceremonial luncheon, it had better not be the wine of Beaune. For the good Doctor told us (*The Sign of Four*, chapter I) that Beaune at lunch made him irritable.

GASOGENE

(January 20, 1934, p. 423)

E. R. (Kalamazoo, Michigan), who has been reading *Jack Robinson* by George Beaton, writes: "That man Beaton can make the wettest rain I ever read in a book, it made me worry all afternoon because the cistern hadn't been cleaned."

She adds a tribute to Sherlock Holmes which will please the Baker Street Irregulars:—

Probably no character in fiction was ever loved or so universally known as Sherlock, and probably no other one character ever gave quite so much—courage and tolerance and joy. When everything else has gone stale and I have reached "the last ditch"—and it seems as if I must plunge out of my slough of desperation and futility, I can talk it out with Holmes and Dr. Watson in Baker St.—and go away laughing at my folly and weakness.

* * *

W. S. H., secretary of the Baker Street Irregulars, has allowed us to look over the minutes of the first meeting of the club. Among other business it appears that the matter of an official toast was discussed. It was agreed that the first health must always be drunk to "*The* Woman." Suggestions for succeeding sentiments, which will have their own overtones for all genuine Holmesians, were:—"Mrs. Hudson," "Mycroft," "The Second Mrs. Watson," "The game is afoot!" and "The second most dangerous man in London."

Also agreed that the club rooms must be exactly seventeen steps up, and the first furnishings to be a gasogene and a tantalus.

(January 27, 1934, p. 439)

THE BAKER STREET IRREGULARS

Of course it is for the study of just such savory problems [referring to a letter by Vincent Starrett about "the Moriarty brothers, James and James"] that the BAKER STREET IRREGULARS propose to meet together. One of the most soundly documented Holmesians now comes forward with a suggested Constitution for the club. It runs as follows:—

ARTICLE I

The name of this society shall be the Baker Street Irregulars.

ARTICLE II

Its purpose shall be the study of the Sacred Writings.

ARTICLE III

All persons shall be eligible for membership who pass an examination in the Sacred Writings set by officers of the society, and who are considered otherwise suitable.

ARTICLE IV

The officers shall be: a Gasogene, a Tantalus, and a Commissionaire.

175

The duties of the Gasogene shall be those commonly performed by a President.

The duties of the Tantalus shall be those commonly performed by a Secretary.

The duties of the Commissionaire shall be to telephone down for ice, White Rock, and whatever else may be required and available; to conduct all negotiations with waiters; and to assess the members pro rata for the cost of same.

BUY LAWS

(1) An annual meeting shall be held on January 6th, at which toasts shall be drunk which were published in the *Saturday Review* of January 27th, 1934; after which the members shall drink at will.

(2) The current round shall be bought by any member who fails to identify, by title of story and context, any quotation from the Sacred Writings submitted by any other member.

Qualification A.—If two or more members fail so to identify, a round shall be bought by each of those so failing.

Qualification B.—If the submitter of the quotation, upon challenge, fails to identify it correctly, he shall buy the round.

(3) Special meetings may be called at any time or any place by any one of three members, two of whom shall constitute a quorum.

Qualification A.—If said two are of opposite sexes, they shall use care in selecting the place of meeting, to avoid misinterpretation (or interpretation, either, for that matter).

Qualification B.—If such two persons of opposite sexes be clients of the Personal Column of the *Saturday Review*, the foregoing does not apply; such persons being presumed to let their consciences be their guides.

(4) All other business shall be left for the monthly meeting.

(5) There shall be no monthly meeting.

ELMER DAVIS

(February 17, 1934, p. 491)

326—DOYLE (A. CONAN). THE MEMOIRS OF SHERLOCK
HOLMES. 1894. £10. The Earl of Rosebery's copy bought
by him on publication when he was Prime Minister of
England and with his 10 Downing Street bookplate. At the
end of the book he has written "again March, 1895 again
Feb. 18, 1901."

This item, which Stephen Benét found in Elkin Mat-
thews' latest catalogue, should really be entered in the
records of the Baker Street Irregulars.

(February 24, 1934, p. 507)

TWO SUPPRESSED HOLMES EPISODES

The number of allusions to Conan Doyle lately seems to
me symptomatic of a widespread revival of interest in that
admirable writer. A healthy sign, indeed; personally I
confess a deliberated assurance that more intellectual vita-
min, and even more sound bourgeois sociology, is to be
found in Doyle than in a large number of Keyserlings and
Spenglers. Good old Sir Arthur! is it not odd how poor a
judge he was of his own work? He singled out as his favorites
those obviously third-rate *Tales of Long Ago*, sentimental
gouache (or do I mean goulash?) of Roman legionaries and
Christian martyrs, etc. . . .

But to the point. If Mr. Vincent Starrett or other Baker
Street Irregulars wish the Sherlock Holmes codex to be
complete they must look at two stories in which Holmes is
not mentioned by name but where he is certainly present
by allusion. The episodes were probably suppressed by
Watson because Holmes guesses wrong both times. The
stories are *The Lost Special* and *The Man with the Watches*, both
mystery tales laid in railway trains; and Holmes's interest
in railroad romance is of course familiar to all. In *The Lost
Special*, dealing with the complete disappearance between
Liverpool and Manchester of a special train on June 3,

177

1890, you will find Holmes referred to as "an amateur reasoner of some celebrity at that date." He wrote a letter to the London *Times* of July 3, 1890, in which the familiar Sherlockian principle was stated: "When the impossible has been eliminated the residuum, *however improbable*, must contain the truth."

In the case of *The Man with the Watches*, which "filled many columns of the daily press in the spring of the year 1892," again we learn that "a well-known criminal investigator" wrote at length to the *Daily Gazette* giving his own reconstruction of the mystery. The letter has all the internal evidences of Holmes's style, though not at his best reasoning power; but it is the more interesting because this was during the time when Holmes—supposed by Watson to be dead—was travelling in Tibet. Even at that distance this remarkable man kept in touch with outrages in Britain. His special interest in this case was undoubtedly the fact that the persons involved were Americans. The number of American malefactors in Holmes's career has often been noted. Does not the typical Sherlockian touch appear in this remark about the unfortunate young man with the watches—"He was probably an American, and also probably a man of weak intellect."

You will find these two stories in the excellent omnibus volume *The Conan Doyle Stories* (John Murray, London, 1200 pp. for 7/6) which reprints all the doctor's short stories other than the Holmes episodes. It has been circulating in England for nearly five years. Among the many mysteries associated with Doyle none is more odd than the enigma of no publisher having issued it here.

(March 3, 1934, p. 523; also in *Streamlines*)

STUDIES ON BAKER STREET

The Speckled Band, the play about Sherlock Holmes written by Conan Doyle himself (the drama known as *Sherlock*

Holmes was written by William Gillette), should be a Must item for the Baker Street Irregulars. (It is published by Samuel French, 25 West 45, and can be had for 75 cents in their paper-bound Acting Edition.) It offers many interesting speculations for the Holmesian researcher. In any imaginative reconstruction of the famous sitting room at 221B Baker Street we must certainly take into account the diagram printed in this book showing the arrangement of the stage-setting. This was presumably plotted by Sir Arthur himself at the time of the first production (Adelphi Theatre, London, June 4, 1910). There are several surprises, notably that above the fireplace is indicated a large settee. ("6 ft. double-ended Chesterfield couch" says the Property Plot.) This is sad, for we had always liked to think of the two armchairs before the hearth, and did not Watson once say that Holmes always kept them so anticipating a visit from the Doctor? More serious still, in the long list of props and furnishings drawn up by Doyle for the sitting-room scene— with "amorous precision," we must suppose—there is no gasogene, no tantalus. And where is the work-table for chemical experiments?

Perhaps after Dr. Watson left Baker Street the landlady, Mrs. Hudson, became more actively supervisory in cleaning the room. I seem to detect her hand in the Property Plot where we are told that there are "four books" on the center table, "four books" on the occasional table in the window recess, and "four books bound in red" on the mantelpiece. That mechanical neatness of disposition was surely not Holmes. One of the volumes, of course, was Winwood Reade's *Martyrdom of Man*. What were the others? Clark Russell, undoubtedly; and if only it had been published in time, Dr. Watson would have Lyman Stowe's *Saints, Sinners and Beechers*.

There is, I repeat, much material in the play of *The Speckled Band* for Mr. Vincent Starrett, Mr. Elmer Davis and other students. There are interesting inconsistencies

179

between the cast of characters listed for the original production and the text of the play as printed. One character, a Mrs. Soames, who had an "American stamped envelope and newspaper cutting" in the Property Plot, has vanished altogether. Who was Mrs. Soames? Dr. Grimesby Roylott of the story becomes Rylott in the play; his stepdaughters Helen and Julia Stoner become Enid and Violet Stonor. Best of all, we observe that it was Dr. Rylott's old butler who was perhaps the first to utter a very contemporary phrase. Of the brutal doctor he ejaculates: "What a man! What a man!"

You will be excited to learn (at least I hope you will) that Dr. Watson's fiancée, Miss Morstan, had red hair.

I leave these matters to be followed up in detail by the experts. But I wish I could get hold of the text of the William Gillette play—apparently it has not been published in this country.

(April 21, 1934, p. 647; also in *Streamlines*)

NEWS FROM BAKER STREET

Mr. A. G. Macdonell—whose *England, Their England* you may remember as a book of most engaging humor—writes from Godalming, Surrey, that the English *Sherlock Holmes Society* has organized and sends greetings to our own *Baker Street Irregulars*. The S. H. S. is to hold its first dinner on June 6th at a restaurant in Baker Street. "June 6th being Derby Day," says Mr. Macdonell, "it was felt that Silver Blaze might well be discussed together with Holmes's extraordinary conduct in running a faked horse."

H. G., prowling along the Rambla de los Estudios in Barcelona, found in a second-hand bookstore a copy of *Les Aventures du Fils de Sherlock Holmes* ("racontées par le Docteur Watson"). This entertaining work was published—no date given, but my guess is about 20 years ago—by Richonnier, 40 rue des Saints Pères, Paris. Dr. Watson settles in New York City in the Late Hansom Cab era and becomes a wealthy and fashionable physician to the Four Hundred. I shall report on this more in detail presently.

(May 12, 1934, p. 690)

SHERLOCK HOLMES CROSSWORD

Lovers of Sherlock Holmes will understand the pleasure with which we received the following letter. It is good to know that our old friend Tobias Gregson, late of Scotland Yard, is still with us. His manner of correspondence has changed not at all since he wrote the famous letter (Chapter III of *A Study in Scarlet*) which was the beginning of so many adventures. He writes from his retirement in Dorset; undoubtedly his love for the full name led him to that county where so many villages have double nomination.

Here is the letter:—

The Laurels, Toller Porcorum, Dorset
10th April 1934

My dear Mr. Christopher Morley:

I have noticed the fun which you gentlemen are having with what you call the Baker Street Irregulars; indeed, the whole affair recalls old times to me. It is not for me to comment on where your correspondents are amiss; but I should like to ask whether Mr. Elmer Davis, who is interested in the Moriarty family, is one of your wealthy book collectors? If so, I know of something that would be to his advantage. I need say no more at this moment; I shall leave everything *in statu quo* until I hear from you. I would esteem it a great kindness if you would favour me with the information,

In the mean time, the name of your club reminded me of an item I picked up a year or more ago at the Diogenes Club. I had to go there to see a late chief of mine who,

181

CROSS-WORD 221 B
(BAKER STREET IRREGULARS)

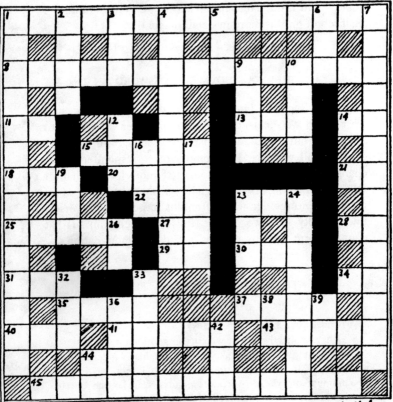

Mycroft Holmes

ACROSS

1 A treatise on this, written at the age of twenty-one, had a European vogue and earned its author a professorship. (2 words, 8, 7)

8 It was of course to see these that Holmes enquired the way from Saxe-Coburg Square to the Strand. (2 words, 10, 5)

11 How the pips were set. (2)

13 Not an Eley's No. 2 (which is an excellent argument with a gentleman who can twist steel pokers into knots) but the weapon in the tragedy of Birlstone. (3)

14 What was done on the opposite wall in bullet-pocks by the patriotic Holmes. (2)

15 What Watson recognized when he put his hand on Bartholomew Sholto's leg. (5)

18 Where Watson met young Stamford, who introduced him to Sherlock Holmes. (3)

20 A kind of pet, over which Dr. Grimesby Roylott hurled the local blacksmith. (4)

21 Holmes should have said this before being so sure of catching the murderers of John Openshaw. (2)

22 The kind of Pedro whence came the tiger. (3)

23 Though he knew the methods, Watson sometimes found it difficult to do this. (3)

25 Patron saint of old Mr. Farquhar's affliction and perhaps of Abe Slaney's men. (5)

27 Perhaps a measure of Holmes's chemicals. (2)

28 In short, Watson. (2)

29 ☿ ☿ (2)

30 Curious that he did nothing in the night-time. (3)

31 This would obviously not describe the empty house opposite 221b Baker Street. (2)

34 It seems likely that Watson's elder brother suffered from this disease. (2)

35 Though you might have taken this at Lodge 29, Chicago, nevertheless, you had to pass a test as well at Lodge 341, Vermissa. (4)

37 The Star of Savannah. (4)

40 Mrs. Barclay's reproach (in The Crooked Man, of course) suggests the parable of this. (3)

41 Scrawled in blood-red letters across the bare plaster at No. 3, Lauriston Gardens. (5)

43 Holmes found this, because he was looking for it, in the muddy hollow where John Straker was killed. (5)

44 Suggests Jonathan Small's leg. (3)

45 The brother who left Watson no choice but to relate The Final Problem. (2 words, 5, 8)

DOWN

1 A country district in the west of England where "Cooee" was a common signal. (2 words, 8, 6)

2 Charles Augustus Milverton dealt with no niggard hand; therefore this would not describe him. (4)

3 The kind of practice indulged by Mr. Williamson, the solitary cyclist's unfrocked clergyman—"there was a man of that name in orders, whose career has been a singularly dark one." (3)

4 There is comparatively as much sense in Hafiz. Indeed, it's a case of identity. (3 words, 2, 2, 6)

5 Caused the rift in the beryl coronet. (3)

6 Many of Holmes's opponents had cause to — (3)

7 Begins: "Whose was it?" "His who is gone." "Who shall have it?" "He who will come." (2 words, 8, 6)

9 of four. (4)

10 The number of Napoleons plus the number of the Randall gang. (4)

12 One of the five sent "S. H. for J. O." (3)

16 To save the dying detective trouble, Mr. Culverton Smith was kind enough to give the signal by turning this up. (3)

17 The blundering constable who failed to gain his sergeant's stripes in the Lauriston Gardens Mystery. (5)

19 One was mentioned by Boscombe Pool; yet it was illusory. There was a giant one of Sumatra; yet it was unwritten. (3)

23 How Watson felt after the Final Problem. (3)

24 He was epollicate. (8)

26 Initials of the second most dangerous man in London. (2)

32 Though Miss Mary Sutherland's boots were not unlike, they were really odd ones; the one having this slightly decorated, and the other plain. (3)

33 You may forgive the plural form of these tobaccos, since Holmes smoked so much of them. (5)

36 Behind this Black Jack of Ballarat waited and smoked an Indian cigar, of the variety which are rolled in Rotterdam. (4)

38 and 39 The best I can make of these is the Latin for the sufferers of the epidemic which pleased Holmes so extremely that he said "A long shot, Watson, a very long shot," and pinched the Doctor's arm. (4)

42 One of the two in the cardboard box. (3)

44 Initials of the street in which Mycroft lodged. (2)

from having seen too much of the world, had become unsociable enough to be a member. He knew that I had been a friend of Mr. Mycroft Holmes, and handed me a scrap of club notepaper which had been found in the crack between the arm and the seat of Mr. Mycroft's favourite armchair. It was an unfinished sketch for a cross-word puzzle; with the heading at the top "No. 221B," and "Baker Street Irregulars," to explain the design. Certain squares were shaded more heavily than others, to bring the initials S. H. out of the pattern. There is evidence to show that Mr. Mycroft was proud of it, for the sketch, though roughly drawn and as yet unnumbered, was signed "Mycroft Holmes." I conjecture that it was intended as a friendly greeting from Mr. Mycroft to his favourite brother; but that he lacked the energy to post it, and it was lost till my late chief happened to find it and give it to me.

In my retirement, I regularly read the agony columns and do the daily cross-words in the *Times* and *Telegraph*; childish pastimes, I admit, but if one is energetic and has some knowledge of the classics, one must do something. So I derived pleasure from fitting my own clues to Mr. Mycroft Holmes's cross-word, and send it to you as an intelligence-test (such as we used to have at the Yard) for your "Irregulars." All the clues are as simple as A. B. C. to any student of Mr. Sherlock Holmes's cases. It is not intended to be a real puzzler; I should expect a man of say Lestrade's ability to do it all in half an hour.

> Yours faithfully,
> TOBIAS GREGSON.

I think perhaps Mr. Gregson—"the smartest of the Scotland Yarders," you remember—a little underestimates the time this puzzle may require for full solution. It took me considerably longer than half an hour; largely because there are some little jokes concealed in the clues which are more ingenious than I had expected. I can't help thinking that it was Mycroft, rather than Gregson, who devised some of them.

I will delay printing the solution of the crossword for two weeks, to give our clients plenty of time to consider it. All those who send me correct solutions—but they must be correct *in every detail*—will automatically become members of the Baker Street Irregulars.

> (May 19, 1934, p. 703; also as *A Sherlock Holmes Crossword Puzzle*)

Speaking of detectives, the always ingenious bookseller George Bates, of 5a Shepherd House, Shepherd Street, London, W.1, has issued a catalogue concisely entitled *Murder*. It is a list of books "illustrating the development of the Detective and Mystery Story," and it is dedicated "to that most lovable and egregious ass, My Dear Watson." The Gutenberg of detectives, remarks Bates, was the famous Frenchman Vidocq (1775–1857), and he offers for £20 a collection of over 60 original letters to and from Vidocq dealing with his cases in the 1830's and '40's. Are the *Memoirs of Vidocq* still in print? That's a book probably well worth reading.

Mr. Bates lists a long run of titles by Anna Katherine Green, going back as far as 1881. Comparative dates gleaned from this catalogue are interesting. Hornung's Raffles began his career in 1899. Arthur Morrison's Martin Hewitt dates back to '94. Freeman's Dr. Thorndyke to 1908 or thereabouts; Arsène Lupin to '09; A. E. W. Mason's Hanaud to 1910; Father Brown to 1911. Ernest Bramah's superb blind detective, Max Carrados, appeared in 1914. Mr. Bailey's Reggie Fortune is still quite a newcomer, 1920.

According to Bates two of the most popular detective romances from France are Gaston Leroux: *The Mystery of the Yellow Room* and Fortuné du Boisgobey: *The Crime of the Opera House*, neither of which we have read. One of the most difficult titles to find in an early printing is Fergus Humes's *The Mystery of a Hansom Cab*, published the same

185

year as Doyle's *Study in Scarlet* (1887). The earliest printing in the British Museum is marked "225th Thousand"; the copy offered by Bates is marked "175th Thousand." Mr. Bates fears that these figures may have been printed on more or less at random by "The Hansom Cab Publishing Co." as a come-on.

Authors' feelings about their own books are often surprising. In one of the prefaces of the collected edition of his Works we find Conan Doyle speaking of "Professor Challenger, a character who has always amused me more than any other which I have invented." Surely he must, for the moment, have forgotten Brigadier Gerard.

(May 26, 1934, p. 715)

DR. WATSON IN FRENCH

The anonymous French author of *Les Aventures du Fils de Sherlock Holmes*, to which we alluded before, has entered with much understanding into the character of Doctor Watson. If the worthy doctor were to have emigrated to New York, and there become a fashionable practitioner, he would doubtless act and think much as described. Holmes, according to the French Autolycus, inherited a huge estate in Devonshire, where "he led the existence of a gentleman, divided between the care of his property and the education of his children." His oldest son, Sherlock Jr., graduated at 23 from the College of Physicians and Surgeons in London and at 26 we find him, at his father's express desire, acting as assistant to Watson who holds a chair at the Post-Graduate Hospital in New York. But Watson also has a wealthy private practice and lives in solid comfort on West 57th Street. His patients are all members of "la haute société New-Yorkaise."

But old Watson finds Holmes Jr. very different from his austere and misogynist father. He is more than a little shocked by young Sherlock's luxurious quarters in an expensive bachelor apartment called the "Croyendon" on 43rd Street, near Fifth Avenue. Junior is the idol of the "Tenderloin," which our Frenchman explains is New York's region of gilded society. He has a box at the Opera, spends his vacations at Narragansett Pier, plays bridge "as skilfully as Elwell," drives a fast Panhard, collects sumptuous bibelots and modern French paintings, frequents the Waldorf, Sherry's, Shanley's, and Delmonico's. The period of the stories appears to be about 1910.

By an ingenious variation of the traditional situation, Dr. Watson suspects (with horror) that his assistant is guilty of the murder of Helen Clawson, a beautiful young governess found dead in a building contractor's shack on Central Park West. But by the aid of a couple of delightful young women from the Riverside telephone exchange, young Sherlock is able to show what actually happens. He proves not only his inherited acumen but also the value of a wide feminine acquaintance. His tall slender figure, pale aquiline face, and always elegant attire ("suivant son habitude le jeune dandie était en frac") are very attractive to ladies.

The three stories in this volume are considerably entertaining. One is bound to enjoy the mixed humor and simplicity of the French Watson. When a wealthy patient offers them champagne, he remarks "Je ne contrarie jamais mes malades. Je bus donc. Holmes, lui, oublia de boire; il ne sera jamais un médecin de famille."—And when one of Watson's lady invalids is in a low nervous state, he tells us that "Desiring to drive away sad thoughts from her mind, I set to work to tell her some of my best and most amusing stories of the clinic."

I wish the Publications Richonnier, 40 rue des Saints Pères, Paris, would tell us the author of these yarns; he must have visited New York at some time or other. Was more than one collection issued?

(May 26, 1934, p. 715)

I print today the correct solution of the Sherlock Holmes crossword puzzle. (Bowling Green, May 19.) Up to the time of this week's issue going to press, six answers had been received which were exact in every respect. These were from:

M. S. Packard (Brooklyn); Stuart Robertson (Philadelphia); Harvey Officer (N. Y. City); Walter Klinefelter (Glen Rock, Pa.); Vincent Starrett (Chicago); Emily S. Coit (Pensacola, Fla.).

The strictly correct answer in 31 across should be *let*, but as the middle letter is unkeyed and *lit* would also be a reasonable answer, solutions offering this, and otherwise entirely letter-perfect, are acceptable and were submitted by:—

Elmer Davis (N. Y. City); Mrs. C. C. Williams (South Hamilton, Mass.); C. Warren Force (N. Y. City); Allan M. Price (N. Y. City); J. DeLancey Ferguson (Cleveland); Velma Long (Winamac, Indiana).

Solutions which were almost wholly correct, but failed in one word only, submitted by:—

Earle Walbridge (N. Y. City); Katherine A. Fellows (Cummington, Mass.); W. S. Hall (N. Y. City); Harrison L. Reinke (Lakeville, Conn.); George Lowther (N. Y. City); Laurence P. Dodge (N. Y. City); R. K. Leavitt (N. Y. City); Malcolm Johnson (Garden City, L. I.).

A number of correspondents pointed out that Mr. Tobias Gregson was in error (in the clue to 16 down) in speaking of "Mr. Chelverton Smith." They remark that it should be "Culverton Smith," and the correction seems just.

Mr. Vincent Starrett accompanied his solution with the interesting news that Constable (London) is to publish in June a volume *Baker Street Studies*, edited by Harold Bell. Mr. Starrett says: "Contributors include Dorothy Sayers, Fr. Ronald Knox, S. C. Roberts, Vernon Rendall, A. G. Macdonell, Helen Simpson, Bell himself and V. S.; Knox has done a paper on *Mycroft*; I have written at considerable length on *Mrs. Hudson* and her entourage. The others deal with highly specialized matters: Miss Sayers, I believe, has settled the argument about Holmes's college career (in favor of Cambridge), and Helen Simpson has shown up poor old Watson's professional limitations."

I cannot help hoping that whoever publishes this alluring volume on this side will put on it the imprint of the Baker Street Irregulars. Mycroft's crossword puzzle would make an appropriate appendix.

(June 2, 1934, p. 727)

AGONY COLUMN

Sir:— You have given a good deal of attention lately to Sherlock Holmes. Did you ever notice, in *The Red Circle*, his comment on the Personals (or "Agony") columns of the London papers? The *Saturday Review*, whose column of Personals has proved such a refreshing and valuable feature, will surely enjoy being reminded of Sherlock's remark:

"What a chorus of groans, cries, and bleatings! What a rag-bag of singular happenings! Surely the most valuable hunting-ground that ever was given to a student of the unusual!"

MORIARTY JR.

Lancaster, Pa.

(June 16, 1934, p. 755)

BAKER STREET IRREGULARS

Supplementary report on the Sherlock Holmes crossword puzzle:

Correct solutions were also sent in by Doris E. Barton, Hartford, Conn.; Dorothy E. Dawson, Salem, Va.; Harry W. Hazard Jr., Montclair, N. J.; Henry H. Jackson and family, Barre, Vt.; Joyce and George Guernsey Jr., University City, Mo.; Staff of Mrs. Cowlin's Open Book Shop, Elgin, Ill.; Norman C. Ford, Springfield, Mass.; Ruth M. Cowdell, Hartford, Conn.; Benjamin March, Ann Arbor, Mich.

Solutions nearly correct, but erring in one or more minutiæ, from: Alexander W. Williams, Boston; L. H. and F. E. Fry, Oakmont, Pa.; Dr. Adele B. Cohn, Newark, N. J.; Basil Davenport, N. Y. City; Cecil Spence, Brooklyn; Horace R. Stahl, Desloge, Mo.; Runyon Colie, Newark, N. J.; E. R. Bartlett and son, Bronxville, N. Y.

It is necessary to remind quite a number of contestants that the story of Eve is not a "parable."

Mr. Edward R. Bartlett writes: "The puzzle has been completed by my son, aged 15, and me, and we would like to issue a challenge to any member of the Irregulars for a father-and-son tournament, to be held under the proper auspices and Marquis of Queensbury rules." This is an excellent idea. Mr. Bartlett may be addressed by Baker Street Fathers-and-Sons at 24 West 40 Street.

Gladys Norton, Katherine McMahon, Dorothy Beverly, constituting the staff of the Open Book Shop, Elgin, Ill., report that they now think so highly of Tobias Gregson's acumen that they have named their new English springer spaniel Toby in his honor.

Joyce Guernsey of University City, Mo., says delightfully, "I have signed it for us both, because while my husband is unusually well grounded in these classics, I know he would have been helpless without me when he hit one or two smarty-cat places. I happen to have that sort of a fool mind. . . . To me, as long as I live, some of the stories will bring back hot summers in a little Pennsylvania town, and a ten-year-old clinging to the shelves in the Study Closet, climbing up to find the yellow paper backs which were the first Sherlock Holmes I knew."

(June 16, 1934, p. 755)

BAKER STREET NOTES

The Baker Street Irregulars were much elated by the news of the dinner held in London last month by the Sherlock Holmes Society. Our special representative writes: "Many interesting comments were made in the course of the evening, some by Miss Dorothy Sayers, who, to the Sherlock Holmes Society, will always be *The* Woman. One bright observation leads to an investigation at which I may only hint. The clue is the two brothers Moriarty, James and James, the one the professor and the other, as you will recall, simultaneously a colonel and stationmaster in the West of England. The bright observation was that this and no other is the Binomial Theorem which occupied the professor's ingenuity."

Speaking of Miss Dorothy Sayers, we hope that all Sherlockians will look up her extremely astute conjectures in the current issue of *The Colophon*, where she tackles the prodigious task of correcting the muddled dates in the case of *The Red-Headed League*. But perhaps the most satisfying triumph of all Sherlockian scholarship is her paper in the forthcoming *Baker Street Studies* (to be published here under the imprint of the Irregulars). She proves conclusively, on irresistible evidence in the stories further fortified by details of university regulations, that Holmes studied at Cambridge; probably at Sidney Sussex College.

Reynard Biemiller has kindly redrawn for us the good old

symbolic design on the cover of the first American edition of *The Memoirs of Sherlock Holmes*. Perhaps it was used also on *The Adventures?* I don't remember.

GORDIUS·NODUS

(July 7, 1934, p. 795)

Mr. A. G. Macdonell, secretary of the Sherlock Holmes Society of London, was a welcome visitor here recently. He was specially pleased by a Department of Justice bulletin posted in a country p. o. on Long Island. It tells how to identify a particularly dangerous murderer now at large. Tattooed on his forearm is a pierced heart and the word *Mother.*

(December 22, 1934, p. 387)

Students of Sherlock Holmes will be interested in *Cornish of Scotland Yard*, a book of reminiscences by former Superintendent G. W. Cornish of the C. I. D.—In his narrative of what he calls "The Great Turf Fraud" Mr. Cornish describes the case of a faked racehorse which has some resemblances to the story of Silver Blaze (in the *Memoirs*). And oddly enough the name of the horse, in the fraud that was perpetrated in 1920, was Silver Badge.

(July 6, 1935, p. 16)

&&&The only serious omission we have noted [in *Mapbook of English Literature*, Holt, 1936] is that the map of London does not include any mention of Sherlock Holmes on Baker Street.&&&That reminds us: it has been a great pleasure to receive several letters indicating that Conan Doyle's *Through the Magic Door* (a book about literature) is by no means forgotten.&&&Mr. James Keddie writes from Boston that he believes he can establish that Mrs. Hudson of 221B Baker Street had another lodger besides Holmes and Watson. We eagerly await details.

(from *Ampersands*, November 7, 1936, p. 13)

Bill Henneman, of the Argus Bookshop, Chicago, generously gave me a copy of a favorite which has long been missing from my shelves—Conan Doyle's *Through the Magic Door* (1908). Those library gossips of good old Sir Arthur's, about his own bookshelves, are always a surprise to readers who knew him only as the writer of adventure and detection. By the Magic Door he means the door that shuts you in with your books—

"You are through the magic portal into that fair land whither worry and vexation can follow you no more. You have left all that is vulgar and all that is sordid behind you. There stand your silent comrades, waiting in their ranks. Choose your man."

It was a strong pleasure to renew acquaintance with this delightful book, in which you get to know Doyle rather intimately. When he speaks of his deep admiration for Dr. Oliver Wendell Holmes, dating from his student days, you can't help wondering whether it did not (subconsciously,

193

may be) influence his choice of a name for Sherlock. Of the Autocrat he says, "Never have I so known and loved a man whom I had never seen."

One of the grandest things about *Through the Magic Door* is that it has long been out of print. Which means that to find it requires some search (or a friend like Bill Henneman) and when you get it you really appreciate it. The books that can be had everywhere, at any moment, how banal they are!

(from *Ampersands*, December 26, 1936, p. 13)

The greatest triumph of the Holmes–Watson mythos is that it has even gotten into *The Lancet*, the world's premier medical journal. Mr. P. M. Stone, a Baker Street Irregular in Waltham, Mass., sends me the *Lancet* of Dec. 26, 1936, which prints an article ("by an Occasional Correspondent") *Was Sherlock Holmes a Drug Addict?* This takes the line that Holmes's behavior shows none of the unmistakable signs of cocaine poisoning: that the wrist-scars were make-up, a form of practical joke at Dr. Watson's expense. *The Lancet*'s correspondent concludes with "unfavourable reflections on the professional competence of Dr. Watson."

I wish I had quit reading *The Lancet* at that point, but I went on into some of the clinical matter, and identified a lot of symptoms. Unquestionably I have arthritis, cystoscopy, chronic nepotism, and intermittent nephalism.

(from "Catalogue of Pleasures," March 6, 1937, p. 10)

&&&This is, someone has already remarked, the Sherlock Holmes season. It is exactly 50 years since readers first found him in print; and the very date we write this (Jan. 6) was astrologically computed by the Baker Street Irregulars as the great detective's birthday. We are the more pleased, therefore, to find announced (Black Cat Press, 4940 Winthrop Ave., Chicago) a book by Walter Klinefelter, *Ex Libris A. Conan Doyle*. It is said to be a study of the genesis and growth of the Holmes idea as reflected in the other writings of Dr. Doyle.&&&In the canon of the Baker Street Irregulars, of course, Conan Doyle has no existence and is never mentioned: their own compilation of essays on Holmes–Watson will some day, it is hoped, be forthcoming; set entirely in Baskerville.

(from Ampersands, January 15, 1938, p. 13)

We are occasionally chaffed for our devotion to Sherlock Holmes; it is good to see him recognized by the canny Carnegians as one of the completely universal creations of the Anglo-American mind. We may be allowed to say Anglo-American as Sherlock has in him so large an infusion of Poe's Dupin. (Even Doyle's initials, has it been remarked, are interchangeable with Dupin's.)

(March 26, 1938, p. 13)

&&&*The Adventure of the Blue Carbuncle* (in *The Adventures of Sherlock Holmes*) is apt for this season.

(from Ampersands, December 31, 1938, p. 12)

CHRISTOPHER MORLEY IN 1939
Doubleday publicity photo for *Kitty Foyle*
Courtesy Haverford College Library

"TRADE WINDS"

As these brief paragraphs show, "Trade Winds," which appeared irregularly in *The Saturday Review of Literature* from July 4, 1925 to November 9, 1940, was a crazy quilt of brief essays, random thoughts, and whatever bookish gossip had caught Kit's eye that week. Writing under the pseudonym of P. E. G. Quercus (from the Latin motto "parvis e glandibus quercus": tall oaks from little acorns grow), "Old Q" tried to keep his readers abreast of trends in the publicity trade and the bookselling world (both new and used). (Many items came directly from dealers' catalogues and thus are of historical interest to the collector.) As a whole, the column offers a wonderfully heady, if purely subjective, view of the book world before World War II.

A collection of material from the column between July 1925 and March 1927 was made and galleys pulled, but the book itself was postponed at the author's request. "Trade Winds" continued under other editors, including a decades-long stint with Bennett Cerf, until almost the end of the *Saturday Review*.

A S GRADUATION PRESENT, don't forget First Editions. Looking over a number of current catalogues I find two firsts listed by Alfred Goldsmith, 42 Lexington Avenue, that seem very reasonable. Conan Doyle's *Rodney Stone* (London, 1896) at $3.00 and Bret Harte's *Tales of the Argonauts* (Boston, 1875) at $4.00. These prices are typical of the bargains that alert browsers can pick up nowadays. This is going to be the best summer that ever was for the intelligent book-hunter. In years to come, how we shall brag of our finds.

(June 11, 1932, p. 783)

Walter Klinefelter, of Glen Rock, Pa., announces "The private emission, for the promotion of gaiety among bibliophiles," of *How Sherlock Holmes Solved the Mystery of Edwin Drood*, by Harry B. Smith, well-known librettist and collector. There are to be 223 copies at $1.50, 27 signed copies at $6.

(June 17, 1933, p. 660)

The "Baker Street Irregulars," a club of Holmes-and-Watson devotees, held its first meeting on January 6, the date now accepted as Sherlock Holmes's birthday. Mr. Malcolm Johnson, editor of the Crime Club books, proposes that the Baker Street Irregulars publish once a year a rare private item of Holmesiana.

(January 13, 1934, p. 416)

Excellent [London bookseller George] Bates: he is a good Conan Doyle man and has even discovered an item of which few have heard—a 3-volume novel, *The Fate of Frenella* (1892), which was written by 24 authors; Doyle did chapter 4. Among the others were F. Anstey, Mrs. Trollope, Bram Stoker, etc. Bates asks 21 bob for it. For the benefit of "Baker Street Irregulars" we note that Mr. Bates touches

199

on a moot point—was the correct title of a famous story, *The Sign of Four* or *The Sign of the Four*? According to Bates it was first issued in *Lippincott's Magazine* (February 1890) as *The Sign of the Four*. Published (later in the same year) in book form without the *the*.

(February 24, 1934, p. 516)

Mr. W. S. Hall, 500 Fifth Avenue, is undertaking a Conan Doyle bibliography for the Baker Street Irregulars. He notes in Arthur Rogers's catalogue (Newcastle-on-Tyne, England) Doyle's excessively rare first appearance in book form, *Dreamland and Ghostland* (3 vols., 1886).

(March 3, 1934, p. 530)

Ray Peck, bookseller at 34 West 47 Street, has delighted the Baker Street Irregulars by gathering some thirty first editions of Conan Doyle.

(December 8, 1934, p. 362)

It's odd that William Gillette's play, *Sherlock Holmes*, was never published until now: Doubleday announce it for Sept. 6 ($2.00) with an introduction by the eminent Baker Street Irregular, Mr. Vincent Starrett.

(August 31, 1935, p. 21)

Be bold, be bold . . . but not too bold; among new books buy something old. Chaucer, Shakespeare, Keats, and Blake, perfect Christmas presents make. Donne, Walt Whitman, Lamb, Montaigne, these will help to keep you sane. And the sun will ne'er go down, on those who read Sir Thomas Browne. For a dish that's spiced and mincy, try A. France or T. De Quincey. Then catch up, a little later, with Melville, Coleridge, and Pater. Beerbohm, Conrad, Conan Doyle, are goods that Time is loth to spoil. O. Henry, Kipling, Oliver Holmes, give you amperes and not

ohms. Yea, hosanna, these and others, gave their sisters and
their brothers, Words of life . . . so while you're at it you'd
Better think a Xmas gratitude.

(December 14, 1935, p. 22)

Q. has the old Sherlock Holmes books spread out by the
hearth, warming them up (like crumpets) for the annual rereading. It may be news to Sherlockians that the present
address 221 Baker Street is the headquarters of a very
important Building and Loan Bank in London, the Abbey
Road Building Society (of which Sir Josiah Stamp is president and the Lord High Chancellor, Viscount Hailsham, is
a trustee). And to their office the occasional letters still
addressed to Mr. Sherlock Holmes are faithfully delivered
by the postoffice. This Q. learns from an amusing article
("Sherlock Doesn't Live Here Any More") by the editor of
the company's magazine, *The Abbey Road Journal*.

(December 28, 1935, p. 24)

Has any secondhander a copy of Conan Doyle's *Through the
Magic Door*, a delightful old book-about-books too much
forgotten?

(October 24, 1936, p. 26)

We were heartily sorry to hear of the death of Leonard L.
Mackall, distinguished bibliographer, who had been a regular contributor to our contemporary the *Herald Tribune
Books* from its beginning in 1924. Innumerable stories are
told of Mr. Mackall's acute instincts in the field of bibli-
ophily; he was sometimes nicknamed "the Sherlock
Holmes of book collectors."

The motto on Old Q.'s bookplate, if he had a bookplate,
would be "Some poor bibliophile, who, either as a trade or
as a hobby, was a collector of obscure volumes." The
speaker is Dr. Watson, in *The Adventure of the Empty House*.

Another good quote from the same volume (*The Return of S. H.*) is Holmes's remark "The Press, Watson, is a most valuable institution, if you only know how to use it." This was after Holmes, for reasons of his own, had given a reporter a misleading steer on a certain story.

(May 29, 1937, p. 21)

The person we most envy this warm summer Sunday is a young woman of our acquaintance, age 14, who is reading *The Hound of the Baskervilles* for the first time. She remarks, "Doctor Watson is just leaving for Baskerville Hall. . . ." She wonders if Maxwell Anderson knows that one of the farmhouses in that region was called *High Tor*.

(July 17, 1937, p. 24)

Vincent Starrett, an old, old friend of Sherlock Holmes and the SRL, blew into the office the other day after a sojourn in China. . . . The eminent collector of the detective novel has recently completed a Conan Doyle bibliography of only the Holmes stories.

(August 7, 1937, p. 24)

At this season we begin to hanker for the annual rereading of Sherlock Holmes: we remember that it was New Year's resolutions (for the year 1881) that occupied Dr. Watson's mind as he stood at the Criterion Bar and felt that historic tap on the shoulder. To every Baker Street Irregular, the first toast of the year should be to Young Stamford (of Bart's Hospital) who introduced the immortal pair to each other.

In our own private collection two of the choicest items are a portrait of the actual bull-terrier that bit Sherlock Holmes at Cambridge, and the copy of Murger's *Vie de Bohème* that Dr. Watson read so inattentively one evening during the *Study in Scarlet*. Holmes's own volume of George Meredith and his pocket Petrarch have never turned up, but we scan the Scribner catalogues in hope to see them listed.

(January 1, 1938, p. 24)

If we thought the Oxford Press would accept it we'd suggest a livelier motto for that Who's Who of the English Church [*Crockford's Clerical Directory*], viz. Sherlock Holmes, in *The Adventure of the Retired Colourman*: "The good vicar's name I took, of course, out of my Crockford." Speaking of Holmes, he—or at any rate Watson—knew his Horace, for another of the Satires (the first) is quoted at the end of *A Study in Scarlet*.

(June 18, 1938, p. 24)

Amused to observe, rereading E. M. Forster's *Aspects of the Novel*, that Mr. Forster says his (Mr. Forster's) "priggishness" prevents him from enjoying Conan Doyle. A pity.

(September 3, 1938, p. 24)

The Black Cat Press, 5062 Winthrop Avenue, Chicago, offers *Ex Libris A. Conan Doyle: Sherlock Holmes* by Walter Klinefelter, a desirable Christmas gift for Sherlockians ($3.50). Mr. Klinefelter examines the genesis of the great detective as shown in Dr. Doyle's personal writings. It appears that the wife of G. T. Bettany (a former Cambridge don then editing MSS for Ward, Lock & Co.) was the first reader who saw the popular possibilities of Sherlock Holmes. That was in October 1886. The first editorial enthusiast in the U. S. was J. M. Stoddart of *Lippincott's Magazine* who hunted out Doyle in 1889.

(October 1, 1938, p. 21)

We always liked Sherlock Holmes's idea of compiling his own Encyclopaedia. It is the perfect occupation for the slackening years. There is probably no other weapon that does as little harm as a pair of scissors.

(December 10, 1938, p. 21)

What sounds like a good buy is the first English edition of *The Hound of the Baskervilles* (1902) listed at $3 by Norman Alexander Hall, 67 Union St., Newton Center, Mass. . . .

Howard Swiggett writes that Baker Street Irregulars must not forget other irregular events that happened on the same highway. He says that the plot to assassinate Napoleon which resulted in the execution of the Duke of Enghien was hatched in 1803 at 46 Baker Street.

(March 4, 1939, p. 24)

NEWS ON BAKER STREET

It is good news that Mr. Vincent Starrett has accepted the editorship of the volume *221B*, being some transactions of the Baker Street Irregulars, and is preparing copy for publication. This year, as noted before, is the 50th anniversary of the first publication of Sherlock Holmes in this country. It was the late Joseph M. Stoddart, the brilliant managing editor of *Lippincott's Magazine* in the '80's and '90's, who got Conan Doyle, Oscar Wilde, Kipling, Amelie Rives, James Lane Allen, Julian Hawthorne, John Habberton and many others for his magazine. Stoddart (1845–1920 were, we believe, his "dates") was a lively fellow. He began at Lippincott's as a youngster; had some soldier experience in the Civil War; then started a subscription book business of his own which included such ventures as Max Adeler's *Out of the Hurly Burly* (illustrated by a young artist named A. B. Frost) and T. S. Arthur's *Ten Nights in a Bar Room*. He leased a theatre and produced Gilbert & Sullivan. He published the famous American reprint of the 9th edition *Encyclopae-*

dia Britannica. He brought Oscar Wilde over here for a lecture tour. He invented new magazines every few years.

(March 18, 1939, p. 21)

A number of Baker Street Irregulars have reported on the movie *The Hound of the Baskervilles*, which sounds like a fine cast in a tripey picture.

(April 8, 1939, p. 21)

It will be fifty years this winter since there first appeared in American ink the two fiction characters who have probably given more innocent pleasure than any others in history— Sherlock Holmes and Dr. Watson, in *Lippincott's Magazine.* Which will make appropriate the forthcoming volume of Baker Street Irregularities edited by Vincent Starrett.

(September 30, 1939, p. 24)

The Chaucer Head Bookshop, now at 22 East 55, has issued an attractive 15th anniversary catalogue. An 1890 *Firm of Girdlestone* (A. Conan Doyle) should be tempting to the Sherlock Holmes collector, as in that book one may find (we maintain) a parallel appearance of the famous landlady Mrs. Hudson.

(November 25, 1939, p. 24)

Old Q.'s greatest personal pleasures, perhaps, were in hearing that Vincent Starrett's volume of Sherlockiana *221B* is now definitely scheduled for January 30 (Macmillan). . . .

(December 23, 1939, p. 21)

The piece that all the eminent tycoons read every Xmas (yes, the Dickens thing) was so overwritten and has been ever since so overtouted that we are fed to the teeth with it. We prefer the Sherlock Holmes story of the Xmas goose,

The Adventure of the Blue Carbuncle. The goose, you remember, was destined for "Mrs. Henry Baker." There are two of that name in the Manhattan phone book and we always think of sending them a Xmas card from Sherlock Holmes, but we never get round to it. . . .

Speaking of Sherlock Holmes, it was the Linotype Company who kept insisting that 1939 was "A Baskerville Year." The story of The Hound was no more exciting than that of the Baskerville type-faces. John Baskerville was printer to Cambridge University in the 18th century. After his death (1775) his types were bought by Beaumarchais, the French writer (how come, we wonder?), and disappeared in the troubles of 1789. The lost almae matrices were rediscovered in 1929 in Paris, and the late Wm. Edwin Rudge carried them back to London in a suitcase which he never allowed out of his sight.

(December 30, 1939, p. 24)

Dave Randall, of Scribner's Rare Books Dept., celebrated the recent convention of the Baker Street Irregulars by showing in a Fifth Avenue window some of Vincent Starrett's remarkable collection of Holmes and Watson firsts. This meeting was held to celebrate the 50th anniversary of Sherlock Holmes's first appearance in American ink (*Lippincott's Magazine*, February 1890).

(February 10, 1940, p. 21)

Mr. Archie Macdonell, Scottish novelist and journalist, was asked in January by his government to fly to Scandinavia to make some talks on Britain's work in the war. At the last moment, due presumably to some diplomatic anxiety, he was asked not to talk about the war but about Sherlock Holmes. (Mr. Macdonell is secretary of the Sherlock Holmes Society in London.) He says:

206

Slightly dazed, I set off, and had a rousing time in Stockholm, Oslo and Copenhagen. They all fancied that they knew their Sherlock pretty well, but I soon set them right about that. I took them through the whole story, beginning with the north country squires and the French grandmother, and ending with a moving description of the work which Sherlock is doing for the Government today.

Although he will be eighty-eight this year, he is back in the Intelligence Department solving cryptograms. Naturally he cannot leave his farm in Sussex because of the physical exertion, but the cryptograms are sent down from the Foreign Office by special messenger, and Mr. Holmes solves them while the messenger is drinking a glass of beer in the hall.

Watson, of course, has been rejected from the R.A.M.C. for a good many reasons. And so he spends most of his time at his club, describing at some length the fatal battle of Maiwand, looking eagerly at the racing news, and dwelling at even greater length upon his "experiences of women in three continents."

(March 2, 1940, p. 24)

Q.'s Holmesian fancy was tickled when he noticed in glancing over the rotogravure that the caption writer had dubbed the recent villainous sun-spots "The Speckled Band." And so they did appear, as photographed by telescopic lens.

(April 6, 1940, p. 38)

W. Orton Tewson, in his always interesting syndicate *An Attic Salt-Shaker*, recalls that in his boyhood in South Norwood, a London suburb, his family doctor was a certain A. Conan Doyle. Dr. Doyle gave his young patient up for lost in some early illness, but Mr. Tewson still carries on cheerfully.

(April 13, 1940, p. 24)

Speaking of surreptitious items, Pamphlet House, Room 1800, 1775 Broadway, N. Y. C., is issuing *Baker Street and Beyond*, a Sherlockian Gazetteer by Edgar W. Smith with admirable maps drawn by Dr. Julian Wolff. This astonishing topography lists and comments 517 streets, towns, places or regions (from Abbas Parva to Zion) that have "fallen under the benevolent shadow of Sherlock Holmes and Dr. Watson." It may be had, in plain envelope, at $1.25 in paper and $2.50 in cloth. We rather suspect also that Dave Randall at Scribner's, who knows his Baker Street, will have copies available for the passer-by.

(June 8, 1940, p. 24)

In his foreword to Edgar W. Smith's *Baker Street and Beyond*, Vincent Starrett remarks that George Gissing lived just around the corner from Baker Street in '84–'87 and must often have met Holmes and Watson on the pavement.

(June 29, 1940, p. 24)

Dave Randall of Scribner's says Sherlock Holmes's bees will take care of any parachute troops that land on the Sussex Downs.

(July 20, 1940, p. 22)

Edgar W. Smith suggests that the remarkable passage about the bitter east wind, at the end of *His Last Bow* (one of the Sherlock Holmes volumes), keeps coming into many minds nowadays and is heartening to reread.

(August 24, 1940, p. 21)

The Membership Committee of the Baker Street Irregulars might take a look at W. Somserset Maugham. His qualifications are peculiar. In *The Saturday Evening Post* [Dec. 28], he has written an article called "Give Me a Murder," in which he says some sharp things about the Sherlock Holmes stories in particular and mystery writing in general. If the Irregulars were not what the word implies, Mr. Maugham would not stand a chance of admittance. He commits heresy at once by mentioning the name of Conan Doyle; then he plunges into an indictment: "I was surprised to discover how poor they [the Holmes stories] were, for like everybody else, I had read them with delight when they first appeared. The introduction is highly effective, the scene is well set, but the anecdote is thin and you are too often left feeling that you have been cheated. There is poverty of invention and there is lack of ingenuity. The thrill has gone out of them."

That last sentence may be more than the Irregulars can take, but our own hope that Mr. Maugham will reach the Initiating Committee lies in the verdict—the pull of the stories is in the charm of Sherlock Holmes himself. "He was drawn on broad and telling lines, a melodramatic figure with marked idiosyncrasies . . . this lay figure, decked out in theatrical properties, has acquired the same sort of life in your imagination as is held by Mr. Micawber. No detective stories have ever had the popularity of Conan Doyle's and because of the invention of Sherlock Holmes I think it must be admitted that none have so well deserved it."

(January 4, 1941, p. 24, by P.E.G. Quercus Associates)

Sharpest crack in the many newspaper pieces about Rex Stout's *SRL* article *Watson Was a Woman*: H. Allen Smith's in the February 28th *New York World-Telegram*—"Quick, Watson, the needlework!"

(March 8, 1941, p. 20, by P.E.G. Quercus Associates)

SHERLOCK HOLMES'S PRAYER

Specially printed for
the Sherlock Holmes dinner
of the Baker Street Irregulars,
March 31, 1944

———————————

Harcourt, Brace and Company
Publishers of
SHERLOCK HOLMES AND DR. WATSON
edited by Christopher Morley

POEMS

From his first book, *The Eighth Sin* (1912), to *Gentlemen's Relish* (1955), poems were the alpha and omega of Kit's work. If a Sherlockian knows any line of Kit's, it is most likely to be: "My only drug is a good long slug of Tincture of Conan Doyle." "Sherlock Holmes's Prayer" is trotted out every year at the Baker Street Irregulars Dinner and other Sherlockian events. These are not great poems, nor would Kit have considered them as more than light verse. But they amuse and, perhaps, instruct.

Several of these poems are of the sort Kit called "Translations from the Chinese," the free verse that he used to great effect in many short and perceptive poems. Kit often referred to himself as "the Old Mandarin" and was known as such by some friends. (His children called him the O.M., for either "The Old Mandarin" or "The Old Man.") Much of his output in the 'fifties was poetry, the work that, he said, gave him his greatest excitement. Kit viewed his poetry with much affection and hoped to be remembered most for his achievements as a poet.

GRADUATE STUDENT

The loveliest pupil I ever had
Was my little samoyed soubrette
Who used to cry, after every lecture,
"When does the drinking begin?"
And declared that Bosanquet's *Essentials of Logic*
Was more fun that Sherlock Holmes.

SRL, November 5, 1938, p. 13; also in *The Middle Kingdom*

SONNET ON BAKER STREET

Quick, Watson, quick! (he says) the game's afoot:
Perhaps it's only Scandal in Bohemia,
Or maybe Speckled Band, or Devil's Root,
Or famous sleuth who's dying of Anaemia—
The Dancing Men, Chicago's smartest crooks
Have given us the code: we'll fool that party:—
These are not merely episodes in books,
But the Crusade of Holmes and Moriarty.

So bring the fiddle and the dressing gown,
And Mrs Hudson, and brave Scotland Yard,
And Watson by the jezail bullet lamed—
We rattle in a hansom back to Town.
If this is fancy, history's debarred:
If this is fiction, let fact be ashamed.

Two Sonnets; also in *Profile by Gaslight*

SHERLOCK HOLMES'S PRAYER

[1] Grant me, O spirit of Reason, matter for Deduction, Intuition, and Analysis; plenty of three-pipe problems, that I may avoid the cowardice of seven per cent cocaine, or at least substitute something a little special in white wines.

[2] Give me newspapers, telegrams, and the grind of carriage wheels against the kerb; the meditative breakfast at morning; the unexpected client in the nighttime. And, occasionally, the alerting word *grotesque*.

[3] Strengthen me not to astonish the good Watson merely for theatrical pleasure; yet always to be impatient of Unmitigated Bleat; and of Guessing, which rots the logical faculty.

[4] If in hours of dulness neither the Turkish bath nor mediaeval charters, nor my scrapbooks nor my fiddle avail to soothe, turn my attention to the infallible reactions of chemistry—or to that rational and edifying insect the Bee.

[5] Remind me that there is a season of forgiveness for misfortune; but never for the incredible imbecility of bunglers (from LeCoq to Lestrade).

[6] In all the joys of action let me not forget the intellectual achievements of lethargy: to wit, Mycroft; and, slightly less to wit, Moriarty.

[7] Burden me not with unrelated facts, but encourage the habit of synthetic observation, collating the distinctions between the various. As the hand of the lithotyper is to that of the cork-cutter, so are the types of the *Morning Mercury* to those of the *Yorkshire Post*.

[8] Remember, O spirit, to Segregate the Queen. Viz., the fair sex is Watson's department. For me, the Mind

is All. But one confession in remembrance: the pistol-shot initials on the sitting-room wall were not what Watson thought. In the name of that Gracious Lady my favourite letters were the last two. I was writing not VR but IA. The Baker Street Underground shook my aim.

[9] Hold fast the doctrine: When all impossibles are eliminated, what remains, however improbable, must be the Truth.

[10] Then, O spirit, be the Game Afoot!

S. H.

NOTE BY J. H. W.

Holmes was always pithy. I think he worked back to this little credo through Winwood Reade. In [7] he makes his usual grammatical error, using *between* when he means *among*. I reproduce here a little verse I found among his papers—his only poem!

ELEMENTARY

> If Baker Street required a mate
> Or Reason crowned a queen,
> The only one to segregate
> Would be, of course, IRENE.

Sherlock Holmes's Prayer, also in *A Baker Street Four-Wheeler*, *The Incunabular Sherlock Holmes*, and BSJ (NS), 40 No. 1 (March 1990). "Elementary" also appeared as one of "Three Poems," BSJ (NS), 11 No. 3 (September 1961).

God rest us merry, gentlemen

God rest us merry, gentlemen,
  Let nothing us disturb;
So be it we may hear again
  The wheel grind at the kerb,
  Regard, with mien acerb,
    The boots with muddy spots on,
  The tardy German verb. . . .
    You know my methods, Watson!

Minutes of the Baker Street Irregulars (1945); also
appeared as one of "Three Poems," BSJ (NS), 11
No. 3 (September 1961)

COCAINE BOTTLE

When influential domes
  See earth to hell proceeding
The library he combs
  For anodyne he's needing
And still finds Sherlock Holmes
  The perfect bathroom reading.

"Clinical Notes," BSJ (os), 1 No. 2 (April 1946);
reprinted BSJ (ns), 40 No. 1 (March 1990)

As brown as nut and thin as lath

As brown as nut and thin as lath
  (Young Stamford said), twice-wounded man
Orontes brought him back the path
  To London from Afghanistan.
Thenceforward, through his mortal span,
  He had no bullpup, kin, nor kith,
Until he met, by perfect plan,
  Our compère, Edgar Wadsworth Smith.

"Clinical Notes," BSJ (os), 3 No. 2 (April 1948)

BAKER STREET EXERCISE

It's often interesting
To walk round someone's property
And try to deduce
What sort of person lives there
But it takes courage to do it
Round one's own.

from *The Old Mandarin*

TE DEUM LAUDANUM

What opiate can best abate
  Anxiety and toil?
Not aspirins, nor treble gins,
  Nor love, nor mineral oil—
My only drug is a good long slug
  Of Tincture of Conan Doyle.

(Christmas 1949)

one of "Three Poems," BSJ (NS), 11 No. 3 (September 1961); also as *Te Deum Laudanum* and as "Te Deum Laudanum," BSJ (NS), 40 No. 1 (March 1990)

When influential domes

When influential domes
    See nations in collision
The world of art he combs
    For happier decision
And in the trade of Holmes
    Finds perfect television. . . .

BSJ (NS), 40 No. 1 (March 1990)

THE NEW HOUSEMAID
(Christmas 1894)

This 'ere's a blinkin' place, 221-B;
You carn't do nothink right, blimey, because
'Oo wants when, and what? Cawfee? Early tea?
Rashers? At nine, snoring a treat they was,
Now 'Olmes's bath's too cold, Doctor's too 'ot;
Their eggs is boiling solid in the shell.
'Ow do you twig 'oo's 'om, and when, and wot?
But Mrs. 'Udson says . . .

         Oh Gord, the Bell!

House, lodgers, maid, all gone. The pavement's there
Which hansom, growler, even royal brougham
Scraped in hot haste for desperate appeals.
Baker Street, your memorial is where
On the way to the consulting room
This was the kerb that ground a thousand wheels.

The Spectator, December 21, 1951, p. 866; also in
Gentlemen's Relish and BSJ (NS), 5 No. 3 (July 1955)

POUR PRENDRE CONGER

Never, Oh never,
Mention your hobbies in public.
I was silly enough to admit
My boyish pleasure
In Sherlock Holmes.
Now I am pooped
By a great following surge
Of innocent correspondents
Whom I have no stenography
To retaliate.

Remember, my dears,
The instant I mention anything
I'm through with it.

from "Translations from Somethingorother," SRL,
July 21, 1951, p. 39

MORNING AFTER

After such long busywork of dying
It was so peaceful in the stratosphere
I wondered, am I going to be bored?
Then old Peter Pearlygate, replying:
"Gosh sake, I never thought to see *you* here;
You'll have to wait a while to see The Lord."
He scanned his book. "You got the breaks, old boy.
While your attendant Angel rests, and combs
His plumage—he looks a little ruffled—
Take it easy. What would you most enjoy?"

I said: To learn again how words, well shuffled,
Can sort miraculously into rhyme;
Or better still, read as for the first time
One of the Adventures of Sherlock Holmes.

Gentlemen's Relish; also in BSJ (NS), 5 No. 3 (July 1955). For a slight variant, see "Clinical Notes," April 1952, below in this volume, p. 369.

ANALYSIS
by Percy Trevelyan, M.D.

Briefly, this becomes my credo:
Watson, for the sake of Holmes,
Rearranged his chromosomes,
Almost conquered his libido:
Set threshold (for the analysts)
With touch of white at neck and wrists.
If you ask why Watson's great, he's
Holmes's Lares and Penates,
Doubles acolyte and Achates.
Watson Fido, Watson Phaedo!

"Clinical Notes," BSJ (NS), 2 No. 4 (October 1952)

BAKER STREET 1952
(contributed by a Postcard Tourist)

Baker Street now
Mostly mammalian on the eastern side,
Milk bars and bust supports.
These latter, with inherited French delicacy,
Sherlock would have accepted as
Simple *soutiens-gorges*.
But the prudent professional Watson
Never notices.

"Clinical Notes," BSJ (NS), 2 No. 4 (October 1952)

VINCENZIO
FROM CHRIS

Said C. M. to Vincent Starrett:
I do my work in an ancient garret,
But you, so pleasantly aquiline—
Your profile's more like his than mine.
Before this paper I make blots on,
You be Holmes and I'll be Watson.

The Last Bookman

FRAGMENTS AND
FUGITIVES

This section contains the flotsam and jetsam of the career of a man of letters. There are letters to the editor, footnotes, errata, and other minor work. There are also those portions of longer essays whose thrust precludes their being reprinted here in their entirety. These pieces offer verification, if any is needed, that Sherlock Holmes was always present in Kit's consciousness.

[ERRATA]

IN THE UNAVOIDABLE ABSENCE of the Editor, a volunteer hand must call attention to the curious incident of what the Proofreader did in the night-time. Indoctrinated students will deduce that (by an innocent misunderstanding) a portion of this work was set from unrevised copy, and this first edition will remain identifiable by a number of irregularities; notably in Mr Edgar Smith's valuable concordance. Anomalies inseparable as between the traditional British and American texts are impossible to reconcile: e.g., is it Riding Thorpe or Ridling Thorpe? was it the first Mrs Watson's mother, or her aunt, whom she was visiting at the time of *The Five Orange Pips*?

JANE NIGHTWORK

errata slip tipped into *221B*

THE MYCROFT MAGIC
SQUARE

YOU ARE OF COURSE FAMILIAR with the theory, advanced by some learned men—Father Ronald Knox, for instance, and (less vigorously) our good friend the late Archie Macdonell—that Mycroft and Moriarty were in cahoots; or even the same person. (The problem of the Colonel Moriarty who was stationmaster in the West of England I reject: this was merely Dr. Watson's muddled misunderstanding of the overheard remark that Colonel Moriarty was "stationed" in the W. of England—perhaps at Weston-super-Mare's Nest).

Wishing to test the matter I applied myself to a magic square of 64 cells. Why 64? Because Sherlock was 64 when he finally retired from any kind of investigations, at the end of the First Great War.

Trusting to automatic writing and subconscious impulse, I began filling in the square. I began by writing the word MYCROFT both horizontally and vertically, since my purpose was to test whether Mycroft was really on the level and equally an upright fellow. Thus:

M	Y	C	R	O	F	T	1
Y	2	3	4	5	6	7	8
C	9	10	11	12	13	14	15
R	16	17	18	19	20	21	22
O	23	24	25	26	27	28	29
F	30	31	32	33	34	35	36
T	37	38	39	40	41	42	43
44	45	46	47	48	49	50	51

Then, filling in the other cells in the usual order, *moving from left to right and downward through all vacancies*, I wrote:

Mycroft's surname (one word of six letters, in boxes 1, 2, 3, 4, 5, and 6).

Then: Mycroft's brother's first name and initial of surname (one word of eight letters, in boxes 7, 8, 9, 10, 11, 12, 13, and 14; and initial in box 15).

Then: the name of the work in which the crucial clue was found (two words of nine letters and seven letters respectively, in boxes 16, 17, 18, 19, 20, 21, 22, 23, 24 (giving, of course, its own cell to the apostrophe!), and 25; and the second word in boxes 26, 27, 28, 29, 30, 31, and 32).

Then: the title and initial of surname of Sherlock's biographer (abbreviated title in boxes 33 and 34; and initial in box 35).

Then: Sherlock's obvious comment (one word of ten letters, in boxes 36, 37, 38, 39, 40, 41, 42, 43, 44, and 45).

And finally: the first word of the title of the story in which the truth becomes known (six letters, in boxes 46, 47, 48, 49, 50, and 51).

ANSWER

M	Y	C	R	O	F	T	H
Y	O	L	M	E	S	S	H
C	E	R	L	O	C	K	H
R	W	H	I	T	A	K	E
O	R	'	S	A	L	M	A
F	N	A	C	D	R	W	E
T	L	E	M	E	N	T	A
R	Y	V	A	L	L	E	Y

233

If Mycroft was on the level and an upright fellow (as demonstrated), could he possibly be one and the same as, or even in cahoots with, Moriarty, who is now proved an obviously oblique fellow?

The defense rests. . . .

EXCERPT FROM LETTER TO ELLERY QUEEN

Dear Ellery:

I still fear you overrate the merit of the Mycroft Magic Square: it was put together to amuse a young nephew who is somewhat stricken with sherlockophily. . . .

C. M.

EXCERPT FROM LETTER TO MR. MORLEY

Dear Chris:

I dissent vigorously.

Any new light thrown on the Sacred Writings—especially so important a revelation as this one, which in one diagonal swoop not only establishes Mycroft's innocence but clears his good name for all time—such new light, I repeat, is of vital interest to all Devotees of Doyle and Sycophants of Sherlock.

If you are still fearful, good Chris, you may henceforth consider the Editor and all readers of this magazine new members of your family-circle—"nephews," equally afflicted with that incurable malady, "sherlockophily."

Your steadfast admirer,

E. Q.

Ellery Queen's Mystery Magazine, 4 (March 1943); the square first appeared in Minutes of the Baker Street Irregulars (1942)

234

A LETTER TO
DAVID A. RANDALL

Roslyn Heights, L.I.
December 22, 1942

Dear Dave Randall—

Say, I think you've got hold of a gorgeous idea in re S. H. and Tom Wise. In the first place the famous photo of Wise in his honorary M.A. Oxon gown (frontis in Partington's book) is the living spit of one's idea of Moriarty. All kinds of corroborations come to mind. Wise did his first collecting along the stalls of Farringdon Road—and that's where the episode of *The Red-Headed League* came to climax. Of course, the Clay connection interests me specially, as my grandmother was Elizabeth Jane Clay of the famous printing family. Sherlock's disguising himself as the old bookseller is a shrewd touch indeed. I am so excited about yr thesis that I hope you'll get it into shape to say something about it at the Dinner. Let Edgar Smith know as I suspect he has collected a plethora of material from all sorts of contributors & he'll have to consider his program.

Copying the *Encyclopaedia Britannica* is exactly the kind of job that Wise wd have thought of to keep the poor red-headed pawnbroker busy. Whether Wise was both Moriarty & John Clay will need meditation. Reading of course was also concerned in the counterfeiting hydraulic press of *The Engineer's Thumb*. You could almost convince me there is some connection between Vincent Spaulding & Vincent Starrett! But be sure to look up the photos of Wise in Partington's book. I shall await with eagerness John Carter's comment on yr magnificent theory. I fear many of the Irregulars are hardly bibliophile enough to appreciate the notable aptness of yr discovery! It rings treble bob majors with me—

Merry Xmas! Yrs,

CHRISTOPHER MORLEY

The Adventure of the Notorious Forger

MYCROSTIC

[The first magic square was revealed to the Baker Street Irregulars at their meeting on Friday, January 9, 1942. The following year, on Friday, January 8, Kit again introduced a "mycrostic." The following is by Edgar W. Smith, acting in his role as "Buttons" of the Irregulars.—S.R.]

The Conanical toasts were proposed and drunk, upon which Mr. Morley offered as the first order of business the collective solution of a new Christophelian Mycrostic—a "Rebus in Arduis"—designed to reveal, or at least to adumbrate, the identity of Dr. Watson's Second Wife. The membership displayed acumen in entering the Clews (Grace, V.D.M., Mrs. S. Clair, Mme. N., H.T.H., Violet Hunter, Hatty D., V.S., Stoper, M. Sutherland, Oakshott, and I.A.N.) in the proper squares beneath the master-line inscribed MRSWATSON, and astonishment and appreciation were duly in evidence at the resultant diagonal reading from upper left to lower right, viz:

M	R	S	W	A	T	S	O	N
G	R	A	C	E	V	D	M	M
R	S	S	C	L	A	I	R	M
M	E	N	H	T	H	V	I	O
L	E	T	H	U	N	T	E	R
H	A	T	T	Y	D	V	S	S
T	O	P	E	R	M	S	U	T
H	E	R	L	A	N	D	O	A
K	S	H	O	T	T	I	A	N

The climax was capped, however, by discovery of the gentle tribute paid to the *first* Mrs. Watson in the right-hand vertical column read downward.

Minutes of the Baker Street Irregulars (1943)

A FOOTNOTE ON
DRESSING GOWNS

IT HAS LONG BEEN ON MY MIND to mention the fact that our beloved Freddie Steele, who has so lately been taken from us, misled us in the matter of that garment. Probably he himself took the notion from William Gillette, who wore one of those robes with satin cuffs and long satin lapels (perhaps even padded or quilted with a kind of diagonal stitch). Bathrobes of that type are definitely American; I don't believe they have ever been seen in Britain. I think it not unlikely that smoking jackets with silk cuffs and lapels might be possible among certain parvenu milieux: perhaps C. A. Milverton's jacket was of that sort; but then he undoubtedly called his sanctum a "snuggery"—one could sink no lower.

The dressing gown with ultra lapels and deep satin cuffs—and even frogs instead of buttons—is surely the Jno Wanamaker or Gimbel Bros. or R. H. Macy idea of what a genteel dressing-gown should be, or possibly even the Galeries Lafayette?? I'm sure Holmes's gown was not like that. It was of substantial wool or wool-flannelette, severely cut, with plenty of pockets, and large horn buttons. Rather than a twisted cord-girdle it was tied round with a strip of the same material.

To be certain on these points one would need to look up an illustrated catalogue of the Army and Navy Stores, or Gamage's, in London of the '90's.

footnote to "The Sartorial Sherlock Holmes" by
Humfrey Michell in *A Baker Street Four-Wheeler*

MR. ELIOT'S
ECHOLALIA

SIRS:

In my thesis on *Echolalia in Modern Verse* I shall of course mention Mr. Eliot's odd repercussion of the Musgrave Ritual, in *Murder in the Cathedral*; which is bien connu.

But has anyone else pointed out—and if so warn me off—another Holmesian ricochet upon that clifflike brow? You will find it in Mr. Eliot's deservedly famous *Four Quartets* (1943). In the first of his quartets, *East Coker*, section II, line 41:—

On the edge of a grimpen, where is no secure foothold.

Sometimes I suspect Mr. Eliot is a bit of a slyboots. I happen to know, from my own footnotes in my thesis, that he is an inveterate reader of the Sacred Writings, and I shall be ill bestead if you do not inveigle him to do something for the B.S.J.—Tell him so, with my, well, with my affectionate homage.

JANE NIGHTWORK

New York, N.Y.

Letter to the Editor, BSJ (OS), 1 No. 2 (April 1946)

ON BELONGING
TO CLUBS

AND STILL, POOR SOUL, I had this morbid hanker for inventing clubs. Surely the most innocent impulse of my life was my boyish passion for the corn of Conan Doyle. I invented something called the Baker Street Irregulars; a simple group of a dozen devotees who met, Dutch, to discuss what amused them. It was taken up by that resonant sounding-board·Woollcott, and then by *Life* magazine. The quiet speakeasy where we met was trampled into covercharge by runners and readers and their dames. Our scrapbook of minutes was stolen by some biblioklept; our simple punchinello (Christ Cella) died of ambitious hypertension. Truly, men in Clubs have an urge toward Deficit, Damnation and Death. Now the scholarly group of Baker Street find themselves swaddled, or saddled, with a publishing business, an annual meeting, and a province of pulp. They have about 30 scionist branches whose letters have to be answered. But not by me.

from "On Belonging to Clubs," *The Colophon*, June 1949, pp. 26–27; also in *The Ironing Board* and *Christopher Morley's New York*

GREAT AND
LITTLE SNORING

OUR VACATION HAS BEEN UNUSUAL for Americans. Instead of rushing straight to London, gravitating to the Great Cesspool was Dr. John H. Watson's phrase, you remember—by the way how much less Dr. Watson would have had to rely on Sherlock Holmes if there had been a National health scheme in the 'eighties and 'nineties—I wonder if there would have been any of his patients still living to testify?—instead of gravitating to the Great Cesspool we cut across country and spent several weeks in that part of England where so much of America began, Lincolnshire and Norfolk and Suffolk.

from "Great and Little Snoring," *The Ironing Board*

SHERLOCKIAN STAMPS

SIR,—I have been too bashful to say how happy the Baker Street Irregulars (of New York) have been in your readers' response to an innocent letter of nostalgia. Even though the letters, whether from Lord Justice Asquith or Mr. Desmond MacCarthy, or others of equal spirit, showed that your Sherlockian students are still balking at some fences that our esoterics cleared long ago.

My only claim at this moment, on your scant Scandinavian pulp, is that one of our scionist groups (The Musgrave Ritualists, of Uptown, N.Y.) appealed to the British G.P.O. to suggest a possible centennial issue of postage stamps for the year 1954, to the mark the one hundredth birthday of Sherlock Holmes. The year 1854 has been oecumenically assigned (by what Chaucer called the "eyrisshe beastes," viz. signs of the zodiac) as Holmes's birth year (6 January).

But H.M. Postmaster-General writes that he "regrets the infeasibility of issuing commemorative Sherlock Holmes stamps in 1954, on the ground that only events of national, international, or Post Office importance are marked in this way."

Is this really final? If so, we can still inculcate the U.S. Post Office, which is always wild for new stamps; but we feel the great Holmes-and-Watson stamp should come from your side.

CHRISTOPHER MORLEY

New York

Letter to the Editor, *The Sunday Times*, London, [February?], 1950; also in *The Sherlock Holmes Letters*

POSSIBLE OSMOSIS

Sir: You haven't printed any parallel columns for a long time. Here is a possible case of literary osmosis—

"Gabriel Rossetti, a true poet, if not a great one, very firmly declared himself not at all sure that the earth really revolved round the sun. He even aggravated this scandalous position by asking, what, after all, did it matter."
—From an address by John Morley at the Mansion House, London, February 26, 1887. (Reprinted in Lord Morley's *Politics and History*.)

"I found incidentally that he [Holmes] was ignorant of the Copernican Theory and of the composition of the Solar System. That any civilized human being in this nineteenth century should not be aware that the earth traveled round the sun appeared to me such an extraordinary fact. . . . 'What the deuce is it to me?' he interrupted."
—From Dr. Watson's analysis of Sherlock Holmes in *A Study in Scarlet*, published in *Beeton's Christmas Annual* for 1887.

CHRISTOPHER MORLEY
Roslyn Heights, N. Y.

Letter to the Editor, SRL, December 2, 1950, p. 31

[UNTITLED LETTER TO *THE TIMES*]

Sir,— As the Michaelmas term approaches in the universities, members of Pembroke College, Cambridge, will note in staircase D in the front court two significant names. At 1A is Mr. Sherlock, at 7 is Mr. Holmes. Of course I presumed this had been arranged by the Master of Pembroke, the eminent Holmesian, Mr. S. C. Roberts. He maintains, however, that he knew nothing of it until I pointed it out to him. In his admirable edition of the stories published last year in the World's Classics, Mr. Roberts (in the full authority of his vice-chancellorship) gave Holmes away from Cambridge to Oxford. It is my duty to warn you, Sir, that this Michaelmas manoeuvre was conjured by Professor Moriarty, who lived at Garden House in Cambridge for many years. He used to listen to the water over the dam at that pleasant spot and say it reminded him of the Reichenbach. Moriarty lived there under another name, but the portrait still preserved there shows the likeness unmistakable. The heirs and assigns of Moriarty are still causing confusion and dismay; pray do not publish my address lest reprisals be incurred.

Yours faithfully,
Christopher Morley

Suffolk, en route.

Letter to the Editor, *The Times*, London, September 19, 1952, p. 7g

RANDOM
LITERARY NOTES

O F COURSE WHAT WE MOST WANTED were posthumous suspirations of our two boyhood heroes, Sherlock Holmes and R. L. S. [Robert Louis Stevenson]. At Southsea, a sort of Cockney-Coney suburb of the great naval works at Portsmouth, we learned what no one has yet told, that the little house in Bush Villas was wiped out in a blitz. It destroyed the ancient Bush Hotel, and the neighboring church, and the adjoining houses. It is wildfare vacancy, deep grown in weeds and rubble. There the young medico Doyle dug himself in for practice, as he faithfully described in *The Stark Munro Letters* (1894); and found time and energy to write *A Study in Scarlet* and *The Sign of the Four*. These were both under the influence of the prevailing literary monsoon which blew in those days from Bournemouth, a few miles southwestward, where R. L. S. was living, or half-living; and that sultry human lioness Fanny Stevenson was encouraging Henry James and hissing out the too insistent Henley. We went of course to the beach, to a notable pavilion of bellying fish and chips; I gathered a bottle of the seashore shingle, in memory of Dr. Watson's always lovingly mentioned vacation optimum (the shingle of Southsea), but when they held a Sherlock Holmes vivarium on Baker Street, and even lately on Fifty-seventh Street, I admit I was too faded to send it in for exhibition. I had a strange feeling that the sponsors of the second litter are a little high-hat about humble Southsea.

from "Random Literary Notes from a Literary Traveler," *The New York Times Book Review*, October 5, 1952, p. 4

245

KEATS AT
KING'S PYLAND?

MUCH GOOD WORK has been done but the *apparatus criticus* is still compiling. I admit that not till this year's rereading of *The Eve of St. Agnes*, which always happens round about St. Agnes' Eve (January 20), did it occur to me where the most famous of all Sherlock's dicta came from. You remember the curious incident of the dog in the night-time in *Silver Blaze*:

"But the dog did nothing?"
"That," said Sherlock Holmes, "was the curious incident."

Turn then to stanza 41 of Keats's immortal poem. The lovers are fleeing into the storm; they pass all the dangers of the castle until the "iron porch"; the porter is drunk—asleep—but the dog! He rises, shakes his great frame—
"But his sagacious eye an inmate owns,"
He was indeed the First Hound of the Baskervilles; and Keats's poem was also laid (in early draft) on Dartmoor!

"from a recent essay by Christopher Morley,"* *Sherlock Holmes Journal*, 2 No. 2 (December 1954)

*Editor's note: I have been unable to identify this essay.—S.R.

CANON-FODDER?

SIR:— Thank you for allowing me to peruse the articles "Sherlock Holmes writes to the Papers" and "The Case Against," by Messrs. Green and Hedgegrove respectively. In 1942, I recall, it was proposed by Mr. Edgar W. Smith of the Baker Street Irregulars of New York to subsume "The Lost Special" and "The Man with the Watches" into the Holmesian Canon. I pointed out at the time, to Mr. Christopher Morley, that the letter in the *Gazette* was the work of Mr. Mycroft Holmes, Sherlock being in Tibet at the time— "doing a polyphonic motet in Lhasa," as Mycroft put it. He added that the stories were, however, potential canon-fodder. Only Mycroft, as a Government employee, would have access to the official columns of the *Gazette*. "The Lost Special" was material which Dr. Watson proposed to amplify as "The Papers of ex-President Murillo." Reference to W. S. Gilbert's "Patience" in Mr. Hedgegrove's article, reminds me that Holmes used to tease me by playing "A Policeman's Lot . . ." to me on his Stradivarius. The mysterious Horace Moore was, of course, Moriarty, the Professor's brother, who later became a stationmaster in the West of England. I am 86 now.

My best to you all,

> Yours, etc.,
> STANLEY HOPKINS, O.B.E.
> Chief Inspector, C.I.D. (retd.).

P.S. Your members can read up the whole business in *Letters from Baker Street* (Pamphlet House, N.Y., 1942).

> Letter to the Editor, *Sherlock Holmes Journal*, 3 No. 1
> (Summer 1956)

CHRISTOPHER MORLEY AT MONTREAL IN THE LATE
'THIRTIES DURING A LECTURE TOUR AND "LOOKING
LIKE AN ARCHDEACON"

"CLINICAL NOTES
BY A RESIDENT
PATIENT"

"Clinical Notes" are, by their punning title, Kit's admission to being a Sherlockoholic. The form is that of a journal or daybook filled with random jottings all united by the single theme of Holmes. Every aspect of the world of Baker Street is explored: dressing gowns, turkish baths, billiards, first editions, names, places, railroads (or -ways). Much is done under the personae of Stanley Hopkins, O.B.E., the retired C.I.D. Chief Inspector and former acquaintance of Holmes and Watson (see *Black Peter*, *The Missing Three-Quarter*, and others) and (out of *King Henry IV*, Part II, Act 3, Scene 2) Jane Nightwork, Litt.D., McGill University, who allowed the Christophalian imagination to fly even higher on matters more or less Sherlockian. Jane Nightwork's letters, for example, feature almost constant reference to dress in the Canon, particularly Holmes's dressing gown and Watson's repeated reference to a "touch of lace at neck and wrist." (This latter became the King Charles's head of the Nightwork letters.)

The spasmodic nature of these columns comes from their method of creation. Kit, who didn't have the time to spend on an unpaid column, wrote frequent letters and postcards to Edgar W. Smith, the *Baker Street Journal* 's editor, on topics Sherlockian. He would occasionally add a small essay on a suitable subject. Edgar would then cut and paste the letters into copy for "Clinical Notes." This continued until Kit's death in 1957. Their correspondence, in which Smith is addressed as "Dear Thorny[croft Huxtable]" and Kit as "Porky [Shinwell Johnson]," is an entertaining one, with letters like this:

Dear Thorny:

I think your little patchwork of Clinical Notes is surprisingly interesting; I had forgotten there were so many topics; I even enclose a quotation from a letter I expect soon to receive from Stanley Hopkins; he plans to write it tomorrow, 6 November, as you will see.

I WAS DELIGHTED TO GET A LETTER today from Chief Inspector (Retired) Stanley Hopkins. The earlier portion is perhaps irrelevant, dealing with his impressions of some Senators who had been traveling in England, but some of his biographical comments on his old friend Mr Sherlock Holmes are interesting:

If the weather is tolerable, [he writes,] I hope to get down to Sussex to see Mr Holmes for his birthday in January—think of it, 90 years!

The last time I saw him he was very much gratified when I told him of the various inquiries made by the members of your club. There were two prime reasons (besides climate) why he retired to Sussex rather than his native Yorkshire. First, the excellent Turkish baths at the Grand Hotel in Eastbourne; a cab used to drive out once a week to his cottage to take him in to Eastbourne for a good steaming. "Pleasant lassitude," he used to say with a chuckle, quoting the Doctor's phrase. The other reason was his admiration for T. H. Huxley, who had also retired to Eastbourne after so much severe mental exertion. When Huxley died (about 1895, I think) Holmes said he thought Eastbourne deserved another rationalist. After his Turkish bath he always went to the Eastbourne concert pavilion, which was famous for good music. He used to sit there waving his hands dreamily, and chuckling "Lassitude and di Lasso."

It was really rather fortunate that all that coast was so carefully barred off in the time of invasion scare. Of course, Mr Holmes was not forced to evacuate; the Ministry made a special exception in his case; but the barbed wire barriers and gun pits and restricted areas prevented Mr Holmes from the rambles which were really hazardous for a man of his years. Did you hear of the time he almost got into trouble by doing some unauthorized digging in the ruins of Wilmington Priory, only a few miles from his cottage? He was convinced that some early English charters were concealed there.

The gift sent me by your Irregulars is warmly appreciated. I think the best proof of the United Nations once more having command of the seas was to get that box of 1000 from Ionides[1] of Alexandria! My salaams to you all.

Hopkins is nearly 78 himself now, and an O.B.E. But, as he says, "I'm still not entirely a crock, and do my share as a Senior Warden—we've had plenty of plastering down here in Kent." His letter led me to get out a Bartholomew Survey Map of Sussex, and I suddenly realized that our admired cartographer Dr Wolff has seriously erred in placing the Fulworth bee-farm.[2] It is expressly stated that it is "five miles from Eastbourne"; whereas Dr Wolff has spotted it westward of Newhaven. Five miles by road over the height of the Downs, westward from Eastbourne, would bring us just about to the famous Seven Sisters (chalk cliffs; there is a gorgeous photo of them in *The Beauty of Britain*, introduction by J. B. Priestley, published by Scribners in 1935—Batsford in London—op. p. 51; if you want to see the view Holmes mentions in *The Adventure of the Lion's Mane*). The village of Fulworth seems to me evidently Cuckmere Haven, between Eastbourne and Seaford. Outside Cuckmere Haven is some sort of formation—rocks or cliffs or breakers, I don't know what—marked as *The Mares*, which suggests Manes. And Birling Gap (between Beachy Head and Cuckmere Haven) has a suggestion of Birlstone, not far away?

* * *

These are but toys; yet pleasing toys. In that region, if Sherlock wanted a drink he would walk over to the famous pub The Star at Alfriston, of which Belloc or someone, or Chesterton or someone, or Theodore Maynard or someone, wrote a ballade: "The Star at Alfriston sells damned good

---

[1]Cf. *The Adventure of the Golden Pince-Nez*, in which Inspector Hopkins figured prominently, if somewhat ineffectually.

[2]Cf. Dr. Wolff's end-papers in *Profile by Gaslight*.

beer." He would then be very near The Long Man of Wilmington—not a pub but a prehistoric figure cut out of the slopes of chalk. . . . Which reminds me, how many American readers, when they hear of the Singular Contents of the Ancient British Barrow, suppose it was a wheel-barrow?

* * *

Holmes himself was no mean cartographer (remember the Priory School terrain) and he would have enjoyed Dr Wolff's maps. Here for the first time we get a tempting glimpse of Uffa, *insula incognita*. I am not *quite* sure of the rig of some of Dr Wolff's vessels: but to pester the matter would put one in a class with the notorious canary trainer. . . . Fulworth might, after all, be really the *Lul*worth remembered for John Keats, though that was in Dorset.

* * *

Vincent Starrett has written delightfully of Mrs Hudson of Sussex and Baker Street.[3] I know it is not quite cricket to go outside the Canon, yet I could not resist suggesting to Vincent that in chapter 2 of *The Firm of Girdlestone* there is a Mrs Hudson, widowed in 1874 by the death of her husband, a bosun in one of the Girdlestone ships, who might quite reasonably have become, a few years later, the landlady of 221B.

* * *

I've been wondering if anyone has ever noted the extreme ingenuity of the publishers' solution of the problem of right- vs. left-hand rule of the road. In the familiar picture of Holmes and Watson on Regent Street, watched by Stapleton *en barbe* from the hansom, the McClure Phillips edition of the *Hound* shows traffic moving on the right-hand side of the street (to placate American readers?) whereas in the George Newnes edition the same picture is printed reversed and the vehicles move in the correct left-hand

[3]Cf. "The Singular Adventures of Martha Hudson" in *Profile by Gaslight*.

direction. What strikes me as thoroughly odd is that the drawing (by Sidney Paget) was plainly done to show *right-hand* rule of the road, for in the English edition the artist's name comes out printed in looking-glass fashion.

Now how does one account for that?

Speaking of *en barbe*, I can't do better than quote again from something Stanley Hopkins once wrote me:

> I was amused, [he said,] by your allusion to one of your members who is writing a monograph on Beards and Sherlock Holmes. What oddities you Americans think of! I can testify that Mr Holmes did think of growing a beard in the later years, because as Mrs Hudson grew older she never got his shaving water hot enough; but I think he was really prejudiced against them because so many rascals in his cases were conspicuous for hairy faces. Also he found a beard interfered with his eating honey, and you know he has always had a catlike neatness.

* * *

Mr Edgar Smith may need to reconsider our old argument whether the famous March 4th in the *Study in Scarlet* was 1881 or 1882. His case for 1882 is plausibly set forth in *The Long Road from Maiwand*—Mr Smith contends that all the things that happened to Watson from the time he was wounded to the time Holmes revealed his profession could not possibly have taken place in the seven and a half months between July 27, 1880, and March 4, 1881. Yet I ask him to remember that in those earliest Baker Street days, when Holmes and Watson had been living together for about six weeks, Watson raised the topic of Carlyle. And why? Because Carlyle died on February 5, 1881! Watson of course had read all the published obituaries, and they were undoubtedly still fresh in his mind, including the one referred to by George Gissing who wrote (in London, February 11, '81) that "I have just risen from the memoir of Carlyle in *The Times*." Obviously, Carlyle's recent death was the occasion for the mention Watson made of him.

It will be argued—in fact it has been—that Holmes responded to this mention by inquiring naïvely who Carlyle was and what he had done—an unlikely question for an omnivorous newspaper reader to ask just a few days after a great man's death, but not quite so unlikely a year later. To this I reply that in suggesting his ignorance in this manner Holmes was gently pulling Watson's leg, for shortly there-after he glibly quotes Carlyle's most famous apothegm.

My theory remains, therefore, that the day of the meet-ing of Watson and Stamford at the Criterion bar was January 1, 1881—a day when Watson would naturally be making resolutions for a more frugal life (though the lunch with wine at the Holborn must have been costly). Also the fact that it was a holiday would account for Holmes being the only student at work in the laboratory. Watson went back to the hotel—could it have been the Craven Hotel, in Craven Street, Strand???—got rid of the bull pup (hence never mentioned again?) and the next day, Sunday, January 2, they went to look at the lodgings.

The two theories could be checked, maybe, by reference to weather bureau files. Was Friday, March 4, 1881—or Saturday, March 4, 1882—a foggy day after a rainy night? (Presumably they both were.)

Yet how are we to clarify the Watsonian muddle? It was on the 4th of March "as I have good reason to remember." But then in chapter 6 the doctor quotes the morning papers. The *Standard* spoke of *"Tuesday, the 4th inst."* What are we to make of that? If the murder took place in the night of the 3rd–4th, certainly Drebber and Stangerson said good-bye to their landlady on the night of the *3rd inst.* If the *3rd inst.* was a Tuesday, according to the calendar the year was either 1874 or 1885. If the *Standard* was correct and the *4th inst.* was a Tuesday, the year must have been either 1879 or 1884. Or was Watson deliberately showing the conservative old *Standard* (not to be confused with the present *Evening Standard*) in a confusion of dates?

It might be well to send to the Public Library for *The Life and Letters of Sir Charles Hallé*, by C. E. and M. Hallé, to see whether he impresarioed a recital by Norman Neruda on the afternoon of March 4, 1881—or 1882. Hallé (1819–1895) was a noted concert manager of the time, and himself a musician of high repute. By the way, he not only impresarioed Neruda, he also married her.

* * *

I said once[4] that "a careful study of the *Strand* magazine text is prerequisite for any solid Sherlockian scholarship." I've been looking over the old volumes again, and call attention to the fact that Watson was a good conscientious plugger for *Strand* magazine features. Is it only coincidence that in the issue of October '91 there was a sea story ("Three in Charge") by Clark Russell; and lo, in the very next number, November '91, we find the good Watson reading Clark Russell by the fire, that stormy evening that began the affair of *The Five Orange Pips*? And then the issue of the *Strand* for March 1892 had an illustrated article about Sarasate . . . now when was it that Holmes and Watson went to hear him play? The point is that both Greenhough Smith, the editor, and good old Watson, the contributor, strengthened each other's hands. There is the further case in point of the *Strand* articles on Ears in the issues of October and November 1893, and Watson's well-synchronized reference[5] to Holmes's trifling monographs "Upon the surface anatomy of the human ear," which had been published in *The Anthropological Journal* about 1886.

* * *

Rereading "John Barrington Cowles," one of the tales in *The Captain of the Polestar*, etc., for a momentary anaesthesia, I find:

---

[4]*The Saturday Review of Literature*, Jan. 28, 1939.
[5]In *The Adventure of the Cardboard Box*, in the *Strand* for January 1893.

... we visited the Isle of May, an island near the mouth of Forth, which, except in the tourist season, is singularly barren and desolate. Beyond the keeper of the lighthouse there are only one or two families of poor fisher-folk, who sustain a precarious existence by their nets, and by the capture of cormorants and solan geese.

Does this cast any further light on the mooted problem of the Politician, Lighthouse, etc.?[6] Was the Politician really a solan goose? ... At any rate I submit that the Lighthouse was the one on the Isle of May. .... The etymology of cormorant is pleasant: *corvus marinus*, viz. sea-crow or sea-raven. ... I think one of our next projects should be a discussion of corroborations and parallels to the S.H. theme found in the writings of his contemporary A.C.D.

* * *

All my life I have wondered just what was a "tide-waiter."[7] Lo and behold the other day I was reading some of Robert Burns's letters (in *Autograph Poems and Letters of Robert Burns in the Collection of R. B. Adam*, privately printed Buffalo, 1922). In August 1795, he wrote to Mrs Riddell discussing the possibilities of a protégé of hers getting a job as a tide-waiter. The context makes it abundantly plain it meant a customs officer—one who waited for ships to come in with the tide. He wrote: "I think there is little doubt but that your interest, if judiciously directed, may procure a tide-waiter's place for your protégé, Shaw; but, alas, that is doing little for him! Fifteen pounds per an: is the salary; and the perquisites, in some lucky stations, may be ten more. ... The appointment is not in the Excise; but in the Customs." I presume Burns was himself in the Customs at that time, hence Mrs Riddell applied to him for information.

[6] Cf. *The Adventure of the Veiled Lodger.*
[7] Cf. *The Adventure of the Noble Bachelor.*

* * *

I remember I said something once about there maybe not being a "jetty" at Portsmouth[8]. . . . In my associations a jetty is always something projecting: like what we call a pier. But I've been looking at the map of Portsmouth, in Muirhead's wonderful *Guide* to England (an absolutely indispensable textbook for every lover of English literature), and I see to my correcting that Portsmouth has all sorts of wharves, docks, piers, landings, whatever we might call 'em, named as "jetties." There are Sheer Jetty, Pitch House Jetty, South Jetty, etc., but obviously where JHW landed was *Troopship Jetty*, marked large as life on the map . . . I can almost see the *Orontes* there unloading . . . at the south end of the Royal Dock Yard, close to the Royal Naval College, and with a spur of railway track (line) running right down to the landing stage so the invalid could be helped aboard an L. & S.W. train and take no time at all to "gravitate" to the waiting "Cesspool" (one and ¾ hrs. by fast train, says the *Guide*, 1920 edition).

I looked up the *Orontes* one time; because there *was* a sailing ship of that name, and if JHW had been aboard her he'd have been a lot later in arriving at Portsmouth. . . .

They also use the old term *Hard* for certain water frontages or dock areas: there is Portsea Hard, both a street and an embankment, adjoining the Royal Dock Yard; and Gosport Hard across the ferry . . . all sorts of delightful nomenclatures in Portsmouth: a ferry is called a "steam floating bridge."

Anyone who comes across Muirhead's *Guide* should snap it up . . . published by Macmillan, but I don't know if it's still in print; it is a treasury of interesting information and splendid maps and plans. There is a companion volume,

---

[8]Cf. *A Study in Scarlet*: "I [Watson] was despatched, accordingly, in the troopship *Orontes*, and landed a month later on Portsmouth jetty, with my health irretrievably ruined."

same editor, *London and Its Environs*. Of course the small Bartholomew *Atlas of London and Suburbs* is classic for pre-blitz London.

* * *

Watson mentions in *The Adventure of the Norwood Builder* "the shocking affair of the Dutch steamship *Friesland*, which so nearly cost us both our lives." There was such a ship, and she was a beauty, a smart little Red Star Liner (registry surely Belgian rather than Dutch) . . . I crossed in her in one of her latest voyages, Phila to L'pool in September 1910; I was on my way to Oxford as a Rhodes Scholar; you know, those fellows who conspire to return the U.S.A. to colonial status. I even took a photo of her lovely forward lines, as seen from the bridge on a smiling day about the equinox of that September . . . I was enormously amused and pleased by a letter written to Mr Edgar Smith by Jephro Rucastle (Lieut. Commander Richard W. Clarke of the U. S. Naval Reserve Midshipmen's School in Chicago), who has constituted himself the Naval and Marine Committee of that Institute of Higher Studies, the Five Orange Pips. Rucastle has established that there was a bark *Lone Star* in the American Registry several years ago, and a *Matilda Briggs* owned by the Oriental Trading Company in 1873. He also claims there was a *Friesland* under Dutch registry, but he has as yet been unable to locate the bark *Sophy Anderson* or the bark *Gloria Scott* or the cutter *Alicia*. His conclusion is that there were three women in Watson's life not heretofore recognized, namely, Sophy, Gloria and Alicia, and that Watson deliberately changed the original names of the vessels in question to suit his own purpose. This would explain much.

* * *

Mr Edgar Smith is wrong, I think, in speaking of "the *Town* of Mycroft" as Sherlock Holmes's birthplace. It was actually the name of the old Yorkshire farmstead where the Holmes family had long been settled.—"*My*-croft," or "my enclosed farm or field"—what a delightful name and what a sturdy assertion of the individual! Holmes himself once told Stanley Hopkins that he, as well as his brother, was almost given a place name; Sherringford or Sherrinford, I think it was; for *Shearing-ford*, a ford in the stream where the sheep were sheared.

* * *

There was one other comment by Chief Inspector Hopkins that pleased me much. "Mr Holmes is still as keenly interested in minutiæ as in the larger issues. The last time I talked with him on the telephone (a restricted number, but of course you know it: Eastbourne 221B) he was grousing about one of your American wireless programmes he had happened to pick up. With his French ancestry of course Mr Holmes is very critical of pronunciations; especially, since Watson developed him into a wine-drinker, of the French vintages. He wanted me to ask if something couldn't be done to persuade that interlocutor *not* to call it 'Sawturn.' *So-tairn, So-tairn!* Mr Holmes kept repeating in that high strident voice."

* * *

What will really be a great moment will be Holmes's first ride in a plane—it seems extraordinary that he has never been up. But the Coastal Command has promised, when the time comes, to give him a flight up to Essex. He wants to see the lights come on again at Harwich—in memory of Von Bork.

Profile by Gaslight

AT LAST ACCOUNTS MY GOOD FRIEND Chief Inspector (Retired) Stanley Hopkins was rusticating in Yoxley, Kent, at his villa (or is it his cottage?) The Bilboes. It came as something of a surprise, therefore, when I heard from him last winter from up in the North of England: he wrote on the letterhead of Morley Manor, Derbyshire, which carries the legend: "Telegrams, Smalley; Telephone, Horsley 47; Station, West Hallam, L.N.E.R." His letter, while it is now of pre-postwar vintage, is worth spreading on the record in full:

You will see by the railway address, my dear Mr. Morley, that this is really the original of the Priory House School (in Hallamshire); I come up here for a visit every winter, with my precious little American portable writing-machine. This region of course has many associations with Dr. Johnson and other writers, and I find it, especially in wintry snowscape, very stimulating for my memoirs. The present Duke of Holderness (in the legitimate line, naturally) is very proud of the Holmes association, and one of the rarest items in his museum is the leaflet written, years later, by Doctor Huxtable about Holmes's visit to Holdernesse Hall. The cloven foot-irons are of course still there, and the thin film of mud has never been removed. Central heating would be an improvement at Holdernesse, I was thinking, when I spent a night there latterly; in the same bedroom where Holmes balanced the paraffin lamp on the bed (how nervous that would have made the Duke if he had known) and upon my word, I think there is still a small oily or greasy stain on the cover-lid. His Grace and family have been at the Hall this winter, despite the rigours of the season, because the house on Carlton Terrace was hit by a buzzbomb—there can be no harm in telling you that now.

I am interested in what you wrote me in your last letter: you spoke of Monsignor Ronald Knox and Mr. S. C. Roberts as the two "incunables" (whatever that meant,) of your modern Baker Street studies, but I don't think you knew that Mr. Roberts's little biography of Watson (1931) was

261

preceded by Mr. Roberts's own trial version of the same, his *A Note on the Watson Problem*[1] of which only 100 copies were printed at the University Press, Camb., in 1929. Very few collectors indeed have this pamphlet, but naturally Mr. Roberts sent me one. I thought you would be interested to know about it. . . . What would Holmes have done in this cigarette shortage?

Yrs faithfully
STANLEY HOPKINS, O.B.E.

* * *

There are so many more important things on hand, I naturally procrastinate them to offer a possible new slant on Dr. Watson and billiards. Is it not possible that JHW was an expert, and perhaps neglected medical practice because he made more £ s d on the green tables? For note: rereading an old essay (*circa* 1905, I think) by E. V. Lucas on famous billiard players, I note that the great championship billiard matches were held in London at Thurston's Hall; and this is confirmed in an allusion to Thurston's Hall in the *Encyc. Brit.* article on Billiards, vol. III, p. 568. . . . Is it possible that Thurston was one of the great billiards masters, and that JHW was good enough to play with him? I shall do some research in this matter when opportunity serves, but I want the readers of the *Journal* to be the first to share with me this exciting conjecture.

My friend Edgar Smith has urged that one phase of this research, when I undertake it, be devoted collaterally to investigation of Watson's habits of cleanliness. Holmes, he reminds me, always had a catlike neatness; but Watson, according to the account of this evening he spent with Thurston, came back to Baker Street with chalk-marks still between his "left finger" and thumb. Holmes's comment

---

[1] Mr. Hopkins is slightly in error. The piece in question is not, actually, a trial version of the classic biography; it is, rather, a gentle but well-merited attack on the atrocious Holmesian scholarship of that other "incunable," Monsignor (then Father) Knox. —Ed. [Edgar W. Smith].

on the fact, actually, was not made until the following morning, and it could even be inferred from the context that the chalk-marks were still there then. "It is hard to believe," Mr. Smith contends, "that a man with medical training—even if he had, as you suggest, abandoned the consulting-room for the pool-room—could so far depart from the elementary principles of hygiene as to forget to wash his hands."

* * *

I've always wondered about the deal-topped table in the room in Baker Street; surely the worst possible surface for chemical experiment. *Deal*, if I understand the English usage, is not a *kind of wood*, but any soft wood, such as pine or fir, sawn into broad planks. Extremely inflammable, I should think, and erodable by acids.

* * *

I discover in Muirhead's *Southern France*, under MONTPEL-LIER, that among the Greuzes in the Musée Fabre in that city is a painting called *Young Mathematician*. How's that for a tie-up with Moriarty?

Just on impulse, I consulted the *Cyclopaedia of Painters and Paintings re* Greuze. In the list of his better-known works I found Young Girl with Doves, Rabbit, Spaniel, Apple, Watch, Broken Jug, Dead Canary—to say nothing of Old Woman with Crutch—but no Young Girl with Lamb: though one feels sure he painted one (probably with a different label).

But as always what I *did* learn is more exciting still: at the Museum in Montpellier are Six Studies of Girls. Certainly Sherlock had seen these, and hence his jealous interest in Greuze. . . . Is there some way to tie up Sherlock with Montpelier, Vermont?

Greuze was a fairly close contemporary in dates of Claude Joseph Vernet. Maybe we should engage some spirited copyist to do us the kind of painting Greuze would have done of the *Jeune Fille à l'Agneau.*

* * *

When, one day a year ago, I had to escort one of my daughters to the altar—or rather, I guess I mean the chancel, to give her away—we checked, in the frontispiece of the Old Harper edn of *The Adventures*, the perfect demeanor of arm and hand (illus. for *The Noble Bachelor*). So do the Sacred Writings shew still another usefulness.

And this leads to: has any sound study ever been devoted to the symbolism of the famous old cover-design of the early Harper editions? I think I once had it redrawn and reproduced in the *Saturday Review*,* but if so I don't know what became of the drawing. . . . Anyhow, take another look at that complicated old design: a circle of handcuffs; through which passes some kind of large man-trap? then the inner circle, a leafy sort of pattern: is it the hangman's noose? top and bottom are the bobby's head and the judge's ditto, with a horned moon above it; East a cherub; West a Medusa; and in the intervening spaces various items: handcuffs, key, dark lantern, skeleton keys, leg-cuffs. And in the center, dagger and Gordian knot . . .

* * *

Now here's something really odd. Looking through the volume of testimony in the Beecher–Tilton trial (1875) I learn that one of the leading figures in the scandal was FRANCIS MOULTON—to be exact, Francis D. Moulton—evidently the Francis Moultons were destined to all sorts of marital uncertainties. This Francis Moulton was a sort of a go-between for Rev. Beecher and Theodore Tilton; and Mrs. Moulton herself was not averse to an embrace from the eloquent parson.

I feel sure that after the delicate-minded Watson had read some of the testimony he decided NOT to buy a frame for the Beecher portrait—though Beecher himself contended through the trial that he *had* been framed.

---

*Editor's note: See above, p. 192, in the "Bowling Green" section, July 7, 1934.—S.R.

* * *

I noticed in a footnote in Swift's *Jnl to Stella* that SCOWRER was a familiar 18th-century term for a night-rover (one who scowred the streets, viz. ran about) meaning a *Mohock*, a gangster, a ruffian generally—vide Letter #43 in Swift's Jnl.

* * *

Old Stanley Hopkins wrote me again, on the date 4 November, that he was getting his Christmas letter off in good time this year. I wish you would tell Mr. Edgar Smith, he says:—

I am well into my memoirs, the 4th chapter deals entirely with Baker Street, and that reminds me: I think I am the first to point out Holmes's curious fixation on the number

265

4. When the B.S.I. finally issue that Baker Street Calendar they have long promised, I almost think the 4th of each month should be rubricated. The sign of the 4 recurred very strangely in Holmes's cases. It was on the 4th of January that he first crossed Professor Moriarty's path. It was 4th March that Watson "had good reason to remember." It was the 4th day after the New Year that the orange pips arrived. The 1st date in the KKK journal was a 4th. On the 4th May died Sir Charles Baskerville; and I don't need to remind you that the date of the Reichenbach Fall was 4 May. The case of the Bruce-Partington Plans began on the 4th day of fog. Sir Charles Damery called at Baker Street on 4th September. Senator Gibson called on 4th October. Violet Hunter got £4 per month at Col Spence Munro's. Jabez Wilson got £4 per week for copying the Encyclopaedia.

I have a feeling that both Holmes and Watson grew superstitious about number 4, and always waked on that date with the feeling that some game might be afoot.

By the bye, did you know that Holmes always maintained he never used so literary a phrase as "the game is afoot." He insisted that Watson, half asleep, misunderstood him. What he said was "Quick, never mind your *game foot*."

I hope to spend Christmas at Holdernesse.

* * *

Rereading *The Murder of Roger Ackroyd* (and on this thought the current series of these Clinical Notes must end) I find a good motto for any B.S.I. publication:—

"It is completely unimportant," said Poirot. "That is why it is so interesting."

BSJ (OS), 1 No. 1 (January 1946)

> "Not out of malevolence, you understand,
> but simply out of a spirit of inquiry."
> —Young Stamford*

IT HAS NOT BEEN PERMITTED until now to explain the seriousness of Holmes's anxiety about Professor Moriarty. Particularly the mood of strange, foreboding, veil-piercing apprehension at the end of *The Valley of Fear*. He had just been reading *The Dynamics of an Asteroid*, and although no one in the scientific press twigged it, Holmes got the idea. Moriarty was on the trail of atomic energy.

* * *

Add influence of S. Holmes on other writers:—Chapter 17 of *Sir Nigel*, published 1906, by A. Conan Doyle; describing sea battle between English and Spaniards, in the Channel, date 1350 or thereabouts:

> The King sprang up with a joyous face. "The game is afoot, my friends!" said he. "Dress, John! Dress, Walter! Squires, bring the harness!"

* * *

Add influence of John H. Watson ditto:—*The White Company*, Chapter XI, description of the lady Maude Loring, anno 1366:

> . . . attired in a long sweeping robe of black velvet, with delicate tracery of white lace at neck and at wrist.

* * *

One of my grandfathers, James Bird, was at one time a junior partner in the famous old publishing house Chapman & Hall (Dickens's publishers, inter alios). Bird was a great collector of autograph letters, especially of writers and musicians. Looking again through one of his old scrapbooks

---

*Editor's note: Morley used this quotation at the beginning of every subsequent "Clinical Notes" through BSJ (os), 4 No. 1 (January 1949).—S.R.

I find the following MS letter—written while Charles Hallé
was impresarioing in Manchester:

> Greenhays,
> Manchester
> 2 Novbr 83

Dear Mr. Watts

Will you kindly, on receipt of this, telegraph to Madame
Norman Neruda (20 Linden Gardens, Bayswater, London)
the name of the Hotel at which you have taken rooms for
her and her particulars about a rehearsal of her pieces?

You will much oblige

> Yours truly
>
> CHARLES HALLÉ

Whether this was before, or after, Hallé's marriage to
Neruda—before, I like sentimentally to think—it shows his
solicitude; and adds her private address (alas, less romantic
than Briony Lodge?) to our files.

* * *

My friend Dr. Henry Pleasants, Jr., of West Chester, Pennsylvania, tells in his book *From Kilts to Pantaloons* (privately
printed, West Chester, Pa., 1945) an anecdote that tempts
me outside the convention of not mentioning Dr. Watson's
literary agent by name.

Dr. Pleasants was a member of the Haverford College
cricket team that played in England in the summer of 1904.
(In the great days of Philadelphia cricket Haverford College
used to send a team every four years to play English
schools, colleges, and clubs.) The climax of the tour was
always the game with the famous Marylebone Cricket
Club. Dr. Pleasants tells how thrilled the Haverford boys
were when they learned that A.C.D. had been chosen to
play for M.C.C. He writes:—

> The M.C.C. started batting; and for a while it looked as
> if we would have an easy time. Our bowling was deadly.
> Then out on the field ambled the great novelist. He was tall

and must have weighed well over 200 pounds. As he approached the wicket, he nodded to each of us and made some dry comment on the progress of the game. He then took his position at bat, and started in. He was an accomplished cricketer. For fully an hour he smashed the ball over the field. Only twice did he give chances. Both of these went to me; and each time I disgraced myself by dropping the ball like a hot potato. We finally put him out in time to win the game; but it was no credit to me. I could have immortalized myself in the cricketing world by catching him out. He was a great sportsman.

* * *

A NOTE ON THE WATSON–JEPHSON PROBLEM

I do not need to remind you of the Curious Incident of Dr. Jephson's wound. The story, *J. Habakuk Jephson's Statement*, first printed in *Cornhill* in the late '80's, was regarded by its author as his first real literary success. (V. *Memories and Adventures*, Chapter VIII.) In his Statement, J. Habakuk Jephson says:—

> When the war broke out I left Brooklyn and accompanied the 113th New York Regiment through the campaign. I was present at the second battle of Bull Run and at the Battle of Gettysburg. Finally, I was severely wounded at Antietam and would probably have perished on the field had it not been for the kindness of a gentleman named Murray, who had me carried to his house and provided me with every comfort.

It is surely tempting to believe that this is not only J. H. Jephson writing, but also J. H. Watson. The congenital uncertainty of dates, the interposition of one Murray, even the familiar and comfortable cadence of the prose, put intuition on the alert.

Let us examine the history of this Dr. Jephson. He was

the son of a Plymouth Brethren preacher in Lowell, Mass., U.S.A. From his evangelical parent young J. Habakuk received his strong zeal for the abolition of slavery. "While I was studying medicine at Harvard University," he tells us, "I had already made a mark as an advanced Abolitionist." After taking his degree, perhaps about 1850, young Dr. Jephson bought a share in a medical practice in Brooklyn. Probably he was attracted to that city by the renown of another great Abolitionist, Rev. Henry Ward Beecher, who was called to the pulpit of the Plymouth Church in 1847. We know that by 1859 Dr. Jephson was well established in Brooklyn, in busy practice, but had also found time to publish his liberal pamphlet *Where Is Thy Brother* which made a great stir. I should like to think it came from the same printing shop where *Leaves of Grass* first grew, but the record is explicit. It bore the imprint of Swarburgh, Lister & Co., so probably Dr. Jephson had it published in his home town of Lowell. Swarburgh is obviously a variant of another respected family name in Lowell, the Swanboroughs. To Harold Swanborough of Lowell, you remember, J. Stark Munro was writing (some years later) those lively letters.

His wound cured, Dr. Habakuk Jephson returned to Brooklyn. He had married a daughter of Josiah Vanburger, "the well-known wood engraver." From Vanburger's shop came a proof copy of the engraving of Dr. Beecher, which he always intended to get framed. It was in these postbellum years that he changed the spelling of his middle name from the Biblical form Habakkuk; he preferred it not to show three K's. He was a busy man; sometimes a certain Dr. Jackson had to help in the practice.[1] But exposure and exertion in the war years had caused a lung congestion; sea voyages were advised, and he probably laid in copies of some of the earliest tales by Clark Russell.

[1] Cf. "I have no doubt Jackson would take my practice."—*The Crooked Man*.

270

To recapitulate, we can see that a son of Dr. Jephson would infallibly inherit certain habits: (1) a vagueness as to the date or place of battles and wounds; (2) being rescued by someone called Murray; (3) sharing medical practice with someone called Jackson; (4) a taste for pamphleteering or brochuring; (5) admiration of Ward Beecher and Clark Russell; (6) a lipsetting, eyesparkling, handclenching and wound-remembering attitude toward the Civil War.

Something else, of course, that a less lucky son could inherit would be the distressing baptismal name Habakuk; enough in itself to lead to irregularity and despair.

In search of health Dr. Jephson (after calling in Jackson) went in 1873 for his strange voyage aboard the *Marie Celeste*. It was not until some years later still that, as his lung trouble grew worse, he set down the facts. One presumes that the appalling scandal of the Beecher–Tilton trial, in 1875, did much to undermine his failing resistance. The publicity, even persecution, caused by his accidental connection with race problems, saddened his last years. About the time of the Beecher trial he advised his two young sons to go to England for their studies and to take a different name. The older boy, also christened Habakuk, asked "If not Jephson, what?" The younger boy, John, mischievously echoed "Whatson!" Even then he had a pawky touch of humor.

This younger boy, already planning to follow his father into medicine, was named in full John Henry Jephson, the Henry of course for Henry Ward Beecher.

The older boy, after intervals of prosperity, took to drink, as shown years later on his heirloom watch. He found, living in England, the family name Habakuk caused so much chaff that he always abbreviated it to the initial. If you think this only surmise, let us check by the proper sortilege. Turn to the Book of Habakuk which you will find near the end of the Old Testament. It has only three chapters; the natural place to look would be chapter 2, 21st verse. But chapter 2 has only 20 verses so naturally one turns back to the 1st verse and reads it again. Then you will see why the scars and dents on H. Watson's timepiece. The 2nd chapter, 1st verse, begins:—

I will stand upon my watch.

The speculation rests. Was Watson an American?

* * *

Perhaps Mr. J. F. Christ, in B.S.J. No. 1 (pp. 24, 25), is too tentative in suggesting that Holmes was named for the famous Bishop Thomas Sherlock ("the stormy petrel of the English religious world"—catalogue of Argosy Bookstore, N.Y.C.). Myself, however, think it may rather have been William Sherlock, father of Thomas, from whom Holmes was christened. Thomas Sherlock was a strong defender of miracles, which might have strong appeal to Holmes's mother; but William Sherlock, who became dean of St. Paul's, was the author of *A Practical Discourse Concerning Death*, which sounds very Baker Street. King Charles's head was still firm on his shoulders when William Sherlock was born: his dates were 1641–1707. Both divines were great brochurists, and both by the way were Cambridge men. There can be little doubt that the detective's full name was either Thomas Sherlock Holmes or William Sherlock Holmes.

To quote Thomas Sherlock himself, in his preface to *The Use and Intent of Prophecy, in Six Discourses* (3rd edition, London, 1732): "If the Notion is not approved, it is at least an innocent one; and I am not so fond of it as to enter further into the Defense of it."

Of course it was Thomas Sherlock whose sermons were so much admired by Dr. Johnson. In that great chrestomathy *Johnsonian Miscellanies* by G. B. Hill, II, 429, I find what might well be an agreeable motto for this *Journal*. It comes among the anecdotes told by Mr. Wickins, "the respectable draper in Lichfield":

"Sir," said he, "do you ever read any others?"

"Yes, Doctor; I read Sherlock."

"Ay, Sir, *there* you drink the cup of salvation to the bottom."

BSJ (OS), 1 No. 2 (April 1946)

As I LOOK OVER MY CASE-BOOKS I can see now (what was mercifully concealed from me at the time) how strangely significant were the spring and summer of 1930. The world is not yet prepared, and very likely never will be, for the full details of some of those episodes. There was the Scandal on the Seacoast of Bohemia (viz. Hoboken); the Affair of Mulligan's Kitchen (opposite the old Doelger Brewery, somewhere in the East 50's); the Decline and Fall of the Grillparzer Club (where I first met Rex Stout); and the Story of the Autographed Bathroom (on Lexington Avenue) where I encountered Bill Hall. As the waters of Long Island Sound grew warmer there were the Singular Circumstances of the Cruiser *Snippet*, Captain Bob Leavitt, a few leagues off the Stamford Yacht Club. But of all these adventures, which mingled comedy and calamity in quantum suff., I think of none which had more bearing upon our present curiosity than the Proffer of the Third Oldfashioned.

There was a basement speakeasy, then momentarily esteemed by the Grub Street Runners of Messrs. Doubleday Doran and Co. There, whether by chance or solicitation, I met my old friend Mr. Francis C. Henry, at that time sales manager of that firm. I am too proud, or too prudent, to look up dates and memos, but my thought is that the author of the Sacred Writings had lately died (date? June 1930?) and his American publishers planned the first complete collected edition of the Holmes stories. I think that Mr. Henry was accompanied and enforced by his faithful assemblymen Messrs. Malcolm Johnson, Charles Halliwell Duell, Daniel Longwell, and Ogden Nash; at any rate they were only a few olives or cherries away down that shining counter. According to the ritual prescribed in the prohibition era no one talked business until the Third Drink—the one which George Herbert, my favorite poet, says is fatal; see *The Church Porch* stanza 8. With the third oldfashioned amberlucent between us (I could still drink bourbon or rye in those days) Mr. Henry and his assiduents suggested I should write a preface for the projected two-volume Holmes. I said if the fee would be generous enough for me to go to Baker Street and back I'd do it. Actually it fell short by about 200 dollars; but that was my fault, not theirs. They paid the largest price I ever heard of for a preface to any book.

By coincidence, July 16 that year, the Book-of-the-Month Club chose the Holmes Omnibus. I think, but am not sure, it was the only time the Club has ever taken an older book as a monthly selection. I did not urge it, but was delighted. What a break for Doubleday!

On July 25, 1930, I wrote my preface.

On July 30, 1930, I got my check.

On August 2, I think it was, I sailed in RMS *Caronia*.

I've just looked it up. I was only 6 minutes wrong. According to the *Abstract of Log*, RMS *Caronia* (Twin Screw) sailed 11.54 p.m. August 1st. She had Ambrose Channel L.V. abeam at 2.06 a.m. She made Eddystone abeam at 1.18 G.M.T., August 9. Captain F. G. Brown, RNR. My wine account, as of August 9, was £2.16.6. Stateroom C 47. Table 29. Saloon steward, Wimbush.—As a matter of historic record (since I've now looked up the chits) in the year 1930, when one bought drinks for cash in the smokeroom, a Martini or a Manhattan cost 21 cents; an Old Fashioned 25 cents; a whiskey sour 37 cents; and a "John Collins" (so Cunard called it) 37 cents. They called a highball a "Long Cocktail." Lemon squash was 13 cents.

I don't remember why, I stayed at the Stafford Hotel (St. James's Place) instead of the good old Wigmore Hotel as in previous years—I once, about 1926, met A.C.D. on Wigmore Street carrying a "gripsack" of ectoplasm slides for his lecture that evening.—I see that at the Stafford in August 1930 one paid 15 bob for room and bath. Breakfast was 4 bob. Newspaper was 2d. I'm chagrined that under the rubric "Wine, cocktails, spirits, liqueurs, ale & stout, minerals" I spent nothing, so I can't check against F. H. Moulton. But I want to record that the 5-shilling lunch at the Hind's Head Hotel at Bray (where the Vicar was) was like this:—Fried fillet of haddock; Steak & Kidney Pudding; Silverside, Marrow, New Potatoes; Treacle Tart; and Cheddar Cheese.

I have always been griped because Holmes never spoke of Mrs. Hudson's treacle tart. I usually took two slices and Watson three. I don't believe there is another B.S.I. who ever had a Baker Street treacle tart; and Watson, with his experience in India, always insisted on kedgeree for breakfast. The *Orontes*, by the way, mushed up a mighty wholesome kedgeree.

* * *

The famous revival of the play *Sherlock Holmes*, by William Gillette, in the winter 1929–30; the lamented death of the Sacred Writer; the wide circulation of the new omnibus edition; and the increasing nostalgia for Victorian comedy and melodrama (certainly stimulated by the Hoboken production of *After Dark* and *The Black Crook*) were all seed on the wind. (I use this phrase à propos; it is the title of Rex Stout's first and best book.) Then came Mr. S. C. Roberts's brilliant little biography *Doctor Watson* (Faber & Faber, 1931). Mr. Vincent Starrett followed in 1933 with his admirable *The Private Life of Sherlock Holmes*. This was reviewed (Dec. 2, 1933) in *The Saturday Review of Literature* by Mr. Elmer Davis, a stunning piece afterward revised into its present classical form "On the Emotional Geology of Baker Street" (in *221B*). The first actual suggestion that some of the devotees might join in an informal sodality, or even whisky-and-sodality, came about by devolution from the many paragraphs uttered in the "Bowling Green" and "Trade Winds" departments of the S.R.L. Mr. Elmer Davis promptly composed a pointed and humorous constitution and buy-laws, first printed in the S.R.L. of Feb. 17, 1934.

There was in those days a small back room, up the canonical count of steps, at Christ Cella's restaurant on East 45 Street. To paint 221B on the door and gather there a few appropriate memorabilia was an agreeable amusement. There were on that upper floor two retiring rooms, which we persuaded Christ Cella to label as SHERLOCK and IRENE. This puzzled some customers, but was effective for segregation. The occult and retentive 3rd Garrideb, F.V.M., amused himself about that time in the smokeroom of a Cunard liner by putting together a crossword puzzle based on Sherlockian allusions. This, printed in the "Bowling Green," was used as a shibboleth for entrance into B.S.I. membership. I think about a dozen correspondents answered it with 100% accuracy and were enrolled as charter members. Unexpectedly, one of these was a charming young woman from Illinois, Miss D. B., who was immediately elevated as *The* Woman and given the statutory luncheon of honor (3 hours) when she visited New York a few months later.* There is an appropriate fogginess of detail as to the earliest proceedings of the Irregulars; due to the fact that when Cella moved from his original quarters to a luxurious renovation next door, some brigandeering bibliophile swiped the scrapbook in which a multitude of clippings and souvenirs had been carefully preserved.

So the B.S.I. never had any strictly formal organization; and since the disappearance of the early memoranda, no one remembers who were the founding fathers. It is sad to record that Miss B. married a man who, so far as we know, has no special interest in Sherlock. The first dinner was held June 5, 1934. Mr. H. G. Wells, who had been in New York about that time, should have been there, but admitted that he could not pass the examination. One member, of a horoscopic bent, announced that zodiacal and astrological study indicated Sherlock's birthday as probably January 6,

*Editor's note: See above, pp. 181–185, 188–191.—S.R.

1854. This pleased me as it coincided with the birthday, in 1894, of the 2nd Garrideb, Dr. Felix Morley. So we decided to hold the annual meeting, if possible, some time during January.

At the first of the more formal meetings, in December 1934, we were lucky enough to have William Gillette as our guest of honor; also Mr. A. G. Macdonell who had been one of the founders of the Sherlock Holmes society in London, which started about the same time as the B.S.I. That was the occasion when the Gasogene scoured the town to find exactly the right kind of Woolworth bauble to represent the Blue Carbuncle in the guts of the Christmas Goose. The worthy Cella was considerably puzzled by our insistence that the goose be cooked with the jewel inside it. That was also the dinner to which Alec Woollcott came unbidden, made himself happily conspicuous, and afterward rather ridiculed our naïveté in his *New Yorker* piece. As none of us had had the slightest appetite for publicity, I think the original group were a trifle annoyed.

The happiest achievement of the B.S.I. was when it attracted the attention of our devoted Edgar Smith. Very different from Woollcott, he wrote in a vein of decorous modesty asking if he could be put on the waiting list and offered to undergo any sort of inquest of suitability. It was plain from the first that here was *The* Man. After the Woollcott condescension most of us were content to go on without any Stated Meetings—indeed, I think several years did go by—but Mr. Edgar Smith's affectionate zeal, not less than his Sherlockian scholarship, his gusto in pamphleteering, his delight in keeping orderly records and his access to mimeographic, and parchment-engrossing and secretarial resources, all these were irresistible. I don't suppose that any society of Amateur Mendicants has ever had a more agreeable or competent fugleman. It was probably Mr. Edgar Smith who took pains to ensure the correct serving of a scroll representing the Naval Treaty, under the

Murray Hill Hotel's largest dish-cover, as in the Sacred Writings; this, I think, was at an early dinner when Dr. Harrison Martland, medical examiner of the City of Newark, was our guest. The Murray Hill kitchen was always able to give us a very satisfactory replica of Mrs. Hudson's catering, including curried chicken. As these notes are written it is likely that the familiar Murray Hill may not again shelter us; Edgar Smith's suggestion of the Chelsea as a possible refuge is certainly worth notice. It is probably the only other hotel in Manhattan that still has some Baker Street flavor; I believe it actually antedates the Murray Hill by two years.

It is odd to recall, thinking back over past dinners, that one of the pleasantest talks we ever had was made by Mr. Denis Conan Doyle. He was naturally and filially moved by the profound homage implied in our proceedings. That he afterward changed his mind, and decided that in some sinister way the B.S.I. were invading the property rights of his father's estate, is likely to become a permanent liptwisting footnote in literary history.

There have been, of course, occasional hard-minded observers who thought it silly for a group of grown men to dally so intently over a literature of entertainment for which even its own author had only moderate regard. Let me repeat what I have said before, that no printed body of modern social history (including Keyserlings, Spenglers, Paretos, and other brows like Dover Cliff) either by purpose or accident contains a richer pandect of the efficient impulses of its age. It has shown itself keen forecast in many ways, and some of its allusions may yet again be painfully timely. I wouldn't be surprised at any moment to see Afghanistan, or the river Orontes, or the Coptic Patriarch, or the dynamics of an asteroid, reappear in the news.

BSJ (OS), 1 No. 3 (July 1946); also in *Sherlock Holmes by Gas-Lamp*

279

THERE ARE CALIBRATIONS AND CURLICUES in the prosody of man. It was Elizabeth Winspear who, coming generously to my aid for a few days to bring me abreast of neglected doings, discovered (for 20 cents) in the Opportunity Shop a copy of that almost completely forgotten Conan Doyle, *The Mystery of Cloomber*. How well I remember reading it in the old Pratt Library in Baltimore, back about 1902; and I don't think I had reread it since. Even in his *Memories and Adventures*, A. C. D. never mentioned it; and it wasn't included in the Collected Edition.

Judge, therefore, of my apex of attention when the well-beloved doctor makes his inevitable confusion between John and James. In the very first sentence the narrator is identified as James Fothergill West; but after that bravura introit ("My name is James Fothergill West"), he is always bespoken, alluded, mentioned and referred to as John.

This I think is so magnificent that no one but La Yuhasova can properly appreciate, and I urge that she note that apocryptic detail.

* * *

The other day I got a letter from one of my idols; one of the truly great poets of our tongue and time: Ralph Hodgson. Bless his old heart (he's now well over 70; comparatively little known; but one of the few pure singing voices, never spoiled by anyone or anything; he has absolute pitch in the English lyric, with both perfect strings, of anger and of ecstasy) he lives now, by some mysterious transmigrancy, at "Owlacres, Route 1, Minerva, Ohio."

I was saying one day to my bro FVM what about Watson's friend Thurston and the billiard parlours? He said, "write to Hodgson, who used many yrs ago to be a professional billiard marker." After long delay I did, and here's Hodgson's letter, arrived today:

OWLACRES,
ROUTE 1, MINERVA, OHIO.

I *can* tell you something about THURSTON. At least I think I can. Many years ago I chanced upon an almost

280

totally uninspired book called *The Commercial Companion*. Almost but not wholly. For there I read this statement: "Sometime prior to 1814 John Thurston received from one of his customers an order for a small size billiard table to take abroad. . . ." I noted this down opposite the name —Thurston, John, Cabinet Maker, 78 Margaret St., Cavendish Sq., in Kent's Directory of London, 1816. Then I looked up the 1820 Edition and found: "Thurston, J., Superior Billiard Table Manuf. 14 Catharine St. Strand." Next I turned to the P. O. London Directory–1823 and read: "Thurston, John, Superior Portable & other Billiard table & Bagatelle Manufacturer, 14 Catherine St. Strand." Then the P. O. London Dir. 1836 & found: "Thurston John, Billiard-Table & Bagatelle Manuf. to his Majesty, 14 Catherine St. Strand."

I turned to the advertising pages at the end of Pigot's National & Commercial Directory 1828–9, & had a good look at the page which I now take out & enclose with this account. About that time Thurston turned publisher and got out a most charming book of Billiards in marbled-board foolscap paper size; the bright green label (like a tiny little B.T. cloth) bearing the legend *"Thurston's Translation of Mingaud's Billiards, 1831."* I do want to speak of the large (torn, unhappily) plate, its frontispiece: a lithograph I take it to be but I'm not sure—there's a touch of aquatint about it. One of the figures—not a player—or at least not playing, is the foxiest looking Billiards wrong'un ever drawn. A marvel of character.

In Roberts' Billiards, 1869 in a note on p. 72 I read: "The chief table-makers are Messrs. Burroughs & Watts, Soho Square [where they still are unless they were bombed out], Messrs. Cox & Yeman [I'm not sure if they still hold on] & *Messrs. Thurston & Coy, Catharine Street, Strand.*" After that I got out the Badminton Billiards, 1896, & looked up Sydenham Dixon's references to the founder of the House, pp. 10, 11 & Arch'd Boyd's tribute to it on p. 55. From these I turned to personal memories of matches played in their room at their present address in Leicester Square— under the Green Room Club. And in *News of the World*, some time in the mid-'30's:—

Playing in his "Daily Mail" Gold Cup tournament heat
against Newman at *Thurston's*, Davis the British Billiards
champion and world's snooker champion made a world's
record break of 1,177 under the new baulk-line rule.

There you are. I have made out a flawless case. Dr. Watson
may have had a friend of the name, who though a billiards
player was not a member of the illustrious family. He *may*
have had. There *were* other Thurstons. I leave it to you and
the other Masters of the Saga.

(Signed) RALPH HODGSON.

Anyhow, read, brood, perpend and consider. And if you
never encountered Rafe Hodgson's poems, look them up.
They are the real miracle.

* * *

In *The New Yorker* for April 20, 1946, I note a paragraph
informing us that The East Side Playboys, Inc., a social
club, is located at 221 Avenue B. When the Murray Hill
Hotel has been taken from us, the B.S.I. may wish to
consider a merger.

282

* * *

Good old Stanley Hopkins writes me (his hand is getting very shaky) that Chapter 18 of his Memoirs (to be entitled, perhaps, *On, Stanley, On?*) proves conclusively that Holmes absented himself during what Edgar Smith has so deftly called "The Great Hiatus" so as not to be implicated in any way with the famous but sordid and disgusting case of NEILL CREAM (1891–1892) . . . "one of the few top-hole murder cases," says old Hopkins, "in which a bookseller was publicized, apparently quite at random. It was a horrible transpontine orgy. Miss Frinywyd Tennyson Jesse and your own Mr. Lester Pearson have written glibly about it; but we here at Scotland Yd had to scavenge the loathly details. Holmes, bless him, was as neat as a cat, even in his taste for crime."

* * *

The Resident Patient, in his slow, patient researches and rereadings of Victorian Corn (the Corn of the Century) marks for you the close of Chapter VI of *Rupert of Hentzau* (1898):

"The game was afoot now; who could tell the issue of it?"

There is something a bit spooky about Rupert of H. also. In Chapter XIII Rupert looks at his watch: "it was ten minutes to ten." Yrs ago (Jan. 17, 1922) my bro FVM was rereading the tale, looked at his watch at those words: exactly 9:50. On Oct. 6, 1934, I was rereading in that same copy, found his memo, looked at my watch: exactly 9:50 P.M.

* * *

Reading Richard Clarke's delightful note on the Nomenclature of Watson's Ships in the April *Journal*, I was led to wonder if he remembered the *Norah Creina* of Stevenson's *The Wrecker*—a fine novel to read or reread any time; and oddly pathetic now when so much has happened in the

Pacific. I was rereading *The Wrecker* about 1938 and put in my copy an Airways tourist folder of that time that is queer reading now:—

> Two perfect islands for complete rest, relaxation and sport . . . WAKE and MIDWAY, isolated from the confusion and conflict of all the rest of the world . . . touched only by the Flying Clipper ships.

Midway Island, and the *Norah Creina*, play an important part in *The Wrecker*. Alan Lang Strout, of Lubbock, Texas, wrote interestingly in *The Saturday Review of Literature* for April 8, 1939, of the closing passage in *The Resident Patient* which tells (in 1893) of this ill-fated steamer "which was lost some years ago with all hands upon the Portuguese coast."

> I always regretted the loss of that ship [Professor Strout says]. Such a pretty Irish name! But I have been glad to discover that Dr. Watson was in error, for, only a year before, the *Norah Creina* carried Mr. Dodd safely into Honolulu: see R. L. Stevenson's *The Wrecker*, which appeared serially in *Scribner's Magazine* in 1891 and as a book in 1892. Possibly the change from the Pacific to the Atlantic proved, ultimately, too severe a one for the gallant barque.

The change was indeed severe: not only from Pacific to Atlantic but from a schooner (not barque) to steamship. Putting engines in her undoubtedly made her cranky.

Clarke notes in his piece that the *Matilda Briggs* was of Shanghai registry. I fear she came to her end in the East, for my grand old Findlay's Sailing Directory of the Indian Archipelago and China and Japan Seas (1878 edition, the one used by Conrad) lists on p. 679 as a hazard of Batavia Bay the *Matilda Rock*. According to the custom of marine geographers, a reef or shoal is named for the vessel that first ran upon it, or surveyed it. Was the *Matilda* on her way to look for the giant rats? Batavia would be a port of call.

* * *

I can't help noticing that some of the correspondence that has frowned upon the publication of the *Journal* as an invasion of proprietary prerogatives, or something or other, has emanated from Minstead (near Lyndhurst), Hants.

Do you remember the Socman of Minstead, the villain and ruffian of *The White Company*, the wicked uncle?

BSJ (os), 1 No. 4 (October 1946)

THE JUNE 1935 ISSUE of *The Railway Magazine* (English) contains a letter (p. 457) referring to Mr. Alan Rannie's article in the preceding issue (on Sherlock Holmes and Railways as listed in *Baker Street Inventory*). This letter, signed by A. G. R. Hickes, B.A., discusses the pleasant point, just about where was it that Sir Henry got from the train his first view of the moor?

Mr. Hickes offers alternatives, but votes for DAINTON (not marked in my atlas) where I gather the GWR line traverses a high embankment. (Page 409 of the same issue shows photo of an express train actually on DAINTON BANK, with moor in background.) The train, Mr. Hickes thinks, was either the Cornishman or its predecessor The Flying Dutchman; Watson seems to have the time wrong for its departure from Paddington.

I wonder if Dr. Mortimer's spaniel would have been allowed in the railway carriage with them?

* * *

I wish I might have joined The Six Napoleons of Baltimore at the meeting which saw their subsumption as a Scion Society last September. I wrote Paul Stephen Clarkson at the time suggesting that they ask one of the old Bonaparte family of Balto to be an honorary member; and also the noble librarian of the Enoch Pratt Library, who might have brought with him pp. 73–74 of a book called *Internal Revenue*.

* * *

The editor of the *Journal* sent me a while back a letter he had received from Chief Inspector Stanley Hopkins (Retired) which would normally have been printed in the Letters to Baker Street pages, but which, by virtue of the proprietary rights I exercise in all matters appertaining to the old boy, I immediately commandeered for incorporation in these Notes. Hopkins is evidently in one of his lighter moods:

The Bilboes,
Yoxley, Kent,
3 Nov., 1946

My dear Mr. Edgar Smith:—

It was good to hear from you again, and kind of you to send Miss Jane Nightwork to me with a letter of introduction. I shd have acknowledged this sooner, but I was working on chapter 12 of my *Memories and Adventures*. Miss Nightwork (what a spirited girl! in an experience of women extending over three continents and several archipelagoes I have never met a more feminine female) happily visited when I was staying in a private hotel in the Strand—leading a comfortless, meaningless existence. She took me one night to the cinema to see Olivier's production of *Henry Fifth* ("Hank Sank" she called it in her blithe American way) and gave me some admirable encouragements.

By pleasing coincidence I had just been totting up Mr. Holmes's allusions to Shakespeare. I never forgot, of course, that in *The Adventure of the Empty House* Mr. Holmes twice quoted from The Bard; but I had forgotten, until Miss Nightwork nudged me (or squeezed, rather) in Act Three, Scene 1, of *Henry Fifth*, that the immortal cry *The game is afoot!* was King Harry's phrase. And then of course (while we were having a Gin and It afterward, at the Criterion) J. N. pointed out that The Bard had used it in her own play, 1st *Henry IV*, Act I, iii, 279. Miss Nightwork knows that piece well; she was born, she tells me, in 2nd *Henry IV*, Act III, ii, 213. I was greatly annoyed when your friend Mr. Morley, in one of his articles, suggested that Mr. Holmes never used the phrase "The game is afoot." He thought it was a literary phrase, when it was nothing but a quotation from Shakespeare. If my book ever gets published, it will put him where he belongs.

What always pleased me about Shakespeare, likewise Mr. Holmes, one forgets their best stuff because one thinks it was one's own. I've also got a good piece about Holmes's geography, for instance you are quite right about Boscombe, it's on the northern border of Somerset and not at all where he pretended to place it (in Hereford). You can check it in your Bartholomew's survey of maps, which if the members haven't got they know nothing of British topography.

There were some other passages in *Henry Fifth* which might well have startled me if Miss Nightwork hadn't been there. She really does make one feel younger than he is.

I hope your dinner in January can still be held at the old Murray Hill Hotel. I remember when I stayed there at the time of the Long Island Cave Mystery.

Forgive an old man, as Miss Jane did, for what Shakespeare called "Small time."

Respftly yrs.,
STANLEY HOPKINS (O.B.E.)

I commend Miss Nightwork's discrimination in taking Stanley to see that Olivier movie *Henry V*. I think it's the most marvelous spectacle, the greatest triumph of representative genius, I've ever seen.

* * *

The interesting question, how much did Mycroft really know about Canada, or those more complicated quaternion problems involving simultaneously the Navy, India, Canada, and bimetallism (v. *Bruce-Partington Plans*) may now come usefully under focus. In Calgary, Alberta, your R.P. encouraged three admirable indoctrinaires to nucleolate as a scion B.S.I. I don't know whether they have yet communicated with Buttons and chosen their symbolism. I learned that Henry Baskerville's ranche was not far from Calgary; in fact he was one of the early members of the famous Ranchmen's Club of that delightful city. I got a vague unconfirmed impression that the ranche bought by Edward Prince of Wales (now Windsor) included some of the cattle-acres first settled upon by Baskerville. The whole gorgeous region of Calgary is rich in overtones of both sacred and semi-sacred writ. Dinosaur Park, for instance, where the creatures of a Lost World, in exact facsimile, startle you among the trees. The Irregulars of Calgary will probably hold an annual picnic or Gymkhana on Baker Creek, which runs into the Bow River northwest of Banff. Your gospeller descended from a Brewster bus, about 51°21' N and 116°4' W, to dip a hand into that cold and precise stream.

Please list Dr. E. P. Scarlett, of the Calgary Associate Clinic, 214 Sixth Avenue West, Calgary, Alta., as point d'appui or tendo Achillis of this new group. Another member, Mr. George B. Coutts, remembers an old cowpuncher who used to ride horseback 40 miles to High River, in the '90's, to get the *Strand* on the day it arrived there. A third member, Miss Kathleen I. Morrison, has already contributed to our archives.

* * *

Speaking of semi-sacred associations, in Winnipeg I had the pleasure of meeting a distinguished physician, Dr. Gerard Allison, who was named for the immortal Brigadier. Dr. Allison's father, well-remembered Canadian critic and man of letters, was strongly infatuated with the Gerard saga at the time of the boy's birth. Dr. Allison is proud of Russian Dressing à la Brigadier which he concocts, and of which he gave me the formula. Both Dr. Gerard Allison and his brother Carlyle Allison (named for the author of whom S.H. had not heard), editor of the Winnipeg *Tribune*, are hereby nominated as out-of-town members of the Calgary conclave.

* * *

My great collection of Victorian Corn is, of course, vigorously cross-indexed; blood-streams of allusion, collusion, and association carry from author to author. An ancient work of claptrap, E. W. Hornung's *The Amateur Cracksman*, was famous in its day; I've been reminded of it lately by a biography of the great Sir Stamford Raffles of Singapore. Hornung, of course, introduced A. J. Raffles, burglar and cricketer. He dedicated his book "To A.C.D., This Form of Flattery." The adventures of Raffles and Bunny seemed, even to a boyish reader, pretty thin stuff, but they helped pass away some of the enormous leisures of childhood, between football or one-old-cat or tadpole dredging.

The only Raffles tale I really resented was *Wilful Murder* (one of the tales in *The Amateur Cracksman*). Here the plot was so completely identical, even sometimes in phrase and setting, with *Charles Augustus Milverton*, that I thought Hornung had trespassed a bit far on his brother-in-law. If you were to reread them side by side you'd be startled. So was I when I happened to notice that *The Amateur Cracksman* was copyright by Scribner in 1902; and I seem to remember that *Milverton* was in *The Return*, which series didn't begin printing until late 1903.

No one is less a bibliographer than I, but won't some expert, maybe Dave Randall, give us the exact relative chronology of these two stories?

* * *

"It may be doubted if the human race is notably happier today than it was in the age of Grover Cleveland and Lord Rosebery and Sherlock Holmes."

—Elmer Davis, in *Saturday Review of Literature*,
August 31, 1946

BSJ (OS), 2 No. 1 (January 1947)

Now that the analysts are beginning to work on Sherlock Holmes, it is just to observe that like everyone else he betrays much that he did not intend. Holmes's generalizations are surely based, like everyone's, on his own personal experience? When he says, in *The Musgrave Ritual*:

> "A man always finds it hard to realize that he may have finally lost a woman's love, however badly he may have treated her."

is it not fair to deduce that he had learned this in his own emotional career? I don't remember whether Mr. Davis quotes this passage in his classic "Emotional Geology of Baker Street"? If not, it belongs there in footnote.

* * *

A few weeks ago I had occasion to take down from a high shelf an old album of postcards collected in youth—you may remember how in those arcadian days of say 1900–1906 one collected picture postcards. A card slipped out, fell on the floor; I stuck it behind something on a bookshelf where it has been standing for several weeks. Tonight, by some curio of chance—perhaps because I am feeling relaxed while waiting for the Sherlock program to go on in a few minutes—I looked at the card.

It was given me (in 1904) by the mother of a boyhood friend, Temple Tweedy of Washington, D.C.—who is alluded to in *Thorofare*, by the way; he is "the boy who lived at 3416 13th Street N.W."—and he actually became an Olympic shotputter; now a lumber merchant in L. I. City, and I sometimes see him on the L. I. trains, to this day—

To Temple's mother (Mrs. Frank Tweedy, as per the card) this was just a postcard from some friend of hers traveling in Switzerland.

But look, please, where it was printed:

ANSTALT BRÜGGER, MEIRINGEN

This shews that there is a printing shop in Meiringen, and I think we should write to them and have them do an insert of some sort for the B.S.J.

The scene shewn on the card is of Brünig (Grand Buffet de la Gare). I've looked up Brünig in the atlas; it seems to be the next station to Meiringen on the railway. There is a lady under a parasol in the picture, walking next to a gentleman—is it Dr. Watson?

* * *

In a book catalog of P. H. Muir (for Elkin Mathews Ltd.), Takeley, Bishop's Stortford, I find a first edition of the *Memoirs* described as "Lord Rosebery's copy, with his pencil note at the end 'again March 1895, again Feb. 18, 1901,' referring to dates of re-reading the book. Also with his 10 Downing Street Bookplate, the book having appeared during the few months that he was Prime Minister." Of course it was old Stanley Hopkins who sent me this cutting. He adds that he himself always notes the dates and times of his rereadings. And when, exactly, in '95 was Rosebery voted out?

I was delighted to learn, by the letter from Hopkins which transmitted this item, that the famous hydro at Tamfield Haw, Staffs., has resumed civilian service. The Chief Inspector (Retired) says he was feeling rheumatic and old, and needed what Watson used to call an alterative. I remembered by his use of those terms that it was Dr. Watson who first sent Hopkins to Tamfield. I wonder if in his memoirs he will at last break down and tell what he once confided to me after an evening of tantalus-cum-gasogene? He didn't mention it in his letter, but the old boy was evidently bucked up by his hydropathic regime, for he had been over to Walsall (a few miles away) to look fondly at the grave of Violet Hunter. I'm surprised he didn't do a mortuary also in Birmingham, for the sister of Victor Trevor.

Old Hopkins says he spent "the octave, from Christmas

Eve till Hogmanay" (there must be Scots in him some-where) at the hydro. I'm roaring from laughter to think how many of the members can guess what is a hydro? But the point about Tamfield Haw is that it is named for the shady and never-till-now mentioned fact that Sherlock had a younger brother. You can find out about it in that com-pletely forgotten story of Watson's, *The Doings of Raffles Haw*. It was written in Vienna in the early winter of 1891, and Sherlock was so sore about it that Watson never alluded to it again—except to sneer at it in his *Memories and Adventures*.

* * *

Raffles Holmes, some five years younger than Sherlock and twelve years younger than Pycroft, I mean Mycroft, was the febrile and mystical member of the family. I don't suppose there are a dozen people living who have read *The Doings of Raffles Haw*, but it is plain to those who have that Haw was a code pseudonym for Holmes. (Why else would Willy Hornung, to tease Watson, have picked on the name Raf-fles?) Poor Raffles, the youngest brother, had all the Sher-lockian mien. He was tall and lean; he was pale and lanky; he had the habit of chuckling. He was an incessant smoker, with special fumigation of a pipe. He had a pale thin face, keen gray eyes, a sharp curving nose with decision and character in the straight thick eyebrows which almost met. He had thin firm lips, and a short straggling beard (which he grew for disguise when he changed Holmes to Haw). When interrupted in the middle of the night he put on a dark dressing gown. He was a fanatical chemist, a before-his-time student of atomic physics. He liked to wear a rough and soiled pea-jacket. He had all the Sherlockian stigmata; but he was hysterical, idealistic, and hypersensi-tive. He was ruined; killed indeed, by his pure love for a woman. Hence, and no one has dared admit it before, Sherlock's horrid cynicism about the sex.

If our fellow members will read this forgotten story (and

I don't know where they'll find it, except in the old pirated editions; they might try The Old Authors' Book Farm, Morrisburg, Ontario, which is pretty good for that sort of corn) they will see with what tender evasion Watson told all without admitting anything. The Welsh country doctor whom Raffles Haw mentions as his father in no way contradicts the country squires Sherlock vaguely claimed as forebears. Raffles Haw was a clever man. He had the taste for chemistry shown by Sherlock, but he put it (by accident) to extraordinary use. He had the shy lethargic reluctance of Mycroft. If you mix the temperaments of Sherlock and Mycroft you get tops in schizophrenia. This he had. He changed his name to Haw (the first rural thing he would see: it means a hedge, or a hawthorn berry) to avoid the publicity the name of Holmes was getting, from 1887 on. He fell in love, and was deluded, two-timed, and bilked. Watson's kindly story was that Raffles died of a broken heart; but I think the truth (which Hopkins won't ever tell) is that he took some tablets. They found him dead in his laboratory, looking easy, natural, and serene. That always means suicide.

Mycroft and Sherlock remained bitterly celibate. That was why Sherlock never followed Miss Hunter to Walsall. It was too close to Tamfield (actually Tamworth; see your atlas). That was why Mycroft never went to Birmingham. The one who went there was Pycroft.

These things have to be studied. They have to be studied with care. Raffles Holmes, who took the name of Raffles Haw because he was troubled by his brothers' publicity, "ran through the whole gamut of metallic nature." He was on the beam, in 1890, of atomic conversion. Read him and weep.

You don't know our blessed old Watson, Hopkins used to say, until you've read everything he wrote. Watson's third wife, by the way, was Lady Frances Carfax.

* * *

I have another letter from Stanley Hopkins, dated from the Bilboes, Yoxley, which is worthy of quoting in full:

> Animadverting upon Mr. Walter P. Armstrong Jr. [he says], why is the idea "ridiculous" of putting shoes on backwards? (B.S.J., Vol. I, p. 400.) The whole point, missed by everyone, is that Mr. Holmes learned in his years in the U.S.A. to wear *shoes*, not boots. You can't easily put boots on backwards, the uppers crumple and hamper; but *shoes* (what you Americans so quaintly call *oxfords*, viz., low shoes) are easily reversed and can be walked in, with care, far enough to leave a misleading spoor. You trample down on the flanges of the shoe, and tie the laces over your ankle. I've been walking round my muddy garden this evening in reversed brogues just to prove it to myself and to puzzle my gardener.
>
> Trickery with shoes, whether human or horsinine, was a speciality of Mr. Holmes, as I remember the Duke of Holdernesse emphasizing, and confirmed by Mr. Myers, that excellent tradesman of Toronto.
>
> I am an old and peevish fellow, but I am constrained to insist that the brandy, about which Mr. Armstrong Jr. makes so much pother, did not *sting*. Not, if it was genuine Hennessy; as Watson said, it *tingled*. And that (as he said) on his lips; Holmes, agitated, spilled most of it outside his mouth. Properly injected, the tingle comes much lower down. This is one of the classic proofs that Holmes was always shaken when anything happened to Watson.
>
> I deal with this *in petto* in chapter 24 of my eventually forthcoming Memoir, in the passage I have subtitled "A Little Brandy Comes in Handy." I should be most obliged if you would let me know the names of some American publishers?

* * *

Reading Thayer Cumings (B.S.J., Vol. I, p. 385), of course I came upon "a hydraulic engineer" and felt a pricking in my epollicate engineering thumb. I knew perfectly damn well that for Sherlock it would be *an* hydraulic engineer. I turned to the old Harper edns, and sure enough. See p. 210, old Harper edn of the *Adventures*. But in the hyperpiddling Jno Murray edn of the Shorts, which we have too readily taken as canon, I find "*a* hydraulic engineer" (p. 201).

It *must* be "*an*" hydraulic engr., just as JHW would say we are going on Jan 3rd to "*an* hotel." See *Thorofare* for attendant sociology. But here's funny: *Strand Magazine* for March 1892 says "*a*" hydraulic engineer.

* * *

I am no ballistician (as Mr. Robert Keith Leavitt is), but I was always shocked by Watson speaking of the lady in *Charles Augustus Milverton* emptying "barrel after barrel" (of her revolver) into the blackmailer's body. Surely in small-arms (hand-guns) it is *chamber*, not *barrel*?

* * *

If it is true, as rumored, that the Countess of Morcar's blue carbuncle was among the gems stolen from the Duchess of Windsor, I cannot feel too grieved. For Windsor was the only man, so far as I know, who ever had an invitation from the Baker Street Irregulars and was so insensible as to ignore it.

* * *

One of the most curious surprises in New York City (it should be a point of pilgrimage to all B. S. I.) is to find against the western outside wall of St. Paul's Chapel, Broadway and Fulton Street, a marble drinking fountain *In Memory of Oscar Slater*.

* * *

I suppose it has been noted that the passengers of the plane that crashed in the Alps last November were taken, when rescued, to Kurhaus Rosenlaui, at Meiringen. This, one presumes, is the later name of the Englischer Hof, now run by Peter Steiler the grandson?

BSJ (os), 2 No. 2 (April 1947)

I HAVE BEEN SO HILARIOUSLY AMUSED by *Sherlock Holmes and Music*, which Denis Brogan sent me from Cambridge (Eng.), that I've written to Terence Holliday (Holliday Book Shop, 49 East 49, specializes in English imports) to send one to the editorial office of the *Journal* for review. It's really comical that (in true British mode) Guy Warrack shews no knowledge whatever of any U. S. Holmesians except Harold Bell, who of course was published in England.

It is hard to forgive Warrack for the note that no one has ever studied S. H. and Music: in *221B: Studies in Sherlock Holmes*, edited by Vincent Starrett and published by Macmillan under the sponsorship of the Baker Street Irregulars, Harvey Officer's essay bore the very title; and the *Journal* has frequently alluded to the topic, including the problem of the gramophone records.

Mr. Warrack should know that Holmesian scholarship has reached a fairly lively tempo over here—after all, the Baker Street Irregulars were founded in 1934—and it is a little comical to find him suggesting that someone should write about such topics as Holmes the Oinosophist or Oenophilist when that theme was so charmingly dealt with by our learned Edgar Smith some ten years ago.

Chaffing apart, it is a delightful little book.

* * *

Mr. J. F. Christ (B. S. J., Vol. II, p. 91) need not be puzzled by absence of reference to any heating, other than the fireplace, at 221B. English lodgings in those days, and most often still, never dreamed of central heating. *Crede experto.*

In regard to the constantly recurring query as to the address 221B, surely it should be pointed out that the "B" probably stood for "bis" (literally meaning *twice*) which was a frequent English identification for a subsidiary address. See for instance Leonard Merrick's genial old story *Conrad in Quest of His Youth* (1903) where one of his chorus girls gives her address thus:

297

Miss Tattie Lascelles
c/o Madame Hermiance,
42 bis, Great Titchfield Street, W.

Mme. Hermiance ran a laundry on the ground floor, and Miss Tattie had rooms up one flight; probably 17 steps.

Therefore the stickler will remember that Mrs. Hudson's address was 221; it was only the suite occupied by Holmes and Watson that was 221B.

* * *

You may remember two middle-aged gentlemen flying westward at fifty miles an hour, on their way to Boscombe Valley. Or again, in the affair of *Silver Blaze*, "flying along en route for Exeter" at 53½ ditto. ("The telegraph posts are 60 yards apart, and the calculation is a simple one.")

Sometimes I have wondered whether Watson had some G. W. R. shares and was trying a little bullish ramp? As a matter of fact the Great Western in those days was famous for lethargy of schedule. I refer you to the classic work *Express Trains, English and Foreign*, by E. Foxwell and T. C. Farrer (Smith, Elder & Co., 1889). This lively compilation, equal in candor and humor (with some vigorous tangents upon North American railroads), speaks particularly of the "timorous conduct" of the G. W. R. management, which "waits dozing till the traffic shall be thrust upon it." In especial of the London–Exeter expresses (Holmes's and Watson's favorites) which averaged 5 hours 20 minutes for a journey of 194 miles. A "discreditable speed," they reckon, of 36½ m.p.h.

It appears that these trains, even the crack *Dutchman* and *Zulu*, had to make prolonged "stoppages" which cut their overall average and compelled the calculable celerity between stations. I never realized until studying Foxwell and Farrer that there was bitterness in Holmes's remark: "We lunch at Swindon." They *had* to lunch at Swindon. Our authorities say:

Inclusive speed of trains on the Great Western is lessened by the obligation to pause ten minutes at Swindon, an obligation from which the refreshment proprietors will not free the company until the year 1940.

How I would love to know whether this 99-year lease, or whatever it was, did actually persist until the savage year 1940! And if so, what ceremonial untrooping of Bath buns was performed in the Swindon Refreshment Rooms?

Probably ten minutes would have been enough for Holmes and Watson, light lunchers. A cup of tea and a sausage roll. They were both solid breakfastmen, and we know that Watson had been at the morning table as late as 10:15. They left Paddington at 11:15, and should have reached Swindon (1889 timetable) about 12:42.

I believe, subject to correction, that the G. W. R. main line was in those days still broad gauge, which accounts for the roomy perspective of the carriages illustrated in the old *Strand Magazine* by Sidney Paget. There is still pleasing research to be done on the railway journeys of Holmes and Watson. If one could only find a Bradshaw of about 1890! In these parts it is *introuvable*.

* * *

It always astounds me [writes old Stanley Hopkins] that you fellows in yr earnest research do so little among the parallaxes (or paralipomena) of Dr. Watson. For instance Mr. Morley's otherwise lucubrated and well-intended study of *A Study in Scarlet* and *The Sign of the Four*. The first draught of these excellent tales, as also of that worthy fellow Hilton's Shangri-La stuff, was obviously *The Mystery of Cloomber*; which everyone has tried hard to obliterate. Your American publisher R. F. Fenno printed it "copyright 1895" but that I do not believe. It is a more difficult problem in bibliography than Hawthorne's *Fanshawe* or Poe's *Tamerlane*. When was it written? Very early, I suggest; and unsalable until after the success of Sherlock and Watson. At my age, an old old man as I am, I have no hesitation to say what I think: it is prothonotary stuff. You will see in it, not only (as Mr. Morley has noticed) the umbilical confusion of James & John, but the Urquelle of the Night-Time, the lurcher dog, and the great Grimpen Mire. What became in *Study in Scarlet* the *second* Afghan War was, in *Cloomber*, the *first* Afghan War. It was a pity, I always thought, that Dorothy Sayers so many years later wrote a story (I forget the title, and even her publisher can't remember it) of mayhem and mortmain in the same county of Wigtown (you will find it in the atlas in SW Scotland) with the fatal Bay of Luce (not Henry) and Stranraer and Kirkmaiden and the Great Hole of Cree. Miss Sayers never even thought to make any acknowledgement; nor did that heavily sponsored man Dr. Watson. Do your members do their collateral reading?

STANLEY HOPKINS, O.B.E.

P.S. If your members were to do a little outside reading, among the things not so easy to acquire (e.g., *Sasassa Valley*, or *Beyond the City*, or *My Friend the Murderer*) or the literary schidzoes such as *Through the Magic Door* (with 16 illustrations) or *A Duet* (which could only be published by a publisher newly married) you would realize how sad it is to be a narrow specialist. Have none of you realized how many corny and lovely things old Watson wrote under another name, so as to avoid the incubus of his (let's be honest) very irritating roommate? I know, as did the Apostles, that the myth outgrows the creator; but I was a competitor of Holmes & he annoyed me. Watson was the greater man. The radio sponsors agreed.

Yrs,

S. HOPKINS

P.S. *bis*:—You will have noticed, or I hope you will, that *The Mystery of Cloomber* is one of Watson's several attempts to rewrite Stevenson's *The Pavilion on the Links*. No one but the often peccant and wrongheaded Mr. Morley seems to have pointed out the persistence of Stevenson in Watson's works (even the name *Branksome* in the Cloomber story is an echo of R.L.S., though only to the initiates). But more important than that, Cloomber is definitely of the pre-neck-and-wrists era. There are two beautiful young heroines; neither of them has a frill of white at those strategic openings. I offer a lace wristlet (a pair of them) to any woman who can find a copy of *The Mystery of Cloomber*. And what became of R. F. Fenno?

S. HOPKINS, O.B.E.

BSJ (OS), 2 No. 3 (July 1947)

I HAVE A FEELING that something might be done in looking up the reason for calling Miss Adler's house Briony Lodge. It was not the Bastard Bryony, I hope; but the regular bryony which Webster says has "powerful cathartic roots." Then there was "a sprig of wild bigamy," if you remember your Chesterton. Could it have been Bigamy Lodge?

* * *

Miss Jane Nightwork has written me a letter which I am happy, with her permission, to pass along to the readers of the *Journal*:

Lake Halibut, Ontario,
c/o Villa Satyre Sejour (F.S.S.V.P.)

My dear M. Morley:

In her delightfully confused and perverse homily on "Dr. Watson's Third Marriage" Miss Dorothy Sayers quotes Mr. Holmes: "Matilda Briggs was not the name of a young woman, Watson. It was a ship." She then proceeds to speak of "the solecism (common today among journalists) of writing the name of the ship without the definite article." Holmes, you notice, did. Hurray for him!

As a seawoman (Canadian Wren 1940–45) and great-grand-daughter of Sir Belcher Nightwork, G.C.B. (Belcher was not a nickname; it was a family name: he was of the family of Lady Belcher who wrote the classic *Mutineers of H.M.S. Bounty and Their Descendants*; reticent as I am it is pleasing to me that I am of the breadfruit blood of Pitcairn Island)—

As a seawoman (C.P.O., mentioned in despatches), I resume: the naming of ships *tout court* is no journalist solecism, but universal mariners' usage. No sailor would dream of saying or writing "The" *Mauretania*, "The" *Abigail Gibbons*, "The" *Aluminium Trader*, "The" *Gripsholm*. That is travel bureau and tourist talk, just as they speak of sailing "on" S.S. *Soandso*. You don't live *on* a house, you don't sail *on* a ship. Miss Sayers, definitely an Inland Girl (from

Oxford, I think; as far from salt water as you can get in England) and busy to assume that everything unfamiliar to herself must be a mannerism, chooses to believe that the journalist's humble attempt to copy maritime lingo must be a "solecism." Not at all, my sweet virago! The name of the famous captivated ship was not *The* Bounty, but *Bounty*; just as Dana's brig was not *The* Pilgrim, but *Pilgrim*, and the Night Boat to Albany (what a night!) was not *The* Charles W. Morse. (When we used to take a return trip—few did— we called her *Remorse*. But that was before Miss Sayers' time? I doubt if she, or any other well-bred Englishwoman, ever travelled in a river steamer? Or am I thinking of *Chester W. Chapin*, that used to churn from N. Y. to New London? Did Miss Sayers ever patronize *Clacton Belle*, or those seasick little beauties from Southampton to Jersey? Or S.S. *May Day*, sidewheeler I hope, from Liverpool to Albert Dock, as in *Cardboard Box*?)

Dana's brig was not *The* Pilgrim, she was *Pilgrim*, like Cunard's *Queen Mary* and U.S. Lines' *America* and D. L. & W.'s *Hopatcong*. It is no "solecism" as per *The* Lord Peter Wimsey, but just sailors' way of mentioning a ship.

I wouldn't bother you with this, but dear old senile Stanley Hopkins, O.B.E., saw Sayers' book (just published in England) and was so upset. Naturally, because he was the one who married Lady Frances Carfax, so illicitly mentioned as Watson's third. Watson really had no third: he remarried (as the B. S. J. has shewn) Mary Morstan, *en secondes noces*. Sayers is fond of Dr. Watson's illegible handwriting: has she never realized that it was not Thurston he played billiards with, but *Morstan*? His bro-in-law, who brought them together again.

Roger!

Yrs, dear sir,
JANE NIGHTWORK, ex-CWRNS

* * *

And speaking of Stanley Hopkins, as Jane does, I have two letters from that good O.B.E., which are also worth sharing with our readers:

303

THE BILBOES,
Yoxley, Kent

My dear Mr. Christopher Morley:

One of your members, perhaps Mr. Peter Greig, very kindly remembered my birthday by sending me a flask of the Oyster Sauce. Our socialist dietary only allows me an egg to my breakfast three times a week, but a poached egg well drenched with Mr. Greig's elixir gives me as good an idea of breakfast as a Scotswoman. How outraged I was, by the way, by Mr. Hesketh Pearson's remark (chapter XI of his Biography) that only people without sensitive palates love curry. An infamy!! I hope to hear if you and your colleagues picked up some amusing odds-and-sods at the auction of the poor old Murray Hill's effects. The newspapers here, to distract us from our political woes, mentioned the matter. . . . By the way, I always thought Holmes was unusually smart to be able to send off a Personal to the evening papers at noon (*A Study in Scarlet*, chapter 5) and get it into that afternoon's edition.

I am up to chapter 20 of my memoirs, which deals with Holmes and Watson as psychiatrists, but still I haven't heard from any of your American publishers. I wrote to Messrs. Schuster & Doubleday; I heard they are one of the most enterprising of your firms, but got no answer.

During the horrible winter we had here I reread the best of all spuriosa, Rev. Knox's *Studies in the Literature of Sherlock Holmes*; I have a horrid notion that very few of your members ever saw it, and think they are having fresh new fun when they are only saying (less wittily?) what Rev. Knox wrote 35 years ago. I have a sad feeling that many of your members only read their own stuff? Tell me I am wrong? For instance Knox's classical analysis of every Holmes–Watson story into its eleven canonical points: pro-oimion, exegesis, ichneusis, etc. I was brutally drilled in all those severities at Bedford Grammar School, but I have a feeling they mean less to your vigorous young men. I was thinking when Mr. Wallace was here how wonderfully young your American men are. I am sure that is their good fortune, but don't your American women, who age rapidly (I remember Miss Nightwork!) get impatient? But this is (alas) none of my business.

304

I remember Mr. Holmes telling me that of course his interest in warships of the future was started by that brilliant but annoying fellow Cullingworth (in *The Stark Munro Letters*) whom Hesketh Pearson identifies with one Budd. I was treated by Dr. Stark Munro when I was a child; my parents took me on holiday to the seaside and I bruised my toes on the shingle of Southsea. They saw Dr. Munro's brass plate (it was so dazzlingly polished) and he bound up my foot with a detergent. He also treated Mr. Raffles Haw. As I grow older I get confused, but so did Watson. You remember, of course, that Dr. Stark Munro treated Lord Saltire long before Watson heard of him. Chapter 4 of *Stark Munro Letters*. I shall deal with all this in a later chapter. Send me the names of some publishers.

STANLEY HOPKINS, O.B.E.

* * *

And here is the other:

THE BILBOES,
Yoxley, Kent

My dear Mr. Christopher Morley:

I write you again because I have just read my Yorkshire *Post* and heard of the death of my old friend Lloyd Osbourne, the stepson of R. L. Stevenson. I tell in my 24th chapter (I am still waiting for the names of some U. S. A. publishers? Schuster & Doubleday refused my offer of £100 advance!) how Lloyd Osbourne, "an American Gentleman," if you remember the immortal dedication of *Treasure Island*, told me how Watson admitted to him that his first real impulse to tell the Holmes episodes was started by Stevenson's *Dynamiter*. That was published in 1885, and one autumn night when the wind was sobbing like a child in the chimney, J. H. W. read it, at Bush Villa. You yourself have already pointed out some of its prenatal quality, but I fear you are no economist, for you did not notice its sinister forecast of fiscal horrors. I quote:

> . . . sat down to compute in English money the value of the figure named. The result of this investigation filled him

with amazement and disgust; but it was now too late; nothing remained but to endure . . . still trying, by various arithmetical expedients, to obtain a more favourable quotation for the dollar.

(*The Dynamiter*, Scribner edition, p. 148.)

As you said in a letter you wrote recently to the Manchester *Guardian*, and as the good Watson had admitted to me privily, it was Stevenson's *Dynamiter* that first actually pushed poor J. H. W. into narration about Holmes.

I am a very old man, and must be brief (as you know, today, The Queen's Birthday, is also mine; age 81. And you haven't forgotten that this year is the 110th anniversary of the Victorian age).

I was very pleased by your letter describing how you went to the Murray Hill Hotel before the sale started, and got away with those items you have told us about. I was equally, and even more than equally, pleased by Miss Nightwork's account of her bidding for the furniture of room 534. I thought it was so characteristic of you to want the copy of the Bible, and of Miss N. to want the rosewood escritoire. What sentimentalists both!

I just wanted to say that if you and Mr. Edgar Smith are coming to England this summer (don't come before September, when Mrs. Hopkins goes to visit her mother, or her aunt, and elemental forces shriek at the bars?) be sure to stop in Southsea and get a copy of the Municipal Guide, which says nice things about Bush Villa. Your most difficult struggle will be, landing at Southampton, not to be sent on automatically to the Great Cesspool. I will meet you at Waterloo (I repeat, Waterloo?) and accompany you to Baker Street to help you put up the tablet the Irregulars have so kindly devised.

Speaking of railways, the April issue of the *Journal* was superb, but of course the locomotive (p. 174) was one of the Underground (Metropolitan) engines, and not an L. B. and S. C. machine. It plainly has the bogies, too. I never love Edgar Smith so much as in his obvious errors. It is the only way that editors get to be loved, as Watson used to say to poor bedevilled Greenhough Smith.

306

I have just looked up some old letters from Lloyd Osbourne, 25 years ago, from Vanumanutangi Ranch, Gilroy,
California. I would like to offer a prize to any publisher
(including Scribner's) who could shew proof of having read
The Wrong Box, in which L. O. was collaborator. As Kipling
said, and George Saintsbury too (both cautious friends of
J. H. W.), that is one of the Test Books.

Send me the names of some publishers?

STANLEY HOPKINS, O.B.E.

BSJ (OS), 2 No. 4 (October 1947)

YOUR RESIDENT PATIENT was profoundly grieved to hear of the death of our foremost scholar and chronological adept, Mr. H. W. Bell. Mr. Bell's devotion to the cause would welcome my mentioning here a small point I had always wished to submit to him. It is with reluctance that one ever takes issue with his masterly and classic Chronology. But I was never quite content with his setting aside Watson's date (1889) for *The Hound of the Baskervilles*. Bell dates it 1886. But in the *Hound*, in the Second Report of Dr. Watson, there is a phrase that shows the strong influence remaining from his meeting the King of Bohemia. Watson writes to Holmes:—

"All these things have by one night's work been thoroughly cleared."

This can be nothing but an unconscious memory of the King's discourtesy to his verbs? The *Scandal in Bohemia* happened in 1888 (this is by all students universally admitted), and I respectfully suggest that Watson's odd usage may confirm the later dating for the Baskerville case.

* * *

It will have been noticed, too, in Rebecca West's remarkable book, *The Meaning of Treason*, what it was that really set Scotland Yard on edge about the late William Joyce, "Lord Haw-haw." His first statement, dictated to an Intelligence officer after his capture in May 1945, spoke of "the resentment that my broadcasts have in many quarters aroused."

It is plain that Joyce was a grandson of the King of Bohemia, off-blanket.

* * *

APPEAL TO BIBLIOPHILES: Please let me know if you ever come across a pamphlet with title something like this:—

UPON THE DISTINCTION BETWEEN
THE VARIOUS PERFUMES
A Monograph on Natural & Synthetic Fragrance
With analyses of the 75 primary scents

by
SHERLOCK HOLMES
And a Memorandum by J.H.W. on the Types of Women
Likely to Favour the Several Modes of Allure
Privately Printed
(on three continents)

The bibliographer would have to list this as N.D. (no date), but it would probably precede the allusion in chapter XV of *The Hound of the Baskervilles* where Mrs. Stapleton (flaming Beryl, but not, as Sir Henry hoped, single) was first suspected by her use of white jessamine.

This monograph is no more conjectural than some of the accepted *desiderata*. No bibliographies of S.H. have listed it—the classic references of course are S. C. Roberts (1931), H. W. Bell (1932), and V. Starrett (1933).

The Resident Patient submits it, therefore, for search by collectors. What assures authenticity is Holmes's familiar use of *Between* when he meant *Among*.

One wonders, of course, if even so oecumenical a gyneolater as Watson could find 75 types to match up with the 75 savours? Baskerville makes one think of Laura Lyons, the sulphur-rose brunette who played nervously on the stops of her typewriter. She still does, maybe; you have noticed that she has written these many years the column about female modes in *The New Yorker*, signed L.L.

* * *

The New York Times carried a story on September 16th of the *Royal Jelly*, on which the queen-bee is fed—and lives 20 times longer than the working bees. It can now be told, this is what Sherlock Holmes was working on when he segregated the queen. It is the royal jelly that has kept him alive so long; and even Watson, the fruit fly, will have his life prolonged by 46%.

Couldn't some honey merchant put up jars of Sussex Royal Jelly, properly labeled, for the members of the B.S.I.?

* * *

When great corporations are looking for masterly advtg copy—I mean for the B.S.I.—how's about that greatest of all brief ads:

> "Try Canadian Pacific Railway," said Holmes.
> —*The Adventure of Black Peter*

The new president of CPR was on the same ship with me (*Empress of Canada*, from Montreal) when I went to Europe last September, but I couldn't induce him to use it. Why doesn't Ben Abramson sell it (as an advt) to the CPR people? It's worth at least $100 of bucks.

The best advt ever written for Pullman was by Walt Whitman, but I never could sell it to them!

* * *

Because it was too long for inclusion in the "Letters to Baker Street" column, the editor of the *Journal* has turned over to me a letter he received last summer from Stanley Hopkins, O.B.E., written from The Bilboes, in Yoxley, Kent:

My dear Mr. Edgar Smith:—

It is the 4th of July (as I have good reason to remember) and I had the pleasure of a visit from Miss Jane Nightwork; she came to England, in a ship astonishingly named *Marine Jumper*, as chaperone of a group of young American girls who were going to visit and search Great Britain this summer and return to tell your State Universities what we are like and what is wrong with us. God speed them; even after all her troubles poor England is embarrassed by the earnestness of the young American.

But I had been saving a few dregs of whisky for Miss Jane (she doesn't care for tea) and showed her the piece by your friend Mr. Morley in the Manchester *Guardian* a month ago, about Stevenson's influence on Dr. Watson. How right he was! Dear old Watson, always influenced by the latest thing he had been reading; and Miss Nightwork exclaimed: "Goodness, hasn't he ever noticed the astounding parallel between the opening paragraphs of *The White Company* (1890) and *The Black Arrow* (in book 1888, but printed serially in *Young Folks* magazine in 1883)?"

Miss Nightwork continued: "I was always specially pleased that most of *The Black Arrow* was written at Royat (Puy de Dôme), France, the place that never was popular with British tourists until a Bishop got into trouble by biting a barmaid in the neck. It was the mountain air and the alkaline mineral springs. It had a lot of publicity, and even, 40 years later, got into *Ellery Queen's Mystery Magazine*."

The only reason why your experts haven't commented more on the curious parallels of Watson and R. L. Stevenson is that obviously most of your catechumens are too young to have read Stevenson. I was so amused that Scribners' famous editor Max Perkins, when he called on me some years ago looking for copy, knew almost nothing about R.L.S.—It used to be uproariously funny to see poor old Lloyd Osbourne, Stevenson's stepson and collaborator, terrified of going to Scribners' office because he had to explain who he was.

Of course that is what is so wonderful about you young Americans, you have no memories and are not disturbed by any thing that ever happened before. I often wonder, is the old Broadway Central Hotel still in existence? I stayed there once in the early '80's, long before the Murray Hill existed? I went there in line of duty, to see the staircase where Fiske shot Stokes; or was it vice versa? Then I tried to find the famous Pfaff's, the rathskeller where Walt Whitman and Poe and Weeping Willie Winter and even Bayard Taylor, on a stallion shod with fire, used to visit. It was gone; I think Lüchow's took its place? Another habitué of Pfaff's was Artemus Ward, and that reminds me—

Your Mr. Morley speaks of Watson imitating Stevenson in his Mormon obsession. But it was Artemus Ward who started it over here. His lectures, which were the sensation of London in my father's time, included some uproarious takeoffs on the Destroying Angels and Brigham Young, etc.

311

I think *Punch* printed a lot of them; anyhow, they made Mormons a subject for public curio. So Stevenson was on a fresh trail, and Watson followed. But I doubt if any of your young fellows know or care about Artemus Ward. That is what pleases me so about Miss Jane Nightwork; her father, a Canadian parson, truly reared her on American literature.

Miss Nightwork said to me: "Ask them if they'll just read the first paragraph of *The Black Arrow*; and also, why do the American editions of *The White Company* omit the famous Anglo-American dedication?"

My hand is rather crippled with gout, but I'm getting on with chapter 30 of my book; it deals with my official visits to America. It always surprises me that no one has ever mentioned the fact that Holmes and I, of course incogniti, were at the World's Fair in Chicago in 1893. We had wonderful times with Eugene Field.—Do you think Scribners wd be interested?

Yrs always,

STANLEY HOPKINS, O.B.E.

* * *

And I had a letter from Inspector Hopkins myself, as late as last September, which is worth incorporating in full:

My dear Mr. Christopher Morley:

The next time I go up to Town I shall stop in at Harrod's and procure that pair of lace wristlets for the lady in Rochester, N. Y., U. S. A., who owns a copy of *The Mystery of Cloomber*.

I am an old man and I get confused now, for instance between Dr. Watson and Dr. Balthazar Walker. Dr. Walker, you may have forgotten, lived at Number 2, The Wilderness, Norwood (*Beyond the City*, 1891). He wrote (chapter 2, *ibid.*) on *The Gouty Diathesis* and, later, on *Affections of the Vaso-Motor System*. I seem to remember that Watson also was interested in these same topics? Then there was his neighbor the Admiral (Hay Denver) R. N. Ret.—"in many climes he had looked upon women of all shades and ages, but never upon a more clear-cut handsome face, nor a more

erect, supple, and womanly figure."—Then there was Dr.
Walker's younger daughter: "in a low chair beneath a red-
shaded standing lamp sat Ida, in a diaphanous evening dress
of *mousseline de soie*"—but, alas, nothing at her neck and
wrists.

I was about to offer a diaphanous garment of *mousseline* to
any lady who has a copy of *Beyond the City*; but I am now
experienced to abstain. But that book is (as none of your
experts have noted) a first draught of *The Speckled Band*;
there you will find the same rock snake, domesticated much
milder than the horrid purposes of Dr. Roylott, hatching
her eggs in front of the drawing room fire, and called *Eliza*.

In chapter 34 of my memoirs I deal exhaustively with
these singular parallels between Watson and his imitators; it
pains me that so few of your students are aware of them.
You have not yet given me any introduction to some repu-
table American publisher.

I trust you have not forgotten the wonderful photo in the
Strand (1892?) of Watson on his tricycle, rotating a busy
treadle round Norwood, Anerley, and Forest Hill. That
same tricycle appears to romantic effect in *Beyond the City*.

I divine your interest in what Watson and I used to call
Romance. So I enclose an editorial from *The Times* of August
4, 1947. It was your old friend Mr. W. S. Hall who shewed
it to me. I think it a pleasant evidence of Britain's detachment that in the middle of her fiscal woe and Domesday
bookkeeping she could emit so genial a spoof apropos the
never-never land of Ruritania. *The Prisoner of Zenda*, about
1894, came just when we needed it. It was written, remember (not even Henry Holt remembers this?), to console us
for Holmes's supposed culbute at Reichenbach. The romance of the Rassendylls is, in its own humble redhead
way, just as significant as Baker Street? I knew Rudy well,
and deal with him in my next chapter. I sometimes worry a
little about your members who don't know the '90's as well
as they think they do. Next after Watson's exequy for
Sherlock, what is so moving as this:—

313

RUDOLFU: Qui in hac civitate nuper regnavit
In corde ipsius in aeternum regnat.

Yrs., dear Mr. Morley,
STANLEY HOPKINS, O.B.E.

Miss Jane Nightwork, too, has been favoring me with her ruminations:

Bon Echo, Ontario,
Sept. 30, 1947.

Dear Mr. Christopher Morley:

I have just got back from my arduous summer abroad, and came here to recuperate in the old Walt Whitman colony. Consumed as you are in important affairs I don't suppose you realize there still is a little *Zollverein* of Walt's disciples up here, and I like to visit occasionally—"to live with the animals," as Walt said. Nothing surprises them.

One of the things I asked dear old Mr. Hopkins was if Holmes ever mentioned Walt Whitman. His only reply was, "Holmes was as neat as a cat."

It was good of you to send me a copy of Mr. Hopkins's letter, because I can add a word or two. Bless his old heart, he is really getting shaky, because he sometimes gets Watson confused with Dr. Doyle. When I got down to The Bilboes he was in his rose garden, and picked me some exquisite blooms; he has bred a sulphur rose of his own, which he calls the Laura Lyons. He was rather resentful of your piece about Stevenson's influence on Doyle or Watson, so I didn't say a few thoughts that occurred to me. But to you, in the austerity of letters, I can mention them.

One reason why Doyle was eager to accept so paltry an offer for *Study in Scarlet*, to be printed in *Beeton's Xmas Annual* for 1887, was that when he heard from Ward Lock & Co. he had just noticed, in *Cassell's Xmas Annual* for 1886, that now quite forgotten story by his idol Stevenson, "The Misadventures of John Nicholson." So he was eager to be in a Xmas Annual too.

Stevenson was so much in Doyle's mind in those days

314

that in 1889 he was busy writing a notable essay on "Mr. Stevenson's Methods in Fiction" which you will find in the *National Review* for January 1890. He thought well of this piece, and subsumed considerable bits of it into his delightful *Through the Magic Door* 18 years later.

Don't forget that probably the only magazine sure to be on Dr. Doyle's waiting room table (only no one ever had to wait?) was *Cornhill*, which had also been Stevenson's prentice vehicle. But it had never printed anything so corny, said the reviewers, as "Habakuk Jephson," in '83.

You must wonder how I think of these things, but you see I took my Master's Degree at McGill for a thesis on Cross-Fertilization in Scots. Just to call it *Scots* makes you safe with Montreal examiners.

I wanted to put in a footnote, but didn't, that one reason Dr. Doyle never cottoned to Walt Whitman was account of Walt's anomalous relations with Peter Doyle, the street car conductor in Washington, D.C. I assure you it is still unwise, in university circles, for a young woman to shew too keen curiosity about the kind of things that happen to writers.

The physiological polarity of Stevenson and Doyle (one the fevered skeleton of a man, the other the great hulking athlete, but both beset by Northern Lights) was obviously an unconscious excitement. I give you Full Marks for guessing this.

I am living in a sleeping bag By Blue Ontario's Shore. But when I get down to N. Y. (I am going to teach Salic Law at Barnard, under Gen Eisenhower, and I wonder a little about him too, but I shan't mispronounce him like Lowell Thomas does (Eisenauer he calls it; the radio cockneys all hiatize their haspirates?)), but after daming a hundred middlewestern gals round the United Kingdom all summer, and how divinely ignorant they are, I think the completely unsullied ignorance of a young American female is one of the most lovely phenomena of our social Niagara. They just go foaming over the granite ledge and don't even know why.

Speaking of Canada, I think we're approaching the centennial of Dr. Osler; who was, as you know, a great friend of Mycroft Holmes and gave him much of the information that made him an expert on this country. According to old Stanley Hopkins—but I admit I don't always trust him now—it was Osler's tact that composed the trouble between Watson and Mary Morstan. Mycroft, then just at the dangerous age for a solitary Diogenes, made passes at Mary M. Watson while Sherlock was in Chicago, in '93.—Osler was one of the saints, and his Life by Dr. Cushing should be catalogued as hagiography.

Sincerely yours,

JANE NIGHTWORK (M.A., McGill)

* * *

And Miss Nightwork has also written the editor in a vein and at a length which lends itself to inclusion in these notes:

"Scented Herbage" (Châlet Feuilles d'Herbe)
Bon Echo, Ontario
November, 1947.

My dear Mr. Edgar Smith:—

I know how extensive are your archives: can you or any other member afford me the timetable of suburban trains on the Southeastern and Chatham Ry as of August 1894? (Or, to satisfy H. W. Bell's chronology, 1895 would do.) It has always bothered me, why could not the unhappy John Hector McFarlane get back from Lower Norwood to Blackheath that night? It was "between eleven and twelve" when he and Jonas Oldacre finished their business. Young McFarlane said that it was so late he couldn't get back to Blackheath.

I meant to test the matter for myself when I was in England last summer, but the troupe of students I had to chaperone gave me no leisure. But according to my large-scale Bartholomew it is only about ½-mile walk from Sydenham Road (where the odious Oldacre lived) to Lower Sydenham Station, and only 3 miles by train (two intermediate stops) from there to Lewisham Junction. Lewisham Junction

316

is practically in Blackheath; or, as we wouldn't need to remind Watson (who must have practised his football there) Blackheath Station is only a mile, after changing trains, from Lewisham Jc.

Or, assuming there was no train from Lower Sydenham about midnight, would it not have been possible to get a tram on the line Bromley Road–Lewisham High Street? That would have been no longer walk, or cab ride, than to the Anerley Arms.

I only mention these points because they provide confirmation of poor Mr. McFarlane's vacillating and ineffective character. What was in his mother only "fluffy" became in John Hector "washed-out, negative, and weakly sensitive." He could certainly have got back to Blackheath that night if he had really wanted to. It was only four miles if he had wanted to walk it. Any experienced B.S.I. can make all sorts of deductions from this.

I haven't told you how I was clever enough to run down dear old Stanley Hopkins. I took my Master's degree at college for a thesis on *Associations of Place in the Life of William Hazlitt.* So when I first went to England I took train to Maidstone, in Kent, where Hazlitt was born. I went for a walk, and about 3 miles out of Maidstone I found myself admiring some ancient ruins of Boxley Abbey. Also the grave of an old governor of Virginia (Sir Francis Wyatt) and the park so humorously described in the prologue of Tennyson's *Princess*—I had always thought it was a description of the Vassar campus. But I kept on saying to myself sotto voice: *Boxley? Boxley?* Seven miles from Chatham, three miles from the railway? Well natuerlich! This was what dear old Stanley Hopkins calls *Yoxley.* So I hunted around until I found The Bilboes.

As you know, I'm a Canadian, so when I knocked on Inspector Hopkins' door I said, "I'm from C.P.R."—He laughed and said, "Oh, I learned that back in the days of Black Peter.—Come in, I have a prescription containing hot water and a lemon."

I said: "Chief Inspector, a little group of us in Winnipeg and Calgary want to put up a tablet at 46 Lord Street, Brixton."

Poor old sweetheart, I had to remind him: that was where he lived when Holmes first knew him, in 1895. (Yes, *Black Peter*.)

There were a lot of questions I wanted to ask the old fellow, but the Maidstone butcher (Allardyce) had just brought him his weekly sausage ration and he was enjoying it so. I wanted to ask him why Holmes dropped that terrible brick, in *Gloria Scott*, to refer to the Norfolk Broads as "the North" (which is like calling Montreal "the West"); and what kind of a pipe is an A.D.P. (*Silver Blaze*)? It is these very simple things that throw me, and until your complete collated and harmonized edition comes along I don't know how I can learn? I am submitting, for doctorate at McGill, my thesis *Some Unelucidated Passages in the Text of Sherlock Holmes*.

But tell that lovely man Dr. J. Wolff—who didn't put Yoxley on his map—that it's really *Boxley*.

Mr. Morley, one of the rudest men I've ever known, doesn't answer my letters, so I send this to you. What will you be doing about February 14th?

Sincerely yours,

JANE NIGHTWORK (ex-CWRNS)

P.S. By the most curious chance I met Mr. Morley on the wharf at Montreal; he was just going abroad in S.S. *Empress of Canada* (late *Duchess of Richmond*, I believe?) and I was debarking from same.

I was able to tell him, and he asked me to remind you, that the christening of Sherlock Holmes, in 1886, was undoubtedly influenced by the fact that Oliver Wendell Holmes made his famous (and enormously publicized) re-visit to England in May of that year. You can check this in recent biographies of O. W. Holmes by Tilton and others, or in the bound vols of *The Atlantic* so long and patiently stocked by Ben-Abramson.

What will you be doing on Thanksgiving Eve?

* * *

India is, natch (as the children say), much in one's mind and I was specially tickled by Mrs. Crighton Sellars's admirable piece about Watson and the Indian Army. Homage to her for apparently spotting an error none of us ever knew, viz. Charasiab. I see that in the great London Times Atlas it is printed as *Charasia*—just south of Kabul. She says there are no Bangalore Pioneers; but the name one most associates with Bangalore is that of a (then) young lieutenant of the 4th Queen's Own Hussars, who wrote his first book there. It is dated from "Cavalry Barracks, Bangalore, 30th December, 1897," and the preface is signed: Winston L. S. Churchill. (The book was *The Malakand Field Force*.)

BSJ (os), 3 No. 1 (January 1948)

WHEN I WAS IN LONDON LAST FALL, I went to the Wigmore Street P. O. to buy "a thick packet of postcards," since I seem to remember Watson once did so.

* * *

Baker Street is the best known street in London. As soon as you get into a bus you see two advtg cards: one, that all Lost Property is deposited at 200 Baker Street (or whatever the address is) and the other is the busiest renter of dress and morning clothes in London. The Great Hiatus is the one in the middle of Baker Street, where almost a whole block was blasted away. The house that Gray Chandler Briggs tried to canonize is obviously impossible. Too big. No sign of Camden House, neither; nor of Elmer Davis's Gowns for the Fuller Figures. But there IS a dentist at # 11 (this will drive Charley Goodman goofy): Mr. V. D. Gross, L.D.S., R.C.S., dental surgeon, 1st floor. I counted; he is 18 steps up, but most remaining Baker Street stairs are in ½ flights, with a turn after the 9th step.

I particularly wish to remark that of houses still standing the one nearest in look and character is the dwelling that has been absorbed into a branch of Barclay's Bank at 121. (Note the number—121, and B for Bank or Barclay.)

The habit of using the suffix B in addresses still persists on Baker Street. The Portman House Restaurant (where Baker Street runs into Portman Square) uses as its side-address "1B, Baker Street."

* * *

England is still, in spite of her troubles, a comfortable country to anyone of my placable tastes. It's very hard not to keep repeating "things are a bit grim," because that's what everyone expects you to say. I don't think I ever felt better than on their spare diet of Fish and Cripps, nor never slept better than in those cold damp sheets. I couldn't read in bed, because they don't have the lamps for it, so all I could do was sleep.

* * *

One of my happiest treasures is the old 16th-century (or maybe 17th-centy) fire-back that was in Hilton Soames's sitting room at St. Luke's (Camb.). It has a long story, too long to tell in type; Hilton Soames was my uncle (by marriage; he married my mother's sister), and after being a classical tutor he was for 50 yrs the bursar of Trinity College, Camb. I shd like to tell about that fire-back (the only other one I ever coveted was in that little old château in the Côte d'Or where I used to stay; the ancestral home of the Suremains de Saiserie—a sure hand to hold; and in that one the open palm was smelted into the iron screen so you saw, in the light of the fire, the right-handed palm welcoming. There, in a 14th-century stone tower, I used to beguile myself with rhymes.

And at this very moment, in an icy chandelier evening (no Metropolitan or Covent Garden Opera ever had so intricated and dangerous an overload of crystal as the willow and locusts down my drive) the fire is shining on the Adam and Eve and appletree design of the old fire-back on my front porch.

* * *

I wish some one would attack a project—the perfect scholar to undertake it would be Mr. S. C. Roberts—for some solid editorial commentary on that very odd case *The Missing Three-Quarter*. It is very evident that Watson was in an unusually muddled state; not only are his comments of exceptional fatuity, and his out-of-touch with profession complete (he had never heard of Leslie Armstrong); he, an old football player, thought Overton's telegram enigmatic, and worse still speaks of *dribbling*. Is there dribbling in *rugby* football? It is an expertise in soccer, of course. I know nothing of rugger, but I am wondering whether it is possible, in any exact sense, to dribble the oval ball?? Of course any rugby player can settle this at once.

But Watson's vein is so odd in this report—he even quotes Holmes as saying "different to"—that one might think he had, for a while, weaned his friend from drugs by taking some himself? So problems of drugger as well as rugger need to be considered.

And there never was (according to Bradshaw) an 11.15 p.m. train to Cambridge, neither from King's X nor L'pool Street. There would be no point, and no passengers, for such a train. The whole purpose of the late trains (10.2 from L'pool St., and 10.25 from King's X, per Bradshaw July 1894) was, and still is, to get students back to the university before midnight, by order of the Vice Chancellor and Proctors.

There are many other small points that shew Watson about ¾ missing. I do not believe the old miser would have said "My name is *Lord* St. James." (Watson always went wrong with lordships.) As a doctor he should have explained that when Staunton was "laid up with a hack" it didn't mean a hacking cough but a gash on the shin. The very odd geography of Cambridge and the neighboring villages can best be examined by Mr. Roberts, well known as topographer and historian of that immortal town. When biking round Chesterton, Histon, Waterbeach, Oakington, of course Holmes passed through Madingley. He would have been strangely moved to know how many young Americans would one day lie there, in the quietest of all universities, the dead. (Over 6000 Americans buried there, mostly of the A. A. F.)

One of Holmes's best touches was the deduction that six words were missing from the telegram. Because he saw, in the earlier message, that Cambridge undergraduates did not go beyond the 12 words for a shilling. I have meant to ascertain whether Western Union would accept a telegram including the phrase *for God's sake*; somehow I doubt it?

I have tried to reproduce the handwriting of the telegram with a broad-pointed quill pen (Am I the only B. S. I. who actually owns a quill pen of the period? But I never mastered the delicate art of trimming it), but it always comes out looking exactly like Holmes's and Stanley Hopkins's. That was no quill pen, but too much Beaune for lunch.

* * *

Add Influence on John H. Watson of Other Writers:

> ". . . a faint flush of pink breaking through her dainty colour, like the deeper flush at the heart of a sulphur rose."
> —*The Great Shadow*, chapter 2,
> by A. CONAN DOYLE

* * *

I seem to remember that Dorothy Sayers once argued laboriously about which varsity S.H. attended. Has no one ever remarked that Holmes *twice* in *The "Gloria Scott"* uses the phrase *"Long Vacation,"* which is exclusively a Camb Term; never used at Oxon?

* * *

It is my pleasure once again to reveal one of Miss Jane Nightwork's private epistles to Mr. Edgar Smith, who seems himself to have no compunctions in the matter of these disclosures. The letter is written from the Ladies' Cloak Room at Marylebone Station, in N.W. [Nightwork?] 1, and it reads:

> Would not a Baker Street Cutting Service be an excellent ancillary or subsidiary branch of any projected Baker Street Enterprises; to provide subscribers with all newspaper & magazine clippings that in one way or another bear upon the saga of the Master?
>
> Think this over. Then there might be (let us consult Mr. Peter Greig) the *Baker Street Breakfasts*, as cooked and served at 221B. Complete, in tin and carton, the kipper, the curried chicken, the devilled bones (how few even of the truly faithful have ever tasted the echt-Britisch devilled bone),

perhaps that now almost extinct perfection the Patum Peperium or Gentleman's Relish. . . . I *must* send a copy of this letter to P. Greig . . . all packed and shipped and just Add Sherlock Holmes and Serve. As prepared by Mrs. Hudson.

Vixere fortes ante Fortnum & Mason, wd say old Waggish Black Peter Greig, whose Oyster Sauce I have striven to promote in three continents.

A sinister little man pressed into my hand a printed bill which troubled me—of course I have heard of these privy attempts to identify one of our great men with Prof. Moriarty; but this, I thought (it was only identified as J. F. Judas), is really angst-making:—

THE FINAL PROBLEM

   . . . a man of good birth and excellent education, endowed by nature with a phenomenal mathematical **F**aculty. At the age of 21 he w**R**ote **A** treatise upo**N** the Binomial Theorem. . . . But the man had hereditary tendencies of the most diabolical **K**ind. A crimina**L** stra**IN** ran in his bloo**D**, which, inst**E**ad of being modified, was increased and rendered infinite**L**y more d**AN**ger**O**us by his ext**R**a-**O**rdinary mental p**O**wer**S**. Dark rumours gath**E**red round him in the uni**VE**rsity town, and eventua**L**ly he was compelled to resign his chair and to come down to London, where he se**T** up as an army coach. . . .
   He is the Napoleon of crime, Watson. . . . He has a brain of the **F**irst or**D**e**R**. . . .

As that wonderful advt for Guinness, on the hoardings of London says (picture two glasses of Stout simpering at each other), "Don't look now, but I think we're being swallowed." I send this, secretly, from the Ladies Cloakroom at Marylebone.

                                                JANE NIGHTWORK.

*   *   *

And Jane, whose circle of friends and confidants is evidently a wide one, has also written a letter to Elmer Davis which bears revelation:

GARDEN HOUSE HOTEL,

PHONE 4259   A.A.

CAMBRIDGE.

GUESTS 236011
(telephone no., not number of guests)   R.A.C.

☞

🖐

4 December, 1947

My Dear Mr. Elmer Davis:—

Mutual friends have told me of your family connection with the Holmes clan, and I cannot resist writing you on a sheet of paper I brought back with me from the little hotel in Camb. which was once the home of the original Professor Moriarty. . . . I mean of course Professor Cayley, 1821–1895, who lived for 31 yrs in the house later enlarged into Garden House Hotel; the study where he meditated his doctrine of matrices & his polynomials (which had an oecumenical vogue) is now used for billiards, pingpong, and televisions. You will hasten, I hope, to look up Professor Cayley & you will find that he only survived a few yrs after the shock of the Reichenbach fall.

Unlike yourself, I did not stay at the Savoy, but at an odd little hotel in Knightsbridge, a kind of goldfish bowl or museum mostly built of glass, porcelain and widows in fur jackets; it is on top of the abandoned old Brompton Road tube station, and during the days of blitz was a notable refuge in that nbrhood; some of the elderly ladies took shelter in the catacombs of the Tube & never found their way out; like that forgotten story by The Master; But like yrself, I went as soon as possible to Baker Street; alas I could nowhere find your affiche about Gowns for the Fuller Figures; but perhaps the modiste has moved across the way, for at 32 Baker Street is *Jou Jou, the World's Best Breast Supporter*. How much I prefer the French term, *soutien-gorge*.

I had no responsibilities of any sort (except some deductions from income taxes) so I didn't have to do anything trivial. I had a drink at the Criterion Bar; I spent a night at

Undershaw (Hindhead, where the *Hound* was written), I paid my shilling at Somerset House & "searched" the will of ACD (to see if he had left any special instructions about Sherlock; he didn't; what he did leave in the way of instructions will grieve you); and I followed in Supt. Fallon's launch (he is head of the Thames River Police) the course down river of the fleeing Andaman Islander; we embarked at Rotherhithe & went all the way to the desolate Plumstead Marshes & on to Erith.

Of course I did other things too: I had kippers for breakfast 45 days running & early morning tea and went to bed with a hot water bottle; I saw Churchill and Attlee doing their stuff in Ho Commons; & Canterbury Cathedral; I took train from Marylebone Station which even few English have ever done, dug some stained glass out of a pile of rubble in blitzed London, and wheeled a baby in a pram up and down Sloane Street & round Lowndes Square. I bought a drink for the editor of *Punch*, I had my coiffure done by a Court hairdresser, I was shocked by Oxford and enchanted by Cambridge. It'll take quite a while to digest all these notions; meanwhile I has a yen to tell you about them; *entre nous*. When you go to England, follow Sherlock's advice: as he said once: "Try Canadian Pacific." (*Black Peter*, was it? I think so.) I even found an 1894 Bradshaw.

Take care of yrself, with yr powerful convex lens.

JANE NIGHTWORK.

BSJ (os), 3 No. 2 (April 1948)

M R. SHERLOCK HOLMES sometimes revisits his old
university; I think he was probably there last fall
during the week of November 13 to attend the lectures
celebrating the centennial of George Boole's *Mathematical
Analysis of Logic*. He is rather old, you say? True, he is over
90, but that isn't so much in Cambridge, the shrine of
longevity. It is a town that still lives more by the pulsations
of thought than of petrol. It hasn't been drawn and quar-
tered by heavy traffic, like Oxford. I even thought, while I
was there, that I saw the old gentleman trundling gently
down Queens Road (behind the Backs) on one of those
legendary tricycles. The town of the Tripos naturally
cleaves to the tricycle.

* * *

Perhaps now more accessible to the softer emotions,
Holmes always goes to Cambridge in autumn, to stroll those
paths of golden litter under the beech avenues; to hear the
rasp of twig besoms on the lawns; to see through archways
a flash of scarlet creeper, flung like a doctor of science gown
on the gray shoulder of a college. Pacing by smooth-sliding
Cam he sees how each curved silvery bridge frames still
another in perspective beyond; a parable of education. And
you may be quite sure he conned on the noticeboards the
warning from the Cambridge Borough Police about some
rascal who has been thieving from students' rooms. The
suspect is "a man about 30, 5 feet 9 or 10 inches, dark hair,
of proportionate build, clean shaven, high cheek bones,
quietly spoken, wearing a dark suit." He does most of his
larcenies between 2:15 and 4:15 on Saturday afternoons.
Surprised on a stairway at Queens, he said he was looking
for "Mr. Harvey." There is no such name in that college.

Elementary, says Holmes; the culprit is a waiter from
one of the hotels or pubs. That time of the afternoon is
their off period, and the first name that came to his mind

was a fish sauce. He is obviously a rank amateur; to prowl round a college unnoticed one would wear horrible old gray bags, a tweed jacket, and a huge woollen scarf of club colours twice round the neck.

* * *

Ironical as always, Mr. Holmes adds that some of the purest examples of clean-limbed pink-tinted young Anglo-Saxon thanes are the P.O.W.'s who ramble solitary at week-ends.

* * *

I doubt if Holmes stays in college when he visits Cambridge. He took his name off the books long ago, piqued because he was not offered a fellowship. That was why (as is well known) he went to the U.S. for graduate study. I also doubt if his college was the one to which Dorothy Sayers assigned him. That particular foundation has a leaning toward high church rites, which were never his choice. I think it likely that Peterhouse was his college; perhaps that is why Peterhouse now has such a lively influx of students from the States, where Holmes is revered even more than in England. Peterhouse was handy to the laboratories, and adjoins Coe Fen. I see the young Holmes of the '70's, issuing onto the Fen in a misty morning, trousers rolled high, carrying net and collecting jar, to dip those drains and ditches for animalculae. I hope he had the room where the poet Gray fixed an iron bar outside the window, to swing a rope ladder for emergency escape. Holmes also always felt precautious against possible disaster. "Gray had an acute horror of fire," he says. "Internationally speaking, so should we all."

* * *

I derive valuable conjectures from my wonderful *Bradshaw* for "7th Month, 1894." (Alas that Bradshaw has abandoned its old Quaker terminology.) I think that in the '90's Holmes stayed at the University Arms; who could resist its advertisement "Frequented by the late Charles Kingsley and Anthony Trollope. Favourite resort of American and

Australian Visitors." Latterly I think he patronizes the little hotel, down by the river, enlarged from the home of the late Professor Cayley of Pure Mathematics. Sometimes, as he grows older, Holmes confuses Cayley with Moriarty; at any rate it tickles him to see young people playing ping-pong in the room that was for 30 years the great mathematician's study. "The daring thought of one generation," he says, "becomes a parlor game for its grandchildren." As you remember, he had always a palate for "something a little choice in white wines," and was hugely pleased when a Cambridge don brought him as tribute a bottle of Montrachet from the college cellar. They cradled it into the dining room, and the head waiter served it exactly chilled. Holmes was amused later to find his bill extended 5 bob for corkage. But, he reflected, "that is precisely what a university should do: cool and uncork for service bright vintages of youth."

* * *

From his hotel Mr. Holmes totters out to revisit favourite memorabilia. He much admires the secret fellows' bowling green at Trinity, where subtle undulations of turf impart a special modulus to the boxwood ballistics. From there he sees the gable at St. John's where Wordsworth gazed across at the marble composure of Isaac Newton in Trinity chapel. "A pity he didn't keep thinking about Newton; it would have saved him much twaddle." Holmes says the handwriting of *Lycidas*, in Trinity library, shows a much stronger mind. He is also fond of the Pepysian library at Magdalene, though he says Pepys's cipher was puerile. He is pleased to see again the warts-and-all portrait of Cromwell at Sidney Sussex, and likes to be driven to Ely Cathedral to revisit the tomb of Merivale, who was "Caustic in Wit." He watches the tame hedgehog on the back lawns of St. John's, probing the turf with its inquisitive little snout; I think he sees in that prickly and investigating creature an emblem of himself.

* * *

When told that General Montgomery's father once did a standing leap up the steps of the hall, in Trinity Great Court, Mr. Holmes got out his tape and measured them (there are eight steps). All he said was "Humph." Then he added "Perhaps it was dinner time."

* * *

He does not attend chapel services, but I have seen him walking in King's to listen while organ and choir were winnowing the bright air. He knows when it is Sunday because the college porter wears a silk hat.

* * *

Mr. Holmes's well-known sympathy for America of course leads him to the U. S. Army cemetery on Madingley Hill. It is a quiet university of the dead; nearly 6000 American boys came a long way to lie on that gentlest and kindest of slopes. Beside some of the little white ballot-crosses (votes for a better world?) are bundles of autumn flowers, from English friends who have not forgotten. In the little chapel is that moving tablet from the residents of Cheshunt and Waltham Cross. It is to remember the ten American airmen who gave their lives "to prevent their aircraft from crashing on our homes."

* * *

The old detective doesn't miss much. Always a lover of trains, he gives his noiseless chuckle to the inscription in Ely Cathedral about the Spiritual Railway:—

> . . . At any station on the line
> If you'll repent and turn from sin
> The train will stop and take you in.

Watson was always a little disconcerted by Holmes's grave-yard humour. In a Cambridge byway he noticed an ancient stone to Ann Argent Christmas. "First mention of a White Christmas," he remarked. He was equally pleased by undergraduate antics to collect pennies for Remembrance Day. For instance the two zealots who "flaming with spirits cast themselves into the icy Cam." He duly laid down his coins to help the Corpus Mile of Coppers along the pavement of King's Parade. Holmes likes high spirits and thinks England needs more of them. He is not dismayed by the vigour of partisan politics, so much of which is either shadow-boxing or showoff. I think what pleased him most lately was an advertisement from a great London shop, recommending a Pair of Duelling Pistols as "a distinguished Christmas Present." "An excellent idea for men in public life."

* * *

Smoking is now so costly that Holmes's revised edition of his monograph on *The Distinction Between the Ashes of the Various Tobaccos* has had to be postponed. If it gets printed, I am sure it will be supervised by Mr. S. C. Roberts of the Cambridge University Press. It was Mr. Roberts who wrote the admirable biography of Dr. Watson.

Of course Watson keeps an eye on Mr. Holmes during these little expeditions. On a college bulletin they saw "The following gentlemen go on Full Training. . . . No Smoking, No Spirits, Early to Bed." For a man of your age, Watson suggests, that is sound advice.

Holmes, who is always pithy, replies with his favourite classical pun: "Non omnis Moriarty."

BSJ (os), 3 No. 3 (July 1948); also in *The Courier*, 9 No. 6 (December 1947)

I WISH I COULD HAVE GONE to the first meeting of the new Philadelphia Scion, The Sons of the Copper Beeches (what a glorious name!), but, as I wrote to Dr. Lysander Starr, or Holmes Watson Starr, I simply had to carry on in the final phases of the grievous task on which I am engaged. If I had gone, I would have taken with me a plover's egg to be shown at the dinner.

Has it occurred to anyone that the christening of Lysander Stark and ditto Starr may have been unconscious echo from a name then much in the public mind: *Leander Starr* Jameson (of the famous Raid)?

Perhaps Prof. Starr would like to collaborate with me on my great eventual monograph on *Watson as Grammarian*, or *Let's Get Down to Syntax*. Watson's solecisms are delicious: one of my favorites is in *The Greek Interpreter:*

> He came back with a companion *whom* I knew could only
> be his brother.

It is a pity to correct such loveliness, as the Murray editions have done.

* * *

The Philadelphians should some day hold their meeting under one of the magnificent copper beeches on the lawn in front of Founders Hall, Haverford College—*sub tegmine fagi*—there are no finer copper beeches in America, I reckon—and then go into the Library to see the collection of Holmesiana. Prof. Ned Snyder would be delighted.

They will, of course, take up the problem whether Alice Rucastle Fowler ever did go to Philadelphia (after Mauritius)—and what became of the cockroach kid little Eddie, who was going to play a considerable part in the history of the country. He probably invented a vermin powder and insecticide.

* * *

A wonderful profitable sideline might be made of a B. S. I. Advt. Service. I have already remarked the possibilities of "Try Canadian Pacific." And what could American Tobacco Co. do with "The Distinction Between . . . the Various Tobaccos." Or a wine merchant with "Something a Little Choice," etc.

* * *

Shouldn't we write to our good Sidney Roberts (now elevated to Master of Pembroke College, Camb.) and insist that he send for the *Journal* a script of the talk he gave recently in London about Holmes's education? I spent an evening with Roberts last November. He is a longtime friend of my brother Frank, and a most admirable caustic soul. And certainly just about the most distinguished Sherlockian living.

* * *

I am sure that the man who took a room across from the Bellevue-Stratford in Philadelphia during the Republican Convention, and kept shooting down the rubber G. O. P. elephant, was the old shikari and big-game hunter Colonel Moran, late Bangalore, etc.

* * *

Miss Jane Nightwork has written me from Hector, B.C., Canada:

> My thesis on *The Principles of Osmosis in Journalism* (together with some Observations on Multiple Enterprise in the Publishing Business) have of course necessitated careful study of old bound volumes of *The Strand Magazine*. It was burthensome to have to transport them all the way to the Rocky Mtns. for privacy, but some of your subscribers . . .
>
> You are familiar of course with the heroical efforts of poor Mr. Greenhough Smith to keep the magazine rolling when there were no stories from Watson; in that critical Volume 4 (July–Dec. 1892) they even published pictures of Mr. Newnes and Mr. Greenhough Smith at their desks; Mr. Smith (p. 598) looks very worried. Another form of osmosis

was to get as many stories as possible illustrated by Sidney Paget so that they looked exactly like stories by Watson.

Volume 4 of *The Strand* is very important to the student; there is the incredibly lovely "A Day with Dr. Watson" showing what the Norwood Builder built for him! There is (p. 239) poor dear Mr. Greenhough Smith's attempt to write a mystery story; he had a wonderful idea, but he was too tired (after a day with Mr. Newnes) to give it what Kipling used to call, and Cutcliffe Hyne always echoed (osmosis again): "fluency and point." You know, osmosis; viz., the reciprocal percolation of fluids, was almost as lively in London in the '90's as it is in Chicago now. No one, until my thesis (*ouvrage couronné*, I hope, by McGill University), has ever written the real zoology, both clinical and cynical, of *Print for Profit*. . . .

It would be fun if two or three of your more comfortable members were here to talk these matters. I should lay special stress on the January 1897 number of *The Strand* in which Dr. Conan Doyle described his seven months as a Greenland whaler, apprentice surgeon in the Peterhead whaleship *Hope* in 1880. The noble Dr. got not only oil and blubber, but even sometimes ambergris, from everything that happened to him; this was the prognosis, of course, of the *Captain of the Pole Star*. But, since I always feel your members are deficient in Ursprung scholarship, I must quote to you what Dr. Doyle said of his return, after seven months at sea in 1880, without any news at all:

> For seven long months no letter and no news. . . . We had left in exciting times. War seemed imminent with Russia. . . . Great events had happened: the defeat of Maiwand and the famous march of Roberts from Cabul to Candahar. But it was all haze to us; and, to this day, I have never been able to get that particular bit of military history straightened out in my own mind.

And no one but Dr. Watson, of course, could straighten it for him.

Yrs. for a few fixed points in a changing age,

JANE NIGHTWORK

And later, as she moved on, Miss Nightwork wrote me again:

> I write from Morrisburg, Ontario, where research for my thesis brought me to examine the stock of Sacred Writings at that most unusual bookshop, Old Authors Farm.
>
> Mr. Edgar Smith (in the July B.S.J.) was plausible and suave, as usual, in his suggestion that "Three in Charge" *might* have been the Clark Russell story Watson was reading. But the presumption is, if Mr. Edgar Smith will carefully construe Watson's statement, that the doctor was reading one of the *storm* stories: "The howl of the gale from without seemed to blend with the text." Surely that implies that the text was stormy too? "Three in Charge" is one of Russell's calm-pieces; even the shipwreck is a very placid one.
>
> I should wish to be just as suave and plausible as Mr. Edgar Smith, in making my suggestion that the book was probably *Round the Galley Fire*, published 1883. This particular book had a special influence on Watson (osmosis again); so much so that he adopted its title for his own *Round the Red Lamp* some years later.
>
> Or I should like to think Watson's reading might have been that little masterpiece "The Mystery of the Ocean Star"—first published in *Longmans' Magazine before* '88—I don't know exact date. It was included in a collection of stories imported to N.Y. by Appleton in '88. I am always brutally precise. This is a fog story, not a storm piece; but the vessel, both in name and rig (*Ocean Star*, a barque), checks with the barque *Lone Star*.
>
> There are not very many readers of Clark Russell any more, but if you should care to reprint it I have a very fine photo of him which I would be happy to send you.

* * *

I am not even an ancillary member of the famous Canadian C.A.I.C. (Christ Am I Confused) Club, which is a kind of permanent intellectual Third Party; but one of its officers told me they held a special meeting, after *The Case of the Man Who Was Wanted* was published, and elected Watson to posthumous honorary membership. I shall, of course, for full scholarship, have to gloss the story for a footnote in my thesis. I give you, for your *droit de seigneur*, a brief preview of some of my notes on its iridescent inconsistencies:

The "Dore and Chinley Tunnel" was of course the famous Totley Tunnel, but is *not* on the main line to Sheffield.—This story, if "subsumed" (your word; I prefer *intussuscepted*) into the canon, raises the spectre of a possible Fourth Mrs. Watson.—New York City never had a "Landing Stage"; only docks or piers.—In 1895 there was no ocean liner, not even the immortal *Lucania*, that could cross from L'pool to N.Y. under six days.—And what doctor under the sigil of Hippocrates, or the caduceus of Hermes, would speak of "one of my best patients"? Perhaps it was Ockendon Senior, the retired oysterman.

I do think you chaps have tremendous fun, but I resent it a little; as Irgun Zwai Leumi used to say in the desert, "What is fun for you is death for the Wogs." I need to get my Mistress of Arts degree at McGill and I have to take these things literally. I must get on with my Nightwork.

JANE

P.S. I must add, while in my literal mood, a memo confirming the Quintessence of Watsonism as exhibited in *The Man Who Was Wanted*. We can suppose that it was only a bank manager in Sheffield who would address a telegram to 221B Baker Street, *S.W.* The postal districts, as everyone knows, have been subdivided later, but Baker Street could never have been South Western. It was either W, or W.C. But we know we are dealing with the authentic Watson when Holmes "crumpled the paper into a ball" (Holmes never gives poor Watson a piece of paper legibly flat) and made one of his habitual solecisms: "the greatest of the two."

Mr. Robert Fawcett, the talented artist who illustrated the story for *Cosmo*, has of course added to our canonical problems. He has equipped Watson, in 1895, with a zipper traveling-bag. He, or Souren Ermoyan (the very young art editor of *Cosmo*), had added a new color (green) to the prism of Holmes's dressing gown, and gone further into the dangerous tradition of deep satin lapels, Ascot cravat and curve-stem pipe. These, initiated by William Gillette, I find out of character for Mr. Holmes? Mr. Fawcett's spats for Lestrade, though I think a new touch, I find quite likely. We shall need to consider the glimpse of the alcove in which Watson sits; I think you might well ask Mr. Fawcett to do you a memo on his problems and how he studied them. The pictures in the Baker Street sitting room are surely more richly framed, with matts, mouldings, etc., than Dr. Ward Beecher might have expected? Watson I find very lifelike, though I believe his cuffs were always round and not linked sideways.

I think it would be wonderfully entertaining to ask Messrs. Ermoyan and Fawcett to tell us about their troubles and how much of the Sacred Writings they had to read to do what is, really, a lively and attractive job. I feared at first that Holmes had lacquered fingernails in the Railway carriage, but I think it is the shadow from the overhead lamp. Always for the canon, yrs, J. NIGHTWORK.

P.P.S. It was either Dr. Humfrey Michell or old Stanley Hopkins, I can't remember which, who pointed out to me that Watson, like Chaucer's prioress, was always "all conscience and tendre heart," and when he mentioned anyone by name it was because he had lifted something of his. The naming of Clark Russell is a psychic clue, and I make quite a note about this in my thesis.

* * *

One of my Favorite Allusions is in Saki's story "The Romancers," in his volume of short stories *Beasts and Superbeasts*, published in England in 1914 and then by comical Viking Press in N.Y., 1928:

My neighbors tell me wonderful, incredible things that their Aberdeens and chows and borzois have done; I never listen to them. On the other hand, I have read *The Hound of the Baskervilles* three times.

BSJ (OS), 3 No. 4 (October 1948)

I HAVE LONG WISHED that Elmer Davis, or some other classics expert, would discover a portion of MS or an ancient copy of the *Sidelights on Horace*; perhaps Dr. Huxtable's comments on Horace's schooling. I find this suggestive:

> Of his [Horace's] teachers only one is known to us, Orbilius Pupillus, of Beneventum, an old cavalry soldier who had resumed his books when his campaigns were over, and at the age of fifty had set up a school in the capital in the year when Cicero was consul. He was a gruff old fellow with a caustic tongue, and his ready resort to the rod Horace remembered many years after.
> —Clement Lawrence Smith, introduction to his edition of *The Odes and Epodes of Horace*; Ginn & Company, 1894.

Awaiting Elmer's prospective revelations from original sources, I tried my own hand at putting words into the mouth of Pupillus, in the form of this "Tail Light on Horace" which was presented, in an interval of relative calm, at the meeting of the Baker Street Irregulars on January 7th:

From Dr. Thorneycroft Huxtable's Projected New Edition
Translated from ORBILIUS PUPILLUS
Endorsed by him "This Xmas, 22 B.C."

Good Flaccus! I have read your scroll:
　　There are some passages I'd edit.
My only comment, on the whole,
　　Is, for the Priory School, some credit.

Now, master of the perfect ode,
　　If ever you feel supercilious
Recall, on fame's long rocky road,
　　The discipline of old Orbilius.

338

Now, easy in your Sabine Farm,
  Maecenas-kept (R.F.D. Tibur)
Remember how I had to warm
  Your britches for the poet's labor.

Your exercises would not pass,
  They were completely hasenpfeffer;
There was no boy in any class
  To lyric matters dumber, deafer.

In sapphic or asclepiad
  (I would admit it now, but dare I?)
Thou wert the idlest sleepyhead
  I had *in statu pupillari*.

Professors who now praise your songs
  Give Chloe, Lydia, Lalage,
The praise; I think as much belongs
  To your old teacher; *viz.*, to me.

You learned, the hard way, language shrewd,
  Not from Maecenas nor from bitches:
So mention, in your gratitude,
  Not old school ties, but old school switches.

Oh master of mind's perfect brief,
  Enjoy longevities! You've got 'em—
But think of me, who cried in grief,
  Bend over, boy! I tanned your bottom.

And speaking of Horace, I wonder how many know that our R. A. Knox had a share in the greatest Horatian spoof in all history, the invented *fifth* book of Horace's Odes, done in Latin and English by Charles Graves and Rudyard Kipling, with editorial help from A. D. Godley and Ronald Knox. Published at Oxford by Basil Blackwell; my copy is *third ed.*, 1920. I am not enough of a classicist to appreciate all its subtleties, but it is one of the finest highbrow

339

transfusions on record. This is a book that should certainly be in T. Huxtable's library.

* * *

I think that *The Baker Street Cook Book*, prepared by Peter Greig, should go on the publication program of the B.S.I. Inc., now that *The Blue Carbuncle* has won such a *succès d'estime*. It would give, of course, the exact recipe for all dishes, and treatment and vintage of all drinks, ever served on Baker Street. Peter and I have been enjoying a brisk correspondence about our favorite kedgeree, which also is not mentioned in the Canon, but (as I have said) was always on the menu aboard the *Orontes*.

* * *

I can't do better than copy out for quotation what I read with great delight on Xmas Day in T. S. Eliot's lecture *From Poe to Valéry*, privately printed as a Xmas present, 1948, by Harcourt Brace & Co.:

> Conan Doyle owes much to Poe, and not merely to Monsieur Dupin of *The Murders in the Rue Morgue*. Sherlock Holmes was deceiving Watson when he told him that he had bought his Stradivarius violin for a few shillings at a second-hand shop in the Tottenham Court Road. There is a close similarity between the musical exercises of Holmes and those of Roderick Usher: those wild and irregular improvisations which, while on one occasion they sent Watson off to sleep, must have been excruciating to any ear trained to music.

Of course Tom Eliot has long been a disciple of Holmes; which is one of the tests of a genuine High Brow: to distinguish the immortal elements in work apparently only popular. It makes me think of Professor Saintsbury's Law (what he calls the First Law of Criticism):

> B is not bad because it is not A, no matter how good A may be.

340

And Osbert Sitwell (in *Laughter in the Next Room*, 1948) contributes what may be regarded as appropriate commentary:

> . . . that sense of truth to an epoch that so pre-eminently, so memorably, distinguishes several books, not least among them *The Adventures* of Sherlock Holmes.

* * *

The Irregular Quarter would not be replete if I did not quote the latest communications that have come to hand from Jane Nightwork. Writing from the Ladies' Lodgings, at McGill University, she has this to say:

> While preparing a footnote (for my thesis) on *Sherlockian Allusions in Chaucer's Summoner's Tale*, I always remembered the special interest that you and Edgar Smith hold in the Priory School and the Duke of Holdernesse. The *Summoner's Tale* begins, you recall:—
>
> > Lordynges, there is in Yorkshire, as I guess,
> > A marshy country called Holdernesse . . .
>
> It is regrettable that a young woman of breeding but vowed to literary study should have to read such marshy matter; but so it is. Sherlock Holmes, with his cat-neat mind, always referred to that story as a monograph on *The Duodecimation of Gases*. But a study of the place-names of the Holdernesse region (between the North Sea and the Humber) assures me that the Yorkshire squirearchy from which Sherlock and Mycroft descended was certainly in his neighborhood. There, more than anywhere in England, one finds all possible variations on the ancient word *holm*—in Middle English a seaside or riverside meadow? or an islet or eyot in a river? That is exactly our geography here at Montreal, but none of our philologists seem to know.
>
> You will find (McGill University Library) plate 67 of the glorious Bartholomew's *Survey Atlas of England & Wales*—you own the only private copy in North America, and you

341

have not brought yourself as yet to lend it even to a student—Holme on the Wolds [how about Holme on the Range?], Holme Wold, Holmedale, Waxholme, Cattle Holms, etc., etc., all near the ancient Holdernesse Drain, one of the innumerable dykes by which that ancient and fertile meadowland was made useful for grazing and culture. Your northbound train from Hull will take you through Beverley, against whose Franciscan Priory Chaucer had some special scunner, we don't now know why. But it is well remembered (see Muriel Bowden: *Commentary on the Prologue to the Canterbury Tales*; Macmillan, 1948) that Chaucer was fined 2 shillings for beating a Franciscan friar not far from Charing Cross. Friar Matthew—from Beverley—knocked out Geoffrey's left canine.

I don't need to remind you that the Duke of Holdernesse was also Baron Beverley. And the literary associations of that ancient country are enforced by a railway station called Kipling Cotes; which is, however, quite a way from Lake Rudyard, in Staffs.

There are many more interesting footnotes to be trodden. From the *Paragon Station* (sic) in Hull you can take train, for instance, to the two ancient churches at Hedon and Patrington, which are locally known as the King and Queen of Holdernesse. I am positive it was one of the two lighthouses on Spurn Head where the untrained politician encountered the trained cormorant. My notion is that next summer you and Edgar Smith and I should hire a couple of appropriate Humber pushbikes and explore that region—including (not very far) *Shandy Hall*, in the North Riding of Yorks., where the Irrev. Laurence Sterne wrote much of his mischief.

I always remember your line: "The best textbook of literature is an atlas."

Sincerely yours,

JANE NIGHTWORK

And again, a little while later, Miss Nightwork, heading her letter this time "McGill University (Women's Graduate Dormitory), Montreal, P.Q. (and mind them!)," gave these thoughts into being:

I am sorry to have to misaddress this letter: actually I am in my berth in the famous old 10½ P.M. sleeper from Grand Central to Montreal. But I found, in a delicatessen store on 47 Street (which you had mentioned to me) a tin of *Lyle's Golden Syrup*, that immortal British succulent and adhesive on which John H. Watson and all children of the British Commonwealth were reared (together with Cooper's Oxford Marmalade). It was of course Lyle's Golden Syrup (in which, according to the tin, "micro-organisms cannot live") of which the Treacle Tart of our childhoods was built. It always made me sad that in the menus and cookbooks of The States the two great nourishments of my innocence do not exist: Treacle Tart, and Kedgeree.

I had to come to N. Y. to trace some further allusions I need in my thesis on Stevensonian Echoes in the Works of John H. Watson. Even Edgar Smith, in his admirable monograph on "A Scandal in Identity," did not exhaust the topic. Though he will have remarked the parallel between the sinister President of the Suicide Club and Professor Moriarty; even to Stevenson's phrase:

the most dangerous hands in Europe,

on which Watson played so many variations. Or consider, in the story of the Rajah's Diamond: "Have you read Gaboriau?" and the allusions to Lecoq. Even the Trichinopoli cigar smoked in that same story had its echo later; and I seem to suspect that the hotel where Watson stayed in his early days in the great cesspool was the Craven Hotel (just off The Strand) where the young American Silas Q (for Quincy?) Scuddamore took the Saratoga Trunk. It is plain to me also that Watson took his cue for using American allusions from Stevenson's highly humorous attitude toward the U.S.A. in those deathless pasticcioes of burlesque.

I could not wait to enjoy some of the Golden Syrup, so I opened the tin in my berth, with my pocket tin-opener which I always carry, but a lurch of the train on that D & H roadbed spilled some of the gummy glucose and I am stuck to my sheets until the porter wakes in the morning and can dishesive me.

343

The train approaches Rouse's Point, the sun is coming up over that northern dribble of Lake Champlain, sturdy old Mr. Mackenzie King is getting ready to retire, and we are all hoping that the one thing Canada has lacked since Leacock may revive in our literature, but only in the French-Canadian contingent: a sense of humour. What grim fellows our Canadian writers are! The English, the Scots, the Irish, go cast-iron in their wits as soon as they face the frontier. As soon as an Englishman has to earn a living it annihilates his sense of humour. No wonder.

The porter is spraying me with some detergent which he uses to get chewing gum off the rugs, and I may be able to get clean of Lyle's Golden Syrup by the time we stop at Westmount, where I unload. Keep in touch with Canada; the Canadians are the luckiest of people, they wear ear-muffs half the year. I was terribly upset by what you-all have done to radio. It was such a lovely little idea.

I shall take my Doctor's Degree, I hope, in the spring; then I shall need a job. Don't the B.S.I. want a delegate on Baker Street? Opposite the Jou-jou soutien-gorges?

Sincerely yours,

Jane Nightwork

* * *

I like Miss Nightwork's idea of Literary Osmosis or inter-fusion of fluids. Perhaps I can supply a footnote for her Thesis, à propos Southsea. I do not remember seeing it mentioned that if Watson had moved to Southsea only a few years earlier (3 or 4) he would have seen, on the shingle beaches, a very shortsighted and odd looking little boy—I don't know whether he yet wore spectacles?—who was only happy when he was escaped from the cruelties of (he uses the same phrase) *The Woman*. She was a boarding-house keeper who took in the helpless children of Anglo-Indian professionals, and the unhappy little boy was Rudyard Kipling.* I have no exact chronology—let us leave exacti-tude to Miss Nightwork—but by the time Watson was

---

*All described in early chapters of *The Light that Failed*.

polishing his brass plate at Bush Villa, the young Beetle was at Westward Ho and ⅓ of Stalky and Co.—but I wish the gigantic young doctor and the dark dwarfish schoolboy might have encountered.

Watson, in his *Memories and Adventures*, pays such lively tribute to R. K. (he says he even bought the *Plain Tales* in the Southsea days when every book was a strain on the exchequer) that I wish R. K. in his extraordinary posthumous memoir, *Something of Myself* (1937), had mentioned Watson. But I don't think Kipling ever forgave Watson for taking the Road to Endor.

Miss Nightwork would be astounded if she were to read Kipling's wonderful gallbladder and chalkstone testament. It is a truly great book, in which without fear or fervor a great artist lancets his own tendons. How much Kipling and Watson had in common, e.g., an imperious mother! What Kipling is proudest of, viz., that until the age of 45 (when they died) he submitted everything he ever wrote to his parents, is I think one of the most tragic confessions ever made by a mature creature. It makes me think of my electric toaster which has just quit working, and I found it was choked with crumbs. Old stale burned-out crumbs. Kipling is one of my idols; I love him best of all when he twangs his sour note because I can see him dreeing his dreadful wyrd, but he was always (as E. V. Lucas said in our cups on 45 Street) "that bitter little man." And our credulous and magnificent Watson (as Nightwork will agree) was never little and never bitter. The gods are never kind, they are like the great cloudy South African diamond that was served on a platter at Mr. Churchill's dinner, and Lady Somebody Something thought it an illjelled blancmange and said to the butler, "No, thank you."

There are only three great literary memoirs, in English, in the past 20 years. I hope Miss Nightwork, the solitudinary cyclist, will quote them all: Watson's *Memories and Adventures*; Kipling's *Something of Myself*; and Sir Eddie

Marsh's *A Number of People.* These could, if temperamentally read, give a number of youngfry a notion of what the world was like. Which, quite rightly, they don't wish to know.

But I beg Mlle. Nightwork, while she is not forgetting things, not to forget R. K., the most broken and beautiful of unfashionable writers. His distaste for Watson is creditable to them both. There is double-entry in the books of literature.

BSJ (os), 4 No. 1 (January 1949)

I DO NOT THINK anyone has done the desirable collation of Baker Street and the *Round the Red Lamp* stories. In *R.R.L.*, the Agent (settled in his new house at Undershaw) really let himself go. Let us check first our eponym story, *The Resident Patient*. There we learn that poor taper-faced, sandy-chopped Percy was the author of a monograph on Obscure Nervous Lesions. But in the story *A Medical Document* in *R.R.L.*, we learn its full title, "Obscure Nervous Lesions *in the Unmarried.*" Percy Trevelyan, if he hadn't been so obscure, was on the way to write the Kinsey Report of 1893.

Of course, as I have noted before, there is the troubling antithesis—which is more anxious-making, "the chest and limbs of a Hercules" (*A Scandal in Bohemia*) or "the limbs and chest of a Hercules" (*The Resident Patient*)? I think it the delicacy of Watson that, under the known circumstances, he put limbs second in the case of Mlle. Adler.

* * *

A note I wd cherish from Miss Nightwork could be provided by the great medical faculty of McGill: the antiseptic precautions of the Watsonian era. In *Round the Red Lamp* (e.g., in that shocking story of sin and revenge, *The Case of Lady Sannox*, which so horrified me as a child) the third most prosperous surgeon in London stuffs his pockets with bandages and lint, apparently without much care for sterility. Even Dr. Percy Trevelyan carried his instruments loose in a wicker basket inside his brougham.

But I think the note to which I would solicit Miss Nightwork's agile foot comes from page 22 of the issue of *The Strand* for July 1893. Here, in Sidney Paget's drawing, Holmes is hanging up his soft hat on the hat stand in Watson's hall—his lobby, the Scots would call it. There are visible (and S. Paget is the most Ursprung scholarship we have) Mrs. Watson's summer parasol; three sturdy umbrellas; and Watson's two walking sticks. Also Watson's carefully burnished professional topper. But—and here the astonishment—on a lower peg, hangs a *deerstalker*. This I think one of the pleasantest glimpses into Watson's character. He so admired Holmes that he even got himself a deerstalker that he thought he might some day, travelling to Yorkshire or Hereford or Norfolk or somewhere, feel warranted to wear. Of course he never did. But there it is; I wish Mr. Edgar Smith would reproduce that picture as evidence.

* * *

Another footnote: that story (*The Crooked Man*) is an additional evidence of Watson's lethargy. Holmes asks him if he could possibly make the 11:10 from Waterloo next morning.

* * *

Students of *The Strand* will have noticed of course that the first thing poor Greenhough Smith (the editor) did when he got the shattering *Final Problem* was to spread *The Naval Treaty* through two issues, and then (December 1893) for the first time Sherlock Holmes, at the Reichenbach Fall, got top billing in the Magazine.

* * *

In the matter of nervous lesions, consider the psychic stunting or diminution caused upon Watson by association with Holmes. One of our psychiatrists might well do a paper on this. Somewhere Watson pathetically remarks "I had become one of his habits." Used as punching bag and Persian slipper, Watson had sunk dangerously low in the scale of self-respect. The best proof is how he rebounds when released from Holmes and on his own footwork. When he was sent down to Devonshire with Baskerville and Mortimer, for example, he was definitely puerile—he spent much of the journey, he tells us, playing with the spaniel—as a child of 12 would have done. But see him rise, in those superb reports from Baskerville Hall. There, brevetted above Baker Street status, we see Watson at his best, the best that Mary Morstan loved (and other women too). It was poor Watson's *Thing* about Holmes that finally

348

wore down Mary Morstan Watson. The theory, often advanced, that Mary went nuts &c, is nonsense. I have proved long ago, in this *Journal*, that she cried ungrammatically "Who did you marry, me or Mr. Holmes?" and went off and started a profitable millinery boutique. This, as Bell (p. 68) has pointed out, was possible by the bequest from Thaddeus Sholto. I have always been interested in the Sholto–Morstan settlement, because (Bell, p. 50) the pearls arrived every year on May 5, which is my own birthday.

* * *

Since we mention the Baskerville codex, may I say—for better scholarship to follow through—the great need for insinuating commentary on a number of points.

1. Why was one page of Watson's letters to Holmes "missing"?

See beginning chapter viii. It was not likely that Holmes lost it in carelessness, and we know that neither the lightfoot skivvy nor the heavyfoot Mrs. Hudson ever removed a paper from the sitting-room.

(Excuse me for interrupting, but I can't help remembering how that simplest of funny old millionaires, Cyrus H. K. Curtis, when he found himself owner of the famous Phila. *Ledger*, always thought the *City Room* was the *Sitting Room*, and alluded to it as such. It was, in those wonderful years 1917–1920, the most superb example of an unspotted old man (with no nervous lesions) who found himself On Top of the World, and didn't know how, or why, or what, not to do about it.)

The page that Holmes deliberately removed from Watson's reports was one that told more about Watson (possibly re Laura Lyons?) than Holmes thought prudent. Remember, it was always Holmes who was the prude, not Watson. And n.b., that Mr. Rex Stout's infamous piece, though factually grotesque, has deep psychological suggestion. There is no more devastating theme for students of schism.

than the whole saga of Holmes, Watson, and The Agent. My only comment (which Jane Nightwork is too puelline to comprehend) is don't do your schism with nail scissors.

2. Queries for students: Free Advertising in the Saga.

E.g., Remington Typewriter, Canadian Pacific, Arcadia Mixture. Of course standard products such as Bradshaw, Whitaker, Crockford don't count. A man came to see me the other day and found on my table a copy of Crockford. He was staggered, he thought Crockford (100 yrs. old or nearly) was something Watson invented. I doubt if you yourself have a copy of Crockford.

3. A number of social allusions in *Baskervilles* that are not pervious to children. Why couldn't they smoke a cigarette until they got away from the dining room? To this day it isn't British *comme il faut*, except in very Bohemian or BBC rallies, to smoke before the coffee.—When he talks about The Yard, he doesn't mean Scotland, but the cab stable— When he talks about the "express office" he means the district messenger service; the case that Bell never listed.

4. I have always wanted to enjoy the game of ecarte, which Sir Henry Baskerville & Dr. Mortimer played. It sounds in Hoyle less than alluring, but I know it was the gin-rummy of the 18th century. Wouldn't someone from the Cavendish or Tankerville Club give us a notionable routine of it?

5. My guess is that the page of Watson's letters that Holmes prudishly destroyed was about the third Flaming Beryl.

* * *

Miss Jane Nightwork has written me from the Ladies' Lounge at the Graduate School of McGill University, in the following vein:

As I dare say I have apprised you, I am still pursuing the infantry of footnotes for my medium opus, my D.Litt. thesis on Unelucidated Coefficients in the Literature of Sherlock Holmes; or, the Semiscience of Induction.

I realized that in my footnotes I had never demorialized one of the great granite cromlechs of the Victorian age: I have maybe too often blown sparm in honor of the noble old Saintsbury; but there was a contemporary (I think about 7 yrs older than G.S.) who was as fantastically rational, liberal, agnostic—and, even to use one of his two favorite adjectives, *sapid* (the other was flangent)—and in prose so crystalline & courageous, as sometimes old softy Saintsbury was wordy and wallowing. His family were Yorkshire, as were Sherlock Holmes's country voorlopers, though himself was born in Lancs. But he was, in the formative yrs of young Holmes and almost as young Watson, the most admired, dreaded, and cold-judging editor & critic; say from 1867–1882 when he was editor of the *Fortnightly Review*. It was unquestionably the *Fortnightly* (whatever Watson, always shuffling the cards, called it) in which S.H. published his essay, *The Book of Life?*

One of the astounding & truly beautiful memorandabilities of this great writer & great statesman is the fact that not until his wife died (in her sleep) two months later than her secretive husband (November and September 1923) did anyone know that he had ever been married. His wife, that notable and carborundum scholar always maintained, was Nobody's Business. I have consulted, in the library of the University of Manchester, the great collection of books which he spent years in gathering and reading, but could not be released to that library (nearest like McGill of all other universities, with its nozzle always on the sill of actuality and scientific spoor, completely devoid of reverence for anything but facts on probation) until his widow's death; and still, I hope, available only to virgin, or at any rate women, students.

I refer, of course, in my footnotes terser than this, to Lord Morley, 1838–1923. It was his incessant references and quotations from Goethe, in the wonderful years when he was editing the *Fortnightly* and the *Pall Mall Gazette* (say 1867–1890) and writing the wonderful reviews and essays reprinted in his later books (you can write to Macmillan, who published the grand set of uncostly reprints in 1923, but I doubt if there's anyone at Macmillan nowadays who ever heard of them) in which you can find the quotes from Goethe that poor Holmes, or poor Watson, or poor Agent, wrote down in his or their commonplace books.

I shall add, somewhere in my footnotes, the modern version of Burke (who was John Morley's first ignition-spark) *On the Origin of Our Ideas of the Low and Hideous*. And of course Holmes got his notion of Irene Adler from Burke's hypostatized description of Marie Antoinette. You never know whither our study will lead us.

Yours

J. N. (Jane Nightwork)

BSJ (NS), 1 No. 1 (January 1951)

I F YOU OPEN your Bartholomew survey map of Norfolk, and study the neighborhood of North Walsham (delicious old town with two railway stations side by side), you will see it was only a short drive from there to the house of Hilton Cubitt, Esq. He lived either at *Edingthorp* or at *Ridlington*; which accounts for the confusion of the two texts, Riding Thorp or Ridlingthorp. The last time I was in England, I went by bus very near both villages, though not actually through them—we were on our way to Mundesley, Paston (where the letters came from), and Bacton-on-Sea. What is particularly interesting is that the Literary Agent took care to choose an indigenous Norfolk name for his squire. The graveyards are rich in Cubitts, and an advertisement in a North Walsham booklet shows that the family also went into trade. It is told that a certain E. R. Cubitt, of 8 King's Arms St., North Walsham, is prepared to entertain negotiations for the sale of his stock of fine carpets, linoleums, blinds, curtains, loose covers and upholstery, etc., etc.

* * *

I always read J. J. Bell's fine book on whaling (*The Whalers*, ca. 1915) alongside *The Captain of the Pole Star* and F. V. Morley et al.'s *Whaling North and South*. And I often feel that most Irregulars don't have time to do their collateral home-work. But the harpoon is that in *1849*, when Herman Melville went to London (see his *Journal*, or Lewis Mumford's biography, p. 123), he also stayed "in a tall draughty room in Craven Street, just off the Strand." The room of the bull pup, and of the Saratoga Trunk?

* * *

In British usage the verb *seconded*, meaning transfer of an officer from his own regiment to some other outfit—or possibly promoted to staff duty—is always pronounced as in French: se*con*ded (like absconded). Then, methought, poor Watson was se*con*ded (at the very beginning of *A Study in Scarlet*)—from his Northumberland Fusiliers to the Berk-

353

shires. But when I look it up, it says "I was removed from my brigade" etc. That *removed* has to me a somewhat sinister sound? It doesn't sound pukka military talk at all, and seems to suggest less than promotion? Perhaps Helen Simpson dealt with this in her medical career of JHW?

* * *

I am in duty bound to remark on Vincent Starrett's apodosis, on page 238 of his *Books and Bipeds*, that, in consequence of Jay Finley Christ's discovery of the juxtaposition of the islands of Ulva and Staffa off the western coast of Scotland, the argument over the location of the island of Uffa is closed.

Like Vincent, I have warm admiration for Prof. Christ's brilliant conjecture that Ulva plus Staffa equals Uffa. But if that is accepted, surely we must conjecture further? Dr. Johnson reported that in Ulva there still continued the traditional *Mercheta Mulierum*—vis., that the bride's virginity had to be bought off from the Laird, who had prescriptive right to it (*jus primae noctis*). The singular adventure(s) were obviously caused by the Laird of Ulva, or Uffa, attempting to exercise upon a Grice Paterson bride this ancient privilege.

But I myself still have a fancy for my own theory, which I think was once printed somewhere—perhaps in the old B.S.J., I don't remember; Edgar Smith would know. Briefly, there are in England many "islands" not surrounded by water. The Isle of Ely is the most famous. Particularly in East Anglia any region rising above fens or meadows, even an isolated hilltop or a woodland surrounded by open country, is often known as an "island."

There was—I think in the 10th century?—a king of East Anglia named Offa or Uffa: his name is preserved in both forms. Just outside Woodbridge in Suffolk is the ancient village of Ufford, named for Uffa's Ford (across the river Deben). This Offa, by the way, is not to be confused with the earlier Offa, the Strong Man of Mercia, who built Offa's

Dyke from the Dee to the Wye to keep out the wild Welsh. Our authority for not confusing them is the scribe Geoffrey de Fontibus; see footnote, p. 139, of *Lives and Legends of the English Saints* (the Bampton Lectures, 1903, by W. H. Hutton).

The "island" of Uffa, to any student of East Anglia and Anglo-Saxon history, will irresistibly suggest some region of hilly ground rising above the tides and meadows of the Deben at Ufford. You will find just such country north and northwest of Woodbridge. It is a neighborhood rich in ancient British barrows and early English charters. Just before the War, in 1939, men digging anti-aircraft emplacements across the river from Woodbridge found the buried shell of some ancient war-galley, Danish I suppose, at Sutton Hoo, or Haugh. Its ceremonial tools and objects are now in the British Museum; I believe the hull of the ship itself was damaged in the hasty digging of the gun-sites.

The ancient East Anglian king Uffa, and his topographical "island," are I think at least as likely as the telescopic condensation of Ulva and Staffa.

My brother Frank—who lives in England—has brooded on this with me; he will perhaps consult East Anglian antiquarians. Myself, I would be inclined to think that Market Hill, in Woodbridge itself, was the Island of Uffa. The late Mr. V. B. Redstone, in his little volume *Bygone Woodbridge* (1893), says:

> Upon the hill, now Market Hill, first arose the dwellings of the Saxon serfs around the conspicuous burial ground of their departed chief, probably Uffa.

I need hardly point out that there are many other possible theories bearing upon this Uffa problem:

Another kind of island, familiar in England, is the "traffic island." There is an Ufford Street in Lambeth and Southwark; perhaps the Grice Patersons took refuge there, on a traffic island, from roaring beer drays and goods lorries of that neighborhood?

Were the Grice Patersons Scottish, as usually thought? Then Grice may have been Watson's misunderstanding of the old Scots verb *grise* or *griese* meaning to frighten, to turn gray with fear (*vide* Jamieson's Scots Dictionary). They were the Frightened Patersons.

Were the Patersons conspirators for Irish Home Rule? Uffa may have been U.F.F.A., United Fenian Freemen's Association.

Was the name Grice the same as Anna Katharine Green's famous detective Mr. Gryce? Why does no one ever remember Mr. Gryce? He first appeared in 1878—just 73 years ago, in *The Leavenworth Case*. If the Grice Patersons were of the same kin, Holmes would of course be interested.

. . . Never let us assume that any problem in the Sacred Writings can be exhausted!

* * *

Jane Nightwork tells me that after finishing the thesis upon which she has been working, she found herself "as beshent as young Dimsdale (the Edinburgh rugger champion in *The Firm of Girdlestone*) when he answered *Cacodyl* to every question." And Miss Nightwork goes on:

> I was always sorry that neither Hesketh Pearson nor John Dickson Carr really piped themselves into the blessed naïveté of that wonderful prenatal book. It shewed, like any clarified dawn or dusk, the very sweetest and worst of weather to come. No reader of *The Copper Beeches*, for example, can reticulate and relish the horror of Hampshire and a green-crusted sinister priory if he hasn't Girdlestoned.

> This book I strongly recommend:
> One of the corniest ever penned.

Poor Mr. Carr—or was it Mr. Pearson?—suggested a twinge of Meredith. That's nonsense. Please, my dear old boys, notice how The Agent took his Major Clutterbuck straight from Thackeray. There are so many delicate anxieties to consider: what (f.G.s.) is a dog's head hat scarf pin? And how, from RLS, the striving young doctor took Nihilists. And dog-carts! You Baker Street Irregulars are all too young to have ridden in a dog-cart—they were just as periculous as anything fabricated by General Motors. I was once thrown from a dog-cart (in West Chester, Penna.) between the horse and the broken shaft. It ruined my new tweed suit; but if I hadn't been felicity in skirts it would have punctured my lung.

Of course there are some wonderful poppings of corn in *Girdlestone.*—E.g., the horrible error where a chap takes ticket to *Colchester* from Waterloo—he means obviously Chichester. The book could only have been written by a young doctor in Southsea, and his shift of names in the Isle of Havant is lovely at low tide. But he gives the most perfect script of Young Watson's college life at Edinburgh. As a child I used to walk miles to read anything under That Name at the old Enoch Pratt Library, and I have less than no respect for people who come crowding in without having read *The Gully of Bluemansdyke* or *The Surgeon of Gaster Fell.* They were imitated from RLS; and who was ever more worth imitating! I roar from laughter as I think of the people who don't even know that he was educating himself by imitating. That is a fine means of education!

BSJ (NS), 1 No. 2 (April 1951)

I HAVE ALWAYS WANTED the Pullman Co. to name two cars for S.H. and J.H.W. Who among our automotive or transportation confrères might be interested and exert influence?

. . . Think what a tohubohu the Detroit Mendicants would make if the NY Central were to put three cars (Sherlock Holmes, Doctor Watson, and The Paradol Chamber) regular on the Wolverine or the Detroiter.

Jane Nightwork suggests that the *Journal* ask for suggestions, if there were a 10-car Pullman train all cars named out of the Canon, what names would one choose as most Pullmanesque?

As a first try, I suggest (omitting *The* as being more Pullmanesque):

> Speckled Band
> Abbey Grange
> Blue Carbuncle
> Engineer's Thumb
> Five Orange Pips (dining car)
> Gloria Scott
> Dancing Men (cabaret and games car)
> Red-Headed League
> Silver Blaze
> Illustrious Client (suites for tycoons)
> Diogenes Club (lounge car)
> Boscombe Valley
> Noble Bachelor (all roomettes)
> Scandal in Bohemia (all drawing rooms)
> Sussex Vampire (hairdressers, baths, etc.)
> 221B (observation car)

That's more than ten, I notice. Anyhow . . . whyn't we sell the idea of a Sherlock Holmes Limited?

* * *

Uncle Felix Morley, the Second Garrideb, has a lot of interesting and speculating ideas about Dr. Mortimer's curly-haired spaniel. He seems to believe that the reason for Dr. (or *Mr.* as he shd be known; just a humble MRCS) Mortimer having brought the dog, which Felix deduces was a bitch, to Town with him was that she was a bitch, and that he didn't like to leave her at home for fear of accidents. Evidently when he called at 221B he hitched her leash to the door scraper. But there is nothing said of her at the Northumberland Hotel, &c, and Uncle Felix divines she was boarded a few days at Pinchin Lane and by accident or design was bred to the lurcher who sired Toby.

Alas, his chronologies here are dubitative. *The Sign of the Four* was certainly two years before the Dartmoor doings. And Holmes said, "I see the dog *himself*." Would so acute an observer have left the sex in doubt?

But Uncle Felix has set me musing on *The Hound*. Why do we never meet Mrs. Mortimer? Her husband says that when he married "It was necessary to make a home of my own." Morstan and Mortimer are adjacent in alphabet: is it possible that Mrs. Mortimer, like Mary Morstan Watson, had some symptoms of hysteria that made a remote residence desirable?

* * *

I do not hear of any record of the meetings of The Hounds of the Baskerville in Chicago, but surely one of their better stunts would be to provide each member, as provender at the annual dinner, with a loaf of bread (of good old Devonshire cottage style, with the bun on top of the loaf), a tinned tongue, and two tins of preserved peaches. As served by Cartwright in the neolithic stone hut. And what, as Jane Nightwork often asks, became of Cartwright in later years? President of the District Messenger Service?

And what about the phases of the moon in *The Hound*? I've never checked the dates, but it has often seemed to me that the moon was always exactly what Watson, or Holmes, needed it to be. It was low, fairly full, about 3 A.M. about October 15—when Dr. W. saw S.H. on the tor in silhouette. It was half-moon about 10 P.M. the night of the crisis (Oct. 19?). These are matters for study: if the moon was out of whack over Dartmoor (and the parishes of Grimpen and High Barrow, and Mr. Frankland hadn't even spotted it with his telescope) very likely Mrs. Mortimer, and Laura Frankland Lyons also, would have noted it. And Beryl Garcia Vandeleur Stapleton too. . . . The Vandeleur, by the way, is another of the Agent's unconscious borrowings from R.L.S.—remember the South American Dictator General Vandeleur in *The New Arabian Nights*, and the Scotch Express in the Night-time.

* * *

Stanley Hopkins says—now that the Stone of Scone (pronounced, but not by radio commentators, "Scoon") has been found—that Sherlock Holmes would instantly have spotted the initials left on the coronation chair when it was lifted. The "JFS" was a Jacobite anagram—"Jamie for Scotland" or "Jacobus filius Stuartorum."

* * *

Here are two questions for the experts:

(1) What evidence is there that Watson also sometimes wore a deerstalker cap?

 A. *Strand Magazine*, July 1893: Sidney Paget's picture of Watson's hat-stand (*The Crooked Man*) shows three umbrellas, one parasol (Mrs. Watson's, of course), one stout walking stick, Watson's professional silk hat, and a *deerstalker*. Watson's familiar bowler is not shown; it was upstairs where Mrs. Watson was brushing it; at that time she still loved him.

(2) When, on account of his shaken health, did Watson "muffle himself nose-high against the keen night air"?

360

A. *Strand Magazine*, August 1893: *The Resident Patient.* In the various shufflings and transposings of the famous introduction (the Henry Ward Beecher portrait episode) two or three paragraphs (including Holmes's broken test tube) in the Ur-text are missing from the usual trade and omnibus editions; and the nose-high muffling escaped even Mr. Edgar Smith's synoptic Limited Editions Club text. Mr. Paget shows Watson so muffled in his illustration of Holmes and Watson strolling on the Strand.

BSJ (NS), 1 No. 3 (July 1951)

I WAS DELIGHTED by Molly Panter-Downes's piece in *The New Yorker* for July 9th. The Who's Who, birthing S.H. in 1853, gripes me, of course, for it seems that the *Last Bow*, which categorically states him at 60 in August 1914, is our only, and sufficient, calendar.

I would like to think, too, that Molly's pants are down in the suggestion that Watson never mentioned the deerstalker. But it would take a textual cross-hatch to establish the truth or falsity of this assertion. One remembers the "ear-flapped travelling cap" in *Silver Blaze*; but this is not positively a deerstalker. "Close-fitting cloth caps" are frequent (*Boscombe Valley, Engineer's Thumb*, etc.), but I wish Jay Finley Christ or someone would tell me, does JHW ever categorically mention the deerstalker? The Oxford Dictionary gives 1881 as the approximate date of the term (for a hat). It ought to be in the *Hound* (profiled-against-the-moon) but, I repeat, I really want to know.

* * *

Speaking of *His Last Bow*, did anyone ever explain why Von Bork served Tokay? He said to Altamont, "Will you take a glass of wine?" To which, in Yank-Erse-Cockney, Altamont replied, "Okye, chief." So Von Bork thought he meant Tokay.

* * *

It isn't strictly, or even loosely, a Sherlockian thought, but I've just realized the wonderful etymologic accuracy of the word "helicopter": a screw-wing: *helix* plus *pterix*. How wonderfully science keeps Greek and Latin alive for anyone who cares!

* * *

At long last I have heard from Jane Nightwork again. Writing from the Ladies' Lounge and Dormitory at McGill University, she has, I am happy to repeat, this to say:

> I have spoken before of Mr. Holmes's not infrequent breakdowns in English syntax; his errors, or possibly sometimes Watson's?, are meticulously listed in one of my foot-

362

notes. Watson wrote with the divine insouciance which we only find in the work of the very greatest artists, for instance Shakespeare or even Korzeniowski (Conrad to you); and this is doubtless one of the reasons why you have always believed that Holmes had his schooling in the U.S.A.; by analysis of schoolboy records and papers I know you have worked out some theory that Holmes was a schoolboy at a famous Quaker academy (coeducational) in Pennsylvania; his enforced association there with the daughters of Philadelphia Friends gave him his lifelong scunner against women. No wonder when he first met a woman of bohemian stripe he was dangerously enchanted.

One of my footnotes (which grow to be more important than my thesis itself) is on the Parallel Naïvetés of Conrad and Holmes in regard to Women. These two great men (you cannot fail to have noted) were near contemporaries. Conrad was born Dec 6, 1857; and Holmes Jan 6, 1854. I think it very likely also that young Conrad, as a student at Warsaw, met Irene Adler; she was the woman of incredible indefinable fascinations whom he attempted (mostly by negatives) to describe in *The Arrow of Gold*—one of the least memorable but most revealing of his feuilletons.

You will surely not have missed the remarkable essay by Mr. Leavis (of Cambridge) on the fantastic naïveté of Conrad in matters of sentiment. See that stark and sinister book *The Great Tradition*, by F. R. Leavis (Chatto & Windus, 1948) which has not been pub'd in USA. I have long devoted Boxing Day (Dec 26 to you) to a re-examination of my file of old *Strand* Mags. These wonderful documents, as important in our own field of study as the "good" and "bad" quartos of *Hamlet*, relish me in the deep freeze of detached cerebration. I have written you of the profound modesty & chastity of Watson: for instance in the critical case of *The Cardboard Box* (Jan. 1893 *Strand*) even on that (as it first was) blazing hot day neither Watson had discarded his coat, nor Holmes his dressing gown. In the glorious old *Strand* you will find, for instance, Watson's phrase (for the father of the claim-jumped bride of *The Noble Bachelor*) about the Pacific Slope; you will find per Sidney Paget a picture of

Watson in his "brown study" with his hands folded whence they wouldn't have far to "steal" to the shameful wound; and even Sherlock, on the visit to Croydon (for which Watson resumed his weskit) wearing this time a straw hat with the Dark Blue Ribbon of Oxford.

Sitting, the day after Xmas (in a P.Q. snowstorm, in the upper quarters of the Ladies' Lounge at McGill—on a pile of shag tobacco), I love and brood these things and contemn yr scionists for their easy acceptance of imagination. What problems they offer! In the *Strand*, it is Baron Mauper*tins*; it is the Reigate *Squire* (singular); and Watson only turns up his trouser cuffs when in the country (Holmes, I think, never does?). I don't need to remind you (see my footnote on solecisms) that Holmes always says the *best* of the two; distinction *between* the various tobaccos; and splits the most delicious infinitives. He and Watson, God bless them, were storytellers; not grammarians.

I neither will nor shall write you again until I have my diploma and an offer to teach in New Jersey—perhaps at Drew University, founded by that quite incredible old thimblerigger Daniel Drew. Did you ever read the book about him by Bouck White? He was of course the original of the Trained Cormorant.

JANE NIGHTWORK

* * *

There has recently been published in England a delightful book which raises questions that should rally and startle all sincere students—to wit, *My Dear Holmes*, by Gavin Brend (Allen and Unwin, 10s 6d).

Mr. Brend was roused by rereading the tales aloud to his daughter (he doesn't tell her age; about thirteen, I hope). He has lovingly and impudently compiled his own Handbook of 221B Culture. He repudiates our American choice of 111 Baker Street (now only a shell) as the putative original of 221B, and offers 59, 61, and 63, to be assigned severally to Sherlock, Dr. Watson, and Mrs. Hudson. My own solution of the problem of a memorial is to inlay into the pavement, wherever the site is determined, a triple medallion of these three.

I wish there were space to argue with Mr. Brend some of his lively speculations. He does his best to harmonize the Watson gospels, to gloss the horrid discrepancy of Reichenbach and Vermissa; he argues a painful quarrel between Holmes and Watson in 1896. I have my own solution of the date of the Watson–Morstan marriage; and we of the Irregulars insist on 1854, as noted first above, as Sherlock's birth year.

* * *

Ten shrewdly chosen shorts, and one of the early novelettes, are now Volume 528 of the Oxford World's Classics series. And Mr. S. C. Roberts, Vice-Chancellor of Cambridge University and Master of Pembroke College, in a crisp and poker-faced introduction even yields Holmes to the Dark Blue for his college years.

Mr. Roberts acutely says that "in some way not easy to define No. 221B has become a focal point of the civilization of the nineties." By some metempsychosis the Holmes–Watson tales have risen far outside and beyond the mood and purpose for which they were written. They have become the mixed genius and *naïveté* of the author, a mythology equally relishable for old and young. Crossing the Atlantic with me this summer was a boy who had brought with him an Omnibus volume: curled like a hedgehog in his deck-chair he was reading *The Hound of the Baskervilles* for the first time, and how I envied him!

BSJ (NS), 1 No. 4 (October 1951)

It was really unfortunate [writes Jane Nightwork] that just before sailing from Montreal I had reread Stevenson's *The Ebb Tide*. The chapter about the Cargo of Champagne gave me such a yen for fizz that when I got settled aboard ship I ordered a bottle of same. The chief steward then called my attention to a note in the steamship brochure which I hadn't observed: *These vessels are operating on an Austerity Basis.* However, I happened to make friends with one of the junior engineers; he asked me down to his cabin and said he had been saving a bottle of York State champagne; it was wrapped in his winter underwear in the locker below his berth. I think his stateroom must have been just above the boilers; for though we gave the bottle ½ hour glaciation, when he turned off the wire binding the cork exploded right up through the engine-room fiddley and most of the vintage followed it in spume. Except for the usual icebergs in the Straits of Belle Isle that was the only adventure of the voyage. I couldn't help remembering that wonderful passage in our great Canadian poet (Ned Pratt) when the gamblers in the *Titanic* are complaining the wine isn't properly iced, and then comes the berg.

There is an old saying that there is no form of secrecy like writing for a newspaper in Philadelphia, but to be a really fine poet in Canada is almost equal privacy.

I only just missed Mr. Bill Hall in Newcastle (I went there to look up the memorabilia of Cutcliffe Hyne and Captain Kettle) but I learn that he returned to U.S. with a first edition copy of *A Study in Scarlet*. I have always divined that Mr. Hall is a man who spares no cost for anything he really wants. He will have a special footnote in the complete version of my Thesis. I have a really lovely supplement on how Doyle imitated Stevenson, and how Cutcliffe Hyne imitated Doyle. Also how poor Mary Conan Doyle was the first to stand up for the First Mrs. Watson, so grievously shadowy in Mr. Dickson Carr's biography. In fact I have a whole chapter on Intra-Family Angst in the Lives of Late-Victorian Authors. You really should hear me on the Merediths, the Leslie Stephens, and the Literary Associations of the Hammersmith Tube.

I went of course to The Bilboes to see our old darling Chief Inspr. (ret) Stanley Hopkins. He is a little senile, now; he is convinced that your late Harry Hopkins was his nephew; and that Lord Milverton, who resigned from the Labour Party in horror of nationalization of Steel, is the son of C. A. Milverton, the Worst Man in London. He may be right, but he gets tedious about it.

I am now bicycling, on a rented Humber (Forever Humber), through the fens of East Yorkshire. In the saloon bar every evening I read Mr. R. W. Chapman's essay on *Lexicography* (Oxford Univ. Press) and wait impatiently for the next pamphlet from Mr. S. C. Roberts, his opposite number at the Camb. Univ. Press. The McGill Univ. Press is so tart with me I plan to offer my own stuff to Rutgers Univ. Press. They came in 10th or somewhere in the regatta at P'keepsie, they must crave some strenuous laurels?

I would not tip off anyone else, for fear of setting collectors in motion, but one of the first desiderata I shall persecute in Embro, Glesga, Manchester, Birmingham, Newcastle, Bristol, &c (only the simpleminded go to London to bookhunt, which is laid out for tourism) is CASSELL'S Xmas Annual for 1887, *Yule-Tide*.

We all know that *Beeton's Xmas Annual* for that Yule is almost introuvable—though I've always suspected some could be found in Melbourne, Australia, where Ward Lock & Co had a depot. But what specially tickled Watson was that in the Xmas trade of 1887 he was competitor with his great idol and master, R.L.S. It so happened that the feature of Cassell's Xmas annual was that odd little freak *The Misadventures of John Nicholson*. It was written at Skerryvore (Bournemouth) in December 1886, never included in any of the authorized works until the Collected Edns, but I read it in an American paper-bound piracy as a child. It is one of the best examples I know of an author getting himself into so ingenious a situation that he can only emerge by the most appalling naïveté. But by throwing down his cards—not only on the table but all over the floor—and counting on the plum-pudding & brandy mood of the British Yuletide reader—Stevenson exerted his incredible charm and emerged Scot-paid.

367

How thrilling to the student are the potboilers of great artists! How, in those capriccioes and fandangoes, they let themselves unbuckle and do human frolic—as when Stevenson took the reader's time out to remember his favorite writer at a cheap restaurant in San Francisco 7 or 8 years before.

So in my thesis on Literary Osmosis I shall go more and more gaily into the Stevensonian transfusion in Watson. You will have noticed of course that in Stevenson's *Memoir of Fleeming Jenkin* (written about 1886, I reckon; I have no books aboard this packet) he mentions in person "the good Dr. Joseph Bell," who was Jenkin's physician. Whichever way you look, in the middle '80's, you can see the sturdy Watson getting radar from the frail Stevenson a few miles away. They echoed back and forth in *Cornhill* (where stories were unsigned) until simple readers wrote to thank each for the other's pieces. Though of course to fingertip sensitives like you and me our darling JHW had never the lepid lilliputian touches of RLS—in whom Mannerisms Makyth Man. They could get tiresome; I know several later generations conspued his frolic of dancing on the needlepoint of style; but what gorgeous pirouette! How the apes and driven cattle of readership are annoyed by the tender farces of art. (No spoonerism, please.)

JANE NIGHTWORK

BSJ (NS), 2 No. 1 (January 1952)

After such long busywork of dying
It was so peaceful in the stratosphere
I wondered, am I going to be bored?
Then old Peter Pearlygate, replying:
"Gosh sake, I never thought to see *you* here;
You'll have to wait a while to see The Lord."
He scanned his book. "You got the breaks, old boy.
Take it easy. What would you most enjoy,
While your Attendant Angel rests, and combs
His plumage; he looks a little ruffled?"

I said: To learn again how words, well shuffled,
Can sort miraculously into rhyme;
Or better still, read as for the first time
One of the Adventures of Sherlock Holmes.*

* * *

I have just been rereading [writes Jane Nightwork] the letter
from Valentine Williams to the *NY Times*, dated Feb. 12,
1935, I mean V.W.'s letter was dated Feb. 12; shortly after
Greenhough Smith's death. A fine tribute to a great
editor . . .

* * *

I understand, Mr. Morley, that you are doing a preface for
the Limited Editions *Case-Book*. However disappointing
that book may be to the old Baker Street zealots, it throws
some curious lights on Holmes's character; not least in the
stories written by himself. No longer can you blame JHW
for inaccuracy or bad memory. He was tutored to be dim on
detail by Mr. Holmes himself. For inst., in *The Blanched
Soldier* Holmes is deliberately wrong in matters of fact. The
Duke of Greyminster, absurd . . . and you can't go to
Bedfordshire via Euston. It was Midland Ry, from St.
Pancras, as every traveller knows. . . . And the oddities in
The Illustrious Client (cf the different layout of the "news-
sheets" in English and U.S. editions, wh always amused
you) give us lots of good canon-fodder.

---

*Editor's note: For a variant, see the version above, p. 225, in the Poems
section of this volume.—S.R.

That story is most interesting to a woman, as shewing the revival, in the last yrs, of poor Mr Holmes's idealism of the female, and his wistful remark about an imagined daughter of his own. If he cd have begotten one he wd have liked to have a daughter; but the undignified horrors of male and female procreation were too much for his cold precise mind.

You will have read, come this spring, the biography of the late Sir Bernard Spilsbury, the famous Home Office pathologist; who lived with death & autopsy & post mortems for 40 yrs, and finally committed a painless suicide. I sometimes wonder (but wdn't dare suggest it) if S.H. didn't, when he felt his cold precise mind failing, take prussic in his honey?? I think in November 1944??

* * *

Among the varices and strumae of my appendix to the Osmosis Holmes–Watson, there is of course a complete calendar of the Adventures untold. Neither Starrett nor Bell nor yourself have ever been exhaustive. One usually omitted is The Dramatic Introduction of Dr Moore Agar to Mr Sherlock Holmes. It happened on Harley Street, as dear old Inspr Hopkins has told me. Dr Agar's bearskin rug smelt so strongly of camphor, adrenalin, shag tobacco cinders and toasted slippers, with drippings of melted butter from Mrs Hudson's crumpets, that Mrs Moore Agar had it put out on the front steps to air. Holmes, passing by (on the rather odd route he sometimes pursued between Baker Street and the Alpha Inn) fainted on the bearskin.

Incidentally, one of the matters never raised in London last summer was the justification, if any, of the *club fender* shewn before the fireplace in the reconstruction of the sitting room at 221B. That type of fender, in those days (and even now), is rarely found except in large club lounges and fairly luxurious houses. Very unlikely in such modest lodgings as Mrs Hudson's; and if there had been one, it wd have been mentioned.

I have long been troubled by the Sidney Paget drawing shewing Holmes & Prof Moriarty grappling on the brink of the Reichenbach; Moriarty's flung-up hand shews all four fingers the same length, which is supposedly a mark of the gorillas and great apes. I am measuring, under controlled conditions, the fingers of all gorillas and greater primates; I have taken membership in the Zoological Society, and only wait an open mtg to raise the question.

JANE NIGHTWORK

* * *

Jane has also sent me her (obviously a little too jocose) announcement of the S.H. Dressing Gown, which she proposes the BSI Inc. shd design, license, and sell under proper restrictions to a few really highclass outlets.

The pattern must be important: perhaps a pipe emitting smoke-rings or a map of Baker Street or a hansom cab—the colours Purple, Blue & Mouse were universally admired when I wore them in my scarf in England last summer. How to dispose them in the right Baker Street pattern? In tartan squares, with VR in the middle of each rectangle? This must be pondered and perpended. And there could be, possibly, a female version of same, in light susurrant nylon, the Irene Adler? Transpicuous enough to reveal the figure against the light, so loved by J.H.W. This commercial idea, Jane thinks, shd be worked upon to be marketed this spring for the autumn 1952 season. And here is the announcement Miss Nightwork suggests:

PURPLE   BLUE   MOUSE

were the colors of Sherlock Holmes's dressing gowns which he wore, for thinking, smoking, and deducing in the famous sitting-room at 221B Baker Street.

Your reasoning may not be as incisive as Holmes's, but you can be as comfortable. And you won't be divorced, as Dr Watson was by his wife, for wearing the department store type of "robe" with satin lapels and cuffs, a hangman's-rope girdle and gewgaw frogs.

371

The Sherlock Holmes Dressing Gown

designed, on the authorized specifications of the Baker Street Irregulars (international condominium of Sherlock Holmes experts) by Jane Nightwork, doctora angelica in texts and textiles, is made to drape the male-at-ease and the homespun homo. As Nightwork has said, homespun philosophers should Stay at home and spin. This dressing gown, the only Holmes-spun garment in the world, is made, in a unique pattern of the three canonical colors, of *Bakstreg* fabric, and tailored to the intelligent man's domestic taste:

> Warm without weight
> Gay without goof
> Canada or Caribbean
> Packable-proof. . . .

> (copr J. Nightwork Associates, 1952)

A few facts: plain masculine cut; easyfast snapper to close the gapping neck for cold foggy nights on Baker St.; *three* pockets—breast for cigarettes (cigars); two midriff pockets, for pipe, pouch, &c, and for a pocket-size detective story, or reading lens, or clippings of *The Times* (London) agony column, or the latest issue of the B.S.J.

Made in 3 sizes: Very tall; tall; medium. (Never ask a man to describe himself as less than medium.) Turn-back cuffs for handkerchief keeping. British warm, and, in the light wonderful Baker Street blacksheep from bachelor south-down Charles lambswool.

BSJ (NS), 2 No. 2 (April 1952)

MISS JANE NIGHTWORK, who says she has been re-proached for omitting her usual memoranda, writes me in a whiff of temper. The fault, however, was mine; I thought her last essay (as usual, about Osmosis, and the chances of escaping from Canada to find a job in the U.S.) was too personal for this nonobjective divan.

> I was very annoyed [she writes] when you accused me of spinning like a fretful midge (as you said some poet, Confetti or Rossetti, had described: I'm grateful you'll never be appointed a job as literature) in the vacancies surrounding the Baker Street frenzy. I am leaving shortly with Violet Smith to resume bicycling on the moors of Yorkshire. Since both you and Mr. Edgar Smith are too timid to mount saddle with me, please send me the address of your most intelligent contributor, Mr. Rolfe Boswell. There is a man I could coddle like an egg. Address me c/o Arthur Rogers, bookseller, Newcastle-on-Tyne. I have been turfed out of my job as precentor in the literary choir at McGill; until I hear the decision of the university of Egg Harbor, N.J., I shall stay around South Shields, the place it took that grand seaman Captain Ellsberg ten hours to reach on the nationalized British phone.
>
> I shall be back just in time to straw-vote a ballot for either Eisenhower or Stevenson; but which? I wrote to the Burlington Pantagraph asking their advice; but they hadn't made up their mind either?

* * *

When, eventually, the perfect *votiva tabella* is planted on Baker Street, I suggest as its most memorable and tenderly evasive text, two lines from V. Starrett's noble sonnet (which wake me at night, Eire perennius, as Russ Mc-Lauchlin might have said when he followed through at Skibbareen?):

> *Here dwell together still two men of note*
> *Who never lived and so can never die.*

* * *

Holmes and Shakespeare: no one has suggested why *Twelfth Night* (the only play he quoted twice) was his favorite. Twelfth Night, Jan 6, was his birthday.

* * *

And, speaking anniversaries, it's just 60 years since dear old Saintsbury, writing in 1892 about the Victorian novel, said how sad it is that aera had created no memorable characters; and at that very month and moment H and W were fresh emergences in print. Let this, but it won't, be a lesson for all students. How confused Walt Whitman was when he got a letter from Tennyson, and was so buffaloed by the embossed address. My suds, he mumbled, what a name for a poet, Farringford Freshwater.

BSJ (NS), 2 No. 4 (October 1952)

A LETTER FROM JANE NIGHTWORK

My dear Mr Edgar Smith:

You know how often I have tried to coax you and Mr Morley to go bicycling with me in Yorkshire; but last September I had the bonne fortune to do the North Riding (Sherlock's homeland) with Mr Morley and his brother F. V., who is Sherlock to C. M.'s Mycroft, the same age-interval and the same difference of temperament? If I'm late in reporting I must explain, since C. M. returned in November (after 3 months' Bummelreise) I've been trying to catch up with his vacancies of correspondence. Since he was mown down by hay fever (*faisons la haie*, as Uncle Tom Eliot cried) 1½ yrs ago, he has wallowed in half-written sonnets. Also he's been rereading some Walt Whitman, who is no good example for any Long Islander who aspires to brevity?

I met the brothers M. at L'pool; did you know that all Cunard ships have a full set of the Murray edns of the Sacred Writings, by gift of the Doyle Estate? You have to ask, as the Library steward may be reading them himself. The first thing the M's wanted to do, after reviewing the Lake District (thank God it was Sunday; Wordsworth Museum at Grasmere was closed, but we had a sandwich lunch in a high breezy sunshine cemetary above Windermere, now very like Bon Echo, Ontario, where Walt wrote a poem—"By Blue Ontario's Shore"—which he used both as poetry and prose; how few of your Irregulars read Canadian poetry?) and then set northeastward to Adrian's Wall; the Iron Curtain of Roman Britain, 2nd centy A.D. At the wonderful high point of the Wall, near Winshield's Crag (1230 feet up)—near the bathhouses where the Roman G.I.'s of A.D. 100 steamed themselves to keep warm, I was almost blown off the parapet by the snell N. W. gale. It was all-same Canada; I was homesick. (Hadrian visited the Wall about A.D. 111. This is important.)

I was most taken by a National Trust warning, where we climbed the ancient stone fortification: *Take Heed not to disturb even one stone.* You'd be astonished by the wild and windy beauty of those remains; fortunately few casual tour-

ists ever hear of them. Like everything best in literature &
all the arts, the dachshunds don't guess. They park and
biddle elsewhere.

On, then, we groaned; through Newcastle, by the famous
High Level Bridge; but without seeing Arthur Rogers, the
kindly bkseller who has more bargains for visitors than
anyone else in Britain; and to see the Captain Kettle country, Wharfedale, where the seaworn skipper set up his
methody chapel; books I've never read, but C. M. reads
them again & again, since his teens; the nearest anodyne,
he says, to Conan Doyle. The absolute brutality of corn,
the perfect rubbish, the tenderness of ho-hum. But not
even the dictionaries will tell you about C. J. Cutcliffe
Hyne.

I had to interrupt here to type C. M.'s piece about Walt
Whitman and the vascular spasm of Jan 23, 1873, which he
wanted to send off to a paper which I'm sure won't print it.
It is full of the most downroarious cracks about Walt's
androgyne or hermaphrodite qualities: he says (imagine!)
even if Walt was a ponce, he was a Ponce de Leon. It took
him a lot of trouble to explain things to me; raised in the
pure air of the Canadian Wrens I just didn't know that sort
of doings were done. Nor how? But faithful to his métier he
managed to get Sherlock into it. He thinks that if Walt
hadn't died (1892) just when the Holmes stories were
beginning in the *Strand*, he (Walt) could have conquered
his bissextile or binomial anomaly, & avoided his European
vogue. C. M. also advances a story of the Agent, *When the
Earth Screamed*, as a parable of *Leaves of Grass*. He says there
are wider & deeper (& shallower) analogues in the Agent's
ancillary writings than anyone except T. S. Eliot has ever
twigged. His essay on *Was Whitman an Ipsomaniac?* (or how
Bulgaria backed the wrong horse?) I thought wise to send
to the vaults at Cox and Co.

So, I haven't had time to describe in detail how the
Morleys discovered Sherlock's birthplace. It was carefully
co-ordinated by geographical plotting: the sum of its lati-
tudes & longitudes add up to 221½ degrees & minutes. It
pleased these experts that it's near the church (Croft on

Tees, Yorkshire) where Lewis Carroll was a child (his father was rector there). The Holmes homestead is in one of the loopy "holms" (Yorkshire word for water-meadows) of the river Tees, and can be identified by the fact that last September they were putting in a large china bathtub, sliding it up a ladder to the first floor. This was indeed the curious, the crucial incident. Because, like the nocturnal dog, a bathtub was what apparently nor Holmes nor Watson ever had. (Except of course Watson's bains à la Turcque.) I *must* tell you what Mr Morley said: that naturally it was on Cranberry Street (in your native Brooklyn) Walt first talked turkey. That was where he set up the type for *L of G*.

I think C. M. wd prefer if I leave himself to recount further ventures, such as the incredible episode (which he reported to the London *Times*) of the 3rd staircase in the front court of Pembroke College, Cambridge. As a genuinely Resident Patient he is under severe régime, and might not be able to cut capers at Cavanagh's. But he tells me his love is toward you all. He adds specially that he encouraged his friend Norman Kark, the imaginative publisher, to take command (as Mr Kark has done) of the *London Mystery Magazine*. Members are urged to report themselves to Mr Kark, at Grand Bldgs., Trafalgar Square, London W.C. 2, for informations & subscriptions. C. M. himself pursues, in Walt Whitman's phrase, his "calm, steady, undeviating procrastination." If any B.S.I. wish to visit Sherlock's birthplace, address the Croft Spa Hotel (a few miles south of Darlington, the famous shrine of *Communication Number 1*, the first steam locomotive) and proceed from there. Mr M says you'll never regret it.

Yrs respfly and still afftly

JANE NIGHTWORK

*　*　*

Here, for all to distinguish, are the types employed by *The Western Morning News* and the *Leeds Mercury*:

The Western Morning News

PLYMOUTH, EXETER, & TRURO,

- - - - - - - - - - - -

Yorkshire 1
and Leeds Mercury
LEEDS, FRIDAY, OCTOBER 10, 1952

BSJ (NS), 3 No. 2 (April 1953)

378

I have [Miss Jane Nightwork writes] been working on a Scotland Yard *schottische* that might be danced at a ballet evening of the B.S.I. I saw Mr. Morley the other day; he is working on 2 sonnets, one about the *Dissembly Line* in which I rather think he has overdrawn his a/c, the other, less philosophical & more within his powers, about *Daffodils with Grey Hair*. He really has a poetical mind if only he wdn't try to put it into poetry. But it is not my business to tell him so. I tried to suggest my feelings by telling him "you set a claptrap but you didn't catch anything." He was annoyed. He is greatly taken with a line of Keats, "delicious diligent indolence," and is celebrating Shakespeare's birthday by living up to it.

Who was the philosopher who said *Omnia abeunt in mysterium*? Mr. M. thinks that would make such a good slogan for a series of detective reprints. Pity it wasn't in S. H.'s Commonplace Book. *Did* S. H. have a Commonplace Book? I can't remember. Certainly JHW did, in which he had copied all those allusions to Goethe, Hafiz, Vanderbilt and the Yegghead, Carlyle, Richter, and the specific gravity of parsley in deliquescing butter. It would have sunk deeper in fresh butter, Mr. M. always insists, than in salt butter; even parsley has its plimsoll rating.

All these minimissima have to be included; stated if not solved, in my Grand Osmosis, which if ever finished will be a kind of Baconian *Novum Organum*. I have just begun to write an appendix on the Horror of *Studio Audience Applause* shewing that it is the application (by Poor Relations counsel) of totalitarian ideas to the humble shewmanship of radio. In other words, as Mr. M. says, when the usher holds up the card saying *Applause*, it is claptrap. Fortunately, only the late Mr. Santayana saw all the implications of our modern hystereses; and Mr. M., who is learning (he says) to make his peace with reality, repeats that the hysterectomy of the fiendish obsessionist J. Ripper is not suitable for public print.

These are only a moment's monument, as someone said;

all that worries Mr. M. (who is not writing letters) is, what news have you of Mr. V. Starrett? He has such a kinsprit feeling for V. S., he says that Mr. Starrett and himself will only be remembered as poets but all their poems have already been forgotten. Even by themselves—but what fun they had between poems!

When are we going bicycling, forever Humber?

* * *

On the night of 3–4th February, 1942, A. Hitler began his evening palaver with his cronies as follows:

You know the story of the Hound of the Baskervilles . . .

Page 283 of the English edition of Hitler's *Table Talk*— soon to be published over here; where of course unless in imported sheets, the pagination may be different. Hitler goes on to mention a time when motoring thru mtns at night, on the way to Bayreuth, his car was attacked by a huge black dog.

BSJ (NS), 3 No. 3 (July 1953)

MANY YEARS AGO—in September 1920—at a little
stationery store uptown (S. Sachs, 385 Amsterdam
Avenue; long since vanished, I expect) I found for a few
cents a copy of Arthur Machen's *The Three Impostors*, published in 1895 by Jno. Lane, and by Roberts Bros. in
Boston. Far too obviously imitated from RLS's *New Arabian
Nights*, it provides a footnote for our continuing study of
Literary Osmosis—part petit larceny, part seepage, maybe
it shews also the earliest reference in contemporary fiction
to Sherlock Holmes. For see page 98—"a problem in the
manner of the inimitable Holmes; there are the facts . . .
summon your acuteness to the solution of the puzzle."

This proves that even by 1895 S. H. was a recognizable
allusion in current fiction.

* * *

There was evidently something about Cambridge which
gave Stevenson a high vibrato of amusement; perhaps
chiefly in satire of his old friend and mentor Sidney Colvin.
In *The Ebb Tide* (begun maybe about 1890, but not published until 1893), RLS, aided by his stepson Lloyd Osbourne, began the tradition of using Trinity Hall, Cambridge, as a comic college; just as the Oxford boys used to
mention Teddy Hall (St. Edmund Hall, the most modest
and beautiful of all the Oxford monkeries) for snob-shad-
ing. The South Pacific muscular-mystic Attwater, in the
Ebb Tide, a sort of combination of Buffalo Bill and Msgr.
Fulton J. Sheen or Msgr. Ronald Knox, was a Trinity Hall
man. It was in that story, surely, that Dr. Watson got the
idea of Kitty Winter's vitriol-throwing. And then along
came C. J. Cutcliffe Hyne, who always attributed his goofi-
est characters to membership in Trinity Hall; usually in
their "second boat," which must have been well down the
river in the May Week races. If you need bibliographic data,
see (if you can find it, which I doubt) that incredibly
amusing book *Atoms of Empire*, Macmillan, 1904.

The only writer left—as he admitted in his interviews in

South Africa—who enjoys a rousing roar of comedy at the expense of the highbrows (but have they noticed it yet?) is T. S. Eliot. The episode of One-Eyed Riley, which so disturbed John Mason Nathan, was of course absolute chaff to annoy or startle the critics of *The Observer, The Sunday Times, The Spectator, The Tablet, The Statesman and Nation, John o' London, Time & Tide, The Listener, Cornhill, The Fortnightly, The Contemporary Review, Life & Letters,* and *Horizon* (obit.). Then of course there's Mr. Darlington, who cables across to the *N. Y. Times,* embarrassing both Messrs. Brooks Benét and Wm. Rose Atkinson who didn't feel the rhythm of verse. Surely we should know, ever since the 1919 rummage sale, that Mr. Eliot is primely a comedian; do you remember his hippopotamus, or whiskey and Sweeney and soda?

* * *

Jane Nightwork would be interested in my own footnotes on *Influence of Other Authors on Dr. John H. Watson,* to which I have added some small pedestriana on *The Refugees,* by A. Conan Doyle (1893, I think?). This is a book that has never been properly studied by Canadian scholars; Dr. Doyle's description of Canadian flora and fauna are incredibly comic; but however or whenever old carbon-copy Watson got ahold of it he didn't forget, for have a look:

Refugees, Chapter 5: "The young man raved with his hands in the air."

Refugees, Chapter 8: ". . . was simply conscious that he was in the presence of a very handsome woman."

These sabbatic qualiaquanta will remind Irregulars of some Baskerville doings. My only contribution to the lore and learning is that in the autumn of 1901, while writing *The Hound,* Dr. Watson was simultaneously rereading and revising *The Refugees.* How lucky it is that few authors are so carefully spoored as I have done deerstalker on You-Know-Whom!

Of course I roar from laughter at Watson's description of

Lake Champlain as "island-studded." How many islands are needed to stud? In the whole length of Lake Champlain (130 miles) there are only about half a dozen? I love to think of Watson in the peacock-feather cosy-corner at South Norwood grinding out his delicious mischief about the Huguenots and Versailles, after a long day on the tricycle.

. . . There is a wonderful example of seepage in that champion corn of 1919, *Bulldog Drummond*, where the brutish Lakington (of Godalming) is described as "the second most dangerous man in Europe."

* * *

Any treatment of the Procrastinative Process in the Life of Watson would have to include the prime example of his sitting down in his armchair for a pleasant little chat before it even occurred to him to examine the hideous mutilation of Mr. Victor Hatherley—indeed, poor Hatherley had to ask him to do his professional duty. Our beloved Watson was just as slow to diagnose the wounds of others as he was of his own wandering jezail bullet. This was the bullet, of course, that traveled from his shoulder to his heel. It was finally diagnosed as a nervous lesion, and was extracted by Dr. Percy Trevelyan.

BSJ (NS), 4 No. 1 (January 1954)

O SMOSIS IN LITERATURE, that remarkable thesis (J. Nightwork, Litt.D.), has pointed out that the first work of fiction mentioned by Dr. Watson in his very first novel (*The Firm of Girdlestone*) was the *New Arabian Nights*. This encourages me to remark that Mr. Dave Randall, or someone, should make a bibliographic résumé of *Girdlestone*. No copyright date is mentioned for it in the collected editions, e.g., the Crowborough; when was it first published in Britain? Not, presumably, until handsomely pirated in U.S.A. A reasoned catalogue of the misdemeaning reprints of that classic of Ceres will placate me almost as much as to decide whether Holmes and Watson knew a tulip from a crocus? See allusions in *The Speckled Band* and *The Empty House*. But, (as Dr. Nightwork always says) the Irregulars simply don't take to doing their corollary or ancillary reading.

Of course, only J. Nightwork or Marianne Moore have really read Professor Saintsbury, who had such suave comments to make on R. L. S. It's odd to remember that though R. L. S. was only five years younger, G. S. outlived him nearly 40 years.

I had just been hearing about the dinner at which the Baker Street Irregulars celebrated the so-called centennial of the birth of Sherlock Holmes. I remembered that in his famous essay in 1891 or so, on late-Victorian fiction, Saintsbury grieved that it had created no characters who were memorable; and at that very moment Holmes was putting on immortality by pretending to die in *The Strand Magazine*. It struck me that the one reader who would have most enjoyed, and most been amused by, the great Holmes tohubohu of recent years, died just too soon. I mean of course Stevenson himself, obit at Vailima in December 1894.

To most older members of the Holmes cult, the Sherlockian zeal was a happily revived gust from our teens; it was tinctured by a proud snob-superiority over schoolmates who pored over such tripe as Nick Carter together with Recruits Little Cigars behind the woodpile and in the alley (off Cathedral Street, Baltimore). But by the time we went to college we were reading Stevenson and the unspoiled intuition of our age showed us at once that our godlike Conan Doyle owed far more than the customers realized to the *New Arabian Nights* and *The Dynamiter*. Stevenson, having laid himself open in his famous confession of the sedulous ape, was certainly too mannerly to rib Dr. Doyle about his obvious borrowings, but Firehound Fanny (a true bitch of the D'Urbervilles) must have been nearly crazed by the Mormon interlude in *A Study in Scarlet*. She herself, you may not recall, had written the gruesome Mormon pastrami in *The Dynamiter*.

You will find in *The Suicide Club* at least two keynotes, even to exact phrase, of the Holmes saga. Our blessed Doyle certainly had no idea of imitation. It just came to him on that prevailing wind (myself have savoured it) that wafts from Bournemouth to Southsea. It's the homely breeze of fish-and-chips and readers love it. The oldtimers have tried sometimes to damp down the literal-minded frenzy of these new Baker Street zealots. They've even tried to suggest that *The Memoirs of Brigadier Gerard* are more subtly rewarding. But there was one flavor that even the kindly-dogged Doyle couldn't emulsify, Stevenson's exquisite mercurial humor. Of this Dr. Doyle, who was fairly heavy-minded Erse, had small notion. Maybe it was too filigree even for Professor Saintsbury, who didn't seem to pay heed to the *New Arabs* and *The Wrong Box*. Stevenson's curse was always to be adored by people who weren't quite The Thing. Even today, when he's dead sixty years, you have to speak carefully of his gloriously tactile delicacy in verbal comedy. Perhaps it's because our young mass-product think of him always as "English," whereas he was always the Scot. Only the Scot could have made such perfect but kindly merriment of the C. of E. and the C. of

I. (Church of England, and Children of Israel). Only a Scot could have impelled the young tourists of my generation to hang about the departure platform at King's Cross, reading the names pasted on sleeping car windows, in hope to find Vandeleur the Dictator and the Young Man in Holy Orders.

My only conclusions: let no one pretend himself a genuine Baker Street urchin until and unless he can show proof that he has rooted in the seedbed of the whole saga, and has relished word by word the *New Arabian Nights*.

* * *

Jane Nightwork tells me she was very happy to have the new B.S.I. edition of Blakeney's *Sherlock Holmes: Fact or Fiction?* She wonders if Mr. Blakeney is aware (p. 14) or for that matter are many BSI's aware that Richter and Jean Paul are the same person. Jean Paul was pseudonym of J. P. F. Richter; the association with Carlyle was obvious: it was old cranky Tammas who introduced J. P.'s works to English readers.

Jane, by the way, is writing a note on Scotswomen's breakfasts; the classic reference is at the beginning of chapter 6 in *The Wrecker*.

Among Miss Nightwork's osmotics she was thinking, in the '80's the most famous literary address in English was Tennyson's home at Farringford (Freshwater, I of W) and quite possy young ACD then living just across the strait at Southsea (within view of I of W) was thus prompted to name his hero Sherringford—but obviously discarded the idea. This (Miss Nightwork muses) is maybe the only ligament between S.H. and Lord T. As Lord T. obit 1892 it is problematic whether he read any of Watson's tales; but J. N. will meditate on the topic. She so often thinks of Lord T. who was a much greater poet than many of you scrannel-pipes realize; and his envenomed cry Bitter barmaid waning fast, Callest thou that thing a leg? has often discomforted her in morbid moments . . .

The obvious linkage between *Silver Blaze* and Keats Miss

N. has pointed out in a small piece soon to be published (she thinks) in the *Herald Tribune Book Review*.

Miss Nightwork is greatly excited by Mr. Elmer Davis's book *But We Were Born Free* (Bobbs Merrill), and has often wondered if you-all know that Mr. Davis's middle name is *Holmes*. Yes, Elmer Holmes Davis.

* * *

It so happens that the great Southdown Bus Service, quite unawares, has a Mandatory Stop within a few hundred yards of that long-sought sacristy, Mr. Holmes's former cottage. Long ago, of course, I drew with compass-pencil the 5-mile arc from Eastbourne Pierhead which bounds the position of Mr. Holmes's retirement. It reaches the sea precisely at the western limit of the Crowlink reservation of the National Trust. And when the great green Southdown omnibus grinds to the crest of the whaleback hill above Eastdean (service #12, between Eastbourne and Brighton) you can be set down at the beautiful little old church of Friston; with a dewpond hard by. I won't be too periculously artifact; it's quite possible that in the bar of The Tiger (Mr. Holmes's favorite pub, below the hill in Eastdean) one of the Moriarty Gang may be waiting for a clue.

Holmes, writing in his own hand in *The Lion's Mane*, was naturally too wary to give away details. His cottage, which I recognized at once (it was built to his own order 50 years ago last October), is deliciously apropos, and right alongside the border of the great Crowlink reserve, now browsed upon more by cattle than the Southdown sheep with their black stockings. You can see how prudently Mr. Holmes planted a windbreak of pine woods to shelter his bees. If he had known as much of apiary as he pretended, of course a cottage right on the crest of the coastal cliffs and in the full push of notorious souwesters, would have been unlikely for those persistent but easily airborne insects. The description given in *The Lion's Mane* was of course to mislead undesired visitors. I shall be equally discreet. The cottage,

with its small sun-trap upstairs porch (where Mr. Holmes
faithfully took his meridian siesta) and the well-tended and
tightly hedged garden (still tended by two gardeners), has
the broad preserve of unspoiled plateau reaching a mile or
so away to the heptarchy of great chalk cliffs west of Birling
Gap. I actually saw dear old Mrs. Hudson (in a blue house-
dress) tottering out to pick an apple for her elevenses. She
is really past domestic chores, and is supplemented by a
middle-aged niece (also in blue denim).

* * *

My brother Frank—the Third Garrideb—writes me that the
father of Neville St. Clair was a schoolteacher in Chesterfield (which he and I visited a couple of years ago, with a
call at the "Mill on the Floss"), and FVM suggests that St.
Clair père was the scholarly assistant who helped Dr.
Thorneycroft Huxtable with the Horace textuals.

BSJ (NS), 4 No. 3 (July 1954)

A LETTER FROM STANLEY HOPKINS, O.B.E.

My dear Mr. Morley:

It is a long while, I fear, since I last wrote; but I am an old man and now nearly finishing my memoirs. No one would or could tell me the name of an American publisher, but then I saw something you wrote (in the *Times Lit. Supp.*) mentioning the Rutgers University Press. I wrote them at once, but frankly am puzzled: what *are* Rutgers?

I have had a windfall! After the terrible detritus of the blitzes were cleaned up, a lot of papers &c were sold at auction, and I learned from Mr. Holmes never to disregard such oddments. In a parcel of wreckage in Camberwell I found a lot of the Forrester Papers, and among them some letters written by Mary Morstan Watson. I always felt that you and your savants were most unfair to Mrs. Watson; when the Dr spoke (in 1894) of his "sad bereavement" he did not mean what you assumed. It was not Mary who had lost her mind, but the Dr who had lost his. (His later work shows it.) At any rate I have copied out one of Mrs. Watson's letters, of autumn 1891, to her Auntie, as she lovingly called Mrs. Forrester.

It is interesting to remember that "the Paddington District" is only a few hansom droppings from St. John's Wood, and Dr. Watson may well have attended Mrs. Norton in her lying-in. I remember that Mrs. Watson was always a trifle contemptuous about Paddington: she would have liked to be in Bayswater. Actually, I think, their address was Farquhar House, St. Vitus Terrace, Formosa Street, Paddington. Not far from the goods depot at Royal Oak. But do read Mary's letter.

What other publishers have you besides Rutgers?

S. Hopkins

The Bilboes
Yoxley, Kent
May, 1949

389

A LETTER FROM MARY MORSTAN WATSON

Paddington, Sunday
[Autumn, 1891]

Dearest Auntie:

Since the tragedy of poor Mr. Holmes, last spring, I have tried my best to keep James happy and amused. As you know, Kate Whitney has the same problem with Isa. It has been all the more trying for her since James wrote his article about Isa and the opium den; the way he put it in his opening sentence, so many people thought that poor Isa, the addict, was the president of the theological college. Never mention this, but Dr. Elias Whitney and his governing board brought legal trouble upon James for mingling them with an opium traffic, and complainants came upon us like cormorants to a lighthouse.

Even with the help of Dr. Jackson or Dr. Anstruther I don't think I can stand it much longer. Mary Jane, the slavey, is less than no help. She is not only a slitter of boots, but also a slattern and a slut. I may come down to Camberwell some night and take refuge. If I do, Auntie dear, just hide me away.

I always urge James to go out, if possible, for an evening's recreation. I've told you how strangely interested he is in anything from America. What did we see in the papers but an announcement from Mr. Henry Irving's Lyceum Theatre. (You know how romantic the Lyceum is for us.) I copy a little of it:

Mr. Augustin Daly's
COMPANY OF COMEDIANS
(from Daly's Theatre, New York, U.S.A.)

Will Play Their Fifth Engagement in London:

Miss Ada Rehan . . .
Mr. John Drew . . . .

A NIGHT OFF, THE LAST WORD, THE RAILROAD
OF LOVE, (etc., etc.)

"A Night Off," I said. "James, just what you need." He was reluctant, and would only take the second cab after Mary Jane's whistle; but we went, and had supper afterward at The Holborn. It was awful. I don't think American comedians have any sense of humour.

Then one night we went to Egyptian Hall, Mr. Maskelyne's Astounding Allusions and So-Called Spiritual Manifestations. Refined Fun and Profound Mystery. Inimitable, Consequently Unique. I know I was vulgar, but when I saw on the program: "Children, half-price. Babies, Ten Guineas Each" (I enclose the paper to shew you) I said "That's more than *you* get for babies."

Poor James, he had just been delivering a swarthy infant, Godfrey Norton, Jr., and he was in his worst of humours. I don't think you can do much with a husband if he is ground down by his practice. If I come to Camberwell, please shew me a plover's egg; is it really so wonderfully freckled? Forgive me, dearest Auntie, I really have been troubled. . . .

MARY M. WATSON

A LETTER FROM JANE NIGHTWORK

Faculty Club (Ladies' Annexe)
McGill University, Montreal

My dear Mr. Edgar Smith:

I wish you to be first to know (as you may twig by the Faculty Club heading) that I have achieved my D.Litt. and am now ancilla assiduissima of the Faculty of Letters. Hardly, I fear, on an ad valorem basis, but I have received a grant to travel (C.P.R.) to Britain to look up some matters in Edinburgh. It has been generally overlooked that in Auld Reekie, in the same year 1859, De Quincey died and The Agent A.C.D. was born. There was an overlappage of dates, but souls are often held in temporal escrow, and it is evident to me that there was some transmigration between the great Opium Eater and author of *Murder as a Fine Art*, and the subtle amateur of fiddles and riddles and cocaine.

This I mention only in footnote in my thesis, but hope to expand for the published version. I hear that your Mr. Morley is Night Watchman for the Columbia University

Press; ask him can he get it published for me? He is, in correspondence, the most dissolute man I know, but you are always courteous. I so often think of you, in the terms of *King Lear*:

> *Enter* EDGAR
> and pat he comes. (Act I, Scene 2.)

In your variorum edition of *The Priory School*, if there is ever such, you will, I hope, notice Shakespeare's description of the Duke of Holdernesse:

> A duke detected for women
> (*Meas. for Meas.*, III, 2)

and you will obviously footnote the fact that Henry Kingsley, in *Ravenshoe* (1861 or thereabouts) had a character named *Lord Saltire*. (Always punctilia, I refer you to p. 349, Vol. II, of the glorious 3 vols of *Collected Essays of George Saintsbury*; Dutton 1923. This wonderful set of obiter stricta has been for me, ever since I commenced scholar, a tomtiddler ground for swiping.)

We are celebrating here, in the Women's Annexe, May 22, with beeswing, the birthday of The Agent, and I am to read a paper on "Watsonian Echoes in Shakespeare." My epigraph is from *Merry Wives*, II, 2—a challenge from Watson:

> Detect my wife.

I want to take a photo, when I am in Edinburgh, of Picardy Place; I was so shocked that Mr. John Dickson Carr, in his biography of The Agent, didn't mention how famous that street was in the old *Noctes Ambrosianae*. But my thesis, if ever printed, will be liable to innumerable & gorgeous footnotes.

I sign myself, for the first time,

JANE NIGHTWORK, *Litt.D.*

BSJ 1956 Christmas Annual

OF COURSE, I have not had time to run down all my byways of research, but I had a wonderful tip lately from good old Stanley Hopkins: he says that Mr. Henry Baker, who was degoosed on Tottenham Court Road, was in actuality George Gissing, who was living in a basement not far from Goodge Street about that time. That was one reason why Holmes did not prosecute, for fear of painful publicity for poor Gissing. Certainly the description Watson gives of Henry Baker's manner and garb is exact to our knowledge of Gissing.

* * *

Another footnote, often adverted upon, is of Holmes's eccentricities in indexing; but I am not sure it has been noted that his Continental Gazetteer was also misalphabeted: "Eglow–Eglonitz–Egria–." Obviously, Eglonitz should precede Eglow.

* * *

Add Great Sayings: "Nothing is so endearing about Dr. Watson as his being two days late in his Christmas greetings."—Jane Nightwork.

* * *

I have long had a suspicion that not even The Sons of the Copper Beeches in Philadelphia know much about plovers's eggs. In my footnote on that topic I quote from the biography of the late E. V. Lucas—one of London's most insistent gourmets in his time—published by his daughter Audrey Lucas (Methuen, 1939) and called to my attention by that high-spirited Irregular, Mr. James Keddie, Jr. It appears that one of Mr. Lucas's lovable habits, after he became rich and important, was taking his mother on an occasional spree. In spite of her Quaker background and her necessarily frugal history, she vastly enjoyed these frolics with her famous son. Now I quote from Audrey Lucas:

> . . . lunch at Jules' in Jermyn Street, where, in the correct season, the same comedy would be played between E. V. and my grandmother on the subject of plovers' eggs, which

were put in their inviting little basket upon the table and regarded by the guest with a mixture of guilt and innocent gluttony. While she began her set piece about reckless extravagance, to say nothing of injustice to the female plover, E. V. would be placidly shelling the eggs, making a little mixture of salt and red pepper to dip them in . . . and would slip the results in front of his mother who would then eat them with considerable placidity.

It appears, therefore, that the eggs, however freckled, must be boiled, and served in an inviting little basket. The chef at the Racquet and Tennis Club would undoubtedly have heard of them; or maybe the Vendome (where I used to buy me that wonderful vintage marmalade, and scrapple, and Mr. Peter Greig's oyster sauce); but now I am living on tinned soups and gin.

* * *

I think that my deduction (based on one of the illustrations in the great Limited Editions omnibus) that Young Stamford took over Watson's bull pup, when Watson went to Baker-street (as the original MSS always spelled it) is entirely sound. The illustration of Young Stamford showed that his clothing was definitely that of a sporting man.

* * *

I am working on a census of Humming and Ha'ing in the career of Mr. Holmes. When Holmes ceased to Hum and Ha (while reading important entries in the dictionaries, &c) he was past his prime.

* * *

Jane Nightwork tells me that the faculty ladies at McGill University are drinking a toast, at this dubitating Christmas festival, to God, to Country, and to Yule.

I am still somewhat beset by some of your members [she says], who try to push a scientific and literary relationship into something more nervous; or do I mean vascular? Quite innocently discussing with a Canadian professor the bachelor status of Lord St. Simon, and his relations with Miss Flora Millar, he spoiled a most innocent evening by quoting that they "were on a *very* friendly footing," but (he added) friendliest of all when they got off their feet. I had to turn him out of the Ladies Lounge after that, because Canadian moeurs do not permit semantic specifications. And, as I come up for my doctorate next spring, I have to be wary.

* * *

This is with the intention of wishing all my fellow-Irregulars the compliments of the season. In my compiled footnotes I have a subsection on the Procrastinative Process in the Life of Watson; of which a prime example is his sitting down in his armchair for a pleasant little chat before it even occurs to him to examine the hideous mutilation of Mr. Victor Hatherley—indeed, poor Hatherley had to ask him to do his professional duty.

Our beloved Watson was just as slow to diagnose the wounds of others as he was of his own wandering jezail bullet.

BSJ 1957 Christmas Annual

These gleanings, from old letters in my files—two of them written on Blue Carbuncle Day, 1948—have not heretofore, to my recollection, been published in the *Journal*. They are shared with our readers now in a spirit of affection and salutation to the founder of the Baker Street Irregulars.—EDGAR W. SMITH*

November 10, 1942

A CATALOGUE from Bertram Rota (London) rises me to a comment. Perhaps you may need to reconsider our old argument whether the famous March 4th in the *Study in Scarlet* was 1881 or 1882. You remember that in those earliest Baker St days Watson raised the topic of Carlyle. And why? My dear sir, Carlyle died in *February, 1881*. Obviously then that was the occasion for his mention. I haven't handy any reference bk that gives the exact *day* of Carlyle's death; but in a vol of the letters of George Gissing he writes (in London, February 11, '81) that "I have just risen from the memoir of Carlyle in *The Times*." Presumably then Carlyle died a day or so before that—and Holmes and Watson had been living together about six weeks.

My theory, you know, remains that the day of the mtg of Watson and Stamford at the Criterion bar was *January 1, 1881*—a day when Watson wd naturally be making resolutions for a more frugal life (though the lunch with wine at the Holborn restaurant must have been costly). Also the fact of its being a Holiday wd account for Holmes being *the only student working in the laboratory*.

Watson went back to the hotel—could it have been the Craven Hotel, in Craven Street, Strand ???—got rid of the bull pup (hence never mentioned again?) & the next day, Sunday January 2, they went to look at the lodgings.

Yr theory could be checked maybe by reference to weather bureau files. Was Friday March 4, 1881—or Satur-

*Editor's note: In fact, the first letter appears in edited form in the first "Clinical Notes" in *Profile by Gaslight*; the second, in BSJ (OS), 1 No. 4 (October 1946); the third, in BSJ (OS), 4 No. 1 (January 1949).—S.R.

day March 4, 1882—a foggy day after a rainy night? (Presumably they both were.)

Yrs, dear sir,

CM

April 12, 1946

I borrowed paged dummy of BSJ #2 from Ben Abramson, to enjoy myself over the week-end; and let me say I think it is a grand job.

Clarke's delightful note on the Nomenclature of Watson's Ships: I wondered if he remembers the *Nora Creina* of Stevenson's *The Wrecker*—a hell of a fine novel to read or reread any time; and oddly pathetic now when so much has happened in the Pacific. I was rereading *The Wrecker* about 1938 and put in my copy an Airways tourist folder of that time that is queer reading now:

> Two perfect islands for complete rest, relaxation and sport . . . WAKE and MIDWAY, isolated from the confusion and conflict of all the rest of the world . . . touched only by the Flying Clipper ships.

Midway Island, and the *Nora Creina*, play an important part in *The Wrecker*. If you've never read it, yourself would find the chapters of student life in Paris particularly entertaining . . .

Richard Clarke notes that *Matilda Briggs* was of Shanghai registry. I fear she came to her end in the East, for my grand old Findlay's Sailing Directory for Indian Archipelago and China & Japan Seas (1878 edition, the one used by Conrad) lists on p. 679 as a hazard of Batavia Bay the *Matilda Rock*. It "carries a beacon on its NE side in 3 fathoms depth, but at low water there is not more than 2 fathoms upon its shoalest spot." According to the custom of marine geographers, a reef or shoal is named for the vessel that first ran upon it, or surveyed it. Was *Matilda Briggs* on her way to look for the giant rats? Batavia would be a port of call.

There is in the China Sea, near Palawan, the *Alicia Annie*

Shoal, but I think the theory of Miss Alice Cutter is too delightful to allow any alternative.

I can't help noticing that the Doyle boys write from Minstead (near Lyndhurst). Do you remember the Socman of Minstead, the villain and ruffian of *The White Company*, the wicked uncle?

Always,

CM

Blue Carbuncle Day, 1948

The compliments of the Season, and how are you, old boy? I can't do better than copy out for you—what I read with great delight on Xmas Day—from T. S. Eliot's lecture *From Poe to Valéry* (privately printed as a Xmas present, 1948, by Harcourt Brace & Co):

> Conan Doyle owes much to Poe, and not merely to Monsieur Dupin of *The Murders in the Rue Morgue*. Sherlock Holmes was deceiving Watson when he told him that he had bought his Stradivarius violin for a few shillings at a second-hand shop in the Tottenham Court Road. He found that violin in the ruins of the house of Usher. There is a close similarity between the musical exercises of Holmes and those of Roderick Usher; those wild and irregular improvisations which, while on one occasion they sent Watson off to sleep, must have been excruciating to any ear trained to music.

How is that for a filler for BSJ? Of course Tom Eliot has long been a disciple of Holmes; which is one of the tests of a genuine High Brow; to distinguish the immortal elements in work apparently only popular. It makes me think of Professor Saintsbury's Law (what he calls the First Law of Criticism): "B is not bad because it is not A; no matter how good A may be." I had thought of asking Eliot to come to our dinner, but the poor fellow is probably run ragged with invitations; also I can't afford another guest!

I have been reading, and quietly drinking and musing; I am grooming myself to write a poem. My annual Xmas

398

Carol was so grim that I let it go up the chimney; all I recall is:

> Ladies, under the Wise Men's Star,
> Rush to and fro like Eleanor R
> And so, in spite of Wise Men's warning
> Jesus nearly dies a-borning.
>
> A little more of mood seraphic!
> A little less Long Gyeland traffic!
> A little less luxurious fare!
> A little less Hark Herald Square!

What wonderful stuff is solid cold bread-&-spice-&-chestnut turkey stuffing for initiating Dreams; and Dreams are always the first onset of a poem? Take care of yourself!

CM

Blue Carbuncle Day

I have invented, in the realm of graphic art, a Sherlock Holmes cherub: the classic head flitting on wings. Did a stage-set for toy theatre to amuse my grown-up gals for Xmas; I'll have to describe it for you some time . . .

I've just read your "Veiled Author." It should not be forgotten, in re Harwich, that it was there that the U-boat fleet surrendered November 20, 1918, as noted by my excellent Bro Frank in his book *Travels in East Anglia* (London, 1923) which shd be in yr reference library; but almost unfindable now . . . Altamont's landlady "down Fratton way": Fratton is next door to "the shingle of Southsea"; another suburb of Portsmouth . . . The allusion to Fords: possibly a prophecy of jeeps??

And so,

CM

November 11, '52

I attended in London a spl mtg of the Council of the SH Society, a cocktail brew they were kind enough to foster for me (at 1a, Baker St) and had from several of them sympathetic approval of my thesis that Bro Frank and I had discovered the Birthplace. It is (still marked on the map as The Holmes Hall) about 2½ miles east of the village of Croft on Tees, in the N.R. of Yorkshire. Lat. 54.29 N., Long. 1.30 W; total of co-ordinates, 221 and 30′, viz 221B. I shall not give complete reasons for thesis (soutenance de thèse) until approved by consultation with FVM whom I shall soon see.

Miss Winifred Paget, Sidney's daughter, entirely agreed that Holmes often used phrases entirely Yorkshire.

Don't count on me for the mtg., if the weather is slidder I no can do. But do ask Adlai Stevenson: I'd go anywhere for him; I found an 18th-centy print that is his spittn image. He is nearest to Sherlock of anyone we've known in boblick life.

I tried to buy a deerstalker at Burberry's (Haymarket) but it was all too small for my skull.

CM

Jan. 12, '54

I'm always very touched when youngsters write in to find out about the BSI. I rather wish we had time & strength to promote & push a Jr auxiliary. Let them subscribe to the Jnl at a cheaper rate. This cd be developed into something really big by a little tactical push . . .

I shall wait eagerly to hear what the dinner was like. I had planned to meet Bill Hall in town tomorrow, but now no can do. How sorry I was to learn of good old Ivar Gunn's death. He and I were in college together at Oxford, way back in '10–'13.

I haven't forgotten I owe for 2 subsrns to the BSJ, but that must wait until I have enough geist to write the check.

I wrote *SH & DR W* (a Textbk of Friendship) for the high school audience, but Harcourt never attempted to reach them.

Yrs

CM

BSJ 1960 Christmas Annual

FICTIONS

This section of Kit's Sherlockian fictions includes his never-before-reprinted dramatization of *A Scandal in Bohemia*. Written to celebrate New Year's Eve 1940, with all parts taken by family and friends, it is an amusing adaptation of one of the most famous of Holmes's adventures, but it is not that close to the canonical original.

"The Adventure of the F.W.L." is a little bit of wartime propaganda that occupies the back of the dust jacket for *Sherlock Holmes and Dr. Watson*.

"Codeine (7 Per Cent)" is only one of a number of tales about Dove Dulcet, poet, literary agent, and literary detective. He first appeared in Kit's writings in the 'twenties in some stories included in *Tales from a Rolltop Desk*. Over the years his name was appended to some occasional poetry. In the 'forties, Kit resurrected Dulcet as detective and/or narrator in a series of short stories. There is a Sherlockian touch in another Dulcet story, "The Adventure of Foggy Bottom," in which Jane Nightwork and Irene Hargreave (grand-niece of the great detective) have walk-on roles, but it does not merit inclusion here.

Kit wrote many short stories and plays in his career, and these three give the reader a glimpse of his later style.

A SCANDAL IN BOHEMIA
(Adapted from the Sacred Writings as a New Year's Eve Pastime)

The Characters

MRS. HUDSON
DR. WATSON
SHERLOCK HOLMES
W. G. S. VON ORMSTEIN, KING OF BOHEMIA
IRENE ADLER

with the assistance of sound effects, walk-ons and Noises Off by competent members of the company

N.B. A few minor liberties have been
taken with the canonical writings

SCENE I: *Baker Street—March 20, 1888*

MRS. HUDSON: 'ow nice to see you again, Doctor. All well at 'ome, we trusts? These narsty March winds are so prelavent for the la grippe.

WATSON: Ah, Mrs. Hudson, I don't know what we doctors would do without the London climate to help us.

MRS. HUDSON: I just took up the spirit case and the gasogene, so you can 'ave a little something to warm you up. Mr. 'Olmes will be *that* tickled to see you. 'e misses you dreadful, Doctor Watson. Sometimes 'e even 'as to call *me* in to get what 'e calls a hunblemished reaction. When 'e told me about that 'orrible affair of the Aluminium Crutch, I was that flustered I didn't 'ave a leg to stand on.

WATSON: Well, Mrs. Hudson, perhaps that was what the

crutch was for. I needn't ask if he's in, I can hear—but that's not the fiddle?

MRS. HUDSON: No, sir, 'e's trying it out with the 'armonica latterly, it don't seem quite so pungent for the neighbors.

WATSON: I suppose anything is better than the cocaine. Hot upon the scent of some new problem, I expect.

MRS. HUDSON: (*Knocking*) Begging your pardon, Mr. 'Olmes,—(*Other half of curtain drawn. Holmes in chair in firelight.*)

HOLMES: Watson! My manner is seldom effusive, but I'm glad to see you. Pull up your old chair. Cigars. Spirit case. Gasogene. Or tobacco? (*Hands slipper.*)

WATSON: Thank you. This is like old times. I should be embarrassed if you were emotional. All emotions are abhorrent to your cold precise mind.

HOLMES: Wedlock suits you. You have put on 7½ pounds since I saw you.

WATSON: Seven.

HOLMES: I should have thought a trifle more. And in practice again, I observe.

WATSON: How do you know?

HOLMES: I deduce it. How do I know that you have been getting yourself very wet, and that you have a most clumsy and careless servant?

WATSON: My dear Holmes, this is too much. You would have been burned if you lived a few centuries ago. It's true that I had a country walk on Thursday and came home in a mess; but I've changed my clothes so I don't see how you deduce it. As for Mary Jane, she's incorrigible and my wife has given her notice; but how did you guess?

HOLMES: (*Chuckles, rubs long nervous hands together*) Simplicity itself. On the inside of your left shoe, just where this comfortable firelight strikes it, the leather is scored by six parallel cuts. Obviously caused by careless scraping to remove mud. Hence my double deduction that you

404

had been out in vile weather, and had a malignant boot-slitting specimen of the London slavey.

WATSON: It was really quite obvious, I suppose.

HOLMES: As to your practice, if a gentleman walks into my rooms smelling of iodoform, and a bulge on his top hat to show where he has secreted his stethoscope, I must be dull indeed not to know him a member of the medical profession.

WATSON: (*Helps himself to a drink*) Well, I can cure the aroma of iodoform.

HOLMES: Cure us both. (*Holmes plays harmonica to cover Watson's work on the drinks.*)

WATSON: You know, Holmes, when I hear you give your reasons, it appears so ridiculously simple I could do it myself; but I'm always baffled until you explain. Yet I believe my eyes are as good as yours.

HOLMES: Quite so. You see, but you do not observe. Since you are interested in these little problems, what do you think of this. It came by the last post. Read it aloud. (*Hands over letter.*)

WATSON: (*Reads aloud*)

> There will call upon you tonight, at a quarter to eight o'clock, a gentleman who desires to consult you upon a matter of the very deepest moment. You have shown that you are one who may safely be trusted with matters which are of an importance which can hardly be exaggerated. This account of you we have from all quarters received. Be in your chamber then at that hour, and do not take it amiss if your visitor wear a mask.

This is indeed a mystery. What do you imagine it means?

HOLMES: It is a capital mistake to theorize before one has data. But the note itself. What do you deduce from it?

WATSON: The man who wrote it was presumably well-to-do. Such paper could not be bought under half a crown a packet. It is peculiarly strong and stiff.

405

HOLMES: Peculiar, that is the very word. It is not an English paper at all. Hold it up to the light.

WATSON: E, G, and then P, and then G, T.—It's woven into the texture of the paper. Why, Holmes, it's a watermark. We should be able to make something of that.

HOLMES: GT, of course, stands for Gesellschaft, German for Company. P probably for Papier.

WATSON: Paper Company!

HOLMES: You're a bloodhound. Now for the EG. Let's glance at the Lippincott Gazetteer. Eglow, Eglonitz, here we are, Egria. In Bohemia, not far from Carlsbad. "Remarkable as being the scene of the death of Wallenstein, and numerous glass factories and paper mills." Ha, ha, my boy, what do you think of that?

WATSON: The paper was made in Bohemia!

HOLMES: Precisely. And the man who wrote the note is a German. Note the construction of the sentence, "This account of you we have from all quarters received." It is only the German who is so uncourteous to his verbs. It remains therefore to discover what is wanted by this German who writes upon Bohemian paper and prefers wearing a mask to showing his face. (*Horses' hoofs*) And here he comes, if I'm not mistaken. (*Holmes whistles*) A pair, by the sound. A nice little brougham and a pair of beauties. 150 guineas apiece. There's money in this, Watson, if there's nothing else.

WATSON: I think I'd better go.

HOLMES: Not a bit, Doctor. Stay where you are. I am lost without my Boswell. (*Heavy steps heard.*)

WATSON: He's coming.

HOLMES: Sit down in that armchair and give us your best attention. (*Heavy knock.*) Come in! (*Enter King of Bohemia.*)

KING: You had my note? I told you I would call.

HOLMES: Pray take a seat. This is my friend and colleague Dr. Watson. Whom have I the honor to address?

KING: You may address me as the Count von Kramm, a Boehmisch nobleman. I understand your friend iss man of honor und discretion? If nod, I prefer to communicate mit your singular self. (*Watson starts to rise. Holmes pushes him back.*)

HOLMES: It is both or none. What you say to this gentleman does not travel very far.

KING: Zo. Den I am binding you both to absolute secrecy for two yearss, at de end of soch time de matter vill be of no importance. At present it is so veighty it might haf influences upon European history.

HOLMES: I promise.

WATSON: And I.

KING: You are excusing dis mask. De august personage who employ me vish his agent to be unknown. De name I just apply to myself is not accurate.

HOLMES: I can think of others. (*Lounges languidly.*)

KING: De circumstance is in great delicacy, und every precautiousness ve take to qvench what might be an immense scandal, compromise one of de reigning families of Europe.

HOLMES: I wouldn't be surprised, my dear Count, some of the reigning families will be compromised by experts.

KING: Enough of soch byplay. Mr. Holmes, de matter implicates de House of Ormstein, hereditary Kings of Bohemia.

HOLMES: If your Majesty would condescend to state your case, I should be better able to advise.

KING: (*Leaps up in agitation; throws off mask*) You are right. I am burning my britches. Vy should I attempt to gonceal it? I am de King.

HOLMES: Quite so. Your Majesty had scarcely spoken before I was aware I was addressing Wilhelm Gottsreich Sigismond von Ormstein, hereditary King of Bohemia.

KING: And Grand Duke of Cassel-Felstein. Don't forget de Grand Duchy, it's de only property dat meets its taxes.— However, you can understand I am not accustomed to do such business in my own person. But de matter is so ticklish how do I confide in an agent mitout putting myself in his power? All de vay from Prague to consult you I haf come.

HOLMES: Then pray consult.

KING: Since five years I am the acquaintance of de well-known adventuress, Irene Adler. Perhaps acquaintance is too feeble a term, Mr. Holmes. I tink you call it boon companions. You understand, gentlemen, she is companion, I am de boon. Maybe she is familiar?

HOLMES: Look her up in my index, Doctor.

WATSON: Yes, here she is. Between a Hebrew rabbi and a staff commander who writes on deep sea fishes.

KING: I don't qvite understand. I don't mind de rabbi, but vot relations did she haf mit dis fish commander?

WATSON: It's quite all right, your Majesty. A merely alpha-betical propinquity.

HOLMES: Born in New Jersey in 1858. Contralto, hum. La Scala, hum. Imperial opera of Warsaw, yes. Retired from operatic stage, ha! Living in London, quite so! Hmmm. I see. So your Majesty became entangled with this young person, wrote her some compromising letters, and is now desirous of getting those letters back.

KING: I don'd know how you guess, but dat is exact. Letters of dreadful varmth, Mr. Holmes. Really lovely letters if day vere only anonymous.

HOLMES: You see, Watson, the pride of authorship.—Was there a secret marriage?

KING: None.

HOLMES: No legal papers or certificates?

KING: Gott! No, noddings.

HOLMES: Then if this young person should produce her

letters for blackmailing or other purposes, how is she to prove their authenticity?

KING: Dere is de writing. It is very strong und recognizable.

HOLMES: Pooh, pooh! Forgery.

KING: Mein private notepaper.

HOLMES: Stolen.

KING: My own seal.

HOLMES: Imitated.

KING: My photograph.

HOLMES: Bought.

KING: Ve vere both in de photograph.

HOLMES: Oh, dear, that's very bad. Your Majesty has indeed committed an indiscretion.

KING: Ach. Unmoegliche Narrheit! I vas insane. I vas den only de Kronprinz. I vas young.

HOLMES: The Ormsteins mature very gradually.—Well, your Majesty, obviously the photograph must be recovered. It must be bought.

KING: She vill not sell.

HOLMES: Stolen, then.

KING: Five attempts ve haf made. Two burglars at my expense account made a ransack in her house. Once ve plunder her luggage ven she is travelling. Tvice ve do feetpad in de Park. Dere iss no result.

HOLMES: Quite a pretty little problem.

KING: Very serious on me. She ruin me mit dis snoopshot.

HOLMES: You are about to be married?

KING: Yes, to Clothilde von Saxe-Meiningen, she spring off second from de old King of Scandinavia. You know how strict is dat family. She iss herself de very soul of delicacy. Any doubts on my conduct vould ruin de whole protocol. De rapture iss rupture.

HOLMES: And I suppose Miss Adler—

KING: Surely. She threaten to send de old King de photograph. If she say so, she vill do it. She has a soul of steel.

Rather dan I shall marry anodder voman, dere are no lengths she vill not go.

HOLMES: You are sure she has not sent the letter yet?

KING: She said she would send it the day the betrothal was made public. That will be next Monday.

HOLMES: (*Yawning*) Oh, then we have three days. That is fortunate, as I have one or two matters of some importance on hand. Your Majesty is staying in London?

KING: You will find me at the Langham, under the name of Graf von Kramm.

HOLMES: And as to money?

KING: Oh, you have carte blanche.

HOLMES: I prefer to have it endorsed.

KING: I am glad to see you so alert. (*Takes out bag of money.*) Here are 300 pounds gold and 700 in notes.

HOLMES: That will do for expenses. (*Gives receipt.*) And Mademoiselle's address?

KING: Briony Lodge, Serpentine Avenue, St. John's Wood.

HOLMES: One more information please. Was the photograph cabinet size?

KING: Shrecklich! It was; and a good likeness.

HOLMES: Hum. Very painful. Well, good night, your Majesty. I trust we shall soon have some good news for you.

KING: Ich lebe in der Hoffnung. Guten Abend, meine Herren. (*Exit.*)

WATSON: I must go too, Holmes. Mrs. Forrester is with my wife this evening, but she will want to get back to Camberwell.

HOLMES: If you will be good enough to call tomorrow afternoon at three, I should like to chat this little matter over with you.

SCENE II: *Baker Street*

MRS. HUDSON: 'e's not back yet, doctor, but 'e said 'e'd expect you if you 'ave no urgent deathbeds.

WATSON: There's a rather nasty case of bronchial pneumonia, but I dare say he'll pull through.

MRS. HUDSON: Mr. 'Olmes went out at eight o'clock this morning. Give me quite a turn 'e did, 'e was dressed as an 'orseman.

WATSON: A Norseman, Mrs. Hudson? You mean a Viking?

MRS. HUDSON: Oh, no, Doctor. I mean one of those chaps what gives 'orses a comb and brush-up. You know, a groom.

WATSON: Disguised, eh? The stage lost a fine actor when Holmes became a specialist in crime.

MRS. HUDSON: You may say so.

WATSON: I can see this case must be more important than I thought. I think I'll just write a postcard to my patient to say I won't be there till tomorrow.

MRS. HUDSON: I think I 'ear 'im now. I better go get the gasogene and the spirit case. (*Exit. Watson writes postcard. Enter Holmes, sketchily made up as groom.*)

WATSON: My dear Holmes! I should never have known you.

HOLMES: (*Sits, stretches legs, laughs*) Well, really! Ha, ha, ha.

WATSON: What is it?

HOLMES: I'm sure you could never guess how I employed my morning.

WATSON: Something to do with horses.

HOLMES: Good man, Watson. Yes, I left the house in the character of a groom out of work. I soon found Briony Lodge. Large sitting room with long windows and those preposterous English fasteners which a child could open. Down the street was a mews. I lent the ostlers a hand rubbing down their horses, and in exchange I received tuppence, a glass of half and half, two fills of shag, and as much information as I could desire about Miss Irene Adler.

WATSON: What about her?

HOLMES: She has turned all the men's heads. The daintiest thing under a bonnet that ever lived. So says Serpentine Mews to a man. She sings at concerts, drives out at five

411

every day, and returns at seven for dinner. Has only one male visitor, but a good deal of him. Mr. Godfrey Norton of the Inner Temple; dark, handsome and dashing. In fact he dashes twice a day.

WATSON: When a lawyer calls twice a day it means trouble for somebody.

HOLMES: Quite so. But is she his client, his friend, or his—

WATSON: Sssh! here's Mrs. Hudson—(*Enter Mrs. Hudson with gasogene and spirit case.*)

HOLMES: Thank you, Mrs. Hudson. This will be all I want. I'm too busy to think of food this evening.

MRS. HUDSON: Nothing to do with firearms I 'ope, Mr. 'Olmes.

HOLMES: I think not. But will you put out my costume for the Non-conformist clergyman. You know, black hat, baggy trousers, white tie. Like Mr. John Hare at the St. James's Theatre.

MRS. HUDSON: Oh, Mr. 'Olmes, I don't think you should tyke liberties with chapel.

HOLMES: And post Dr. Watson's card for him. I can see there's one gone from the rack.

WATSON: Dear me. I had quite forgotten. (*Gives card to Mrs. Hudson, who exits.*)

HOLMES: Well, to continue. This Godfrey Norton, was he Miss Adler's friend, solicitor, or paramour? If he was her attorney, she had probably transferred the photograph to his keeping. I was pondering this when a hansom drove up to Briony Lodge. A gentleman sprang out, handsome, dark, aquiline, moustached. Evidently Mr. Norton himself.

WATSON: What astonishing luck.

HOLMES: Remember your Hafiz, my dear Watson. "Luck is infatuated with the efficient." Mr. Norton was in a great hurry, shouted to the cabby to wait, and rushed into the house. He was there half an hour. I could catch glimpses of him through the windows, pacing up and down, waving his arms.

WATSON: He must feel himself very much *chez soi* to behave like that?

HOLMES: Presently he rushed out again, looking more flurried than before. He pulled out a gold watch and looked at it. "Drive like the devil," he shouted, "first to Gross & Hankey's in Regent Street, then to St. Monica's Church. Half a guinea if you do it in 20 minutes."

WATSON: Gross & Hankey's? Holmes, it's a jeweler's. Perhaps there was something wrong with his gold watch?

HOLMES: I was wondering whether to follow when up the lane came a neat little landau, the coachman with his tie under his ear and the harness tags all sticking out of the buckles. Our heroine shot out of the hall door and into the carriage. A lovely woman, Watson, with a face that a man might die for.

WATSON: Really, Holmes; this from you?

HOLMES: And what do you think she cried to the coachman? "The Church of St. Monica; and half a sovereign if you reach it in 20 minutes."

WATSON: Norton offered sixpence more.

HOLMES: I noticed that, of course; feminine thrift. A cab came through the street and I jumped in. It was 25 minutes to 12, so I knew what was in the wind. When I got to the church there were the two and a surpliced clergyman expostulating. I lounged up the side aisle. Suddenly Godfrey Norton came running towards me. "Thank God," he cried, "you'll do. Hurry! Only 3 minutes or it won't be legal." In short I found myself mumbling responses and vouching for things and generally assisting in the secure tying up of Irene Adler, technical spinster, to Godfrey Norton, bachelor.

WATSON: This is a very unexpected turn of affairs!

HOLMES: Quite so. I found my plans seriously menaced. At the church door they separated, he driving back to the

Temple and she to her own house. So I went off to make my own arrangements.

WATSON: What are they?

HOLMES: Spirit case and gasogene, Watson. And I shall want your co-operation.

WATSON: I shall be delighted.

HOLMES: You don't mind breaking the law?

WATSON: Not in the least.

HOLMES: Nor running a chance of arrest?

WATSON: Not in a good cause.

HOLMES: In two hours we must be on the scene of action. Miss Irene, or Madame rather, returns from her drive at seven. We must be at Briony Lodge to meet her.

WATSON: And what then?

HOLMES: You must leave that to me. I have arranged what is to occur. There will probably be some small unpleasantness. Do not join in it. It will end in my being conveyed into the house. Four or five minutes afterwards the sitting room window will open. You are to station yourself close to that window.

WATSON: Yes?

HOLMES: When I wave my hand you will throw into the room what I give you to throw, and at the same time raise the cry of *Fire!* You follow me?

WATSON: Entirely.

HOLMES: It is nothing very formidable. (*Takes out cigar-shaped object.*) An ordinary plumber's smoke-rocket. When you raise your cry of fire, it will be taken up by a number of people. Walk, not run, to the end of the street and I will rejoin you.

WATSON: You may rely on me.

SCENE III: *Briony Lodge*
(*Sound of horses' hoofs. Then sound of brawl offstage.*)
VOICE: 'ere, stand aht o' the lydy's wye.
VOICE: 'oo's shoving in 'ere?

VOICE: Open the kerridge door, lydy.

VOICE: *I* opened, it, lydy.

VOICE: Gang o' roughs, that's what you are.

VOICE: A copper for a poor old bloke, lydy.

HOLMES'S VOICE: Let me help you, madam. Stand aside, please—

VOICE: Blymey, it's a parson!

VOICE: Give 'im one on the napper!

VOICE: Nah you've done it. (*Sounds of struggle. Enter Irene Adler, very swanky.*)

IRENE: (*Looking back, agitated*) Is the poor gentleman much hurt?

VOICE: 'e got a conky one, pore ole christer.

VOICE: 'e's dead.

VOICE: There's life in 'im.

VOICE: 'e'll be gorn afore you git 'im to the orspital.

VOICE: 'e's a bryve ole chap. Theyda 'ad the lydy's purse.

VOICE: 'e carnt lie in the street. Can we bring 'im in, miss?

IRENE: Bring him into the sitting room. Put him on the sofa. This way, please. (*Holmes carried in by three or four supers.*) Oh, my poor fellow, what dreadful injuries. (*She wipes off blood.*)

HOLMES: (*Feebly*) I'm all right. Just a little air. Air!

IRENE: At once, you poor soul. (*Opens window. Holmes waves his hand. Smoke rocket thrown into room. Everyone cries* Fire! *Irene, in panic, rushes to hiding place and gets photo, clutches it to her breast. Holmes watching her movements.*)

SCENE IV: *Baker Street*

(*Holmes and Watson at breakfast.*)

HOLMES: You did very nicely, Doctor. Nothing could have been better.

WATSON: You have the photograph?

HOLMES: I know where it is.

WATSON: How did you find out?

HOLMES: She showed me, as I told you she would.

WATSON: I am still in the dark.

HOLMES: A pity, Watson, a pity. However, I wired the King last night and he will be here any moment. Then we shall go to Briony Lodge and retrieve the picture.

WATSON: Suppose she has it secreted on her own person?

HOLMES: You forget, it is cabinet size. Mrs. Hudson could do so, but Madam Irene is not ample enough. (*King of Bohemia rushes in.*)

KING: You have really got it?

HOLMES: Not yet.

KING: But you haf hopes?

HOLMES: I have hopes.

KING: Prachtvoll! I am impatience himself.

HOLMES: I had better tell you at once, your Majesty, Irene Adler is married.

KING: Married! Ven?

HOLMES: Yesterday.

KING: Teufelsdroeck! But mit whom?

HOLMES: An English lawyer named Norton.

KING: She could not love him.

HOLMES: I am in hopes she does.

KING: Lèse majesté. How so?

HOLMES: It would spare your Majesty all fear of future embarrassment.

KING: Wahrscheinlich! It is true. Yet—I vish she had been in my own station. Vot a Queen she would have made. (*Enter Mrs. Hudson with letter.*)

MRS. HUDSON: By messenger, Mr. 'Olmes.

HOLMES: Thank you. (*Mrs. H. exits.*) From the lady herself. What can this be? And a photograph with it!

KING: It is herself. I should know. I gave her that dress. Gott! (*Holmes reads the letter.*)

HOLMES: (*Reading*)

My dear Mr. Sherlock Holmes:

You really did it very well. Until after the alarm of fire, I had not a suspicion. Then, when I found how I had

416

betrayed myself, I began to think. I had been warned against you months ago. You know I have been trained as an actress. Male costume is nothing to me. I often take advantage of the freedom it gives. I got into my walking clothes, as I call them, and came down just as you departed.

I followed you to your door, and so made sure that I was really an object of interest to the celebrated Mr. Sherlock Holmes. Did you notice that slender young man who bade you goodnight just as you were getting out your latchkey? That was I.

My husband and I both thought the best resource was flight when pursued by so formidable an antagonist. We are taking the 5:15 a.m. from Charing Cross for the Continent. As to the photograph, your client may rest in peace. I love and am loved by a better man than he. I keep it only to safeguard myself, and leave instead a picture he might care to possess. And I remain, dear Mr. Sherlock Holmes, very truly yours,

IRENE NORTON; née ADLER

KING: Potztausend Blaufeuer! Etwas weibliches! Vot a woman. Did I not tell you how qvick und resolute she was? Vould she not make an admirable qveen? Vot a pity she was not on my level.

HOLMES: She seems indeed to be on a different level. I am sorry I have not been able to bring your Majesty's business to a more successful conclusion.

KING: On the contrary, vot could be more successful? Her vord is always inviolate. De photo is as safe as if it vere in de fire.

HOLMES: I am glad to hear your Majesty say so.

KING: Tell me how I can reward you. Dis ring, it iss a snake emerald. (*Offers ring.*)

HOLMES: Your Majesty has something I should value even more highly.

KING: You have but to name it.

HOLMES: This photograph!

KING: (*Amazed*) Irene's photograph? Vy certainly, if you vish it.

HOLMES: I thank your Majesty. Then there is no more to be done in the matter. I have the honor to wish you a very good morning. (*Turns away without shaking the King's hand. Comes down to footlights, gazing at picture.*)

HOLMES: *The* Woman!

(*Curtain*)

Ellery Queen's Mystery Magazine, 5 No. 14 (January 1944)

THE ADVENTURE OF
THE F.W.L.
Being a reprint from the
Reminiscences of
John H. Watson, M.D.

I T WAS IN THE SPRING OF 1944, as I have good reason to remember, that a heavy brown-gray fog rolled over Baker Street. Sherlock Holmes sat moodily in his velvet armchair, using both bull's-eye lantern and convex lens to examine a letter that had been delivered by the commissionaire. He was always at his worst in such weather, and as his medical adviser I kept my eye anxiously on the cocaine bottle. I was eager to divert him.

"Atmospheric opacity produces strange optical effects," I said. "This pervading obscurity is so exactly the mouse-color of your old dressing gown, I can hardly see you."

He made no reply, and then I noticed he was wearing the ear-flapped travelling cap. I was puzzled: he could not be planning a journey, for Bradshaw was still on the shelf. I sought to please him with a compliment.

"Speaking as a medical man," said I, "I think you wise to wear your deerstalker, even indoors. This abominable dampness can be very mischievous on a bare skull."

"My dear Watson, ear muffs have various uses," he observed. "If you wish something to occupy your mind, let me recommend this book." He pushed it towards me. "It is Erskine Childers's *The Riddle of the Sands*, one of the most remarkable ever penned. Very timely, this invasion weather."

I felt it my duty to remind him that several clients were waiting in the lobby downstairs. Knowing Holmes's methods I had identified them as a Cambridge economist, a typist, a tide-waiter, the American ambassador, General Eisenhower, and one of His Majesty's principal secretaries for Foreign Affairs.

"I can't see them until I have deciphered this note," he said. "The precise handwriting is certainly Mycroft's; the poor quality of the stationery is due to government economies of paper. But the message, Watson, the message! Is it a code? It says: *Must see you at once about F.W.L.—Mature at 54. Coming in person. M.H. for H.M.*"

"Who is F.W.L.?" I asked. "It sounds like a medical case. Some obscure nervous lesion may have arrested his or her development? Almost anyone should have matured before 54."

He looked at me irritably and seemed to check some retort. "*M.H. for H.M.* undoubtedly means 'Mycroft Holmes for His Majesty,'" he mused. "A neat way of suggesting official authority."

"You once told me," said I, "that there are times when Mycroft practically *is* the government. If information were needed on a matter involving, let us say, the Navy, Canada, Poland, the South Pacific, the North Sea, the Corn Belt and the Panama Canal—"

Even through the haze of fog and shag I could see Holmes's eyes brighten under their tufted brows.

"Quite so," he said. "Hum.—Ha!"

At that moment Mycroft entered, accompanied by a tall handsome gentleman of distinguished and courteous bearing. He was muffled in a woolen cravat and the intonation of his "Pleased to meet you" suggested that he was an American who had caught a slight rhinitis in our beastly climate.

Mycroft, massive and portly, had the usual subtle play of expression in his steel-engraving eyes.

"You understood my message?" he asked.

"At once," said Holmes.

"Mr. Mycroft very kindly sponsored my appeal," said

the other gentleman. "Since we on our side think of you as at least half American, I presumed you would be eager to say something in favor of—"

"The Fourth War Loan!" interjected Holmes. "Matures in 1954. My dear Mr. Henry Morgenthau, there is little enough we old fellows can do. But at least there still remains the cheque book."

He reached his long white hand up for it.

"And by the bye," he added, "I keep Watson's cheque book here too."

Sherlock Holmes and Dr. Watson; also as *The Adventure of the F.W.L.*

CODEINE (7 PER CENT)

I HADN'T SEEN DOVE DULCET, former literary agent and
amateur detective, for a long time—not since he went
into Naval Intelligence in '39. But last winter the Baker
Street Irregulars, that famous club of Sherlock Holmes
devotees, invited him to be a guest at their annual dinner.
Dulcet is shy and would have preferred not to speak, but of
course he was called on and made a very agreeable little
impromptu which I supposed the B & O from Washington
had given him time to think out.

What Dulcet did was propose a toast to Sherlock
Holmes's unknown sister. She was a good deal younger
than either Mycroft or Sherlock, he suggested. The basis
of his fancy was Sherlock's famous remark to Miss Hunter
when she was offered that dubious position as governess at
the Copper Beeches. "It is not the situation which I should
like to see a sister of mine apply for," said Sherlock
Holmes. Dulcet maintained that no man would say that
unless he actually *did* have a sister; and offered ingenious
suggestions why Watson had never mentioned her.

The Irregulars, who were getting a bit noisy by then (it
was late in the evening), accused Dulcet of being "whim-
sical," and chaffed him a good deal. There's something in
Dove's innocent demeanor, his broad bland face and sel-
vage of saffron-colored hair under an ivory scalp, that
encourages good-natured teasing. He was twitted about the
supposed inefficiency of our Intelligence Services—how
G2, for instance, was caught actually moving its offices on
D-Day, with all its phones and devices cut off so they
didn't even know what was happening. He replied that
maybe that was exactly what G2 wanted people to think;
perhaps they had Planned It That Way. He suggested
gently (he speaks in a voice so soft that people really keep

quiet in order to listen) that sometimes the Intelligence people work longer ahead than we suppose. I noticed that he paused then a moment, as though he had more to say and thought better of it. "And now, gentlemen," he concluded, "you'll pardon me if I excuse myself and retire. I've got one of those delicious fin de siècle rooms here at the old Murray Hill and I can't wait to get to it. You know the kind of thing, a big brass bedstead, and lace drapes, and a rose-colored secretary with wonderful scroll work." Of course this gave the stags a laugh, and I caught a small private wink from him as he sat down. So presently I followed him up to his room.

"That was an ingenious surmise of yours," I said, "about Holmes having a sister."

"No surmise at all," he said. "I knew her. Or rather, to be exact, I know her daughter. Violet Hargreave; she works for me."

"Good heavens!" I exclaimed. "*Hargreave*? The New York Police Department? As mentioned in *The Dancing Men*?"

"Of course. Violet's mother married Sherlock's friend, Wilson Hargreave. She was Sibyl Holmes, one of the Holmeses who stayed in this country. I didn't want to mention names at your dinner. In our kind of job you don't do it. When I went into Intelligence I took Violet with me. She's absolutely indispensable. Wonderful gift for languages; we use her mostly as an agent overseas."

If I had asked further questions Dove would have shut up; he always says that the first shot you take in Government work is a transfusion of clam-juice. But we are very old friends and he trusts me. He poured me a drink and then fetched his wallet from under his pillow.

"I had this in my pocket tonight," he said, taking out a letter. "I would have loved to mention it when one of your members was talking about cryptography, codes, ciphers, and so on. The best codes are the simplest, not methodical at all but based on some completely personal association. She's safe at home now, so I can show you how Violet used to get her stuff out of Berlin when it wasn't easy. Sometimes it was only a few words on a picture postcard; the Nazis never seemed to suspect anything so naïve as that. When she had more to say she used some stationery she swiped from the Museum of Natural History, to look professional, and then overprinted a new letterhead."

I examined the paper. At the top of the sheet was the legend AMERICAN MUSEUM OF NATURAL HISTORY, and under it:

Professor Challenger's Expedition
Oceanic Ornithology
c/o S.Y. Matilda Briggs

"She couldn't get much on a postcard, not with a handwriting like that," I said, glancing at the lines of large heavily-inked script. "Very different from the small neat hand of her uncle."

"She has several handwritings, as occasion requires. Go ahead and read the letter."

It went thus:

Dear Friend:

Everything very interesting, and German scientists most helpful. Hope to come back by way of Pacific, Hawaii and Alleutians, studying migrations of gulls and goonies. If can take Kodiak will have wonderful pictures. Goonies (*phalacrocorax carbo*, a kind of cormorant, dangerous to lighthouse keepers) have regular schedule, fly Midway or Wake in October, Alleutians in June. Hope to get mail at Honolulu before you take up Conk-Singleton papers.

Yours always,

VIOLET H. HARGREAVE

"She really is an ornithologist, isn't she," I said.

"So the Berlin censor thought, as he let it come through. Does nothing else strike you?"

"Well, I haven't got my convex lens," I said. "Are there any secret watermarks in the paper? The only thing I notice is that surely a scientific investigator should spell geography correctly. Isn't there only one l in Aleutians?"

"Good man. Of course that would tickle the German censor; he'd just think another ignorant American. You can be quite sure any member of the Holmes family would know how to spell. That's our private signal. Whenever Violet spells something wrong I know there's a double meaning. So the gulls and goonies are Japs."

"Say, she's good! And the allusions to the Holmes cases—sure, I get it. Cormorant and lighthouse keeper—that suggests politician; the story of *The Veiled Lodger*; it means get this warning across to the government. But what about Conk-Singleton?"

"Don't you remember the end of *The Six Napoleons*? Holmes says, before you get out the Conk-Singleton papers *put the pearl in the safe*. Just what we didn't do with Pearl Harbor."

"But what's the date of this letter?" I exclaimed. "Why, it's spring of '41, six months before Pearl Harbor."

"I told you we have to work ahead of time," Dove said. "Violet had just been tipped off, in Berlin, about the secret terms of the German–Japanese alliance. Hitler told the Japs he'd be in Moscow by Christmas, they'd be perfectly safe to strike in December. And you can check those goony dates, which by the way are correct for the bird migrations. The Japs landed at Attu and Kiska in June, just as she said."

"I always wondered what they thought they could do up there on those godforsaken rocks."

"Maybe they were attracted by the name of that group. Ever notice it on the map? The Rat Islands."

I was beginning to get the inwardness of this Baker Street code. "Goodness, even the name of the yacht, *Matilda Briggs*—in the *Sussex Vampire*; why, yes, that was the story of the Giant Rat of Sumatra—"

"For which the world *is not prepared*," Dove finished for me.

"Golly, the State Department must have turned handsprings when you decoded this for them."

Dove was discreetly silent.

I looked over the letter once more. "Kodiak . . . they thought she meant Kodak. I suppose you couldn't make any mistake, it was sure to refer to the Japanese?"

"Well, there Violet was really cute. You spoke of the handwriting."

"Yes, she must have used a very broad pen, a stub."

"She picked up the idea from her Uncle Mycroft. Don't you remember his immortal remark, in *The Greek Interpreter*—about the letter written with a J-pen, that is a stub pen—by a middle-aged man with a weak constitution."

"I guess that's me," I said feebly. "Still I don't get it."

"J-pen, Japan."

We finished what Dove called our auld lang snort. I was thinking hard. "Whenever you get a letter with a wrong spelling," I said guiltily, "do you suspect a secret meaning?—Gosh, do you suppose when broadcasters mispronounce a word on the radio it's really a code?"

"Get out of here," said Dove. "I want my rest."

Ellery Queen's Mystery Magazine, 6 No. 25 (November 1945); also in *To the Queen's Taste* and *The Ironing Board*

WORKS CITED

(Books by Morley that are mentioned only in passing in the Introduction are not included here.)

Ashby, Anna Lou Samuelson. "A Publishing Bibliography of Christopher Morley." Ph.D. dissertation, University of Texas at Austin, 1974.

Doyle, Arthur Conan. *The Blue Carbuncle*. New York: Baker Street Irregulars, 1948.

Green, Richard Lancelyn (Ed.). *The Sherlock Holmes Letters*. Iowa City: University of Iowa Press, 1986.

Haining, Peter (Ed.). *The Sherlock Holmes Scrapbook*. New York: Clarkson N. Potter, 1974.

Lee, Alfred P. *A Bibliography of Christopher Morley*. New York: Doubleday, Doran, 1935.

Lyle, Guy R., and H. Tatnall Brown, Jr. *A Bibliography of Christopher Morley*. Washington, D.C.: Scarecrow Press, 1952.

Morley, Christopher. *Parsons' Pleasure*. New York: George H. Doran, 1923.

——. *John Mistletoe*. Garden City, N.Y.: Doubleday, Doran, 1931.

——. *Internal Revenue*. Garden City, N.Y.: Doubleday, Doran, 1933.

——. *The Old Mandarin*. Garden City, N.Y.: Doubleday, Doran, 1933.

——. *Streamlines*. Garden City, N.Y.: Doubleday, Doran, 1936.

——. *The Middle Kingdom*. New York: Harcourt, Brace, 1944.

——. *Sherlock Holmes's Prayer*. [New York:] Harcourt, Brace, 1944.

——. *The Ironing Board*. London: Faber & Faber, 1950. Contains material not in the first edition—Garden City, N.Y.: Doubleday, 1949.

——. *Gentlemen's Relish*. New York: W. W. Norton, 1955.

——. *Introducing Mr. Sherlock Holmes*. Morristown, N.J.: Baker Street Irregulars, 1959.

——. *The Adventure of the F.W.L.* Pittsfield, Mass.: Published for the Annual Dinner of the Baker Street Irregulars by the Spermaceti Press [Peter Blau], January 9, 1970.

——. *Prefaces without Books*. Austin, Tex.: Humanities Research Center, 1970.

——. *Te Deum Laudanum*. Stanford, Cal.: Printed for Members of The Grillparzer Club of California at the Pequod Press [John Ruyle], August 1987.

——. *Christopher Morley's New York*. New York: Fordham University Press, 1988.

Morley, Christopher (Ed.). *Sherlock Holmes and Dr. Watson: A Textbook of Friendship*. New York: Harcourt, Brace, 1944.

Morley, Christopher, and Vincent Starrett. *Two Sonnets*. Ysleta, Tex.: Edwin B. Hill, 1942.

Morley, Felix. *For the Record*. South Bend, Ind.: Regnery/Gateway, 1979.

[Morley, Frank.] *A Sherlock Holmes Cross-word Puzzle by Mycroft Holmes*. Privately printed for the Friends of Walter Klinefelter. [Portland, Me.: Southworth–Anthoensen Press, 1938.]

Morley, F[rank]. V. *My One Contribution to Chess*. New York: B. W. Huebsch, 1945.

Morley, Frank. *Christopher Morley or The Treasure of the Abandoned Mine*. [Haverford, Pa.: Library Associates of Haverford College], 1959.

Oakley, Helen McK. *Three Hours for Lunch*. Searingtown, N.Y.: Watermill, 1976.

Queen, Ellery (Ed.). *To the Queen's Taste*. Boston: Little, Brown, 1946.

Randall, David A., with a letter from Christopher Morley. *The Adventure of the Notorious Forger*. San Francisco: Randall & Windle, 1978.

Riesenberg, Felix. *Living Again: An Autobiography*. Garden City, N.Y.: Doubleday, Doran, 1939.

Ruber, Peter (Ed.). *The Last Bookman*. New York: Candlelight Press, 1968.

Shreffler, Philip A. (Ed.). *Sherlock Holmes by Gas-Lamp: Highlights from the First Four Decades of The Baker Street Journal*. New York: Fordham University Press, 1989.

Smith, Edgar W. *Baker Street and Beyond*. New York: Pamphlet House, 1940.

Smith, Edgar W. (Ed.). *Letters from Baker Street*. New York: Pamphlet House, 1942.